SPEAKING TRUTH TO POWER

THE DÓNAL DE RÓISTE AFFAIR

To the memory of Christina de Róiste. May she and her husband Seán rest in peace knowing that the state which they helped to establish and to which they remained loyal gave their first child, Dónal, a fair and just opportunity to restore his and their good name

and

To Corporal Michael Donnelly, Military Police, Defence Forces, who, since 1975, has – like Lt Dónal Roche – been forced to fight an epic battle against the phantoms of 'Military and State Security' in order to have his innocence declared before the nation and his good name restored.

SPEAKING TRUTH TO POWER

THE DÓNAL DE RÓISTE AFFAIR

DON MULLAN

WITH THE ASSISTANCE OF
BARRY WHYTE

FOREWORD BY JANE WINTER

CURRACH
PRESS

First published in 2006 by

CURRACH PRESS

55A Spruce Avenue, Stillorgan Industrial Park, Blackrock, Co. Dublin

www.currach.ie

1 3 5 4 2

Cover by Bluett

Origination by Currach Press

Printed by ColourBooks Baldoyle Industrial Estate Dublin 13

ISBN: 1-85607-908 2

CONTENTS

Foreword by *Jane Winter, British Irish Rights Watch*   7

Acknowledgements   14

Introduction   18

1 The Emergency Years   22

2 Clonmel   28

3 Army Career, 1963–8   34

4 Public Auction and Interrogation   50

5 Rejection, Rumours and Exile   86

6 The 1997 Presidential Campaign   108

7 Picking up the Pieces   131

8 A Lone Man *Versus* the Power of the State   137

9 First Contact   172

10 Car Crash – a Plausible Hypothesis   198

11 State-Sponsored Spin   226

12 The Judge Advocate General's Report   247

13 The Shinkwin Affair   303

14 Supermarket for Bombers   316

Closing Statement by Dónal de Róiste   334

Afterword by
Lieutenant Colonel (Retired) Gerry Swan   340

Appendix A: Documents Referred to
in Judge Advocate General's Report   342

Appendix B: The Michael Donnelly affair   361

As you are aware we would have preferred to develop this case more fully before moving on ROCHE but in view of the extreme sensitivity of Clancy Barracks it was felt that delay in bringing the association into the open would NOT have been an acceptable risk.

It has not been possible to confirm ROCHE's association with the other members of the group as reported by our confidential source. We were somewhat handicapped by our inability to question directly the original source of information although the questioning and requestioning through a third party was reasonably satisfactory.

While an unsupported report must be viewed with reserve, it is significant that the report was accurate in its other aspects and my view is that it must be considered as likely to be accurate on this count as well.

Colonel M. Hefferon, Director of Intelligence, in a letter to the Chief of Staff, marked 'Secret', 1 May 1969

FOREWORD

The misinterpretation of flawed intelligence and the abuse of power are a deadly combination. Although Dónal de Róiste was the first victim of this syndrome to contact us, he is one of three former soldiers in the Irish Army – the second of whom is Michael Donnelly, to whom this book is dedicated and the third, Corporal Hugh Kearney is from Northern Ireland. All three have come to us with completely unrelated stories that bear an uncanny resemblance, and form, we believe, part of a pattern.

Anyone can make a mistake, but an institution that continues to make the same mistake has a problem. A country that cannot recognise a pattern of mistakes within one of its key organisations, especially when those mistakes were made a long time ago, does not just have a problem; it is in denial.

To serve one's country is a noble calling. It carries with it the potential of having to lay down one's life for the country one loves. When these three young men joined the army, it was no doubt with mixed feelings of pride and apprehension, and, of course, there was also an element of economic necessity. Two things are certain: none of them joined up with the intention of betraying Ireland, and none of them expected Ireland to betray them.

What happened to Dónal de Róiste would be farcical if it were not so serious. There he was, a young man who loved music, seen in one of the most popular bars in Dublin, talking to one or more 'subversives'. An 'intelligence' report – a misnomer if ever there was one – is compiled, quoting a 'confidential source' – always a bad sign – and his superiors take it seriously. The trouble with those who work in the area of security intelligence is that they inhabit a world of smoke and mirrors. The smoke can get in their eyes and lead them to miss important information, often with tragic consequences, while the mirrors can distort and magnify small glimpses of the real world so that they appear to be massive conspiracies.

Such mistakes are human, and as such deserving of forgiveness.

What was unforgivable in Dónal de Róiste's case was the way his superiors treated him. The only sensible way to deal with an intelligence report which alleges that a young officer has been seen in the company of paramilitaries is to tell him to report, stand him to attention, and ask him straight out what he has to say for himself. Had Dónal de Róiste been given that chance, he would no doubt have remained in the army and served his country to the best of his ability, despite the patchy nature of the training he had been offered, maybe even with distinction.

Instead, he was treated completely unfairly. Commandant Gerry O'Sullivan apparently never stopped to ask himself whether the allegations made against Dónal de Róiste were true or not, and he certainly never asked the one person who knew the answer to that question, Dónal de Róiste himself. Instead, he treated him as guilty from the outset. Commandant O'Sullivan did not want to know the truth; what he wanted was a confession, which is what all bad interrogators want. No wonder Dónal de Róiste was confused; he had not the faintest idea what the Commandant was talking about. Like all honest people, he reacted by racking his brains to see if he had inadvertently done something wrong.

The treatment Dónal de Róiste received was shameful. He was summoned to headquarters, taken there by an escort, believing himself to be under arrest, locked up, bullied, exhorted to confess to an unspecified crime, and induced to resign his post. His solicitor's attempt to sort matters out was ignored. Dónal de Róiste's own request to be allowed to defend himself before a court martial was refused. Then, after a brief lull during which he thought it was all over and that he had actually been offered a sought-after appointment, he was dishonourably and involuntarily retired from the army he had so ardently wanted to join. No reasons have ever been given for this 'retirement' – which was in reality a summary dismissal carried out in contravention of the army's own rules – other than that it was 'in the interests of the service'. As a result, Dónal de Róiste lost his good name, but worse than that, he lost his father's confidence and respect. It has been obvious as I have got to know him that both the dismissal itself and the manner of that dismissal have left an indelible mark on Dónal de Róiste.

It falls to the President of Ireland to retire or dismiss any officer from the army, but he or she may do so only on the advice of the government. The memorandum prepared for the cabinet, concerning

Dónal de Róiste's enforced retirement, said that the Minister for Defence considered that 'the retention of Lieutenant Roche in the Army would involve a grave hazard to military security and the safety of the State'. Thus the distorting mirror had magnified a chance encounter of no account, with the result that a loyal soldier had been transmogrified into a serious threat to the state, who must be got rid of without delay and at all costs. Ironically enough, Dónal de Róiste was not considered by the army to be such a blackguard that he was not eligible for his retirement gratuity, which was paid to him in full six months later.

Don Mullan's meticulous research shows that very few people inside the army knew much, if anything, about the circumstances surrounding his removal. Those in high office, including the Minister for Defence, the government and the President – at that time, Eamon De Valera, a hero to Dónal de Róiste's parents – apparently took no personal interest and exercised no care; they simply rubber-stamped a decision which seems to have been made much lower down the chain of command. Moreover, the steps that brought about his retirement were carefully choreographed to coincide with the 1969 general election, when the entire cabinet was otherwise preoccupied.

Those who wanted Dónal de Róiste out of the army were not satisfied with his dishonourable retirement. After he had left the army, they spread rumours about him, the most serious allegation being that he was an IRA man – an untruth that put his life at risk. It was not long before Dónal de Róiste moved to England, and ultimately to America. It seems that his tormentors really wanted him out of the country.

In 1987, he finally returned to Ireland, where he settled into the quiet life of a school bus driver. A decade later, his sister Adi Roche was nominated by the Labour Party, Democratic Left and the Green Party as a presidential candidate. There were four others competing for the office, which had been vacated by Mary Robinson, Ireland's first woman President and a hard act to follow. At the outset of the campaign, Adi Roche was in the lead, but she was up against powerful political opponents. A vicious personal campaign was waged against her. The final straw came when, to the eternal discredit of those responsible, Dónal de Róiste's removal from the army was used against her. Mary McAleese won the election for Fianna Fáil and the Progressive Democrats.

At first, Dónal de Róiste found himself drawn back into the nightmare that he had tried so hard to put behind him. However, seeing his sister very nearly destroyed, certainly politically but also personally, ultimately kindled in him a determination to clear his name. He consulted a Cork solicitor, Eamonn Carroll, who has worked diligently and pro bono for almost a decade. Attempts to obtain official records about Dónal de Róiste's case under the 30-Year Rule and the Freedom of Information Act hit a blank wall. The Department of Defence refused to disclose key papers 'in the interests of national security' – a phrase which all too frequently spells 'cover-up'. In 1998, Dónal de Róiste's legal team, now enlarged to include Ercus Stewart SC and Gerard Humphreys BL, launched an action for judicial review, seeking discovery of all documents held by the Minister for Defence and the Attorney General in relation to Dónal de Róiste. During the hearings, the Ministry for Defence seriously misrepresented the true facts of the case and 'lost' a number of documents. Ultimately, they need not have bothered, because the judge, Mr Justice McCracken, threw the case out because Dónal de Róiste had delayed so long in coming to court. His lawyers appealed, but, in 2001, the Supreme Court affirmed the order of the High Court. The Chief Justice, Mr Justice Keane, heard the case with two other judges, Mrs Justice Denham and Mr Justice Fennelly. Eamonn Carroll did not give up; he took the case to the European Court of Human Rights, even though he knew that he would face the delay question there as well.

Now that he had been failed by both the army and the courts, Dónal de Róiste turned to other means of raising his case. He contacted Don Mullan, who was a friend of his sister, Adi. That contact led to a number of developments, including the support of former Superintendent William Geary, unfairly dismissed by the Garda Síochána; and film star Gabriel Byrne. Dónal de Róiste's mother, Christina, wrote a letter to *The Irish Times*, asserting her son's innocence. There was further press coverage and questions were asked in the Dáil. Dónal de Róiste's two children wrote to the Taoiseach, Bertie Ahern TD, and to President Mary McAleese. Ultimately, it led to the writing of this book.

Don Mullan also asked my organisation, British Irish Rights Watch, to help Dónal de Róiste. British Irish Rights Watch (BIRW) is an independent non-governmental organisation that has been monitoring the human rights dimension of the conflict, and the peace process, in Northern Ireland since 1990. Our services are available, free of charge, to anyone whose human rights have been violated because of the conflict, regardless of religious, political or community affiliations. We take no position on the eventual constitutional outcome of the conflict. Dónal de Róiste's case fell squarely within our remit and I had no hesitation in offering our help. As has been mentioned earlier, he turned out not to be the only soldier to have been kicked out of the army for associating with 'subversives' on evidence that did not bear scrutiny. BIRW wrote to the Taoiseach, repeatedly, to the Department of Defence, and ultimately to the President. None of them was prepared to help. It became clear that the army's only concern was to cover up the reasons for Dónal de Róiste's removal, while the Taoiseach clearly lacked the political will to help Adi Roche's brother. I had hoped for better from him, who has been so staunch in his support for the families of victims of human rights abuses in Northern Ireland, such as those of Patrick Finucane, Rosemary Nelson and Robert Hamill. I had also hoped for better from the President, who is a lawyer and a champion of justice. I understood that she has no power to intervene in political matters, but Dónal de Róiste's case is not a political matter – it is purely a matter of justice. Furthermore, unwittingly I am sure, the good name of the presidency has been besmirched by the manner of Dónal de Róiste's dismissal.

All this flurry of activity did finally prompt some action on the part of the Irish authorities in the immediate aftermath of a two-page *Irish Times* article by Don Mullan, published at the end of June 2002. On 2 July 2002, they asked the Judge Advocate General, Oonah McCrann, to look into Dónal de Róiste's case. At first, this seemed like a hopeful development, but it rapidly became apparent that such hope was misplaced. The Judge Advocate General chose not to interview Dónal de Róiste or other key witnesses, instead relying entirely on documentary evidence. Furthermore, she completely ignored important and compelling representations made by the respected researcher and author Don Mullan, which potentially shed considerable light on events. During this process, the Minister for Defence deliberately withheld documents, legitimately requested by Dónal de Róiste under the Freedom of Information Act, until after the Judge Advocate General had delivered her report. She did so in the autumn of 2002. She concluded that there was no need for further action by the Department of Defence, stating that it was not unreasonable for Dónal de Róiste to have been retired given the evidence available at the time about his connections with a 'known subversive'.

Once again, Dónal de Róiste had been deprived of any due process, denied his rights, and seen his name blackened without having any clear account of the case against him. It was only when Dónal de Róiste was finally given access to his own army file that the Judge Advocate General's report was exposed as a document that was not worth the paper on which it was written. On 27 July 2005, the High Court in Dublin quite rightly quashed the Judge Advocate General's report on grounds of procedural unfairness.

Don Mullan has reproduced several crucial documents from Dónal de Róiste's army file in an appendix, and in the body of this book he painstakingly analyses their contents and provides a rigorous critique of the Judge Advocate General's report. I do not doubt that anyone who reads the book will conclude that Dónal de Róiste was entirely innocent of the allegations made against him. I also expect that anyone reading this foreword will by now be asking themselves just one question: why? What was it that caused the mighty Irish Army to train its sights on one humble soldier and cause the Taoiseach and the President to turn their backs on him in his hour of need? Well, Don Mullan thinks he has some of the answers, which are all set out here. I will not steal his thunder by summarising them, but let the readers find out for themselves and draw their own conclusions.

Although I am not Irish, Ireland is a country I love and admire. It saddens me greatly to see her treat one of her citizens as shamefully as Dónal de Róiste has been treated. It saddens me even more that he is not the only soldier who has been dealt with grossly unfairly. Recently, the government has appointed an Ombudsman for the Defence Forces, Paulyn Marrinan Quinn SC. At last there is someone to whom any member of the armed forces can turn if they feel they have been treated unfairly. However, her powers are not retrospective – which means she cannot examine Dónal de Róiste's case or the other two mentioned above – and, worryingly, the Minster for Defence retains the power to request her to drop an investigation, so her office is not immune from political interference. BIRW has written to her urging her to seek retrospective powers and complete independence. I hope that those who read this book will write to their TDs urging them to lobby the government for all that Dónal de Róiste has ever asked for: a fair, independent, and transparent process and access to *all* relevant files. I also hope that they will urge similar treatment for Michael Donnelly, Hugh Kearney and any other soldier who finds himself or herself in a similar predicament, and proper powers for the Ombudsman for the Defence Forces. Above all, I hope that Ireland will take a long, hard look at what Dónal de Róiste's story tells her about herself, and vow that in future she will treat those who volunteer to serve her at the risk of their lives with the dignity, respect and justice that such service deserves.

Jane Winter
Director
British Irish Rights Watch
May 2006

ACKNOWLEDGEMENTS

I am grateful to a great many people for their help and support with this book. First and foremost, I must thank Dónal de Róiste who trusted me with his life. When we first met, I established two ground rules: (1) I reserved the right to ask him any question I thought appropriate concerning this affair; and (2) If I felt at any time he was being untruthful, I would not continue. More than three years later, after many ups and downs, I believe in his innocence, and this book will, I hope, assist his long campaign to clear his name.

I must also thank his family: his late mother Christina who, sadly, did not live to see this book published and her son's good name restored; Conchubhar and Jackie; Helen and Chris, and Adi Roche and Seán Dunne. I am also indebted to his American family: Leah Martin and their children, Dara and Sinead. They all gave of their time and knowledge with enormous generosity.

I am particularly indebted to his longstanding army friend, retired Commandant Patrick Walshe, his wife Carmel and their family. In Patrick Walshe, Dónal de Róiste had a true friend. Commandant Walshe is, indeed, an officer and a gentleman, whose devotion to truth and tireless dedication to helping De Róiste finally achieve justice, is admirable and inspiring. Thanks also to their friend, Erik Hoffmann from Denmark.

Gratitude is also extended to retired Lt Col. Gerry Swan, another longstanding friend of Dónal de Róiste, whose advice and support were equally invaluable. At all times it was clear that he and Commandant Walshe had a profound respect for the defence forces through which they served the nation, at home and abroad, with valour and distinction.

I wish to thank retired Commandant Edward Horgan who shared his time and knowledge with generosity. In addition, I wish to thank Lt Col. Patrick Kelly, from Cork, who provided insights and knowledge that are crucial.

I am deeply indebted to Dónal de Róiste's legal team: solicitor Eamonn Carroll and barristers Ger Humphries SC, Ercus Stewart SC and Conleth Bradley SC. They have proven to be a formidable and loyal team since 1997, and a bedrock of encouragement during many dark days. I am especially grateful to Eamonn Carroll of Noonan Linehan Carroll Coffey Solicitors, Cork, for his generosity in making available to me enormous quantities of documentation relevant to the Lt Dónal Roche case.

Thanks are also expressed to Micheál W. Ó Murchú for his assistance with the translation of several Irish documents that have proven crucial in trying to solve the jigsaw of Dónal de Róiste's 1969 retirement and to Colm Feeney for assistance of the same kind.

Immense gratitude is offered to Gabriel Byrne and Sr Helen Prejean for their public support and participation in the Dónal de Róiste Truth Campaign. In both Dublin and New York, they spoke eloquently on De Róiste's behalf. Thanks are also expressed to actress Ellen Barkin who, in the immediate aftermath of the damaging report by Ms Oonah McCrann, Judge Advocate General, became the first person to restate our determination to continue the struggle to clear the name of Dónal de Róiste.

The defence forces press office was always courteous and helpful. I am grateful to John Nolan and especially to Commandant Brian Cleary who never showed any annoyance at the scores of requests for information and clarification sent over the past few years. Thank you.

At the Department of Defence I wish to thank Patricia Troy and Kathleen McAuliffe from the Minister's office and the ever-courteous Jack McConnell of the Department's press office.

I am indebted to forensic linguists Professor Malcolm Coulthard and Sue Blackwell of the Department of English at the University of Birmingham, who were immensely generous with their time and expertise. I must also thank Francis Nolan, Reader in Phonetics in the Department of Linguistics, University of Cambridge, for help and direction.

Immense gratitude is expressed also to the following who gave me help and support in various ways: Grainne Mooney, Áras an Uachtaráin; John Nolan, Irish Sugar Company, Carlow; Carmel Nolan, Sugar Distributors Ltd, Carlow; Roisin McIlduff, the Gate Theatre, Dublin; Marie Heading, Ulster Historical Foundation; Dr Brian Barton, author of *The Blitz – Belfast in the War Years* (Blackstaff Press, 1999); Bernie Bergin and Cynthia Post.

I am grateful to several journalists for their help and advice. These include: Frank Doherty, Peter Murtagh, *The Irish Times*; Dónal Musgrave and Neans McSweeney, the *Examiner*; Terry McGeehan, the *Star*: Mark Hennessy, *The Irish Times*; and Niall Stanage, former Editor of *Magill* magazine.

I am immensely grateful to the following archivists and librarians for their help and support: Tom Quinlan and Dr Gregory O'Connor, the National Archives; Anne M. Byrnes, Westmeath County Library, Mullingar; M. Costello, Mayo Country Library, Castlebar; Gerry Kavanagh of the National Library of Ireland; Declan Ryan, librarian at the *Examiner*; and Alessia Kharkonova and Nori McGregor of the Children of Chernobyl Project for documentation and press cuttings from the 1997 presidential election.

One of the great privileges of the past three years was meeting the late great Superintendent William Geary and his godson, Judge John P. Collins, New York. It was inspiring to witness the generosity of spirit so evident in the efforts of 103-year-old William Geary in helping Dónal de Róiste to achieve the same official acknowledgement of innocence which he achieved at the age of 100.

I am grateful also to the following people who gave me enormous personal support: Assistant District Attorney, Brian Meagher, Brooklyn, New York; Pauline Turley, Director, Irish Arts Centre, New York; Kit De Fever, New York; Liam Costello, Institute of Technology, Tallaght; Matt Doyle, National Graves Association; Brian O'Brien and the staff of Prontaprint, Walkinstown; Mick and Peggy Burke and their family who cared for Dónal in Urlingford; Criostóir de Baróid, of the 'Between' Organisation, Cork; and Kathy Tynan, Communications Office, Irish Cancer Society.

Thanks are also extended to Seamus Cashman, retired Wolfhound Press Publisher, a good friend and mentor. Immense gratitude is extended to my trusted editor, Emer Ryan, the best in the publishing sector. Thanks to John Scally for his continuing encouragement and support. Thanks to Jane Winter, Director of British Irish Rights Watch who listened attentively when I brought the cases of Dónal de Róiste and Michael Donnelly to her organisation and, after assessment, decided to take on board their cause for justice. She is a tower of integrity and an Englishwoman who is a true friend of Ireland. I wish also to thank Brian Lynch and Jo O'Donoghue, Currach Press, for their dedication, belief and interest in this book.

Finally, I wish to thank Gary Burke, RIP, for his undying interest and encouragement, and my family, Margaret, Thérèse, Carl and Emma, who got used to living with a hermit during the last six months of the writing of this book. I am indebted to them for their love, support and understanding always.

RESEARCH ASSISTANCE

Barry Whyte: I wish to thank Barry Whyte, a young journalist with a bright future. Barry worked with me for three months, helping with research and additional interviews, and on preparing the initial drafts for Chapters 2, 6, 8 and 11. I am indebted to him for his enthusiastic assistance.

Carl Mullan: My son Carl joined me as part of his Transition Year work experience, helping me with photographic research and photography.

Joseph Rowntree Charitable Trust: Finally, I am enormously indebted to Stephen Pittam, Nick Perks and the trustees of the Joseph Rowntree Charitable Trust for the generosity of a research grant which allowed me to work on this book. Without this support it would have been difficult to commit the necessary time required to undertake the research.

All the opinions expressed in this book are entirely those of the author and contributors.

INTRODUCTION

Every tragedy falls into two parts: complication and unravelling.... By the complication I mean all that extends from the beginning of the action to the part which marks the turning-point to good or bad fortune. The unravelling is that which extends from the beginning of the change to the end.

Aristotle

My involvement with Dónal de Róiste over a four-year period, during which this book was conceived, researched and written, has been a roller-coaster experience. There were many highs and many lows. Unquestionably, the deepest low was the disappointment and dismay at the quality and outcome of the findings of the Judge Advocate General (JAG), Oonah McCrann, in her 'Report of Inquiry into the circumstances surrounding the retirement "in the interests of the service" of Lt Dónal Roche on 27th June 1969.' That report was published on 2 October 2002, its findings and conclusions having been leaked to *TV3 News* at least one day before the report was received by Dónal de Róiste and his lawyers.

The leak was just another of many examples of how elements of the defence forces and the Department of Defence have assiduously attempted to close down De Róiste's lonely campaign for truth and justice. To a growing number of former defence force personnel, who served their country with distinction at home and as UN peacekeepers abroad, the failure to deal with the Lt Roche case in a thoroughly independent and transparent manner has been a source of bewilderment and dismay.

Lt Roche was accused by very senior officers, including the Chief of Staff, of being a threat to military and state security and of consorting with one, and possibly four, alleged subversives – subversives who, if allegations in secret documents in his files are true, were guilty of nothing short of treason, as defined by Article 39 of the Irish Constitution. Many of these secret documents – which Roche and the public were never intended to see, but which were available to Ms

McCrann for the purposes of her inquiry – are published for the first time in this book.

At the outset I would like to register my disappointment with key figures who declined to be interviewed for this book. They are: Minister for Defence, William O'Dea TD; former Chief of Staff, Lieutenant General Gerry O'Sullivan; Colonel Denis Murphy, Military Intelligence; former Captain Patrick Dixon; the Judge Advocate General, Oonah McCrann SC.

One very pertinent question, which the JAG did not consider – because of the restricted terms of references given to her by the Minister for Defence – was this:

Why was Lt Dónal Roche not 'dismissed' as opposed to being 'retired' 'in the interests of the service' in 1969?

Both dismissal and retirement required the recommendation of the government and the ultimate imprimatur of the President.

There is a very simple answer to the above question. If Lt Roche had been 'dismissed', in any defined category of the 1954 Defence Act, as a commissioned officer of the defence forces he had corresponding rights of redress. However, of the six categories of 'retirement', referenced in 1969 as subparagraphs 18(1)(a–f), under Defence Force Regulations A.15, Subsection 47(2), five had rights of redress and only one did not. The lone category, 'in the interests of the service', subparagraph 18(1)(f), deprived Lt Roche of all rights of redress and protected those rushing to expel him from having to defend the unspecified and unsubstantiated allegations being levelled against the young officer.

Fortunately, this loophole in the Defence Act was amended in 1985 so that no officer can ever again be 'retired' without having the right to defend their good name and reputation.

It is also a source of disappointment that Ms McCrann did not express concern that the Chief of Staff made his recommendation that Lt Roche be retired 'in the interests of the service' just eight days after his first interrogation and while the 'investigation' into his alleged contact with alleged subversives was still ongoing. That alone should have raised the first of many red flags.

Ms McCrann's failure to insist that Lt Roche and his legal team should have available to them the documentation that she was reviewing for the purpose of her Inquiry resulted in her findings being quashed by the High Court in July 2005. Had she afforded Lt Roche his constitutional right to have access to the documents she was reviewing, Lt Roche would have had the opportunity to deny several unsubstantiated assertions and allegations contained in these secret documents and of which he was unaware until he was given sight of them, after her Inquiry.

In the interests of basic human rights, there is a need for legislation that ensures the constitutional protection of individual officers and other ranks of the defence forces and members of the Garda Síochána who find themselves caught in the nightmare of state agents claiming privilege on the grounds of state and military security. In the case of the late Superintendent William Geary, such privilege forced him to engage in a dignified struggle to clear his name, which struggle was resolved only when the government decided to intervene, when Geary reached the age of 100. As a nation, we should feel relieved and grateful that the old man survived long enough to see such an injustice against him righted – an injustice perpetrated by the phantom of a 'confidential source' and protected by the cloak of 'national security'.

Dónal de Róiste comes from a decent Irish family whose members have contributed much to Irish society and, indeed, have done much to make us proud by their humanitarian contribution on the international stage. De Róiste's long and often lonely pleas of innocence can no longer be ignored. It is time his case was properly, fairly and independently reviewed. However, the involvement of the current JAG can no longer be considered appropriate.

If it is found that, as others and I suspect, the government was misled by senior officers of the defence forces in order to achieve the fast-track removal of Lt Dónal Roche in 1969, he is entitled to the following remedies:

- The restoration of his good name by an official declaration acknowledging that he was the victim of wrongdoing by agents of the state
- The restoration of his army commission
- An independent inquiry to investigate how the government could have been so misled that it became an unwitting associate in an injustice against

an individual officer whose constitutional rights and rights to natural justice were horrendously denied

• The findings of the inquiry to inform and indicate appropriate steps and recommendations to ensure that this cannot happen to a member of the defence forces, or a servant of the state, ever again

I have decided to conclude this introduction and my conclusion to this book, with the following quotation from Dónal de Róiste's mother who celebrated her eighty-fifth birthday on Christmas Day 2005 but who, sadly, passed away in January 2006. With a mother's intuition, even before Ms McCrann delivered her Inquiry report and recommended the release of her son's secret files, Christina De Róiste's senses knew what had been done to her son in 1969:

I believe my son Dónal is innocent. I believe he was wrongfully 'retired'. I believe the case against him was so spurious that he was denied proper procedures. I believe the government have been misled in the information presented to it by Dónal's accusers and that our one-time great hero, Éamon de Valera, may, in turn, have been wrongly advised.

Don Mullan
Dublin, May 2006

AUTHOR'S NOTE

Throughout the book the main subject is referred to under both the Irish and the English forms of this name: Lt Dónal de Róiste and Lt Dónal Roche.

Two key documents, the report of the Judge Advocate General (October 2002) and the High Court judgment of Mr Justice Quirke which quashed the JAG's report (July 2005) are available on the Currach Press website www.currach.ie.

I

THE EMERGENCY YEARS

There must be nothing worse than knowing you are telling the truth, yet having no one believe you.

Margaret Beatty

Dónal Roche was born in Cork city on the late afternoon of 12 February 1945 on the eve of the Allied bombing of the German city of Dresden. He was to be the first of four children born to Seán and Christina (née Murphy) Roche. Christina recalled that snow was gently falling outside Glenvera Nursing Home, Wellington Road, at the time of his birth.

He was born into 'The Emergency' years, in an Ireland that was partitioned, relatively poor and struggling to find its feet, having finally achieved a partial independence. Political transformation was in the air, at home and abroad. Seán Roche had been born in the year of the Easter Rising and Christina two years later, on the eve of the setting up of Dáil Éireann and the bitterly fought Anglo-Irish War. As children, Dónal Roche's parents lived through the Irish Civil War and were the first generation of the Irish Free State (*Saorstát Éireann*).

Seán and Christina first met in the summer of 1936 in one of Cork's Gaeltacht areas. He was twenty and she was eighteen. They first noticed one another at a céilí. 'He was very handsome,' Christina recalled. 'But right from the beginning there was a union of minds, and it lasted.'

Seán Roche had come of age and Christina was nineteen when, on 29 December 1937, a new constitution, Bunreacht na hÉireann, came into being. It heralded the replacement of the Irish Free State with a new state named Éire (Ireland). Little did they realise, as their love blossomed, that the new constitutional structures, which provided for a President of Ireland instead of the British monarch, would have such a profound and cruel impact in the twilight of their lives.

The six-year courtship of Seán Roche and Christina Murphy was filled with many lively conversations about Irish history and politics, and deepening concern at the escalation of the Second World War. In spite of Ireland's neutrality, the First World War dictum of the Irish Republican Brotherhood, which had paved the way for the 1916 Rising – 'England's difficulty is Ireland's opportunity' – still held currency and there were signs of increased IRA activity. Seán Roche and Christina Murphy were beginning their fourth year of courtship when, on 30 May 1939, the Irish government introduced the Treason Act in response to a revival in IRA militancy. Two weeks later, it introduced the Offences Against the State Act, giving it power to take, if necessary, repressive measures to curtail the IRA. On Christmas Day that same year, Christina Murphy's twenty-first birthday, the IRA staged a daring raid on an Irish army depot in Dublin's Phoenix Park, stealing an estimated one million rounds of ammunition.

Fearing both an internal and external threat, a Department for Co-ordination of Defensive Measures was established at the beginning of 1940, under Frank Aiken. A recruitment campaign boosted the Irish Free State's regular and reserve forces to 54,000 men and women. Seán Roche, who by then had taken up employment with Comhlucht Siúcra Éireann (the Irish Sugar Company), was given leave of absence to join the reserves and was posted to Crosshaven. Christina recalled how her heart raced when she heard the postman approach her home in Liscarroll, Co. Cork, and how it almost skipped a beat when she saw a Crosshaven postmark on an envelope. 'Seán was very nationalist,' she recalled. 'He was ready to help the government of Ireland in any way he could. Now that Ireland had won partial independence and had a standing army, he saw no role for the IRA. He was a great Dev supporter and willing to help in whatever way he asked of loyal citizens.'

Reminiscing about her husband's experience in the Irish army, Christina Roche recalled:

> Seán loved his time in the army. When later Dónal joined the FCA [Fórsa Cosanta Áitiúil – Local Defence Force] he did so with his father's encouragement. When he eventually received his commission in the regular army, Seán was the proudest father imaginable.

With a deep sigh of sadness at the memory of how it was, in time, to turn so sour, she continued, 'Eventually Seán was given an honourable discharge.' 'Now hear me,' she said before repeating the phrase with emphasis. 'He was given an honourable discharge.' (The emphasis was to highlight the very different army discharge forced upon their first child, many years later.)

After two years' service, Seán returned to the Sugar Company. An avid reader, he scoured the newspapers every day, monitoring major developments throughout the course of the war. He knew that Ireland's declared neutrality was by no means safe should any of the big powers decide that the island might provide their war strategy with an essential advantage.

While the Taoiseach, Eamon de Valera, indicated that he would strongly object to the imposition of conscription in Northern Ireland, he did not object to volunteers from both sides of the border joining the war effort. In spite of Ireland's neutral stance, some 43,000 men from the twenty-six counties joined an estimated 38,000 from the six northern counties and marched to the front in British army uniforms.

In January 1940, in the wake of the theft of Irish army ammunition in the Phoenix Park, Justice Minister Gerard Boland extended the Emergency Powers Act to enable the internment of suspected IRA members and their accomplices. An estimated 600 IRA members were imprisoned and 500 interned during the Second World War. In September 1940, the Local Defence Force, the forerunner to the FCA, was established and numbered 100,000 members during the Emergency.

Seán Roche and Christina Murphy were confused by sporadic bombing incidents over Ireland, despite the government's declared neutrality. Christina recalled the shock and terror which, even in faraway Liscarroll and Mallow, families, friends and neighbours felt throughout the months of April and May 1941, as news arrived of bombs in Belfast and Dublin's North Strand, where thirty people were killed in the early hours of 31 May. 'It was appalling,' she said. 'The blitz on Belfast and the bombing of Dublin terrified everybody and we worried that the whole island might find itself in the throes of war. It was a very natural fear.'

The Emergency continued to impact in Ireland but Seán Roche and Christina Murphy were in love, and the war, while worrying and sometimes causing relative hardship, was largely offshore and still somewhat distant, especially in rural Cork. As Christmas Day approached, Christina Murphy's twenty-fourth birthday, Seán Roche proposed to her. They were married on 11 April 1944 at St Joseph's Chapel, Liscarrol, the same church where Christina Murphy had been baptised. The wedding reception was held at the Hibernian Hotel, Mallow, an establishment owned by Christina's Aunt Polly, and the couple honeymooned in Dublin.

The newlyweds were fortunate to find a comfortable house for rent in Waterloo, about five miles from Mallow. Christina recalled Seán's intense interest in the changing fortunes of the war and winced at the memory of the static and high-pitched whistle as he changed radio channels. In the evenings, after returning from work at the sugar factory, he would tune into the BBC World Service for news. In the morning, it was Radio Éireann. Stockpiles of the *Cork Examiner*, *Irish Times*, *Irish Press* and *Irish Independent* were to be found in various corners of the house and under the bed.

As they settled into their first summer together, it was clear the tide was turning. Less than two months after their marriage, there was news of Allied troops entering Rome and the D-Day landings at Normandy. By 25 August, Paris was liberated. The news coincided with the first stirrings of new life within Christina.

In Ireland, domestic politics saw Christina and Seán canvass together to help Fianna Fáil win its sixth consecutive general election under the leadership of Eamon de Valera. 'Those were innocent days,' Christina recalled:

> We would have willingly fought and died for the big man. There were hardships to be endured throughout the Emergency, and 1944 was a particularly harsh year. It was the year the government established Bord na Móna (the Irish Peat Board), because of coal shortages and our inability to obtain shipments due to the war. But we never dreamed of blaming Dev. Those were exceptional times and they required, we told ourselves, exceptional leadership and loyalty.

Dónal Roche was born on 12 February 1945. The fire-bombing of Dresden began the following evening. At least 35,000 people died during the bombing which totally destroyed an area of 15 square kilometres. As a teenager, Dónal Roche would travel with his father around the midlands of Ireland and listen attentively as his father recounted stories of the war and especially the day Dónal was born. It was clear to Dónal that his father had been attuned to the progress of the war and worried about its ultimate impact on the world and the future of his family.

Christina recalled little of the war at this stage as her life was completely absorbed with the responsibilities of taking care of her new baby. 'It was a wonderful thrill when Dónal was born, my first baby. It was wonderful.' That was her abiding memory of that period of her life.

On 2 May 1945, German forces surrendered in Berlin and Italy. Five days later, Germany surrendered to the Allies in Rheims, France. The following day, Europe celebrated VE Day. Christina had no sense of the jubilation erupting across Europe at the ending of major hostilities.

> I was alone during the day, living in the country and still learning to change nappies and deal with the responsibilities and demands of a growing baby and the running of our new home. Seán and I were certainly relieved to know the war was drawing to a close. At heart, Seán was a pacifist. As stories of the Holocaust emerged, we were shocked. The depth of new lows the Second World War reached seemed to be endless. Little did we know that the landmarks of Hiroshima and Nagasaki were still to be reached. But, in all honesty, we were finding it hard to make ends meet and we had plenty to occupy our minds simply in trying to keep our heads above water.

Throughout their courtship, Christina and Seán, along with most of the rest of the world, had no idea that the race to create the first nuclear bomb was in progress. On 6 August, the first atomic bomb was dropped on Hiroshima and, three days later, the second fell on Nagasaki. As images emerged and eyewitnesses and survivors told their stories, time momentarily stopped. Humanity had come face to face with its greatest nightmare. For the first time since the birth of humankind we had invented the seeds of our own destruction.

Within days of the apocalyptic devastation of the atomic bombs, the Japanese Emperor unconditionally surrendered on behalf of his people. The following day, 15 August 1945, the Allies celebrated victory over Japan. The war was now at an end – almost. With the loss of 40 million lives in just six years of conflict, including deaths from the birth of nuclear weapons, humanity was at a crossroads.

The words that permeated their conversations during their early years together – peace, neutrality, respect for government, sovereignty, the rights of small nations, national security, international law, the right to life, targeting of civilians, holocausts, Hiroshima, Nagasaki, atomic bombs, human suffering and compassion – were, in due course, to dominate the lives of Christina and Seán Roche and their family.

As 1945 closed, Dónal Roche took his first steps. On Christmas Day, 1945, Christina Roche's twenty-seventh birthday, those steps were her greatest joy and her Christmas and birthday gift all wrapped into one. She remembered those early days with deep affection and love:

> I loved Dónal; I loved him as a small boy. He was very
> sensitive and very affectionate. He was all that I could
> have hoped for as a young mother living in rural Ireland.
> I had no idea what lay ahead of him.

There was irony in Christina's voice as she recalled the day she received a phone call from her Aunt Polly informing her that President Eamon de Valera was on his way and would be staying at the Hibernian Hotel in Mallow. Polly invited Christina to come quickly and to bring her firstborn son to receive the President's blessing and best wishes. 'Dev would call if passing through to Killarney,' she recalled. 'He sometimes stayed at the hotel with his bodyguard. I remember him smiling as he looked at baby Dónal and gently stroking his forehead. He then signed a hotel menu card for me.'

She retained, somewhere in her belongings, the hotel menu card personally inscribed to her by Eamon de Valera. She watched, with pride and admiration as the great man penned his name, and hers, on the card. Three decades later, that same hand and signature was to drive a stake through her heart. 'I used to be very sentimental about that card,' Christina recalled. 'But I have lost all sentiment now.'

The sadness in her voice was born of trust betrayed.

CLONMEL

The world that young Dónal Roche grew up in was one of hardship and often quite severe poverty for many. The first decade of his life was known as the Hungry Fifties – a decade during which many Irish men and women emigrated to England, the US, Canada and elsewhere in search of work on building sites and in the service industries.

In many respects, the Roche family was blessed, because of the drive and determination of Seán and Christina Roche. Both parents hoped that the stability and security they created would provide an environment conducive to their children's education and, consequently, an increased possibility for work at home as teachers or civil servants.

Seán Roche had hoped to become a teacher before his father's untimely death. He had already achieved the necessary qualifications to enter teacher-training college, but his sense of duty had caused him to abandon this path and return home to run the family hardware shop. An idealist, especially during the early years of Ireland's independence, Seán came from a strong nationalist family and, for him, an independent Ireland, though partitioned, was the fulfilment of the hopes and dreams of his and earlier generations. According to Christina:

> Seán's mother was a tremendous nationalist, and they had a business in Doneraile, Co. Cork. When the first Dáil started, the government asked all business people to contribute towards helping to get the economy on its feet by buying government bonds. Seán's mother sent £100, which was a lot at the time. She was nationalist to the core. Her brother [Seán's uncle] was one of the first to sit on the Sinn Féin courts [a pre-independence court system established as an alternative to British rule in Ireland], and she used to boast about that.

The Roche family sided with Éamon de Valera, and, like many in the country, saw 'The Long Fellow' as being synonymous with Ireland. They also saw themselves as part of the generation of men and women whose years of struggle and hard work ensured the survival of the Irish state, then in its infancy. These were difficult and challenging times for an emergent state, requiring loyalty and commitment from its first post-independence citizens. Seán and Christina Roche were determined to play their part. Christina recalled:

> We had the interest of the Irish state at heart. When it wasn't always popular, we bought Irish manufacture. And we spoke Gaeilge, and things like that.

In 1943, Seán Roche participated in the largest manufacturing campaign in the history of the Irish Sugar Company when over 700 employees began working in three shifts without pause for eighteen weeks until some 230,000 acres of beet were processed. However, his idealism suffered a severe setback when, as a loyal employee of the state-owned company, he found himself in dispute with management over pay and working conditions. During the 1950s, the workers at Irish Sugar went on strike. According to Christina:

> Comhlucht Siúicre Éireann wouldn't give in to the boys. When they were employed first, they had been promised a certain salary and when the time came, they wouldn't give them the increase they had been promised. Anyway, they went on strike which was a major incident in my life, because I knew nothing about strikes. Eventually, they had to go back to work on the company's terms.

For Seán Roche it was a bitter blow. When it became clear that all his years of loyalty to the state were not about to be recognised, he grew disillusioned. He was not only a proud man, but also a stubborn one. In what might be considered an act of recklessness, he decided that he would never again work for the state-owned company.

In the 1950s, this was a major and risky decision for the sole breadwinner of a young family. With thousands of unemployed men and women flooding out of the country at the time, Seán Roche's decision was also courageous, particularly since he decided to leave the familiarity of his native Cork and travel with his family to neighbouring Tipperary.

He found employment at Curran's enamel factory as a fitter/turner and, while he was looking for a home in Clonmel for his family, Christina stayed in Cork with their two sons, Dónal and Conchubhar. Conchubhar had been born in Cork in 1947, two years after Dónal.

As the two boys developed, Christina recalled, so too did their friendship with one another. Dónal was less robust, due in part to a prolonged bout of bronchitis he developed as a very small child. He was quiet and recalls being somewhat introspective and never dreaming of questioning authority. Conchubhar was more rebellious, but recalls his childhood as close to idyllic:

> I suppose you only remember the sunny days, but we had a car when we were children, which was unusual at the time. We used to go to our grandparents in Cork at Christmas. We'd get to go to the Gaeltacht every summer. We'd have regular family holidays and Sunday drives. The atmosphere in the house was generally harmonious apart from the odd blow-up that is part and parcel of every normal family.

Seán's move to Tipperary prospered. He bought a house for his growing family at 'Awbeg', Western Park, Clonmel. Helen (Len) was born on 22 January 1952 and Adi on 11 July 1955.

The town of Clonmel had a major and positive influence on all the Roche family and they all recall their days there with great fondness. They remember a close-knit community in which people looked out for each other, and a town that truly embodied the old Irish saying: 'Is ar scáth a chéile a mhaireann na daoine' ('It's in the shadow of each other that we live'). Clonmel was, according to the Roches, a town that lived up to the idea of active citizenship before the term had ever been coined and in which a belief in community participation and responsibility was strong.

The four Roche children, thanks to Seán and Christina, were imbued with a deep and active social conscience. They were concerned about the plight of suffering humanity and were dedicated to working to alleviate the pain of those less fortunate. The town was filled with charitable organisations and the Roche family was involved with almost all of them: St Vincent de Paul; the Legion of Mary; Meals on Wheels; and various charities set up by the Irish missionary movement and by lay people, for the purpose of relieving poverty and hunger in the Third World.

'In a very real sense,' states Adi Roche, 'the cornerstone for all of this work [The Children of Chernobyl Project] can be traced right back to Clonmel and the values and ethics we learned growing up there from our parents and the good people of our home town.'

There was also a sense of balance in the Roche family home. While they were actively involved in various charitable works, the children were also encouraged to participate in sporting and cultural activities. Len recalls the family home as always filled with the sound of song and music:

> Both my mother and father had lovely voices and were always singing around the house. Dad would often play the piano and mum would sing ... Dónal, Conchubhar and myself all went to piano lessons ... We also have Dónal recorded, singing 'Kevin Barry'. The wireless was always on and we would listen to all kinds of music programmes from traditional Irish music to Jazz ... Dónal learned to play the guitar and when he came back from Cadet School and the army for weekends, we sometimes had the odd singsong around the fireplace.

The children were, variously, sent to elocution lessons and ballet, had unrivalled access to films, and enjoyed music and theatre. Christina Roche, who was also known for her great ability to dance the charleston, was the anchor of the family. She was a sharp, intelligent woman, who, like her husband, valued education. Her father had been a principal in the primary school in Liscarrol. Christina had hopes that all her children would become teachers. But while instilling in her children her desire for education, it was always, as Adi recalls, 'education in the broadest sense'.

Conchubhar and Len became teachers; Adi founded the Chernobyl Children's charity and became a formidable anti-nuclear campaigner in

Ireland and throughout the world. Dónal, the eldest, went on to achieve a commission as a young officer in the Irish army.

Christina believed that their life choices had much to do with the manner in which they were raised: 'They came out of a home where we said everything out. There were no secrets or anything.' This she attributed to Seán, who was sometimes brutally frank:

> Seán wouldn't tell a lie to save his life. To the point of being undiplomatic … they were taught the same … we were in a very truthful home, I can tell you, because you couldn't tell a lie to Seán.

Adi confirms this, adding that his brutal honesty was sometimes uncalled-for, and that he was quite likely to walk into a house and check the shoes that people wore or the cups they drank from to see if they were Irish made and would often berate the owner if they weren't.

Dónal recalls his childhood and adolescent relationship with his dad as one of affection and friendship. Seán Roche, though a full-time employee at Curran's enamel factory, displayed his entrepreneurial skills by establishing a second job – travelling around the countryside with a 16mm projector to show popular films of the day. He brought the movies to rural areas, often filling local halls to capacity. Dónal travelled the length and breadth of Tipperary, and sometimes neighbouring counties, with him. It is a time remembered with great fondness by Dónal.

When not with his father, Dónal Roche spent many evenings and weekends studying or playing with friends. Although he did not have a particular aptitude for sport, he was, nonetheless, physically fit and active. However, he had a real passion for the written word. 'He was an avid reader,' recalled Christina. 'A lot of his time was spent with books.'

In the 1950s, the *Sunday Independent* ran a regular comic strip about the adventures of a superhero called 'The Phantom'. Dónal once wrote a story about the Phantom for a competition. His essay won him a bicycle – a superb prize for a boy who would soon develop a taste for outdoor activities such as camping and fishing.

'Dónal was a clever boy,' recalled his mother. 'He won a scholarship to go to secondary school and came second in the county!'

Christina sensed that Dónal had inherited more of her temperament than he had of his father's: 'I knew he was very sensitive, like myself. When he decided to join the army, I often wondered was it his forte.' She knew, however, that a cadetship in the army was as prestigious as a place in college. He had enjoyed his voluntary service with the FCA, and officers there encouraged him to apply for the cadetship, recognising his intelligence and application.

Alas, Christina's fears would later prove to be well founded, compounded by the rejection he suffered at the hands of his father, a man who, according to his widow, 'saw everything in black and white'.

3

ARMY CAREER, 1963–8

We still have the photographs of Dónal saluting and the gleaming ceremonial sword. To see him standing in his officer's uniform was one of the proudest moments in my mother and father's life. We had such pride in how he represented the family.

Adi Roche

CADET SCHOOL

Brother Finnegan was Dónal Roche's headmaster at Ard Scoil na mBráthar, Clonmel. In 1963, following young Roche's application for a cadetship, Finnegan received a confidential questionnaire from the defence forces. Amongst the answers he gave, he wrote the following:

> Dónal Roche is a boy of excellent character – reliable, obliging, nice personality, obedient and good-humoured. He has all the qualities one would like to discover in a boy of his age. He is one of the best lads we had in our Leaving Cert class (1962–1963). If Dónal decides to go for a career in the army, he will make a success of it.

In the reference, Finnegan described Roche as an honours student who was in the top third of his class, with a noted improvement in his performance and who had a marked aptitude for study. He wrote that Roche expressed himself 'very readily and intelligently' and was 'mature, realistic, reflective, calm, easily stimulated and courageous'. He stated that, depending on the circumstances, Dónal could be either 'independent or dependent'. In a similar vein, he found it difficult to say whether young Roche was 'dominant or submissive'. The headmaster considered Roche to have a 'fair ability' in games and sports and noted that outdoor activities were 'among his interests'.

Dónal Roche enlisted in the Officer Cadet School on 7 November 1963 and was assigned Officer Cadet number 814417. Prior to this, he had been a member of the local defence forces (FCA) and would remain a member until 16 November 1963, bringing his total FCA service to two years and 333 days. The latter indicates dedication and commitment by a young and enthusiastic schoolboy over many weekends and holidays.

In an email to me, dated 9 March 2004, Roche recalled:

> In Clonmel, growing up, there was no boy scouts organisation. The trick was to lie about your age and join the FCA. I was about 16 at the time. It was great: money, training and holidays. The Cadet School came from both my Uncle Gerard Madden (Commandant and godfather) and Commandant Gerry Mulligan, my commander in the 3rd Motor Squadron [FCA].
>
> After Leaving Cert one applied for any and all jobs. Back then it was either the boat, the Civil Service, the Priesthood or the army for young working class fellas like me. You got it by interview and medical test. My dad, a factory worker was determined that we should ascend to a 'higher rung' on the social ladder than himself.

There is no doubt that, with proper training and encouragement, Roche had the potential to mature into an officer of substance. A good indicator arises out of unusual circumstances associated with the 38th Cadet Class in which he was granted a place.

Commandant Edward Horgan served with UN peacekeeping forces in Cyprus and the Middle East and worked as a UN election observer in the Balkans, Indonesia and Africa. He handed back his UN Nobel Peace medal when Ireland agreed to participate in the European Rapid Reaction Force. According to retired Commandant Horgan, 1963 proved to be a particularly challenging year for cadets. In an email, dated 7 October 2003, retired Commandant Horgan stated:

> The 38th Cadet Class was something of a special group of people … The normal intake of cadets in the economically challenged early 1960s was about 35 cadets, and this was the number of cadets requested by the army,

and the number of cadets actually called up in the first round for cadet training.

Anecdotal evidence suggests that a government or ministerial decision was taken to call up 55 cadets that year. Accordingly the army had no option but to call up an additional 20 cadets ...

Over the two years, about two cadets left on their own initiative, and 18 cadets [were dismissed] ... and a further four [were retained with their junior class for an extra year's] training. Out of the original 55 called, only 31 were commissioned in September 1965 [including Dónal Roche] ...

I ... was posted to the Cavalry or Armoured Corps. Because our two years' cadet training was a traumatic experience for many of the class ... a bond was established between most of us which survived until relatively recently. It became the custom to invite back as many of the original 55 class members as possible. One of the few exceptions to this rule was Lieutenant Dónal Roche.... The majority of the 38th Cadet Class accepted the army's version of Dónal Roche's dismissal, on the basis that our fellow officers at army HQ would not have behaved in a dishonourable manner towards a fellow officer. It is now clear to me that the army behaved dishonourably in the case of Dónal Roche, and that he was unjustly dismissed.

The first of Roche's six-monthly Cadet School evaluations, dated 30 April 1964 and signed by Lt Col. Cyril M. Mattimoe, Cadet Master of the Cadet School, and Col. Carl O'Sullivan, Commandant of the Military College, states that academically Roche 'has reasonable ability and test results are fair'. His conduct is noted as 'satisfactory'.

Regarding leadership, his commanding officers noted: 'Though lacking mature confidence he has shown a reasonable amount of potential.' The two senior officers recommended: 'That he continue on the course.'

Roche's second year report, dated 10 November 1964, and signed by Lt Col. Mattimoe and Col. Eugene O'Neill, Commandant, Military College, is somewhat terse and reflects the displeasure of Roche's senior officers at his having committed 'a serious offence'.

During his second and final year of Cadet School, young Roche provided his training officers with a perfect excuse to get rid of him if they had thought him to be unsuitable. One evening, on his return to barracks, his personal property was searched and two condoms were discovered in his wallet. Absurd as it might seem now, condoms were at that time illegal to import or sell within the state. Moreover, given the moral climate at the time, the discovery of such items in his possession would have been regarded by individuals within the military system, including the military chaplain, as a grievous sin, facilitating both sex outside marriage and, more importantly, protected sex, which was forbidden even for married couples.

Roche was paraded before his class and made to apologise for having committed, in the words of a report, 'the serious offence of bringing two contraceptives into the school'. He recalls his fear and concern that he would be the next cadet to be expelled. Instead, he was placed on probation. He states that he was confined to barracks for a period and assigned extra duties.

His humiliation over the affair was compounded by an order forcing him to write home to his parents in Clonmel to inform them of his misdemeanour and to apologise. Christina remembered the incident clearly:

> We nearly died over it. I couldn't explain to you my disappointment, my shock. I had a sheltered rearing ... I was horrified, I really was. I thought it was dreadful. How could he do something like that? It upset me.

The bond between Dónal Roche and his father was severely undermined.

Roche says that he had had the condoms in his wallet for a long time and may even have forgotten about them. He had retained them as a curiosity and out of youthful bravado, since the opportunity to meet the opposite sex in Cadet School was very limited.

The report of Lt Col. Mattimoe and Col. O'Neill describes his conduct thus:

> Guilty of the serious offence of bringing two contra-
> ceptives into the School. His conduct otherwise is
> satisfactory.

It should be noted that, in strictly legal terms, possession of condoms was not an offence. However, it might have been regarded as 'conduct detrimental to good order and discipline' although such a charge would be highly subjective. Subsequently, he was dropped from the top third of his class to second last in rankings. The senior officers state:

> Not as balanced and stable as he might be. Since the
> offence mentioned above [the condom incident] he has
> become more serious-minded in his outlook.

Under the heading 'Special Features', Mattimoe and O'Neill state:

> Is at present on Probation for the offence of bringing
> contraceptives into the School. He still has many
> deficiencies to overcome before attaining the requisite
> standard.

Nonetheless, the two senior officers recommended that 'he continue for the present'.

At the end of her life Christina looked back and laughed at the innocence and stupidity of the condom incident, but following receipt of her son's letter, she worried that the incident might adversely affect his career. However, Dónal's godfather, Ger Madden, a Commandant in the army, put her fears to rest: 'I went to Ger and I remember asking him if it would do Dónal any harm, and Ger said "No, that's his private life." So that satisfied me for the time being.'

And so it seemed. Despite the entire furore and the poor report in the immediate aftermath of the condom affair, it was recommended that Dónal should, indeed, be commissioned in September 1965. Commandant Horgan says that four members of the class were obliged to undergo a further year's training and were commissioned the following year. He states:

> This is a clear indication that Dónal de Róiste was
> considered suitable in September 1965 to be an officer.
> He was considered more suitable than these four
> officers who were commissioned a year later, and he was
> considered more suitable than the eighteen cadets who
> were dismissed during the two-year cadetship.

COMMISSIONING AND POSTING

Dónal Roche graduated from Cadet School as a second lieutenant and took the officer's oath on 27 September 1965 at the Curragh, Kildare, before the Minister for Defence.

Roche swore solemnly to be faithful to Ireland and loyal to the Constitution. He swore that while he was an officer of the permanent defence force he would obey all lawful orders issued to him by his superior officers. He swore that he would not join, or be a member of, or subscribe to, any political organisation or society, or any secret society whatsoever.

We can imagine the pride that Seán Roche felt that day as he watched his son receive his commission as an officer of the defence forces. The words of his eldest son's oath of allegiance would have had special resonance for this man for whom honour and ethics meant everything. To see his son pledge himself to uphold this oath through his loyalty to the Irish state and Constitution would have been the culmination of all his hard work over the years.

Dónal Roche's youngest sister, Adi, was just ten at the time but recalls the day vividly:

> I can remember the day he was commissioned in Kildare.
> It was such a proud day and a great occasion for the
> family. At that time it was the proudest moment of our
> lives. It was like a wedding. I remember the hotel where
> we went for a meal afterwards and I remember what I
> wore and even the hat my mother wore.

Although Dónal's godfather had told Christina that her son would not suffer for being guilty of 'the serious offence of bringing two contraceptives into the [cadet] school', the posting Dónal was given after graduation suggests that the condom affair may not have been forgotten.

On the day of his commissioning, twenty-year-old Second Lieutenant Dónal Roche was assigned to the 4th Field Signal Company, Athlone, Co. Westmeath, a posting for which he had not applied. Official documents confirm that 'Lt Roche opted initially for posting to [Supply and Transport Corps]'.

The normal practice for young officers on posting to a corps from Cadet School was to undergo a Young Officers' (YO) introductory course shortly after their arrival in their first unit. Their next mandatory course would be a Corps Standard Course, normally completed six to seven years after the YO Course. The final mandatory course for officers was a Command and Staff Course, usually completed six to ten years following completion of the Standard Course. When Roche was posted to the Signal Corps, no YO Course was held, possibly because of the small numbers of newly commissioned officers entering his corps that year. Instead, he was required to undergo a corps Standard Course without the benefit of the six-month YO course. A Standard Course would have involved a lot of science and radio theory and would have been doubly difficult for Roche and, in fact, he did not achieve what would have been regarded as a satisfactorily high standard on the course. Despite this, he was happy in his new Signal unit. He settled in well and recalls a number of senior officers with fondness:

> Commandant Eric Gregan was a renaissance man who was as much interested in civilian life as he was in military life. He was a very fatherly figure and gave him great encouragement and advice, particularly how to deal with stress.
>
> I was very happy in my unit … I harboured the hope that I might be transferred to a university town where the army would allow me to study for a degree. I particularly remember one of my commanding officers, Commandant Michael Begley. Like Commandant Gregan, he too was a decent man. We used to swap classical music records such as Rossini and Andrés Segovia. Commandant Begley introduced me to Segovia, the Spanish classical guitarist

who had spurred interest in the guitar as an instrument for classical music through his arrangements of the works of Bach, Handel and other composers.

Apart from the Standard Signal Officers' Course that he undertook, Roche had other assignments during his period with the Signal Corps. Part of Lt Roche's duties following his commission was to 'perform duties with recruit training classes'. He recalls the help and encouragement he received from ordinary soldiers and NCOs:

> I was like a junior manager in Dunnes Stores, learning his trade. I was a rookie and men twice my age obeyed me, not because they respected me, but because they had to. I felt I had a good rapport with the NCOs and ordinary decent soldiers who, despite the rough and tumble of the army, actually introduced me to my role as their commander.

Also amongst the duties assigned to Lt Roche at that time was that of Mess Caterer at the officers' mess in Athlone. It was in Athlone that Lt Roche first met Commandant Seán T. O'Kelly, a visiting officer from Cork, who agreed to give Roche and Lt Michael Cleary a partial lift home one winter's evening in November 1967, during which they were involved in a collision with another car. The controversial circumstances of this car crash, and its possible impact on Lt Roche's career, are dealt with in Chapter 10.

ANNUAL OFFICER REPORTS
1965
At the end of December 1965, after just three months, Lt Roche received his first 'Annual Confidential Officer's Report'. Officers receive their annual reports at the end of each calendar year.

His Service Number: 0.8159, first appears on this report. The report was prepared by Lt Col. J.P. Kane. Lt Col. Kane noted that 2nd Lt Roche was in good health and kept himself physically fit. He was keen on all outdoor sports. His performance of duty called for no adverse comment. Kane stated: 'Lt Roche is very young – this is an easily corrected problem [sic]. He tackles all jobs with enthusiasm.' He reported that Lt Roche's dress and bearing 'leave nothing to be desired'. He stated that his general conduct called for no adverse comment and that he received no warnings, admonishments nor had he been found guilty of any offences. Lt Col. Kane considered Lt Roche suitable for his present appointment. In response to a question regarding an appointment for which he might be better suited, Kane wrote: 'He is so young in the army that it is difficult to say at this early stage.'

Asked to comment on Roche's reliability, devotion to duty, zeal, industry, ability, initiative and, where applicable, the faculty of leadership, Lt Col. Kane wrote: 'He seems to show promise of having these desirable qualities.'

With regard to standards acceptable to his profession, Kane wrote: 'He is keen, eager, energetic and should turn out to be very suitable material.'

In consideration of all of the above, Lt Col. J.P. Kane awarded 2nd Lt Roche a 'satisfactory' rating.

A brigade commander, a superior reporting officer and a corps director endorsed the report. All signed their agreement with Kane's report and rating. Commandant Eric Gregan noted on the report: 'From the little I saw of him I would say however that he is promising material, even if a little boyish.'

1966

The report at the end of 1966 is also marked 'satisfactory'. Commandant Gregan filed it and there is one particularly noteworthy comment made by him:

> He strikes one as being rather 'present generation' and all
> that that connotes. However, I think he will mature into
> a useful officer.

Describing Lt Roche as 'present generation' indicates that he, no doubt along with other young officers, had been imbued by the spirit of the 1960s.

A remark on the report, signed and dated on 15 May (or possibly June) 1967, by the Corps Director reads: '… Has made a poor showing so far on Standard Signal Officers' Course.'

Notwithstanding his struggle with the technical side of the Standard Signal Officers' Course, Roche was promoted on 27 October 1967 from second lieutenant to full lieutenant. Clearly his commanding officers – in particular, Commandant Gregan – had confidence in his potential. Once again, Gregan gave him a rating of 'satisfactory' for the year ended 1967. The commandant also makes one particularly noteworthy comment in response to the standard inquiry regarding promotion in due course:

> Being only recently promoted LIEUTENANT (27 Oct 67) there would be NO question of his promotion for several years. I would expect him to qualify in time however.

Lt Roche's struggle with the technical side of the Signals Corps became evident in 1967. Because of his lack of technical knowledge and wider aspects of signal theory and practice, he did not achieve a satisfactory standard on completion of his Standard Signal Course. The officer in charge of the course was forthright in an assessment that might equally be read as a criticism of the decision to assign Lt Roche to the Signal Corps. On 12 January 1968, he writes:

> Lt Roche, I feel, should not have been appointed to the Signal Corps on commissioning. It is evident that his talents do not lie in the electronics field. He himself opted for [Supply and Transport Corps]. He began the course without having undergone any previous Sig. Corps course … He is undoubtedly intelligent but lacks in method, application and neatness of work … perhaps he could be utilised in the Corps as a motorcycle instructor. His conduct on the course was fair, since knowing that he was unprepared, he did not, in my opinion, devote sufficient time to private study to make up the deficiency.

Lt Roche was given the right of reply and the opportunity to explain his failure on the course. On 24 January 1968 he wrote:

Sir,

I am very disappointed to learn that I have failed the Standard Signal Officers course. While not registering a protest or complaining of the result in any way, I would like the following factors to be borne in mind:

a.   Due to various postings on temporary duty in my home command prior to my going on the course I was unable to prepare for the course by way of private study.

b.   Unlike most of the other students I had NOT done the Basic Signal Officers course of 6 months duration.

However, the knowledge and experience I have gained on the course will NOT be wasted as I intend to further my studies at the earliest opportunity and attain a satisfactory standard.

There is certainly no hint that Lt Roche wanted to throw in the towel. This quality was recognised by his Brigade Commander in his 1967 report:

His [Lt Roche's] outstanding quality would appear to be dour endurance. He works earnestly and zealously.

Just eighteen days later, Lt Roche was transferred out of the 4th Field Signal Corps to 4th Garrison Supply and Transport Company, Athlone.

1968 – Unexpected Transfer

As the spring of 1968 began, Roche was attached temporarily to the Air Squadron at Baldonnell in Dublin. He was posted there on 5 February 1968 and remained there until his transfer from Signals to the 4th Garrison Supply and Transport Company, at the beginning of June. While at Baldonnell, he was involved in the air and sea search for Aer Lingus Flight 712 which disappeared in perfect flying conditions shortly after midday on 24 March 1968. *St Phelim*, a Viscount turboprop, crashed into the Irish Sea near Tuskar Rock, just off the Wexford coast. All sixty-one passengers and crew on board died.

On 3 June 1968, without notice or a transfer request, Roche was unexpectedly moved from the Signal Corps to 4th Garrison Supply and Transport Company. As a consequence of this transfer, Roche now found himself in another corps in which he had no qualification and, as a result, he was somewhat isolated. He states:

> When I found myself in hot water less than a year later, I was without senior officers who knew me and were prepared to stand up for me. I feel sure that Commandant Gregan would have supported me had I remained in the Signal Corps. However, I was now in a different section of the army and felt very isolated and vulnerable.

Roche's penultimate annual report, covering 1968, contains no evidence that he had come to undue attention. The report, written by Commandant Michael Begley, states that Lt Roche, while not participating in sporting activities 'is otherwise quite active, on and off duty'. Roche enjoyed both physical training and long-distance running. Begley notes that Lt Roche 'performs his duties satisfactorily but lacks experience in staff work'. His dress and bearing had called for no adverse comment. Nor had his conduct. Indeed, Begley comments:

> He is well behaved and has NOT [Begley's emphasis] given cause for adverse comment from me.

The report states that he received no warnings or admonishments, and nor had he been found guilty of any offences. He is considered suitable for his present appointment. Commandant Begley notes, 'he has no technical qualifications as yet', suggesting that he expected him to achieve them eventually. With regard to 'Appointments Recommended' Begley writes:

> Suitable for staff or unit appointments in his present rank which do NOT require the knowledge of [transport matters].

In reply to the question regarding evidence of suitability for promotion in due course, Begley answers: 'Yes'.

When asked to explain why he wasn't recommending Lt Roche 'for promotion now', he writes:

> He has NOT completed a Basic S&T [Supply and Transport] Course nor an S&T Standard Course nor is he sufficiently experienced.

With regard to the 'acceptable standards' of his profession as an officer, Begley writes:

> He has served in the Signal Corps until June 68. As yet he has NO [Supply and Transport] qualifications. He lacks experience 'A' adm but is proving satisfactory in his appointment.

Lt Roche receives a 'satisfactory' rating for 1968. The report was signed by Commandant Begley on 21 January 1969. One week later, on 28 January 1969, the commanding officer of Air Signals Squadron, M. O'Riordan, countersigned the report with the handwritten comment: 'I agree with the above remarks.'

As 1969 began, Lt Roche found himself working quietly as an administration officer with 4th Garrison Supply and Transport Company in Custume Barracks, Athlone. In less than six months, his career in the army would be over and his life changed forever.

OFF-DUTY

Within the army, Dónal Roche had two close friends: Lt (later Commandant) Patrick Walshe and Lt (later Lt Col.) Gerry Swan. All three had come from families where love of music had been cultivated and they would regularly meet on evenings off and at weekends to indulge their passion. Walshe was then a training officer of the 3rd Field Artillery Regiment, headquartered in Templemore. He resided in Birr, Co. Offaly. Gerry Swan was a training officer in Thurles, residing at Foley's Hotel, Templemore.

The three young officers would often travel the length and breadth of the country to attend fleadh ceoil or traditional sessions. They had a civilian friend who travelled with them, Brendan Doherty. Doherty worked at various jobs including helping his father, Frank, with 'The Golden Goose' cancer research fundraising initiative. His father later became the first CEO of the Irish Cancer Society, established in the mid-1960s, from which he retired in 1981.

The chief haunts of the three officers and their civilian friend were venues in which they could make their own music. Roche played the guitar; Walshe played the tin whistle and box-accordion, while Swan was, says Roche, 'a tin whistle man renowned for his delivery of songs and monologues and a great composer of poetry.' Roche describes Doherty as a raconteur of note, with 'a very melodious voice'.

To this day, the three former officers laugh as they reminisce over their antics and immaturity. They laugh especially at their nicknames: Roche was called 'Duck', a nickname he had acquired from Clonmel mates who called him 'Donal[d] Duck'; Walshe was 'Pini'; and Swan was simply 'Swannie'. Their civilian friend, Brendan Doherty, now deceased, was nicknamed 'The Dog', because of the frequent misspelling of his name, 'Dogherty'.

Their time in the army coincided with the Irish 'ballad boom' of the 1960s. Singer/songwriters and groups of musicians were beginning to enjoy great success around the country and a strong music scene was growing up around O'Donoghue's public house on Merrion Row in Dublin. Its musical history, according to the current manager, Con Kavanagh, began to take shape in the mid-1960s with artists such as the Dubliners, the Furey Brothers, Christy Moore and Val Doonican performing there. The walls of the famous pub are adorned with drawings and photographs of some of Ireland's finest traditional performers, all of whom played their part in adding to what is a unique heritage.

Famous visitors to O'Donoghue's included the brothers of the 35th President of the United States of America, Robert and Ted Kennedy; the German Chancellor, Gerhard Schröder, and the Prime Minister of Norway, Kjell Magne Bondevik. Its reputation also attracted many visiting celebrities.

Roche describes O'Donoghue's as 'the Temple Bar of its day, without the puke'. He recalls knowing many of the musicians there and having the opportunity to buy them the odd drink. According to retired Commandant Patrick Walshe:

The mid-60s brought a bit of prosperity and freedom. We [Roche, Swan, Doherty and himself] were regular companions almost every weekend, since we were stationed close to one another, travelling the country to various music sessions.

Walshe recalls that, while popular, the meetings with Dónal Roche and Gerry Swan at O'Donoghue's were infrequent. This is also a view supported by Roche's girlfriend of the time, Mary O'Callaghan, who told me on 23 May 2004 that she had little recollection of frequenting O'Donoghue's.

Walshe states:

O'Donoghue's was more often a rendezvous point than a venue that we went to regularly. We used O'Donoghue's purely as a meeting point. We'd meet there and head off to points generally on the outskirts of the city where we would make our own music. In O'Donoghue's there'd be music that you'd sit and listen to, but that wasn't really our scene. We preferred to go and make our own music....

In O'Donoghue's everybody was there for the music. We'd meet different people every night. Sometimes you'd meet the same people and it wasn't unusual to greet a familiar acquaintance. But I seldom asked any of these people their names and they seldom asked me who I was. And they certainly never tried to influence me in any way because everyone was there for the music. There was no other reason for being present at these occasions.

However, unknown to Walshe, Roche and Swan, O'Donoghue's would be named as the location of alleged subversive 'contact' during 1968 and 1969 – an allegation that would ultimately result in Lt Roche's forced 'retirement' from the army.

Beginning on 25 April 1969, Roche and Walshe were interrogated and accused of having amongst their O'Donoghue's acquaintances one, and possibly four, alleged members of an IRA splinter group. It remains a puzzle that despite visits to O'Donoghue's by other army officers at this time, only some of those in Lt Roche's immediate circle of friends were questioned or interrogated. Even within that circle, not all were questioned. It is highly probable that Gerry Swan, for example, spoke to the very same people as Roche; however, he was never questioned.

In addition, it should be noted that Lt Roche was questioned directly in relation to his acquaintances in O'Donoghue's while Patrick Walshe's interrogation appears to have been slanted towards Roche's acquaintances, rather than his own.

While Walshe, Roche and Swan all agree that they had, along with the rest of the nation, a growing interest in the 'Troubles', that period of history was in its infancy, with little evidence of significant IRA activity. Furthermore, Roche's family background was such that he saw no legitimacy for an illegal army.

The first two fatalities of the modern 'Troubles' resulted from the use of batons wielded by RUC officers on Francis McCloskey, a 67-year-old unmarried Catholic pensioner in Dungiven, Co. Derry, on 14 July 1969; and Samuel Devenney, a 42-year-old Catholic father of nine, who died on 16 July 1969, from a beating he received at his home on William Street, Derry, two months earlier. By then, Lt Dónal Roche had been 'retired' from the permanent defence forces.

The circumstances of Lt Roche's 'retirement', including his arrest and interrogations, and those of then Captain Patrick Walshe, are dealt with in the following chapter.

4

PUBLIC AUCTION AND

INTERROGATION

It is not because I cannot explain that you won't understand, but because you won't understand that I cannot explain.

Elie Wiesel

On 12 February 1969, Lt Dónal Roche celebrated his twenty-fourth birthday at Custume Barracks, Athlone, where he was assigned as an acting administration officer to 4th Garrison Field Supply & Transport Company, from 6 August the previous year.

Part of his responsibilities involved helping to organise, on behalf of the Western Command, the public auction of old motor vehicles and motorcycles at Clancy Barracks, Dublin, on 23 April 1969. It was quite a sizable logistical task. The catalogue for the auction shows that there were in total 217 vehicles and motorcycles for sale. An advertisement appeared in *The Irish Times*, *Irish Independent*, *Irish Press* and the *Cork Examiner* on Wednesday, 16 April 1969. The advertisement states twice that the auction was public.

Lt Roche was sent to Dublin for a month to help organise the Western Command's contribution to the auction. Clearly, he was considered a responsible and competent officer to be given such an assignment.

In the event, the auction was a huge success, with most of the 217 vehicles and cycles listed in the catalogue being sold, to a total of fifty-two purchasers. Lot 77, a 1941 Morris Quadrant Gun-Tower, was purchased by the Transport Museum and was pictured on page 7 of the *Irish Press*, on Thursday, 24 April 1969 (see photograph section), the day that Lt Dónal Roche returned to his base at Custume Barracks, Athlone. Later, the Chief of Staff would send a 'Security Report' to the

Minister for Defence in which Clancy Barracks is described as a 'highly sensitive army post'. What is meant by this reference is unclear and, to a civilian mind, it seems strange that a press photographer was allowed to take a photograph, and stranger that the photographer's camera is looking down over the gathering, indicating that he was given access to an upstairs window within the 'highly sensitive army post'. We can be sure that if the *Irish Press* photographer took one picture, he took a dozen or more, and one wonders from what locations he did so.

According to military sources, Clancy Barracks was staffed largely by civilian personnel and housed mainly furniture workshops, transport workshops, optical workshops, engineer stores, clothing stores, and reserve rations. It contained no operational units and probably few weapons stores. The main repository for explosives and ammunitions at this time was the army's magazine in the Curragh.

The press photograph shows just a section of the auction. Approximately forty-five army vehicles can be counted, plus nine cars which may or may not be part of the auction. In the foreground there are over 100 people, including some military personnel. Commandant Patrick Walshe likened the gathering, when first shown the photograph, to 'a fair day in Fermoy in the 1950s'. The gathering looks relaxed with the majority of the crowd huddled around what appears to be an open-topped jeep with two men standing on the left and a woman, presumably an administrative assistant, sitting on the right rear. Military personnel can be seen observing and mingling with the crowd. On the bottom left of the picture, a mother, holding the hand of her child, can be seen exiting the frame of the photograph.

Former Lt Roche states that the following day, Friday, 25 April 1969, without warning or caution, he was arrested by an armed officer and driven back to Dublin:

> I vividly recall the shock and confusion I felt as I was ordered out of my office into a waiting staff car in front of everyone. The arresting officer, Captain Pat Dixon, couldn't tell me what it was all about. He mumbled something about it being 'a mix up perhaps'. He was a fellow officer. We had worked for almost a year in the same Unit of the 4th Field Supply and Transport Company. Now he sat in silence throughout the journey

between Athlone and Dublin staring straight ahead.

Captain Dixon disputes Roche's recollections. He states that Lt Roche was not arrested and that he was simply asked by higher command to accompany him in a staff car to Dublin. Unknown to Roche, he was on his way to an interrogation. A few days later, Captain Patrick Walshe would also be interrogated. However, a more senior officer did not accompany him to army headquarters in Dublin in a staff car. He was ordered to report there and drove himself. It should be noted that at no time from the beginning until the end of the Lt Roche affair was he charged with any offence. Military rules would require that an officer be charged prior to an arrest. It is probable, therefore, that Roche was given the impression that he was under arrest without actually being so. In any event, he had no option but to accompany Captain Dixon.

On 25 August 2005, I spoke by telephone with former Captain Dixon, who retired from the army as a brigadier general. I asked him to explain how it was that Walshe had been asked to attend for 'interview', and did so voluntarily, but Lt Roche was accompanied. 'Does this not suggest Roche was arrested?' I asked him. He replied, 'I was told to accompany him, there and back. That's all I can tell you.'

Roche recalls being placed in a locked room at army headquarters. His principal interrogator was Commandant Gerry O'Sullivan, of the Intelligence Section. O'Sullivan would later be appointed to the rank of Chief of Staff.

Former Lt Roche states that at no point during the first day of interrogation was he told specifically why he was being questioned. He recalls that when he would ask why he was being detained, his interrogator would reply, 'That's for you to tell us.'

He states that sometime after his first interrogation, he contacted his uncle, Ger Madden, a former commandant in the army. Madden advised him to co-operate fully with the Intelligence Section and to be completely honest and truthful. He says the process was so traumatic and confusing that he cannot recall if he was returned to Athlone or kept in Dublin at McKee Barracks. On Monday, 28 April, he returned to army HQ in Dublin for further questioning.

The following reconstruction of an interrogation by Commandant Gerry O'Sullivan is based on Roche's recollection of an exchange:

Interrogator: You know why you are here?

Lt Roche: No, sir.

Interrogator: Why do you think you are here?

Lt Roche: I don't know, sir.

Interrogator: (*shouting*) Do you think we are stupid?

Lt Roche: No, Sir!

Interrogator: Then make this easy for all of us and confess!

Lt Roche: Confess what, sir?

Interrogator: (*pacing and shouting louder*) That is for you to tell us.

Lt Roche: Tell you what, sir?

Interrogator: Don't try and play the old soldier with me, Lieutenant.

(*Interrogator leaves abruptly and returns some time later*)

Interrogator: Have you thought about your position?

Lt Roche: What do you want me to talk about, sir?

Interrogator: That is for you to tell us!

Lt Roche: Why am I here, sir?

Interrogator: Very serious allegations have been made against you.

Lt Roche: Who is making these allegations, sir?

Interrogator: Security.

Lt Roche: What are the allegations, sir?

Interrogator: Pay attention, Lieutenant. I said that it is for you to tell us. This may lead to a court martial or worse.

Recalling his experience, primarily with Commandant O'Sullivan, Roche states:

> I didn't know it at first but I was in his sights for a long merciless torture, a whole lifetime as it has turned out. He has haunted my nightmares for over thirty years. He was an defence forces intelligence officer with ambition. He could smell commies, traitors and subversives a mile off. And, seemingly, because I liked Irish music, I was somehow collaborating with them.

Roche says that O'Sullivan's threat of a court martial shocked him. A court martial, he realised, could lead to dismissal from the army. He responded, 'I don't know what to say, sir.'

He recalls shuddering and his mind racing. 'I wondered if it was some sort of SAS-type endurance test I was undergoing and why.' He further recalls moments during the ordeal when he wept with frustration and fear.

> Thoughts of my family flashed through my mind. My father, a factory worker, would never understand this. The disgrace would kill him. He gloried in the fact that he had placed me a step higher on the [social] ladder than himself. His pride and joy at having a son an officer knew no bounds. My respect for authority was such that I began to think they knew something awful about me that I had yet to discover myself. Waves of nausea came over me. I remember thinking: 'This is madness!'

Lt Roche recalls his interrogator suggesting that it would be better for him to make a clean breast of things, that if he resigned his commission, he would be provided with a good reference and whatever monies were due to him.

The young lieutenant was getting more shocked by the minute. 'I knew that my service had been satisfactory, as I had had my annual assessment at the beginning of the year.' He recalls that his interrogator produced papers and pushed them towards him before leaving the room.

> My mind was in turmoil. I wished to help but not knowing what I was supposed to have done, I felt frightened and helpless. Time, I remember, stood still. My thoughts were racing. The interrogator had also stated that in war times my behaviour would warrant a firing squad. I wondered if he had the wrong person. I resolved to help him, in order to get out of the predicament. But I was equally determined not to resign even though the pressure to do so was enormous. I was determined to vindicate myself.

Roche recalls that his interrogator had him feeling caged and rattled. He admits that thoughts of escape ran through his mind, but he felt rooted, as if drugged.

> If I try to escape, I am admitting guilt, but of what? It is obvious that O'Sullivan already has me classed as guilty of something.

Roche recalls his interrogator screaming at him: 'Lieutenant Roche, an officer must be like Caesar's wife, Caligula. Do you understand that?'

The young lieutenant replied, 'No, sir.'

'You must be above suspicion, Lieutenant Roche,' was the reply

Roche began to trawl his mind to try to figure out what he might be suspected of. He recalled his Uncle Ger's advice about being honest and truthful. The only thing he could think of was a set of hubcaps a sergeant had switched from a car for auction onto his own during the auction. Perhaps this was it. Perhaps he had been arrested for theft. He told his interrogator who clearly wasn't interested.

Roche also recalls a curious twist during one of the interrogations. His interrogator pointed to some papers which he said were Roche's Cadet School records. Roche recalls trembling.

> *Interrogator*: Have you ever had a homosexual experience, Roche?
>
> *Lt Roche*: No, sir!
>
> *Interrogator*: Why are you having such a tense reaction?
>
> *Lt Roche*: I am not, sir.
>
> *Interrogator*: Are you stating that you are not a homosexual?
>
> *Lt Roche*: Definitely not, sir.
>
> *Interrogator*: What, never? All through the Cadet School, locked up in the Curragh Camp with only sheep, and soldiers? No sexual thoughts?
>
> *Lt Roche*: No, sir.
>
> *Interrogator*: Aren't cadets forbidden to date local women? What did you do?
>
> *Lt Roche*: Yes, sir. They are, sir.

The young lieutenant suspected that his interrogator was drawing on the condom incident and drawing inferences that were intended to shock and embarrass.

He recalls that the interrogations then began to centre on his attendance at music venues and public bars while in Dublin before and during the period of the auction of army vehicles at Clancy Barracks. It later emerged that Commandant O'Sullivan was primarily interested in O'Donoghue's public house, the specific nights Roche went there, with whom, and his relationship with a Mr Padraig Dwyer. He states that on occasions the interrogation process was so intimidating that he was afraid for his physical safety.

Roche had no idea why O'Sullivan was interested in Padraig Dwyer. Recalling the advice of his uncle, he truthfully told O'Sullivan that he had been introduced to a Padraig Dwyer by an Australian singer, Brian Mooney, in early 1968, in O'Donoghue's. He told O'Sullivan that Mooney was a gregarious character who knew every-one and was for-ever introducing people to one another; he thought they might have something in common as Lt Roche served with the Signal Corps at Baldonnell Aerodrome – a defence force facility – and Padraig Dwyer frequented the place because he had a connection with a glider club that operated out of Baldonnell in the late 1960s. Roche never met Dwyer there, principally because he had no interest in gliding and no interest in Dwyer. On one other occasion, he and his 'civvy' friend, Brendan (the 'Dog') Doherty, had taken a lift from Dwyer and a German girlfriend as far as Galway where they had arranged to meet up with Captain Patrick Walshe and Lt Gerry Swan for the weekend. That was the ex-tent of their 'relationship' apart from friendly banter on occasions when they came across one another in the crowded confines of O'Donoghue's where great traditional music was the magnet.

Almost four decades later, recalling the advice offered by his uncle, Dónal de Róiste wryly says:

> My godfather, Uncle Ger Madden, an army commandant, advised me to tell the truth and that everything would be all right. I did that. I told the truth and, sadly, in retrospect, it appears to have been the worst thing I could have done because it was twisted to be used against me.

He recalls his mind being in utter turmoil:

> I felt denigrated and very emotional. After my confession about the hubcaps I felt that if I could just get out of the room, I could clear up the evident mistake as I was not guilty of anything. I felt that it was a clear case of mistaken identity as I sought to reconcile my innocence with the apparent conviction of my superiors that I was somehow guilty. During the period of interrogation I lost the concept of space and time. I cannot recall the duration of the interrogations, how or where I slept or ate during this period. I was in a state of confusion and disorientation.

Captain Patrick Walshe has a much clearer memory of his ordeal. Amazingly, while there are 'notes' in existence alleging the contents of Roche's interrogations, Walshe has been informed under the Freedom of Information Act that there are no such records in existence regarding his interrogations by Commandant Gerry O'Sullivan. Chapter 12 deals with the 'notes' that allegedly detail the three interrogations of Lt Roche.

THE INTERROGATION OF PATRICK WALSHE

The alleged non-existence of notes from the Captain Patrick Walshe interrogations is suspicious and curious. In the absence of such documentation, Captain Walshe cannot pinpoint precisely the dates he was interrogated. He was ordered to report to Intelligence Section at Parkgate Street, Dublin, where Commandant Gerry O'Sullivan questioned him about his relationship with Lt Roche and Roche's relationship with unspecified people. He recalls:

> I answered all the questions put to me to the best of my knowledge, but Commandant O'Sullivan continued to repeat the same questions endlessly. It appeared to me that he wanted certain answers to his questions, particularly about persons that Dónal and I had allegedly met. The questioning went on for a number of days. During the final day of questioning I asked him to tell

me the names of the persons in question, but he refused. I asked Commandant O'Sullivan to describe them or to show me a photograph so that I might assist with the answers and he refused this request also.

He spent the first half-day that I was up with him harassing me to find out where and when we had met two weeks before that. And I wasn't sure if it had been a Friday or a Saturday. Funnily enough, he wasn't interested in the days in between, because I had met Dónal since that. He was just interested in a meeting two weeks before.

I was called up to Dublin again two days later and he started into the same thing…. He tried to compel me to say whether it was one evening or the other and I couldn't. I'd have been lying if I'd said one or the other because I couldn't remember.

As the thing went on, he gave me slight bits of information. He said that Dónal and I had been meeting people. I asked for names but he wouldn't give me a thing. On the second day, halfway through, he said that Lt Roche had made a statement saying that I had met 'these people', rather than 'that person'. I let it go and he went on badgering. However, after five minutes I called a halt to it and I said, 'Excuse me, sir, you stated that Lieutenant Roche has made a statement to you that I had been meeting "these people". I want Lieutenant Roche to be brought into my presence to make that statement in front of me; otherwise I'm not answering any more questions here.

… He appeared to have been taken off guard … I knew by his reaction that he had been making it up.

He asked me then did I know anyone named Padraig. I told him I knew several Padraigs around the country and that he would have to be more specific. I asked had he a photograph of him, or what his surname was but I got no response.

He gave me the full name at the next interrogation session, Padraig Dwyer, and I told him I was not aware of anyone of that name. It was quite possible that I had met with someone of that name, but I needed to see a photograph of him. If he was that important, surely he would have a photograph of him.

Commandant Walshe recalls O'Sullivan continuing to press him to answer his questions, while he continued to make it clear that he was unable to do so without a picture of Mr Dwyer. He then recalls that O'Sullivan made a strange statement. 'He looks not unlike yourself,' he said.

Some years later, an acquaintance who knew Dwyer told Walshe that he was, 'a small, chubby fellow with a beard. There is no way, in any respect, that he could be considered to look like you.' Walshe says that he has spent many years trying to figure out this conundrum:

> If the guy was so important Sullivan must have known what he looked like. He must have had some description of him. Dwyer wasn't remotely like me, yet he told me that he was. I don't think that O'Sullivan was interested in my alleged connection with Dwyer. I think it was window dressing and an attempt to get information out of me that might be slanted against Dónal. I always harboured that suspicion and some thirty years later, my suspicions proved to be well founded.

Like Dónal de Róiste, Walshe recalls the experience as 'quite a traumatic affair'. He had met O'Sullivan previously at a debriefing following a trip Walshe had made to Poland, as part of a study group interested in the Polish fishing industry. On that occasion, he considered him to be quite a gentleman.

Initially Walshe thought that he had been invited back to the Intelligence Section to discuss some aspect of his visit to Communist Poland during the previous year. He recalls being stunned and taken off guard by his encounter. He recalls:

> This man that I had thought to be a reasonable man suddenly changed. That was quite shocking. If I had never met Commandant O'Sullivan before and a raging

bully had came into the room, that wouldn't have affected me as much. But I knew him and had considered him a decent man and it was quite shocking for me how he had changed.

While there are three alleged 'notes' related to Lt Roche's interrogations, Captain Walshe believes that Roche was interrogated on more occasions and more intensely than himself. Both he and Roche are very clear that Commandant O'Sullivan was their principal interrogator. They recall that he frequently left them alone in the interrogation room. They also recall that he did not take notes while in their presence. In the files that have been released, there are no notes detailing the 'interviews' with Captain Walshe.

POST-INTERROGATION

Captain Walshe was aware that while he and Roche were under intense investigation, it was likely that their movements and contact with one another would be monitored. He remained confused as to the nature of the investigation but feared that if he and Roche were seen together, it might be construed that they were colluding to ensure that their stories were compatible. He deliberately kept his distance for about two weeks.

As mentioned, Roche had been taken to Dublin for his first interrogation on Friday, 25 April 1969. Walshe believes that his first interrogation by O'Sullivan was the following Tuesday, 29 April. He recalls that his three interrogations took place over a ten-day period. This would suggest that he last met O'Sullivan on or around Thursday, 8 May 1969. He recalls that it was approximately another ten days after this before Lt Roche contacted him by telephone at Magee Barracks, Kildare.

He recalls Roche being very stressed and worried. Primarily, he recalls him being confused.

> During the phone call, Dónal asked me if I would accompany him to visit his maternal uncle, Pat Murphy, who was, ironically, Assistant Secretary at the Department of Defence. He felt that if anyone could help him it would surely be his Uncle Pat. We met in Dublin

and travelled together to Clondalkin where Murphy lived.

We arrived at his home, by arrangement, at about seven o'clock and I recall I did most of the talking….

I remember Pat Murphy sitting before us, tight-lipped for an hour and a half and he hardly spoke, nor did he ask me a question. That was the thing that I remember most; he just sat there. I left Murphy's house with a weight in the pit of my stomach. I hadn't the heart to say it, but I knew that Murphy knew something that we didn't and I sensed whatever it was, it wasn't good for Dónal.

As Pat Murphy closed his front door behind us, I felt an overwhelming sense of sadness and numbness. Dónal had been very quiet throughout the meeting. He was even quieter as we drove back into Dublin.

I knew it had something to do with the gentleman whom O'Sullivan seemed very reluctant to name, Padraig Dwyer. But when he eventually did, he gave no specifics. It was clear from discussing the matter with Dónal that O'Sullivan seemed to be primarily interested in creating confusion. It was all innuendo, mind games and intrigue. I knew too he had attempted to mislead me with the allegation that Dónal had stated that I had met with 'these people'. The question was, who were 'these people'? Dónal Roche and I were completely flummoxed and at a loss to know what we had, allegedly, done wrong. One thing is absolutely certain; it was impossible that Dónal alone was uniquely guilty of some crime solely consequent upon meeting the same people as myself and other army officers, including Gerry Swan. I know I was totally innocent, so does Gerry Swan and we both were certain of Dónal's innocence in this regard.

The ultimate question, of course, is why the secrecy? Why so much cloak-and-dagger posturing and, as we will see, so many rumours and unspecified allegations? Furthermore, there is also a very peculiar absence throughout this entire process: Lt Roche's commanding officers in Custume Barracks, Athlone, or Boyle, made no attempt to come to his assistance or plead his case, although one might reasonably have expected them to do so. Roche recalls a growing coldness and distance amongst the general officer corps.

It was recommended to Roche that he should seek the help of a solicitor. Originally he approached the practice of Barry Turnbull & Co., Cork, but Turnbull recommended that he see Michael B. O'Maoileoin & Co in Dublin. It is clear from documentation that Roche secured from O'Maoileoin in 1978 that he visited the practice on 1 May 1969. It was agreed that O'Maoileoin would write to the army authorities seeking clarification on behalf of his client.

Both Roche and Walshe recall a lull when it appeared that the matter might have passed. However, on 28 May 1969, Lt Roche was asked to meet with a senior legal officer. To this day he has no clear recollection of the meeting, such was the state of his confusion. It now appears that the person he met was the Deputy Judge Advocate General (DJAG), Col. Arthur Cullen, the chief military legal officer of the defence forces.

Based on the tenor of the meeting with the DJAG, Roche realised that his solicitor had, apparently, not yet written to his superiors, seeking clarification. This added to his confusion, as he had been under the assumption that his legal entitlements under the Defence Act and the Constitution were being taken care of.

It is clear from the files released to Lt Roche in 2002 that senior officers, including the army's most senior legal adviser, wanted Lt Roche to provide a written statement. The DJAG, by his own admission, requested Lt Roche to return the following day with such a statement. Captain Walshe recalls Roche telephoning him immediately after his meeting with a senior officer whom Walshe believes was the DJAG:

> His state of mind seemed very bad indeed. It was as though the world was falling in on him. I felt I had a duty to see if I could in any way help him out. I told him to go to his solicitor immediately and report everything that had happened.

Roche returned the following morning, 29 May 1969, as arranged, to Col. Cullen's office. He informed the DJAG that, on the advice of his solicitor, he would not be submitting a written statement. Despite the fact that he was acting on legal advice, and informed the DJAG accordingly, this would later, in secret documents, be used against him, as an indication of guilt.

It is clear from the following letter written by O'Maoileoin to the Chief of Staff that he had questioned Roche carefully and asked him precisely what he was being accused of, and that Roche told him that he honestly was not sure:

> We act for 1st. Lieutenant Dónal Roche who has instructed us to act on his behalf with regard to various serious accusations and charges made against him by the army.
>
> Our client states that he has been brought before various officials and officers of various ranks and accused of misconduct, indiscretion, being a security risk etc. On one occasion he was charged with the offence of being a security risk and on another occasion gross misconduct and so on, with the result that our client does not know where he stands. He is being pressurised and badgered which is quite unfair, due to the fact that he has not yet been formally charged and notice given to him, and an opportunity afforded him to make his own case in his own Defence. Every action that has been taken up to now against him has been completely to his prejudice. We must point out that in the Defence Act, 1954 there are various protections given to officers which have been ignored in our client's case.
>
> Our client would therefore like to know what charge, if any, is being preferred against him.

A clear indication decision and intent of Chief of Staff Lt General Mac Eoin is contained in a secret letter he wrote, and allegedly sent, to the Minister for Defence, Michael Hilliard, on 3 May 1969:

> As a security precaution it has been considered prudent to transfer Lt Roche to an appointment in BOYLE.

There is no evidence in files released to Lt Roche's solicitors in 2002 of even a letter from defence forces HQ to Boyle, giving reasons for Roche's transfer. The move was, in the words of the Chief of Staff, 'a security precaution'.But Roche points out that whereas Custume Barracks, Athlone, is virtually the bull's eye of Ireland, Boyle, Co. Roscommon, was further north and much closer to the border. One would have thought that if the transfer was genuinely 'a security precaution', the prudent posting by the military authorities should have been south, not north.

It is inconceivable that a paper trail of sorts was not created between HQ, Custume Barracks, Athlone, and Boyle, explaining why. But, where is it?

As Lt Roche settled into his new posting in Boyle, he felt justified in assuming that his superiors had realised their mistake. He recalls that his duties as a training officer with the 19th Infantry Battalion, FCA, included organising FCA parades and looking after members' supplies, which included supervising small arms training on the firing range. This also included ensuring that all weapons and ammunition were properly accounted for. As he went about fulfilling the new duties assigned to him, he had little idea that several minds were in overdrive planning the demise of his career.

Dónal de Róiste says that he was ordered to appear before Col. Harry Byrne and other officers at Custume Barracks, Athlone, at 11 a.m. on 26 June 1969. He recalls Byrne handing him a letter. The letter, dated 25 June 1969, had, according to secret files released in 2002, been delivered by Captain P.P. Redmond, a military police officer from the Adjutant General's Branch, Dublin, to Col. E. Shortall, moments before.

The young lieutenant had arrived clueless to the gallows. In retrospect, the only indication that something was afoot was the fact that he had been asked to undergo a medical examination, a legal imperative prior to dismissal or retirement. In an email, dated 11 September 2005, he wrote:

> My recollection is that he [Byrne] gave me a sealed letter
> saying, 'We both know what is in it.' He made me open
> it in front of him and then told me 'You have 12 hours to
> leave.' There were other officers present.

The letter stated:

> I am directed by an tAire Cosanta [the Minister for Defence] to inform you that an tUachtarán has, in pursuance of the powers vested in him by Section 47(2), Defence Act, 1954, and paragraph 18(1)(f), Defence Force Regulation A 15, retired you with effect from the 27th day of June 1969.

Lt Roche walked to his car. He has absolutely no memory of the drive back to Boyle. He doesn't even remember if he cried. However, he does recall feeling that his world had fallen apart. Most of all he worried about the impact on his parents. Rather than face them, he spent the night of 26 June 1969 alone, huddling in his car, into which he had packed his belongings.

He awoke the next morning as an unemployed civilian, with no option but to join the dole queue. That same day, the official journal, *Iris Oifigiúil*, recorded his retirement by the President, 'in the interests of the service'.

1969 IRISH GENERAL RLECTION

How informed of the detail of the Lt Roche affair was the Minister for Defence, Michael Hilliard? The reality is that the Minister was under enormous pressure and was about to lose his seat in the cabinet. On 21 May 1969, the Taoiseach, Jack Lynch, announced a general election and immediately sought the dissolution of the twelfth Dáil. Voting date was set for 18 June 1969.

Despite topping the poll in Meath, Hilliard's days as Minister for Defence were over. Two suspicions seem appropriate. One is that the Minister was so preoccupied with the election that he may have been too easily directed towards an outcome that certain officers in the defence forces wanted. The other is that, in spite of documentation, a superficial reading of which might imply the contrary, he actually knew very little about Lt Roche's predicament. Either way, the Minister for Defence, wittingly or otherwise, may have failed to ensure that Lt Roche's rights as an officer of the permanent defence forces were properly protected. Roche was only a junior officer, perched precariously on the second lowest rung of a nine-rung ladder.

Contained in Lt Roche's 'secret' files is a letter from the Chief of Staff, Lt General Seán Mac Eoin, addressed to the Minister, in which he states:

> In accordance with your request I arranged for [Lt Roche] to be interviewed by the Deputy Judge Advocate General. This interview took place on 28/29 May 1969.
>
> The report of the Deputy Judge Advocate General dated 29 May 1969 is attached hereto and reinforces the conclusions already arrived at by me after consultations with the Adjutant General, the Quartermaster General, the Assistant Chief of Staff and the Director of Intelligence.

The DJAG's report is equally interesting. It too is marked 'secret' and typed on untitled paper. This document will be dealt with in greater detail later in the book but it is interesting to note one fact. According to Lt General Mac Eoin, the meeting between Roche and the DJAG was at the request of the Minister for Defence. Col. Cullen, the DJAG, addressing his report to the Chief of Staff, states: 'In accordance with *your directions* [my emphasis] this officer reported to my office ... I informed Lt Roche that ... the General Staff ... had called upon me ... to advise....' There is no mention of the Minister's request. One would have expected such a request to be conveyed to Lt Roche, emphasising the gravity of the situation, which was, apparently, exercising the mind of a government minister.

It seems fair to ask how the Minister for Defence conveyed his request that the army's chief legal officer should interview Lt Roche. Was it during a personal meeting with the Chief of Staff or his representative? If so, where and when? Was it by means of a letter? If so, where is the letter? Was it by telephone? If so, where is the army's memo recording such an apparently crucial intervention from the member of government to whom the Chief of Staff was ultimately answerable? Is there any evidence to support the Minister's seemingly detailed engagement with Lt Roche's predicament at this time?

Lt General Mac Eoin's letter is headed 'secret', and it is undated, adding to confusion. All that we can deduce is that it was allegedly sent to the Minister subsequent to the meetings that Lt Roche had with the DJAG, Col. Arthur Cullen. It may even have been sent after the Chief of Staff had received the letter from Lt Roche's solicitor, Michael O'Maoileoin, and this may explain why the letter is undated. This is certainly a suspicion held by De Róiste's current solicitor, Eamonn Carroll. He states:

> The reason that the letter … is undated (and is the only undated letter in the sequence) was because the letter from O'Maoileoin had been received and to date the letter subsequent to receipt of O'Maoileoin's letter could prove at a later date that the representations of Dónal's Solicitor was being ignored.

The records indicate that the letter to the Chief of Staff dated 30 May, 1969 from Michael B. O'Maoileoin & Co, Solicitors, was transmitted by the military authorities to the Secretary of the Department of Defence on 6 June, 1969:

> Dear Secretary,
> Please see attached which was sent to the Chief of Staff..
> I understand you have a knowledge of the background.
>   Joseph Emphy
>
> Please prepare a draft answer for Mr O'Cleirigh and discuss with him on Monday if possible.

It is reasonable to assume that the Minister should have been made aware of this letter in the context of the preparation of the memorandum for government and related briefings from the Chief of Staff and the Secretary of the Department. However there is no actual record of this.

As 6 June was a Friday, the draft response to Lt Roche's solicitor's letter would seem to have been written almost immediately. It is clear from the draft that two hands were involved in its drafting (see Appendix A, Document 15). There are two crucial points about the draft which are worth noting. The first is that those drafting the response do not deal with Mr O'Maoileoin's concluding request for clarification, '… what charge, if any, is being preferred against [Lt Roche]'.

The second important point is that the officers drafting the response clearly believed that Lt Roche did have an avenue of redress available to him. Before drafting a response, they consulted the Defence Act upon which they based their response. They indicated that if he thought himself wronged in any matter by any officer, 'it is open to him to take action in accordance with Section 114(1) of the Defence Act 1954'.

Under 'Redress of Wrongs' the Defence Act 1954 states:

> 114.—(1) If an officer thinks himself wronged in any matter by any superior or other officer, including his commanding officer, he may complain thereof to his commanding officer and if, but only if, his commanding officer does not deal with the complaint to such officer's satisfaction, he may complain in the prescribed manner to the Minister who shall inquire into the complaint and give his directions thereon.

Was this draft response discussed with the Secretary to the Department of Defence on the following Monday, 9 June 1969? If it was, and if – as the letter I received from the Department on 20 October 2005 suggests – the Secretary was made aware of Lt Roche's solicitor's letter, the matter begins to take on a very sinister turn. It can only be concluded that a decision was taken at a very high level within the Department of Defence and the defence forces to ignore Lt Roche's military and constitutional rights. All we know for certain is that the draft response was never finalised and was not sent to the young lieutenant's solicitor.

However, a memo from the Secretary of the Department, headed, 'Retirement of Lieutenant Dónal Roche in the interests of the service,' referenced *S. 636* and dated 9 June 1969, states:

> Minister,
> The attached draft memorandum for the government is submitted for your approval.

A memo from Commandant Gerry O'Sullivan in the secret documents released to De Róiste in 2002 states: 'Please open new file in 491 series in name of 0.8159 Lt Dónal ROCHE and pass to me.' It is initialled GOS and dated 12 June 1969. It should be noted that this was six days in advance of the general election and one week in advance of the memorandum prepared for the government, recommending Lt Roche's retirement 'in the interests of the service'.

A file was opened with reference 'G2 C/491/32' with the title: 'Defence Forces. Members engaged in Subversive Activities. 0.8159 Lt Dónal Roche.' O'Sullivan retained possession of this file until either 16 or 17 July 1969, throughout the period when, without Lt Roche's knowledge or suspicion, his 'retirement' was being put in place. O'Sullivan retrieved this file on 11 August 1969 and returned it the same day. He retrieved it again on 10 April 1970 and returned it on 13 April 1970.

The cover letter to the Chief of Staff accompanying the 'Security Report' of the Director of Intelligence, Col. Hefferon, and dated 1 May 1969, also bears the reference 'G2/C/491'. (See Appendix A, Document 8a.)

The question is, given that a file in this category already existed, at such an early stage in the proceedings, why would O'Sullivan request the opening of a 'new file in 491 series' on 12 June 1969? File 491 is G2's 'subversive' file.

It should be recalled that while all of the pieces were being set up for Lt Roche's 'retirement', he was still functioning as a commissioned officer in Boyle, Co. Roscommon. This was a man considered by the DJAG to be a 'grave security risk', and by the Chief of Staff to be a 'hazard [to] military security and the safety of the state'. Why was he not placed under military detention until his 'retirement' was in place if, in fact, he was such a threat?

What is clear from the memorandum for government is that minds were now officially made up. The memorandum simply reflects the recommendation of the Chief of Staff in one of two almost identical letters addressed to the Minister for Defence and dated 3 May 1969 (Appendix A, Documents 10a and 10b).

There are six paragraphs. The crucial paragraph in the draft memorandum states:

> The Minister for Defence considers that, for reasons which he will explain to the government, the retention of Lt Roche in the army would involve a grave hazard to military security and the safety of the state.

Once again, there are no documents to confirm that the Minister received, let alone thoroughly reviewed, the draft memorandum, and we must not lose sight of the fact that he was, during this period, preoccupied with a general election. And here is where another sinister twist in the Lt Roche saga enters the frame. On the first day of counting of votes in the general election, the removal of Lt Roche becomes an urgent matter that *must* be considered by the government. The memorandum for government appears in its final form on 19 June 1969. However, on the same date, an Irish -language document, 'Togra Don Rialtas' (Submission to the Government), Form A, and addressed to the Taoiseach, was prepared. It was headed, 'Recommendation that an officer of the Defence Forces be retired by the President'. The form states the desirability of circulating written documents related to the matter indicated by the heading and of putting it on the agenda for the meeting of the government to be held on Friday, 20 June 1969 (the following day).

The form is standardised and allows room for additional information to be given. This additional information is given in italics below. The second paragraph states:

> I confirm that this is an urgent matter and it should be considered at the meeting referred to above because *it is necessary to pay attention to the case detailed with this Memorandum as soon as possible.*
>
> I confirm also that it was not possible for the Department to complete the required proceedings so that notice could be given in the normal time in advance because *it was not possible to complete the administrative formality before now.*

A second Irish-language document, 'Togra Don Rialtas' (Submission to the Government), Form B, was prepared by the Department of Defence for the Secretary to the Government. It too is headed, 'Recommendation that an officer of the Defence Forces be retired by the President'.

Section 3 of the form states: 'If action by the Government is required under the Constitution or Statute, cite the relevant Article or Statute and the Section and Sub-section.' A handwritten response states:

'Sub-Section 47(2) and Section 51, Defence Act 1954 and Article 13, Section 9 of the Constitution'.

Sub-Section 47(2) of the 1954 Defence Act states:

> An officer [of the Permanent Defence Force] may, for any prescribed reason, be retired by the President.

Section 51 of the Defence Act is also being invoked. This section has three sub-sections and seven sub-paragraphs. The precise sub-section and sub-paragraph are not specified. The document should have stated that Lt Roche was being 'retired' under Section 51(1)(b), that is: an officer may, for any prescribed reason, be retired by the President and 'the retirement ... shall, in each case, take effect from such date as the President may fix'.

The failure to specify the precise sub-section and sub-paragraph confused me for a period. For example, Section 51(1)(e) states:

> ... the dismissal of an officer under section 50, shall, in each case, take effect from such date as the President may fix.
> 50.—(1) The President may dismiss any officer.
> (2) ... an officer shall not be dismissed under this section unless or until the reasons for the proposed dismissal have been communicated to him and such officer has been given a reasonable opportunity of making such representation as he may think proper in relation to the proposed dismissal.

Even though the Chief of Staff was recommending this course of action as early as 3 May 1969 – while the investigation of Lt Roche was still ongoing – when eventually Lt Roche met with the army's chief legal officer, the DJAG, on 28 and 29 May 1969, allegedly to be 'advised of the legal position' (Appendix A, Document 17), the DJAG did not inform the young officer of the specific section of the Defence Act which was being invoked against him.

Article 13, Section 9 of the Constitution, also invoked, states:

The powers and functions conferred on the President by this Constitution shall be exercisable and performable by him only on the advice of the Government.

The real issue, I believe, is that the case against Lt Roche was so weak that those masterminding his expulsion needed to pick their time very carefully to minimise all possible risk of a spanner being put in the works by an over-conscientious cabinet minister, apart from the Minister for Defence, who might raise questions and possibly seek further information or clarification, thereby delaying the process.

The 'Memorandum for the Government', dated 19 June 1969, appears to be the penultimate nail in the coffin for Lt Roche. It reads as follows:

OIFIG AN AIRE COSANTA
MEMORANDUM FOR THE GOVERNMENT
Recommendation that an Officer of the Permanent Defence Force be retired by the President pursuant to subsection 47(2) of the Defence Act, 1954.

1. Subsection 47(2) of the Defence Act, 1954, provides that an Officer of the Permanent Defence Force may, for any prescribed reason, be retired by the President.
2. Subparagraph 18(1)(f) of Defence Force Regulations A.15 prescribes that an Officer of the Permanent Defence Force may be retired pursuant to subsection 47(2) of the Act, in the interests of the service.
3. An Lefteanant Dónal de Róiste (Lieutenant Dónal Roche), born on the 12th February, 1945, entered the Permanent Defence Force as a Cadet on the 7th October, 1963. He was appointed to permanent commissioned rank on the 27th September, 1965. Prior to being awarded a cadetship, he had almost three years' service in An Fórsa Cosanta Áitiúil.
4. The Minister for Defence considers that, for reasons which he will explain to the Government, the retention of Lt Roche in the army would involve a grave hazard to military security and the safety of the state.

5. The Minister, accordingly, recommends that the government should advise the President to retire Lt Roche in the interests of the service, pursuant to subsection 47(2) of the Defence Act, 1954, and subparagraph 18(1)(f) of Defence Force Regulations A.15., with effect from the seventh day after the date of the decision of the government.

6. Retirement in the interests of the service does not involve forfeiture of any entitlement an officer may have under the Defence Forces (Pensions) Schemes. Prima Facie, Lt Roche would be eligible for a small gratuity based on his service on retirement.

A letter in Irish, dated 24 June 1969, from the Department of the Taoiseach, addressed to the Secretary of the Deparement of Defence, with file reference S.17418 states:

> With reference to memorandum number S.636 of 19 June, 1969, submitted by the Minister for Defence, I must inform you that the President today decided, on the advice of the government, to retire Lieutenant Dónal Roche from the Permanent Defence Forces from 27 June, 1969, for the reason that it is in the interests of the service to retire him from the Permanent defence forces.
>
> Arrangements are being made by the Department to publish a suitable notice in *Iris Oifigiúil* (the Official Journal).

CABINET MEETING 20 JUNE 1969

There are two separate 'Minutes Books' in the National Archives in respect of the meeting of the government under which Lt Roche was 'retired'. Both books need to be examined in parallel as they generally record two distinct sets of minutes for the same meeting, recording decisions made by the twelfth government. One of these appears to record decisions made by the government while exercising its power under the Constitution and under statute. The other appears to record more informal decisions concerning matters of government policy. The following summary of items covered in both sets of minutes will help the reader to consider the context of the seventy-minute meeting at which a decisions was made that would blight the remainder of a young man's life.

[MINUTES ONE]

S. 18050   1. PARLIAMENTARY SECRETARIES: Reappointments (4)

S. 1689 D 2. PARLIAMENTARY SECRETARIES: Salaries

S. 18176   3. CIVIL SERVICE: Dismissal.

S. 18186   4. DEFENCE FORCES: Appointments (2) to Reserve Defence Force.

S. 17418   5. DEFENCE FORCES: Retirement from Permanent Defence Force.

Following consideration of a memorandum dated the 19th June, 1969, submitted by the Minister for Defence, it was decided to advise the President to retire

> An Lefteanant Donal De Róiste
> (Lieutenant Donal Roche)

from the Permanent Defence Force with effect from the 27th June, 1969, for the reasons that such retirement would be in the interests of the service.

S. 13869B 6. BORD NA MONA: Re-appointment of Chairman and Members (2)

S. 18168B 7. INDUSTRIAL GRANT: Barbour Threads Limited, Lisburn, County Antrim.

S. 18168B 8. INDUSTRIAL GRANT: Killarney Hosiery Company Limited.

S. 18378   9. INDUSTRIAL GRANT: Pfizer Chemical Corporation, New York.

S. 18092   10. INDUSTRIAL GRANT: Pfizer Chemical Corporation, New York (Quigley Magnesite Branch, Dungarvan, County Waterford).

S. 18168B 11. INDUSTRIAL GRANT: Roto-Finish Limited, Hemel-Hempstead, England.

[MINUTES TWO]

1. REPORT ON VITAL STATISTICS, 1967

2. REPORT ON ACCOUNTS, YEAR ENDED 30 September 1968

3.   CIVIL SERVICE ARBITRATION BOARD: Report on claim for allowances for Clerical Assistants on Sickness — Visitation duties, Department of Social Welfare, April, 1969.

4.   CIVIL SERVICE ARBITRATION BOARD: Reports (2) on claims for travelling allowance for unestablished Local Agents (part-time), Department of Social Welfare, and driving allowance for certain grades — Engineering Branch, Department of Posts and Telegraphs, May, 1969.

5.   ARBITRATION BOARD FOR CERTAIN GRADES OF EMPLOYEES OF COMMITTEES OF AGRICULTURE: Appointment of Chairman

6.   MERCHANDISE MARKS COMMISSION: Reports on Vitreous Enamelled Ware, May, 1969.

7.   EUROPEAN AGREEMENT ON ABOLITION OF VISAS FOR REFUGEES, Strasbourg, April, 1959: Signature.

8.   CONVENTION FOR INTERNATIONAL COUNCIL FOR EXPLORATION OF SEA, COPENHAGEN, SEPT, 1964: Signatures of Protocol, October 1968.

This meeting was the third last meeting of the twelfth government of Ireland, and occurred just two days after the general election of that year and during the second day of the election count. The cabinet consisted of fourteen ministers, including the Taoiseach. Five ministers were absent from this meeting, the largest absence in the first half of 1969, and the entire life of the government. It was the shortest government meeting during 1969, lasting only seventy minutes. And it also had the most crowded agenda, dealing, as it did, with a total of nineteen items. This averages out at three minutes and 41 seconds per item considered.

The average minimum lead-in time for memoranda prepared for the government by various government departments appears to be three to four days. In some cases, it is clear that memoranda had been prepared weeks in advance. However, the memorandum recommending the 'retirement' of Lt Roche was prepared the day before, making it the fastest-produced memorandum in 1969 and, subject to correction, in the life of the twelfth government of Ireland. A defence force memorandum, dated 18 June 1969, accepting the resignation of the commission tendered by Commandant Patrick John Haran and Second Lieutenant John Joseph Cleary, was not presented until the penultimate government meeting, held on 24 June 1969, which lasted two hours and considered a total of eleven items, allowing an average of almost eleven minutes' consideration per item.

It seems reasonable, therefore, to question why the memorandum in respect of Haran and Cleary was not presented to the meeting of government of 20 June. Moreover, given the alleged security threat posed by Lt Roche and, therefore, the urgency of expelling him from the defence forces, it also seems reasonable to question why the memorandum was not prepared and placed much earlier on a government agenda. Why was Lt Roche's memorandum of 19 June permitted to leapfrog over the Haran and Cleary memorandum and to be placed on the agenda of a very crowded meeting on 20 June, where it could not be given the due consideration it deserved?

Despite the thirty-year rule, the material available in the National Archives does not include a copy of more detailed minutes recording the input of various ministers which would help clarify exactly what the Minister for Defence said, if anything, regarding the reasons and desirability of young Lt Roche's 'retirement'.

The timing of the presentation of the memorandum and the speed at which it was dealt with once again raises suspicions that Roche was on an unstoppable fast-track removal from the defence forces. It also appears that civil servants within the Department of Defence were assisting senior officers within the defence forces. This fact is a source of grave hurt for Dónal de Róiste in that his maternal uncle, Patrick Murphy, was an assistant secretary in that very department and appears either to have acquiesced in his removal or was impotent in attempting to help his young nephew.

On 20 May 2002, Dónal de Róiste's mother, Christina, had a letter published in *The Irish Times*, in which she wrote:

> I believe the government may have been misled in the information presented to it by Dónal's accusers....

Mrs de Róiste had these comments published some five months before her son was given access to 'secret' army files. There is nothing in those files that indicates that the Minister, and by extension, the government, were in fact made aware of the letter from Lt Roche's solicitor or of the draft response to it. There is absolutely no reference to the existence of such a letter in the memorandum, drafted by civil servants for the

Minister on 9 June, for presentation to the government. In response to a question as to whether the Minister had been told about the solicitor's letter, the Department of Defence stated on 20 October 2005, that it would 'be reasonable to assume that the Minister would have been made aware of it in the context of the preparation of the Memorandum for Government and related briefings from the Chief of Staff and the Secretary of the Department. However, there is no actual record of this.'

The fact that there is no record allows room for suspicion. There should, at the very least, be a briefing note to the Minister accompanying a copy of the solicitor's letter. One might have expected that knowledge of the letter would have made the Minister cautious. The question remains: Who made the decision to ignore the solicitor's letter and to proceed with the drafting of a memorandum to the government on the very day that the existence of the letter was to be discussed with the Secretary to the Department?

If the cabinet members of the twelfth government were not in possession of the full facts that were required to make such an important decision, the failure to disclose the existence of the letter from Roche's solicitor – and the contents of the unsent draft letter outlining mechanisms of redress available to the young officer under the Defence Act 1954 – demonstrates a degree of predetermination and intent. It also suggests a clear disregard for the institutions of government and Lt Roche's constitutional rights.

While there are copies on file of letters presumably addressed to the Minister for Defence from the Chief of Staff, they are on plain paper and there is no evidence of any reply from the Minister to Lt General Mac Eoin, or any other senior officer of the defence forces, with respect to the developing case against Lt Roche. Despite the claims of his being a 'serious security risk' to the state, how knowledgeable of Lt Roche's case, therefore, was the Minister for Defence, Michael Hilliard, particularly regarding the unanswered letter from his solicitor? Consequently, it seems reasonable to ask: 'Was Lt Dónal Roche's presidential 'retirement', on the recommendation of the government, entirely legal?'

ANNUAL OFFICER REPORTS 1969
Captain Patrick Dixon, the officer who had accompanied Lt Roche to his first interrogation on 25 April, completed Lt Roche's fifth and

final Annual Officer's Confidential Report, for the year ending 1969. The report is signed and dated 17 July 1969. Captain Dixon indicates that his assessment on Lieutenant de Róiste is based on just over two months' observations, 25 February–2 May 1969. With regard to Lt Roche's physical fitness he records:

> Not an active participant in games or sports but otherwise apparently physically fit.
> The performance of his duties as administration officer was inclined to be careless and indifferent.

In response to whether or not Lt Roche had received any warnings, Dixon writes:

> He was informally advised that he was failing to give satisfaction in the performance of his duties.

Roche has no recollection of this. When asked if Roche was 'suitable in his present appointment', he writes, 'Not Applicable' and then comments, 'This officer has now retired from PDF'.

When asked if Lt Roche had given evidence of reliability, devotion to duty, zeal, industry, ability, initiative and, where applicable, the faculty of leadership, Dixon writes, 'Not applicable'.

Finally, Dixon gives Lt Roche the rating of 'unsatisfactory', the only such rating he had received throughout his military career.

Section F of the report is blank, despite the fact that it should be 'completed in respect of periods NOT covered' under Dixon's watch. His period in Boyle, therefore, appears unworthy of comment.

Section G, to be completed by the Brigade Commander, is also blank. This includes the question, 'Do you agree with the RATING?'

Section H, to be completed by a Superior Reporting Officer, is signed and dated by the Officer Commanding, Western Command. The date is 17 July 1969. Col. Shortall agrees with the rating given by Captain Dixon. When asked for additional remarks he writes:

> Has been retired from the defence forces for security reasons.

Section J, to be completed only where an 'unsatisfactory' rating is awarded – by the officer so rated [in this case, Lt Roche] – is blank.

Section K, 'For Use in Adjutant-General's Branch', to be completed where disagreement is expressed with the rating, is blank.

I contacted former Captain Patrick Dixon by telephone on 24 August 2005, and asked him if he could explain how all previous annual reports had given Lt Roche a 'satisfactory' rating while he had given him 'unsatisfactory'. 'Can you explain what had gone wrong in the interim?' I asked him. He replied, 'I have no recollection of that. It was my opinion at the time, I presume.'

I offered to bring the report to Dixon and show him the comments he had written, in the hope of refreshing his memory. He rather tersely informed me before our brief telephone conversation ended: 'I don't want to discuss the matter with you, good, bad or indifferent.'

According to a defence forces source, it is not normal military procedure to complete a report in respect of the year in which an officer retires, as such report would serve no function. These reports are given in the first instance to the officer subject of the report and, if rated 'unsatisfactory', he is given an opportunity to make a submission and he is required to sign the report. In this instance, Roche has not signed the report, nor was he shown it and it was completed after he was retired and apparently for the sole purpose of having an 'unsatisfactory' report on his record.

COMMANDANT EDWARD HORGAN ON DÓNAL
Recting to the 'unsatisfactory' rating given to Lt Roche, retired Commandant Edward Hogan offered the following observations:

> I passed my Leaving Certificate with two honours, but I suspect that Dónal de Róiste may have had a better Leaving result, which probably meant that he was placed higher than me by the original Cadet Interview Board, and that he was one of the original group of 35 who were called by the army authorities.
>
> With regard to Dónal's behaviour, progress and characteristics, both during the two-year cadetship and afterwards, I can offer the following opinions. I do so by comparing him with myself as I recall both of us with the

benefit of hindsight.

First, with regard to the suggestion that Dónal de Róiste was immature, my recollections are to the contrary. Several other cadets, including myself, who were from a more rural and conservative background, and who did not have previous FCA or army experience, tended to be shy and less mature than cadets such as Dónal de Róiste. A significant number of the 38th Cadet Class had served in the FCA and a small number had served for a short time in the Permanent Defence Forces (PDF). Additional points were allotted at the Cadet Interview Board for FCA or PDF service.

I would have been one of a group of cadets who did not drink and tended to socialise less than Dónal de Róiste. With hindsight I would consider that I was less mature than Dónal and more 'boyish'. Dónal was a far more outgoing and more socially aware individual...

To suggest that Dónal's more active social life indicated that he was immature and therefore possibly unsuitable as an officer is simply false. The type of exuberance exhibited by Dónal would have been more indicative of the type of characteristics needed for a junior army officer [rather] than the contrary.

I knew Dónal well during our two years as cadets. We were in the same platoon and in the same accommodation corridor, and therefore would have met and worked closely together not only on a daily but on an hourly basis. It was a very intensive and enclosed working and social environment. Also, the particular regime that our cadet class was exposed to was unusually strict and severe, probably due to the political interference at the early stages of our selections as cadets. As cadets we were very clearly aware that we were much more severely treated than the class ahead of us and the class behind us. This resulted in an almost unique toughening process being applied to those that survived this tough regime.

With regard to my own career, it is reasonable to assume that Dónal's military career should have taken a similar path to mine. We both opted for the smaller corps in the army. In my case, I chose the Cavalry or Armoured Corps, and Dónal requested the Supply and Transport Corps. Both of our jobs were of a technical nature. Career advancement and promotion for Dónal de Róiste should have been quite similar to my career.

We were both promoted from 2-Lieutenant to Lieutenant in September 1967. I was promoted to the rank of Captain in 1972. Dónal de Róiste should have been promoted Captain within about a year of this. In my case, I was promoted to the rank of Commandant in January 1979. Dónal's promotion to the rank of Commandant would have depended on his class placing and also on promotion opportunities in the Supply and Transport Corps. However, it is most likely that Dónal should have been promoted to the rank of Commandant within about one or two years of my date of promotion…

My army career included three six-month tours of duty with the United Nations, up to 1973. For family reasons, I did not volunteer for overseas service after 1973. Officers in the Transport Corps could normally expect to get such a UN tour of duty about every three or four years. My army appointments included about eight years in logistics … very similar to the duties that an officer in the Transport Corps would be doing.

I had a very successful army career. My appointments included troop or platoon commander, instructor in the Cavalry Corps technical school, barrack quartermaster or logistics officer, School Commandant of the Cavalry Technical School, Deputy Governor of the Curragh Prison, Commanding Officer of the 1st Tank Squadron, and Lecturer in the Command and Staff College. I decided to take early retirement in 1986 after serving for twenty-two and-a-half years. This enabled me to receive a pension, which now amounts to about €28,000 per annum. I have been in receipt of this pension, or its equivalent at the applicable rates, since February 1986. This is in addition to any other remuneration I have received from other employment. Because of my military training and background, I was able to achieve employment, first as chief security officer at Trinity College Dublin, 1986/87, and then as security manager and fire chief at Aughinish Alumina, a large chemical plant in Askeaton, Co. Limerick, from 1987 to 1995.

Between 1995 and 1997, I worked in a variety of positions including work with the EU and UN in places such as Bosnia, Croatia [and] Nigeria. My military training and experiences were important factors in my getting each of these opportunities. In 1997 I decided to go back to college as a full-time student and have completed a BA in History and Politics and a masters M.Phil. in Peace Studies. I am now completing a PhD in international relations. I have also drawn on my military training and experiences for the purposes of these further educational opportunities.

I see no reason why Dónal de Róiste's military and civilian careers should not have been very similar to my careers and life experiences. He had a very similar education and level of education, and would have been exposed to very similar opportunities as I have been, if he had not been dismissed from the army. If he had decided to remain in the army until full retirement age, it is likely that he would have reached the rank of Lieutenant Colonel and possibly Colonel. At least two members of the 38th Class have reached the rank of General, Frederick Swords and Gerard McNamara.

GRATUITY

Following Lt Roche's 'retirement', an interesting collection of internal defence forces correspondence and memos ensues concerning whether or not he was entitled to a gratuity. They are contained in Pensions File: 37/SP/5473.

On 6 August 1969, a handwritten minute headed: '0.8159 Lieut. Dónal Roche – retired' and referenced 37/SP/5473 states:

In connection with the question of the award of a gratuity to the above-named under the Defence Forces (Pensions) Schemes will you please arrange to forward a copy of the Memorandum which was submitted to the government regarding his retirement. As Lieut. Roche was retired 'in the interests of the service' it will be necessary to submit his case to An tAire who has discretion under the Schemes to grant or refuse a gratuity or grant a gratuity at a reduced rate.

The above generates two particularly enlightening handwritten responses. The first is a note which states:

Will you please see minute of the 6th instant from A3 (c) regarding the retirement of Lt D. Roche.

The submission to the government in this case was not handled by R6.

Perhaps a copy of the Memorandum for the Government could be made available to A3(c) by An Rúnaí Cúnta [Assistant Secretary].

This note is dated 8 August 1969.

The above received the following response, bearing the same date:

The memorandum for the government did not set out the specific reasons for the proposal that the government should advise the President to retire Lt Roche in the interests of the service. The relevant 'S' file will, of course, be available to An tAire in connection with the gratuity question.

This note is highly significant. The person writing it clearly had sight of the memorandum that was passed to the government with the recommendation that Lt Roche be 'retired'. However, this document states that the memorandum does not 'set out the specific reasons' for Lt Roche's proposed 'retirement' by the President. This is precisely what Lt Dónal Roche has consistently pleaded for over thirty years and was the basis for his solicitor's letter to the Chief of Staff on 30 May 1969. In effect, this is an official confirmation of what Lt Roche has consistently claimed.

Lt Roche's Pensions File contains other noteworthy documents.

On 15 August 1969, a typewritten note is addressed to 'Oifigeach Airgeadais' (Finance Officer), with what appears to be the incorrect reference of 37/SP/5072. Having outlined the relevant section of the Defence Act under which he was 'retired', it states that Lt Roche 'is eligible under the Defence Forces (Pensions) Schemes for a gratuity of £350.4.7d.' The note continues:

> In view of the circumstances in which Lt Roche was retired, the case is submitted for the favour of a direction from An tAire who may in his absolute discretion grant or refuse the gratuity (article 36 of the Principle Scheme) or grant a gratuity of a lesser amount if, in his opinion, the officer's defaults or demerits warrant such a course (Article 43 of the 1947 Scheme).

Immediately below this typewritten note there is a neatly handwritten remark, dated 15 August 1969:

> Rúnaí,
> ... Not knowing the circumstances, I cannot make a recommendation ...

'Not knowing the circumstances' seems a remarkable admission by what must be a senior civilian or military employee of either the defence forces or the Department of Defence. In truth, there were few, if any, who knew the real circumstances of Lt Roche's 'retirement'.

The pensions file also contains two letters from Lt Roche's solicitor, Michael B. O'Maoileoin, dated 26 August and 22 October 1969, seeking clarification on Lt Roche's gratuity. There is also an undated handwritten letter, allegedly from Dónal de Róiste, asking that all correspondence relating to his gratuity be forwarded to his Clonmel address. However, De Róiste points out that the letter is not in his handwriting and – in comparison to other samples of his handwriting and signature that are on file – it is clearly not his. Nor is it the handwriting of his mother. Why, therefore, is this undated letter on his file and who placed it there? Is it an attempt to create the impression that the young lieutenant had accepted his fate? That the acceptance of his gratuity indicated that he wished to settle the last outstanding matter of his army career?

On 19 December 1969, Lt Dónal Roche was awarded a £383.3.6d gratuity 'due under the Defence Forces (Pensions) Scheme'. A revision, dated 30 June 1971, grants a balance of £37-50.

Two days earlier, on 17 December 1969, as Lt Roche approached the season of goodwill in his very early 'retirement', an enlightening exchange of internal communication occurred. A note, addressed to 'Aire', states:

> The history of this case is given in the attached file.
>
> Since Lt Roche's retirement in the interests of the service in June last nothing has come to notice that would adversely affect a decision on the question of granting him the gratuity for which he is eligible.
>
> The maximum gratuity payable is £350.4.7. If you decide that a gratuity should be paid I feel that it should be less than the maximum – knock off say £50.

There is a curt response, presumably by someone in higher authority, dated 18 December 1969. It simply states: 'Pay in full.' It is initialled 'JG'.

Apart from the meanness apparent in the above note, there is something of far greater importance. Does the note imply that, following his 'retirement' on 27 June 1969, Lt Roche had been under surveillance? Or perhaps it betrays the recognition that Roche was an innocent wronged. Either way, the note acknowledges that nothing had been discovered, by way of 'contact' with alleged subversives, to compromise his gratuity entitlement.

5

REJECTION, RUMOURS AND EXILE

Who steals my purse steals trash; 'tis something, nothing/'Twas mine, 'tis his, and has been slave to thousands/But he that filches from me my good name'Robs me of that which not enriches him/And makes me poor indeed.
William Shakespeare, Othello, Act III, Scene 3

Lt Dónal Roche's father found it impossible to accept that the state, especially his hero, President Eamon de Valera, could be so terribly wrong concerning his eldest boy. For the now-former Lt Dónal Roche, it was the beginning of a new nightmare – the nightmare of knowing he was telling the truth but sensing that no one believed him, particularly his father.

The fact that Seán Roche went to his grave in January 2002 never having been reconciled with his first-born child is, in many respects, incomprehensible. Yet, he had two very credible touchstones within the family circle who were telling him that the military authorities the state and the President, had good grounds for the dismissal of his son.

All manner of rumours and unspecified and uncontested allegations began to circulate just prior to, and in the immediate aftermath of, Roche's 'retirement'. Some of these rumours were fed back, as fact, to Seán Roche. How could he question the veracity of information supplied by his wife's brother, Pat Murphy, Assistant Secretary at the Department of Defence? Murphy told his brother-in-law that 'they' had a photograph of Dónal coming out of an IRA meeting in Lahinch, Co. Clare.

Dónal de Róiste recalls:

> My mum and I also met Uncle Pat in a hotel in D'Olier Street, Dublin, some months after my 'retirement'. I remember my mother crying, her loyalty divided by the

injustice of it all. He told us then that 'they' had a photo of me at the Barnes McCormick funeral. My head was spinning. They seemed to know more about me than I did myself.

'Have you seen the photograph?' asked the unemployed lieutenant.

'No,' replied his uncle.

'Well, why don't they produce it as proof?' Dónal replied.

His question fell on deaf ears. Later, according to De Róiste, Murphy admitted that they had no case against him.

Equally, how was Seán Roche to question the veracity of information from another brother-in-law, married to his sister Carmel, retired Commandant Gerard Madden, Dónal's godfather? He too parroted the rumours that he had heard from 'inside' army sources.

For Seán Roche, his son's pleas of innocence seemed hollow. And to top it all, de Valera, a historical hero and a national icon who, as President of Ireland, was the final authority in the dismissal process, would surely not have ended his son's career unless he was sure.

RUMOURS AND ALLEGATIONS

Several rumours and allegations were doing the circuit through the defence forces' bush telegraph, many of which survive to this day. They have a resonance with the tone of the interrogations that Lt Roche underwent. They also have a resonance with the letter that was written by his solicitor, Michael O'Maoileoin, and ignored by the Chief of Staff, on 30 May 1969:

> Our client states that he has been … accused of misconduct, indiscretion, being a security risk … and on another occasion gross misconduct and so on, with the result that our client does not know where he stands….
> Our client would therefore like to know what charge, if any, is being preferred against him.

And therein is the nub of the issue. Therein is the very heart of Lt Dónal Roche's consistent protests of innocence across almost four decades. He asked for a court martial and was refused. He asked that he be allowed to defend his good name and was refused. He asked that he might face his accusers, and their unspecified and uncontested allegations, and was refused. He still asks the right to defend his good name, and yet the defence forces and the state refuse him that right to the present day. Why?

A former Minister for Defence, Michael Smith TD, has stated in the Dáil, and in various press releases issued by the Department of Defence, that Lt Roche knew the reasons why he was 'retired'. It has been implied that Roche's protestations of innocence and/or ignorance are disingenuous – adding to a depiction of him as something of a shifty character.

Lt Roche certainly heard the rumours and allegations. But his constitutional right to defend his good name required the defence forces and the state to be more forthright and fair.

I have heard, in total, nine rumours and allegations concerning why Lt Roche was 'retired' from the army, including the one about the photograph of the Barnes McCormick funeral. It is important to remember that these are largely the tittle-tattle that circulated in the officers' messes of various army barracks throughout the country. I believe that they were deliberately circulated to convince and confuse, and that was the effect they had. Having served for six years in the Officer Corps, twenty-four-year-old Dónal Roche became a leper – ignored, abandoned and shunned by former officer colleagues, with only a few honourable exceptions. Below are the eight other rumours that turned Lt Roche, a gregarious and popular man, into an embittered and bewildered outcast and exile.

Rumours

1 *Dónal Roche was selling guns and ammunition to the IRA.*

This rumour has overtones of the Shinkwin affair which we will discuss in Chapter 13. If Lt Roche had been engaged in such activity, why was he sent to the 19th Infantry Battalion, Boyle, Co. Roscommon, where his responsibilities, close to the Irish border, involved the security of rifles and ammunitions used in the training of FCA recruits? This rumour, when taken in conjunction with the abject failure of senior officers and members of government to secure properly the Irish Industrial Explosives Factory at Clonagh in Co. Meath (see Chapter 14) is farcical.

2. *Lt Roche was warned to discontinue associating with the crowd he was meeting.*
There is no evidence that a warning was given to Roche about any of his associations prior to his interrogations, beginning on 25 April 1969. In his 'secret' files, there is a highly suspect reference in an interrogation memo, and alleged interview note, that Lt Roche 'casually' informed a Commandant P. Maguire that he had a friend in the IRA with whom he discussed zeroing of rifles and 9mm ammunition. This will be dealt with in Chapter 12.

Throughout this whole sordid process, the state has been reluctant to name Padraig Dwyer as the person with whom Roche was, allegedly, 'associating'. In her report, the Judge Advocate General, Ms McCrann, confers on Dwyer a cloak of mystery, referring to him only as 'Mr X' when, in fact, his name has been in the public domain since 1968. Padraig Dwyer has been dead for several years and I see no reason to hide his name from the public – unless, of course, the state has something to hide in this regard.

As far as Roche is concerned, he knew Padraig Dwyer as a very casual acquaintance in O'Donoghue's pub. Commandant Patrick Walshe and Lt Col. Gerry Swan are equally sure that they too would have known Dwyer as a casual acquaintance. If Roche was guilty of subversion simply for knowing Dwyer, then, by implication, they must have been also and, indeed, so was anyone else who spoke to Dwyer. All are adamant, however, that until Roche and Walshe were interrogated by Commandant Gerry O'Sullivan, they were unaware of any alleged criminal or subversive connections.

There is no evidence that Roche ever again met with Padraig Dwyer or any of Dwyer's associates, after his 'retirement'. Indeed, one document in the files clearly states that nothing had come to light, in the six months after his expulsion from the army, to suggest that Roche had any subversive contacts.

3. *Authorities had to change all the security locks at Athlone Military Barracks because Lt Roche had been stationed there.*

While it is possible that such an action did occur, even on a limited scale, Commandant Patrick Walshe believes that it might have been done 'to augment the justification of Lt Roche's expulsion'.

4. *Lt Roche was selling used army vehicles and spare parts to the IRA.*

This rumour obviously has its roots in the public auction at Clancy Barracks on 23 April 1969. Indeed, it is clear from Roche's 'secret' files that Commandant O'Sullivan, his chief interrogator, actually checked to see if he had bought a vehicle. In a 'secret' memo he wrote: 'A reliable source reports that Roche may have bought a Land Rover.' As Lt Roche did not buy a vehicle, the reliability of the source is called into question.

5. *Not one senior officer in Athlone had a good word to say for Lt Roche.*

There is no record of any senior officer in the Western Command, with a direct command responsibility to Roche, questioning what was happening to this junior officer. Furthermore, apart from Commandant Edward Horgan, no one from his Commissioning Class of 1965 has spoken in his defence and, indeed, some even shunned an attempt to have Roche invited to a class reunion in 2003.

6. *Lt Roche was homosexual.*

This rumour may have arisen from the condom affair in Cadet School and suggestions made to him during his interrogations. This rumour survived long enough for him to be asked about it by a journalist during an Irish-language radio interview in 2002.

7. *Lt Roche was a member of Saor Éire.*

I heard this rumour myself from the mouth of the young woman who had been seriously injured in the car crash that is dealt with in Chapter 10. Knowing that the senior officer who had crashed into her car had three passengers with him (including two junior officers), she enquired why none was in attendance at a High Court appearance in Dublin, circa 1971, as witnesses on behalf of Commandant Seán T. O'Kelly. She was informed that one of the young officers (Roche) had been 'thrown out of the army because he was a member of Saor Éire'. She said that she didn't know who or what Saor Éire was.

8. *Lt Roche was on the firing party at the Barnes McCormick funeral.*

Of all the rumours, this one is, perhaps, the most colourful. In the opinion of Commandant Patrick Walshe, it was also the most damaging. He states:

> I believe this rumour was designed by defence forces headquarters to totally discredit Dónal and to wipe out any concern amongst the officer body for the way he had been treated and in particular amongst those who served with him in Athlone, the Curragh and Baldonnell. Most damaging of all, this rumour was presented as fact to Dónal's family by Pat Murphy, the Assistant Secretary of the Department of Defence who was a brother of Dónal's mother. This was very likely the catalyst for the action by Dónal's father that resulted in Dónal becoming an outcast from the family home in Clonmel.

Commandant Walshe recalls first hearing this rumour in July 1969, while he was still a captain in the army. He was attending a meeting at Devoy Barracks, Naas, involving apprentice intake interviews. Walshe says that near the end of a morning coffee break, Lt Col. Jack Kilcullen, 'a decent and honourable man', joined the meeting, having just arrived back from a conference at defence forces' headquarters. Walshe was surprised when Kilcullen announced to those present that Roche had been on the firing party of the Barnes McCormick funeral.

Commandant Walshe says that he immediately addressed Lt Col. Kilcullen in the presence of those gathered in the coffee room, and informed him that, 'Dónal Roche could not have been at the funeral for I was with him in Dublin on that day.' An embarrassed silence enveloped the small gathering, as it was not the done thing for a junior officer to contradict a senior officer so publicly. There was no further discussion on the matter with Lt Col. Kilcullen.

The reason Walshe is so certain of the day he met Dónal Roche is that the Barnes McCormick funeral was a high-profile event. Peadar Barnes and Seamus McCormick had been hanged in Winston Green Prison, Birmingham, in 1940, found guilty of being in possession of a bomb which had exploded on 25 August 1939 in the centre of Coventry, killing five people and injuring 100 more. Both had pleaded their innocence.

A repatriation committee worked for several years to have the bodies of Barnes and McCormick exhumed and returned to Ireland. On 4 July 1969, their tricolour-draped coffins were flown into Dublin Airport and taken to Adam and Eve's Church in Dublin, where thousands of people filed past their remains to pay their respect. The following day, the remains were brought to the Cathedral of Christ the King in Mullingar, and the next day, Sunday, 6 July 1969, following Requiem Mass in Irish, the two men were buried in Ballyglass cemetery, with over 7,000 in attendance. On Monday, 7 July 1969, a front-page *Irish Times* report stated: 'At the graveside a group of young men removed their jackets exposing pistols which they raised to fire a three-volley salute.'

The Sunday Times later published a confession from a former IRA man who said that he had planted the bomb. The newly elected Fianna Fáil government ignored the funerals and remained silent about the new evidence.

Lt Col. Kilcullen made his comments about Lt Roche being on the firing party within a few days of the funerals. Walshe says that he took a risk in making it known that he had met with Roche as, by now, the ex-lieutenant was an outcast. He was surprised that no one from the senior staff came to question him on the veracity of his statement to Lt Col. Kilcullen .

Walshe firmly believes that defence forces' headquarters orchestrated the rumour which was widespread and believed by officers of all ranks. He says that they even believed that Roche's photograph had appeared in a newspaper, as a member of the firing party. Lt Gerry Swan confirms that he too was told the rumour as if it were fact.

IMPACT ON ROCHE FAMILY

The impact on young Lt Roche's family was devastating. In a forthright and hard-hitting interview I conducted with his youngest sister, Adi, in April 2002, she did not mince her words:

> I am saying categorically that I believe my eldest brother Dónal is innocent.
>
> I remember how distraught our household was when the incident happened. I remember the arguments and the stress. And what saddens me most is that there was no peace or reconciliation between my father and his eldest son before he died in January this year. I want to ensure that the same doesn't happen to my mother. She should be able to go to meet my father and say, 'Dónal is innocent and the Irish state has declared him so.'
>
> I remember my family's commitment to Fianna Fáil. I feel the party turned their backs on our family over this. My father couldn't believe or accept that the Irish state could be criminal or that it could callously create such an injustice against his family....
>
> It set Dónal on a path of isolation and, understandably, he became very bitter. Everything in his life, thereafter, was overshadowed by what happened ... Dónal is a very intelligent person. He had such a bright future.... When he received the cadetship to train to become an officer in the Irish army it was the *crème de la crème*.
>
> And then, suddenly, inexplicably, he was thrown out of the army in a move that required the imprimatur of President Eamon de Valera. Can you imagine the impact this had on our entire family, especially my parents? Dev and the government were their heroes. How could you question or disbelieve them?
>
> In their narrow world they had to believe the state

because they couldn't deal with the possibility that the criminal act was, in fact, done by the state and not by their son.

... A terrible sadness enveloped the house and a terrible sense of disgrace. It was almost as if we had a murderer in our midst ... we had to face neighbours and town folk who knew that Dónal had been dishonourably discharged for some undisclosed secretive reason. Rumours were rampant in the small town. Our dad brought us up always to be honest and truthful people. He was a very honourable person who believed in truth. He was, however, very black and white and could be intransigent. Once he formed an opinion it was very hard to shift him.

When he died, he died a stranger to Dónal. And the seeds of the disintegrating relationship between him and his eldest son, his golden boy, began in 1969. Prior to that, they had a great relationship.... They idolised one another.

And we idolised Dónal. Dónal was apolitical. He was more interested in singing ballads in O'Donoghue's and other traditional public houses than in politics.

Is that a crime?

I also interviewed 85-year-old Christina de Róiste, Lt Roche's mother. I was particularly interested in trying to understand what it was that caused her husband to reject his son so totally. She replied:

That has been such heartache to me I couldn't explain it. We never ever disagreed about anything ... I remember somebody saying one time, we were two minds with but a single thought, and that's true. Until this – Dónal's dismissal from the army.

For some reason or other, Seán couldn't take it. Of course it was very disappointing and I can tell you, in the beginning for me too. I used to say to myself, 'My God, what in the name of providence did he do?'

He had an uncle who had retired from the army at

that time … Commandant Gerard Madden. I remember we confided in Gerard… He had a whole lot of army friends but he could not get any specific information about why Dónal was dismissed … which of course increased the mystery for us because we didn't know what to do. We didn't know.

Gerard learned that they were talking about him being in subversive company. I just remember I nearly died when he said it. Because when your child leaves the home you don't know what he is going to do, you don't keep tabs on them to that extent, so I didn't know what to think. I was very frightened when Ger said that.

I also remember Gerard saying to me, 'You know, the IRA could take him down a field and shoot him.' You couldn't believe what that did to me. I went through hell, I really went through hell over all that, because, you could say, we were ignorant of those things and we only knew one way, which was the straight way.…

Later I went to a fellow who had been teaching in Clonmel who became something in Fianna Fáil. As usual, they all tell you they will do something.

Then came along that fellow Gerry Cronin, as Minister for Defence [9 May 1970–14 March 1973]. Gerry Cronin had worked in the Sugar Company … when Seán was there so I suggested to Seán that we approach him. I can always remember the day we went to Mallow, it was pouring out of the heavens, and we went in anyway to Gerry. After that we just got a statement of Dónal's years [of Service]. It was worthless. Dónal could have been a murderer, he could have been anything. I knew it wouldn't take him into a dogfight and so I wrote then to the old Commanding Officer and the Minister for Defence about it – all to no avail. [See Appendix A, Documents 18 and 19].

While worried about the reaction of his parents and the effect his dismissal would have on them, Dónal never expected the total and utter rejection by his father. When Seán Roche turned his back on his son and refused to acknowledge his presence, Dónal left home.

THE BEGINNING OF EXILE
Roche left Clonmel and headed north-east to Dublin and his brother
Conchubhar, then teaching in Dublin's Liberties. Conchubhar recalls
Dónal's turmoil and worried about his mental stability. He recalls him
uncharacteristically getting drunk on one occasion:

> He got really drunk. We wouldn't have looked favourably
> on drunkenness and he got very aggressive, which was
> unusual for him. It was out of sync with everything else.
> That's the only indication that I had that he was out of
> control. He was like a guy who hadn't a clue what he was
> doing.

There is one important matter about which Roche's younger brother is
definite – something that is supported by a memo from the 'secret' files
released in 2002:

> Where were the subversives Dónal allegedly was
> consorting with? Dónal spent many nights telling his
> story to me and the lads [his house-mates]. Dónal told
> us about his interrogations and what was said and what
> he was accused of. We all knew there was a suggestion
> that he had been associated with subversives. We would
> have been alert to any suspicious behaviour and visitors.
> There was never a whiff of it. When he wasn't with us, he
> was with Mary, his girlfriend, whose father was a senior
> garda. We all felt sorry for him. How else could we feel?

Over the summer of 1969, Roche found a job with Ryan's Motor
Company on Townsend Street, with the help of his girlfriend, Mary
O'Callaghan, who was employed there at the time. But Dublin and
Ireland were beginning to make him feel claustrophobic. As the 1970s
began, Dónal and Conchubhar casually met Billy Rowell, an old friend
from Clonmel who had done service with the British army. Billy was
something of a free spirit and one day, on the spur of the moment, he
and Dónal decided to pack their bags and head for London. On the

Lt Gen Gerry O'Sullivan

Cononel Arthur Cullen,
Deputy Judge Advocate General, 1969

Lt. General Sean Mac Eoin, Chief of Staff, 1969

38Ú RANG DALTAÍ 1963-'65.

Tuí Rang: 2/LT. P.ÓSÉ, LT.F.STUDDERT LT.T.MacCORMAIC, LT.P.ÓHEARÁIN, CAPT.C.ÓDUBHTHAIGH, CAPT. P.ÓMUINEACHÁIN,
LT.COL.C M.ÓMAOLMUAIDH, 2/LT.S.ÓCEARBHAILL, CFT.E.ÓCONDÚN CAPT.C.ÓDUBHGHAILL, LT.CÓMADAGÁIN, LT.P.Ó CAOCHLAIGH,
CAPT. T.Ó CAOINDEALBHÁIN, 2/LT. S.MacCONMARA.

Lár-Rang: 2/LT. S.Mac CATHMAOIL, S.ÓCEARBHALLÁIN, C.ÓhAIRT, LÓCATHASAIGH, T.Ó SCEALLAIGH, B.ÓCONCHUBHAIR, P.MacCUARTA,
T.Ó STANDÚN, M.ÓCRIAGÁIN, F.Ó SÓRD, A.ÓMÁIRTÍN, S.MacCONNCRADHA, D.DeRÓISTE, B.MacCANNA,
2/LT. L.Ó COLMÁIN E.Ó DÁLAIGH, T.Ó PLÉIMIONN, G.MacCONMARA, S.ÓCONCHUBHAIR, T.ÓhALLAGÁIN, S.ÓMIONÁIN,

Cúl-Rang: 2/LT. L.Ó COLMÁIN E.Ó DÁLAIGH, T.Ó PLÉIMIONN, G.MacCONMARA, S.ÓCONCHUBHAIR, T.ÓhALLAGÁIN, S.ÓMIONÁIN,
C.ÓDUINSHLÉIBHE, S.ÓMAOLALAIDH, E.ÓhARGÁIN, T.ÓCONCUBHAR, C.WORN, D.ÓhAODHA, M.ÓhAODHA.

38th Cadet Class 1963–5
Dónal De Róiste is second from the right, centre row

Lt G. Swan. Lt P. Walshe, B. Doherty and Dónal in Galway. The photo is thought to have been taken during the weekend Dónal allegedly spent with Mr X, Padraig Dwyer.

Brendan 'The Dog' Doherty (Photo: Patrick Walshe)

il of photo of the public auction of surplus army vehicles held at Clancy Barracks, Dublin, on 23 April 1969. The photo was published the following day in the *Irish Press*.

Page from Dónal's passport stating 'Profession deleted officially' in Irish and English (Photo: Patrick Walshe)

1. A confidential source reported that Lt. ROCHE was in the company of members of the Dublin IRA Athletic Group on the days 16/17 April '69. It was apparent that he knew ██████████ and ██████████ ██████████ well.

2. During the conversation ROCHE mentioned that there was an auction of Army vehs at Clancy Bks on 23rd April 69 and that he would advise on a good car if anyone wanted to buy one.

3. Not possible at this stage to say whether connection is subversive or not.

4. ROCHE is described by a reliable source as rather immature & Bohemian in tastes.

5. Def Fors Sean / was briefed on the background info on 22/4/69. Def Fors Sean o will attend the auction at Clancy Bks on 23 April.
   Gso Offr. 22/4/69

The document, initialled by Commandant Gerry O'Sullivan, that allegedly sparked off the investigation into Lt Roche's 'subversive' associations (Photo: Carl Mullan)

Memo.

Lt. ROCHE was interviewed by DTAG at 1430 hrs on 28 Dec 69.

He was advised of the legal position and informed that he had until 1000 hours on 29 Dec 69, to submit an explanation of his conduct. ROCHE said he proposed to see his solicitor.

At 0940 hours on 29 Dec 69 Lt ROCHE informed DTAG that his solicitor had advised him "to do nothing".

DTAG informed CP & A adn accordingly.

Gos   12/6/69.

Memo by Commandant Gerry O'Sullivan clearly acknowledging that Lt Roche refused to give a written statement on the advice of his solicitor (Photo: Carl Mullan)

Dónal revists the scene of his 1969 interrogation, the former Army Intelligence Headquarter Infirmary Road, Dublin. It was known as the 'Red House' (Photo: Carl Mullan)

Dónal with his wife, Leah Martin, and son Dara, 1978

way, Dónal was held overnight in Holyhead and questioned by British Special Branch officers before being allowed to proceed. He was questioned specifically about why his passport carried the notation 'profession deleted officially'. This notation was also to cause him difficulties in the US.

On his arrival in London, Roche had little trouble finding a job, first as a barman in a pub in Croydon, and later as a small crane operator in the construction industry. It was during this period that hiss relationship with his girlfriend broke up. Even though he was living away from Ireland, with the Irish Sea in between, he still felt vulnerable. He began to make the shift from the Anglicised version of his name, Roche, to the Irish, De Róiste. He readily admits that it was an attempt to disguise his identity and escape his nightmare. It was also, he felt, because nothing bad had ever happened to him when, in the past, he had used the Irish version of his name.

He continued to wonder how he could explain his retirement from the army to a prospective employer. Moreover, as the 'Troubles' intensified, former Lt Roche began to feel that his service to his country had suddenly become a liability, especially in England.

EMIGRATION AND NEW FRIENDS

During the summer of 1972, Roche met a young Irish-American who was on a short hitchhiking visit to Ireland. Jimmy McCarthy was a decorated Vietnam veteran, who had served with the US Marine Corps from February until August 1968. McCarthy had learned to fly when only sixteen and went on to achieve a full commercial pilot's licence. Today, he flies large turbo-prop aircraft for a division of USAirways.

McCarthy took an instant liking to De Róiste, whom he met in O'Donoghue's pub; within hours, they had established a bond that has survived to the present day. Over a few pints, they shared stories of their respective experiences in the service of their countries. The former Marine Corps combat soldier says that the more he listened to De Róiste's story, 'it just didn't seem kosher'. He recalls leaving Ireland with a strong hunch that 'this guy has taken a fall for somebody.' McCarthy understood the rigid structures of the military which too often operated like a machine and forgot that it was stockpiled with human beings.

McCarthy encouraged his Irish friend to contact him if ever he visited the United States. Within a few months, De Róiste had packed his bags and was headed for Pennsylvania. He had $35 in his pocket on his arrival at JFK Airport, New York, enough to get to the bus station in Manhattan and buy a ticket to Harrisburg. McCarthy met De Róiste off a Greyhound Bus in downtown Harrisburg and brought him to his family home, where Dónal was welcomed with open arms. 'Our whole family loved him,' recalls McCarthy. 'My grandparents and parents, God rest them, accepted him like an extension of the family. My two brothers … and our sister … welcomed him like another brother.' McCarthy's late father, Charles 'Cook' McCarthy, taught young De Róiste how to drive a truck and gave him a temporary job as a driver with his fruit and vegetable firm. After the trauma of rejection he had experienced back home, the McCarthy home was a healing haven. In a 1998 affidavit, presented at the Irish High Court, McCarthy recalled:

> Dónal responded very well to the secure family environment in our household and he applied himself to the work as provided by my father. My family and I believed at that time that Dónal would not have been able to hold the employment, were it not for the secure environment provided.

The entire McCarthy family could see that Dónal de Róiste had been traumatised by his enforced retirement and the subsequent rejection by his father and, in a real sense, Irish society as a whole. 'The signs of trauma shown by Dónal de Róiste were the same characteristics as shown by a number of my former military colleagues who had suffered shock and trauma in Vietnam,' McCarthy stated.

After three months with the McCarthys, Dónal de Róiste temporarily returned to Ireland before emigrating to the United States. Harrisburg, Pennsylvania, became his home, and he and McCarthy shared a rented apartment for several months. De Róiste seemed to have no difficulty finding odd jobs, although he seldom settled for a prolonged period.

One evening, he and McCarthy were invited to a party where McCarthy introduced him to an old girlfriend, Leah Martin. Leah was amused at his nickname, 'Duck', which, to this day, she still affectionately calls him. Dónal was impressed by the exuberance of the young African-American. A television advertisement about a brand of soap called 'Irish Spring' intrigued her and so she decided to quiz Duck De Róiste about it. 'Is it true,' she asked, 'that the summer sun stays up in Ireland until ten o'clock at night?' At first, the Irishman thought that she was poking fun at his homeland and became defensive. But Leah recalls that De Róiste came over to her later and apologised. The next time they met, a few days later, was on their first date.

As their relationship developed, Leah began to realise that her Irish boyfriend had a dark side. She recalls that one evening when she had gone to De Róiste's flat to have dinner with him, she began to ask him about his day at work, 'and he went off screaming, "Why are you interrogating me?"' Leah was stunned when Dónal told her that he had been given no reason for his expulsion from the Irish army. Each time he told her his story, she personally became more outraged and, yet, she could not fathom how her boyfriend appeared no longer to have the will to fight back. She saw an inherent contradiction in Dónal de Róiste who, on the one hand, seemed tough and determined about life in general yet, on the other, was fearful and timid about his army background. She confesses to losing her patience with him on the matter.

On 17 February 1973, a Baptist pastor married Dónal de Róiste and Leah Martin in her family home. Respectful of Dónal's Irish Catholic roots, the future Leah de Róiste tried to find a priest to officiate also at the service, but her request was turned down, much to her sadness and bewilderment. She affectionately recalls their wedding day: 'It was an amazing ceremony. It was very intimate. It was a very happy wedding. We didn't have the money to splash out on all the trimmings that young people seem to expect nowadays. We didn't need them, as we were very much in love.'

De Róiste recalls the welcome he received from Leah Martin's family. 'Black people were beginning to develop confidence in themselves,' he says.

> And when we discussed black history and Irish history, we realised we had a lot in common. There was racism amongst the Irish community, in keeping with the general white European population, but there were also strong bonds between Irish and black and I felt privileged to be part of one. Leah's family made me very welcome

and I felt very comfortable in the company of black America.

Leah recalls Dónal de Róiste's first Thanksgiving with her family:

> Thanksgiving dinner was a big deal in our house. And with seven children, that's a lot of people at the table. My mother would put the food out in bowls to serve yourself. The first time Duck had Thanksgiving dinner, my stepfather said Grace and then the plates started to go all over the place, with people trying to get their share. Duck just sat there, watching the chaos. My mother was going back and forth and she made everyone put their plates down and fixed him a huge plate of dinner.

He was later teased about his table manners and told that, in future, if he didn't join the scrum, he would just have to starve.

During 1974, De Róiste decided to return to Ireland with his young wife. Leah was excited with the new adventure, now having the opportunity to see for herself whether or not the sun really did stay up until 10 o'clock at night. She instantly fell in love with the Irish countryside.

Dónal managed to get a six-month electronics training placement with AnCO (An Comhairle Oiliúna, the Industrial Training Authority, which preceded FÁS). The training qualified him as a television repairman. De Róiste says that the knowledge he had acquired while struggling in the Irish Army Signal Corps proved beneficial. It was another indication that, given the right opportunity, Lt Roche was well capable of mastering the technical requirements.

Leah recalls that their time in Ireland was generally happy, living as they were in the first flush of romance. However, the strains between Dónal and his father saddened her deeply. Seán Roche welcomed her, but there was ever an uncomfortable truce when she and Dónal visited the family home in Clonmel.

While in Ireland, Leah became pregnant and gave birth to their first of two children, Dara, a baby boy, born on 1 May 1977 at the Rotunda Hospital in Dublin. Even with a baby in tow, the young couple travelled all around the country. In the late 1970s, jobs were hard to come by in

Ireland and Dónal de Róiste considered himself fortunate to find a job driving a van for a cousin and eventually to get a job with a television rental company, fixing televisions. Money was tight, the hours were long and the pay packet barely got them through the week, especially after paying their rent. Yet, recalls Leah Martin: 'We coped well and I never wanted for anything.'

In 1970s Ireland, as an African-American Baptist, Leah Martin-De Róiste was unique:

> I got used to little kids following me around in supermarkets and in streets. In my first week, I was sitting on a bench near St Luke's in Cork and a child sat next to me and took my hand and started rubbing it. He paused and looked at me. Then he rubbed it again. Eventually he stopped and asked, 'Are you black all over?' I told him I was. 'Really?' he asked. I told him I was. Then he asked, 'Even your bum?' I was hysterical with laughter.

Leah continued to monitor the effect her husband's presidential 'retirement' had on him. Many nights, she knew that he was reliving the nightmare of his interrogations. When she woke him, there was real fear and anxiety in his eyes. He never slept in the dark. Occasionally, he was prone to outbursts of anger and cutting sarcasm. And yet, there was also a tenderness and gentleness that told a tale of two seemingly different men. As time went on, the swings became more extreme and ever more difficult to live with. Despite the pain and anguish, however, Leah understood her husband's sense of injustice and his anger at his father and maternal uncle for not supporting him.

The day they had exchanged vows, Leah had done so believing that marriage is forever. But she began to worry about their future. If their marriage had any long-term hope of survival, a large part of it would depend on Dónal somehow finding closure. The problem was, however, that what he had was like a phantom itch tormenting a man with a lost limb. It was real, but there was nothing to scratch.

Leah encouraged her husband to start seeking answers. She recalls how they both travelled to Dublin to visit De Róiste's former solicitor, Michael O'Maoileoin. Leah was not encouraged by the visit and she left his office angry. In a very real sense, that encounter with O'Maoileoin advanced the rot of hopelessness in Dónal de Róiste's heart. Friends had recommended O'Maoileoin and, unquestionably, his practice wrote a very crucial letter to the Chief of Staff prior to Lt Roche's 'retirement'. In any event, Dónal and Leah de Róiste decided to return to the US in 1978. Before their departure, Leah discovered that she was again pregnant.

Both Dónal and Leah vividly recall the morning of 28 March 1979. There were plenty of military helicopters in the air but, strangely, no birds. They appeared to have disappeared and the metallic taste in the air was the reason. That was the first recognisable sign that all was not well in their locality. They lived just ten miles from the Three Mile Island nuclear power facility, located on an island in the Susquehanna River, south-east of the city of Harrisburg, Pennsylvania. An accident had occurred causing a partial meltdown and the release of radioactive material into the atmosphere. As the authorities began to inform the public, panic ensued, and over 100,000 residents fled the area, fearing a total meltdown. The De Róistes could not afford to join them. 'I was very scared,' Leah frankly admits.

Tragedy was averted by a whisker and as locals retuned and began to take stock, the full realisation of the near disaster began to dawn. Few in the world knew of the Belarusian town of Chernobyl then, but what happened there on 26 April 1986 had been narrowly averted in Harrisburg, Pennsylvania, just seven years before.

Local committees called 'Three Mile Island Alert' were set up, demanding a full investigation and the closure of the facility. The De Róistes became active members in their neighbourhood.

A young Adi Roche, then an Aer Lingus air hostess, recalls her shock and concern for her brother and his family as news of the Three Mile Island accident broke around the world. She had just married Seán Dunne and remembers asking him following a newsflash: 'What is nuclear power?' She had been invited to be the godmother of baby Sinead, born in Harrisburg on 9 May 1979, and, when she arrived in Harrisburg, she discovered that Dónal and Leah were preparing to participate in a major protest rally outside the Three Mile Island facility. She went with them and recalls:

That experience and the potential horror of what had been narrowly averted really frightened me. Three Mile Island caused me to join the anti-nuclear lobby. It caused me to commit wholeheartedly to the anti-nuclear movement. When Chernobyl happened in 1986, I kept thinking of Three Mile Island and the fact that my own brother's family, and their neighbours, could so easily have been the first victims of the world's first nuclear disaster.

Leah Martin has no doubt that her husband's social conscience had a profound influence on his young sister, particularly her work on behalf of the Children of Chernobyl.

After the birth of their daughter, Leah busied herself with the affairs of a full-time mother while Dónal found various jobs. In 1980, he was employed at a steel mill in Harrisburg where he worked until 1987, the year of his marriage break-up and his return to Ireland. He joined the Local 1688 Branch of the United Steel Workers of America (USWA) and while the work was tough, he revelled in the comradeship and the protection the union gave him.

It is obvious as one speaks with Leah Martin today that she still has a deep affection for her ex-husband. 'He was an excellent father,' she says. 'He was very attentive to his children. Even though, in hindsight, the signs were there, I was shocked when he left. For a while, he just wasn't the caring person I knew him to be.'

In her heart, Leah knew that her marriage was slipping. Whereas before she had had time to support Dónal during moments of depression, now, with two young children, her tolerance waned. 'I watched him let the injustice of 1969 eat him up,' she says. 'He became a very difficult person to be around. I got to the point where I couldn't tolerate it any more.'

She has no doubt that 1969 played a major part in the eventual break-up of their marriage. Today she harbours no bitterness.

He could be such fun to be around. But, when he went into depression, it was clear his self-confidence and self-esteem had been beaten down and he was finding it impossible to recover without an acknowledgement of

the injustice he had experienced. I am delighted he has
found the strength to really fight back now and I hope
and pray that he wins a just fight.

Leah Martin has an interesting insight on Seán Roche, her father-in-
law:

I saw him sometimes being very condescending towards
Dónal. That hurt and upset me. He talked down to
Dónal and always seemed to be ready to pick a fight, even
down to his finger nails being dirty. He was nice to me,
although, I admit, we too bumped heads on occasions.
There was even a time when he allowed me into the
family home in Clonmel but not Duck.

The strange thing is, I often felt he reacted to Dónal
out of guilt and inadequacy. I often felt that deep down
he felt he had let his son down because he was unable
to do anything to help him and was too proud and too
stubborn to show his own helplessness and vulnerability.
Mr Roche wasn't a bad man – far from it. He felt horribly
betrayed by a system in which he had placed his entire
faith. When it turned against his son, the only way he
could cope was by shutting down, which meant he shut
Dónal out.

How was Dónal to cope with that? Feeling ostracised
by his father, as well as people he thought were his
friends, he gave up. But is it surprising? When you've
been beaten down like that, it's hard to come back up.

After the second encounter with his old solicitor, O'Maoileoin, Dónal
de Róiste effectively gave up. It was simply too exhausting to chase
shadows and illusions.

Meanwhile, his old army friend, Commandant Patrick Walshe, had
not seen De Róiste since the day of the Barnes McCormick funeral
in July 1969. He was delighted, one day in 1985, when Dónal and the
two children called to see him in Newbridge, during a visit to Ireland.
Walshe recalls that as De Róiste's children played happily with his
own around the house, the two men became engrossed in conversation

about the past. Walshe decided to broach the subject of De Róiste's 'retirement' and the possibility of his beginning some kind of action to clear his name.

Walshe says that he can still remember De Róiste's reaction. 'I can still see him going completely white, falling silent and staring off into space.' Walshe says that he had only once encountered a similar reaction – when he had to tell a soldier under his command in the Congo about the death of his mother. 'Just like the soldier, Dónal seemed catatonic and his lips were trembling. I was afraid that the children would burst in and see him this way, so I quickly changed the subject.'

RETURN TO IRELAND

When Leah Martin and Dónal de Róiste finally split up in 1987, De Róiste returned to Ireland where Adi and her husband welcomed him for six months until he got settled. Through the employment agency, FÁS, he found a job with a voluntary organisation called 'Between', which arranged holidays in the Republic for children from Northern Ireland. The organisation had a house where the children stayed and De Róiste worked as head of the house and drove the bus.

During the summers, his children, Dara and Sinead, often came to holiday with him and he enjoyed bringing them to meet the children from the northern 'Troubles'. Leah Martin had a very balanced approach regarding allowing her children go to Ireland.

> I trusted Dónal and his family … I never once worried that Duck would keep the children in Ireland. It simply never crossed my mind for I knew that, despite their internal family difficulties, the entire De Róiste family were good, decent people, with a strong sense of justice, fair play and moral integrity.

Relations with his father were still strained. Christina, however, would occasionally pick her moment to bring up the possibility of a rapprochement between the father and son. Because both she and her husband were regular mass-goers, she would wait in particular for the parable of the prodigal son:

Every time there would be a sermon, you know periodically, about the prodigal son, I would always watch my time to mention it to Seán. He would say to me, 'The prodigal son repented.' I would counter that in the parable it is made clear that 'The father went out to meet his son before he ever knew he was repenting.'

Seán, however, never made that initial approach to Dónal, while Dónal was never quite sure of what he was supposed to repent. And so the whole affair hung over them all, the elephant in the living room.

As the years passed, Dónal began to settle back in Ireland. He was allocated a small house in Ballincollig by the local authorities. He was on the organising committee of Between, joined a choir and found steady work during the school year as bus driver with Coláiste Colm, where he was respected by teachers and parents and popular amongst the students. During the short journey to and from school, he got to know each of the children individually, their hobbies and heroes, and the songs that they loved. His rapport was such that in 2002, the school wrote to the Taoiseach in support of his campaign to clear his name.

Speaking in September 2005, school principal Pat Kinsella recalled De Róiste's time as the school driver:

He was a great character. I remember on one occasion we had a group of distinguished educationalists from Denmark, who were visiting second-level educational facilities in Ireland. After their visit with us, we had to transport them to another school. I was a bit embarrassed as all we had was an old banger of a bus, driven by Dónal. I mentioned this to him and he had me doubled with laugher with his quick wit. He replied, 'Don't worry about it. They were in wooden boats the last time they were here.' He had such a wealth of one-liners. He wasn't just a bus driver. He was always reliable as well as entertaining and full of fun. The kids loved him.

The children knew too that their bus driver's sister was the famous Adi Roche who had come to national prominence in 1986 following the world's worst non-military nuclear disaster. Under her leadership, the Chernobyl Children's Project initiated aid programmes which, to date, have delivered tens of millions of euros worth of humanitarian and medical aid to areas most affected by the disaster. In addition, the Project has organised rest and recuperation programmes for many thousands of sick children to come to Ireland for medical treatment and holidays. The children of Coláiste Colm had enthusiastically helped to fundraise for the Project and several of the children's families had hosted children from Chernobyl.

One day, in 1997, excitement gripped the school and especially the children on Dónal de Róiste's bus. Adi Roche, their bus driver's sister, had been nominated to run for the presidency of Ireland. As her candidacy was announced, the response throughout Ireland seemed very favourable and bookies immediately made Adi Roche their favourite. As the children mounted the bus, they congratulated Dónal with smiles and hugs and handshakes.

6

THE 1997 PRESIDENTIAL CAMPAIGN

Nobody wanted a butterfly broken on the wheel.

Nell McCafferty

Writing in *Ireland on Sunday*, less than a year after the 1997 presidential election, Rachel Borrill commented: 'The viciousness of last year's presidential campaign certainly took even hardened political pundits by surprise.'

And vicious it was.

Five candidates were declared: Adi Roche, 'the People's Candidate', endorsed by the Labour Party, Democratic Left and the Green Party; Mary Banotti, endorsed by Fine Gael; Mary McAleese, supported by Fianna Fáil and the Progressive Democrats; and Dana Rosemary Scallon and Derek Nally, two independent candidates, supported by various local county councils.

Banotti's suitability for the office was called into question by those who objected to the fact that she was a divorcee. Dana's worst bruising was an encounter with RTÉ radio presenter Vincent Browne, resulting in an official complaint and an apology from RTÉ. Mary McAleese, with less than two weeks to polling day, and by then the clear leader, found herself being accused of 'pushing a Sinn Féin agenda' and much controversy being created following a courteous exchange with Gerry Adams on board a commercial flight. Her primary accusations arose from 'leaked' Department of Foreign Affairs documents that resulted in an investigation by the Garda Síochána.

The combined bruising of Banotti, McAleese and Dana, however, paled in comparison to a relentless two-week assault on Adi Roche even before she registered as a candidate for the race. At the dawn of her campaign, Roche was the bookies' favourite, appeared unassailable, had the backing of U2's Bono and, in the wake of the recent deaths of

Princess Diana and Mother Teresa, might even have filled the vacuum left by their passing. There was impatience, however, amongst some hard-nosed journalists who feared that the race to fill the vacancy – left when President Mary Robinson took up the post of UN High Commissioner for Human Rights – would be so cordial and nice that it would be agonisingly boring. What ensued was not Irish journalism's finest hour. Indeed, there was much to be positively ashamed of. At times it was more akin to ravenous wolves spoiling for scraps of any information that might steal a headline.

By the time the campaign concluded, Adi Roche had dropped from favourite to second-last, losing her deposit with just under 7 per cent of the electorate having voted for her. Kathy Sheridan, writing in *The Irish Times* on Saturday, 1 November 1997, the day after the count, quoted 'a still-baffled' Senator Pat Magnier, Adi's campaign tour manager:

> I don't think it's ever happened in Irish political history that a candidate at 38 per cent in the polls fell from such a height. And I don't think you'll find two people to agree on the cause of it.

Despite a fiercely fought campaign with, at times, saturation media coverage, the majority of the eligible electorate, some 53 per cent, voted by staying at home or spoiling their vote. At 47 per cent, the turnout was the lowest in the history of any Irish presidential election. While President Mary McAleese proved to be both a successful and popular choice, achieving a second term in 2004 unopposed, the 21 per cent of the vote she won in 1997 was the lowest in the history of the presidency.

This chapter is not an analysis of the 1997 presidential election. Instead, its focus is on how that election impacted on the Roche family, in particular Dónal's youngest sister, Adi, and how his departure from the Irish army was cynically used to maximise the irreparable damage she suffered in her presidential campaign.

Journalist Nell McCafferty has never hidden her admiration for Adi Roche. She travelled with the then forty-two-year-old Clonmel woman on one of her famous convoys to Chernobyl. What she witnessed during the arduous journey from Ireland to Belarus so convinced her that Roche had the mettle and the skills to navigate the presidency that she bet, and lost, £900 on Roche winning the election.

In an opinion piece, published in *The Irish Times* on 1 November 1997, Dick Walsh wrote:

> Adi Roche was, in a sense, the right candidate, young, able and idealistic, in the wrong election: someone chosen to meet the version of old Ireland that Albert Reynolds or Michael O'Kennedy represent; unprepared for the fiercely competitive new right of Mary McAleese.

It was known that former Taoiseach Albert Reynolds wanted the Fianna Fáil nomination for the presidency. There was a time when a man such as Reynolds could almost have assumed it was his without having to endure the humiliation that would confound him. For many in Fianna Fáil, Reynolds' undoubted key role in the Northern Ireland peace process was inconsequential history when compared to the threat of handing the presidency to the Labour Party for another seven years. The past did not count. All that mattered was winning this election, whatever it took.

In a very real sense, Adi Roche accelerated the sunset of Reynolds' public life and the dawn of President McAleese. If Roche had not been persuaded by the Labour Party to run for the Áras, it is possible that Mary McAleese would still be lecturing in Queen's University, Belfast. Labour's strategy was based on a bright, intelligent and much-loved charismatic young woman running against a senior politician. The party leadership was confident it could repeat its outstanding coup over Fianna Fáil in 1990 when Mary Robinson became not only the first woman President of Ireland, but also the first President to be elected without the support of Fianna Fáil.

There was no sentiment, therefore, in the decision by Fianna Fáil to strategise the defeat of Reynolds in favour of McAleese.

UNDER STARTER'S ORDERS

Adi Roche was well known for her activities as an anti-nuclear campaigner and a tireless worker on behalf of the children of Chernobyl. She was known to favour Irish neutrality and the positive peacekeeping role that Ireland could serve as a non-aligned nation. She was also conscious of Ireland's responsibility to help the poorest nations of the world, particularly given our own history of famine, hunger, injustice and colonial abuse. There is no doubt that her youthful idealism was viewed as a danger by conservative elements in the state, and perhaps beyond.

Initially Adi Roche had little interest in running for the presidency. However, with the 1997 presidential election on the horizon, both Fianna Fáil and the Labour Party touted her as a potential candidate for their respective parties. Journalists such as Fintan O'Toole in *The Irish Times* and Gráinne Cunningham in the *Examiner* had written of the qualities that Adi Roche might bring to the office.

On 16 September 1997, the Labour Party, Democratic Left and the Green Party selected Adi Roche as a 'people's candidate'. On the same day, Fine Gael announced Mary Banotti as its candidate. There were rumours of conflict in Fianna Fáil and of a campaign with the slogan, 'Anybody but Albert'. The following afternoon, the party announced that Belfast Law Professor Mary McAleese had been chosen as its candidate; she had defeated Reynolds in a secret ballot.

Adi Roche began her first day of campaigning by telling a packed press conference in Dublin:

> This is the most exciting day of my life. There are times when I feel that my heart will burst with nerves and anxiety. But there is another part of me that feels that it is so right – that my time is now.

Curiously, she was questioned about fears of a 'dirty' campaign, to which she responded:

> I would have no hand, act or part in any downgrading, or any gossip or anything negative. I respect all the other candidates, and I wish them well. No matter how dirty the game would get politically, I would not enter myself into that in any way, or support it.

Roche outlined her hopes for Northern Ireland and a new millennium of peace, harmony and co-existence. On the issue of a new abortion referendum, she stated that this would be decided by the will of the people. On neutrality, she expressed the hope that Ireland would enter the new millennium with 'our neutrality intact'. Ironically, she was questioned about the President's role as commander-in-chief of the armed forces. She stated:

> I would always see our army in that tremendous role of peacemakers, peacekeepers. I have a very close identification with the Irish army.

On Thursday, 18 September 1997, Kevin Myers wrote in *The Irish Times*:

> ... this is the year for presidential moulds to be broken. Of the 2,688,316 adults in the Republic, only two have been endorsed as candidates.
>
> One of them works in Brussels, the other is famous for her work in the Ukraine. The other two candidates are from the United Kingdom, where one of them lives. The other lives in Alabama.

On the same day, the *Irish Independent* gave the bookies' ratings of the four women now declared for the race to the Áras: Adi Roche (4/6) favourite, Mary McAleese (5/2), Mary Banotti (4/1) and Dana (8/1). Derek Nally – who was campaigning on a platform of supporting youth, the disabled, and old people – had not yet been nominated as an independent candidate.

The *Irish Mirror* carried a photograph of candidates Mary Banotti and Adi Roche sharing a coffee at a fundraising event. The headline was: 'Adi and Mary Agree: "We won't play dirty".' Roche was quoted as saying:

> This campaign will not resort to dirty tactics or underhand dealings. We came to a ladies' agreement that we'd be very careful with each other and run a dignified and quality campaign.

Whatever about Banotti, a politician with many political campaigns under her belt, it was a sign of Roche's innocence and naïvety. She was just days away from a two-week mauling that would destroy her promising campaign, almost break her health and damage her family.

Kathy Sheridan, assigned by *The Irish Times* to follow Adi Roche in her campaigning trail around the country, gave an insightful commentary in her first of several reports on Saturday, 20 September 1997:

> Although [Roche] refused to be rattled by Mary McAleese's nomination, it gave pause to some in Labour HQ. But they recovered. 'She's the first Fianna Fáil candidate in respect of whom headquarters will have to send out a CV to its own membership,' said one. Their candidate by comparison begins with the inestimable benefit of over 70 organised Project groups around the state, with the tentacles of 900 families reaching deep into the hearts and minds of Ireland's broadest constituency.

Sheridan also reported:

> ... although she earnestly hopes for a dignified campaign, she knows there are tough times ahead. Last Monday she asked her parents to stop reading the newspapers: 'They're very protective of me and would find some of the writing too hurtful.'
>
> But she and all around her know that the backlash will get worse. In the coming days she will be required to assess herself and her style as never before...

On the same day, in an extensive article for the *Examiner*, Mark Hennessy reflected:

> [Roche] is vulnerable on the question of experience. A formidable activist, with an earned reputation for improving the common weal, she faces a rough time as her FF and Fine Gael backed opponents – with good manners, no doubt – target her... On her list of advantages, Roche can point to an incredible network of people around the country from her Chernobyl work, who place her somewhere between Mother Teresa and Princess Diana. No other candidate is her equal.

To destroy Roche's chances for the presidency, 'The Angel of Chernobyl' needed to be turned into a wolf disguised as a lamb. The very next day, it began. A new Sunday newspaper was born with the 'exclusive' front-page headlines: 'Split Rocks Adi's Campaign'. *Ireland on Sunday*'s first issue reported that Roche's campaign 'has been rocked by revelations of a split in the Chernobyl Children's Project which she founded'. Written by Ken Whelan and Mairead Carey, the article stated that the split revolved around a 'row over internal management in the organisation' and had occurred before her decision to run for the presidency.

Helen Callanan, in a more detailed article in the *Sunday Tribune* on the same day, reported that her paper had the names of some thirteen disaffected former colleagues of Roche who were in the process of meeting to discuss what they wished to do publicly. The list was soon to be anonymously distributed amongst Dáil deputies and other media sources. It was reported that some among the group claimed that 'the public face of Adi Roche is not the woman they worked with.'

People on the list openly criticised the Children of Chernobyl Project. The article referred to a memo Roche had written the previous year 'outlining her vision of the organisation, but staff who read the 10-page document found it contained mainly personal criticisms of office workers.' The following day, Laura Monaghan in the *Examiner* wrote that the report had resulted in two committee members, two directors and an accountant resigning from the Chernobyl Project. In the document, it is clear that Roche is expressing frustration and reacting to what she considers unfair criticism from some staff:

> I know the way employers can be abused by manipulative
> or lazy employees ... I did it myself and am ashamed of it
> now that I know what it is like to be at the end of misuse
> and abuse by workers.

The article also quoted an unnamed former FÁS worker who alleged that she had made an official complaint to 'the FÁS office, but they sided with her and my complaints were not looked at.' The former worker complained of being overworked, stating, 'There was no such thing as a family life with her.' On Thursday, 25 September 1997, the *Irish Independent* reported that FÁS, the state training agency, 'said no official complaints from any trainees in relation to the conduct of Ms

Roche while chief of the Chernobyl Children's Project were listed in their files.'

In the *Examiner*, Liam Grant, who worked with Roche for five years before leaving to set up his own charity organisation, Chernobyl Aid Ireland, was quoted defending his former colleague:

> Without Adi Roche, we would never have found out what was going on out there. The only people who can suffer as a result of this are the children lying in sick beds in Belarus.

His sentiments were echoed in a statement 'by key representatives of the Chernobyl charity'.

Roche was now hitting the front page of most national newspapers, with very damaging headlines. The farce gathered heat with several newspapers reporting a Cork meeting of the disaffected who had given themselves the name: The Concerned Group Not Supporting Adi Roche For President [CGNSARFP]. The group, which described Roche's management style as 'Stalinist', claimed that its members were neither politically motivated nor engaging in a personal vendetta against Ms Roche.

Roche had just been hit by the first wave of a turbulent sea being whipped up by a storm, the source of which was hidden from radar. Another was on its way, involving her brother, Dónal, and would leave her almost drowning.

FIRST PUBLIC AIRING OF LT DÓNAL ROCHE'S ARMY 'RETIREMENT'
I first met Dónal de Róiste in the home of his sister, Adi Roche, shortly after he had returned to Ireland in 1988. Like the rest of the nation, I was completely unaware of his 'retirement' from the Irish army in 1969. The first time the public was introduced to it was with headlines on the front of the *Star* and the *Examiner* on Tuesday, 23 September 1997.

The Star *Report*
The *Star* article, written by Barry O'Kelly, stated: 'Adi Roche's brother left the army amid allegations that he was a Republican sympathiser. But Dónal de Róiste said he left the defence forces of his own free will.'

De Róiste is then quoted as follows:

> They said I was linked with people I was not – I am not a
> member of any subversive group. I'm a republican living
> in a republican country.

The article also states that, 'Mr de Róiste is now a bus driver in Cork –
resigned as a lieutenant through a rare order from the President in June
1969. An army spokesman said no reason was shown in army records
for his resignation.'

The above, including the 1½ inch front-page banner headline:
'ADI'S BROTHER QUIT ARMY AFTER IRA SLUR' is entirely
inaccurate. Lt Roche did not quit the army. He was 'retired' by the
President on the recommendation of the government.

In the follow-up article inside the paper, a smaller headline repeats
the assertion above that 'Roche brother says he chose to leave army.'
O'Kelly quotes De Róiste as follows:

> They said I was linked with people I was not. I'm not a
> member of Saoirse Éireann. I am not a member of any
> subversive group. I'm a republican living in a republican
> country.

O'Kelly then reports:

> … De Róiste said he was fully behind his sister's
> campaign for the presidency and labelled her detractors
> as whingers. He said they should 'put up or shut up'. Ms
> Roche was not perfect – but she had done a lot of great
> work and was very well disposed towards the people,
> he said. Mr de Róiste said he had no difficulty with Ms
> Roche becoming Commander in Chief of the defence
> forces – a position held by the President.

The article states that a spokesman for Adi Roche's campaign issued
a one-line response to the breaking story the night before. 'She has
nothing to say about something that happened when she was 14.'

The article also quotes an army spokesman confirming: 'Mr Roche
was resigned by the President on June 29, 1969 under [rarely exercised]
provisions of the Defence Forces Act.'

As previously emphasised, Lt Roche was 'retired'; he did not resign. We will see later in the book that the army was monitoring his case long before it hit the headlines in such a dramatic and unexpected manner. It seems odd that both former Lt Roche and an official army spokesman would, therefore, make the same mistake. Furthermore, an army spokesperson – presumably the same army spokesman – accurately stated to the *Examiner* newspaper, on the same day, 'Mr de Róiste was retired by the President'.

O'Kelly continues: 'Mr de Róiste denied at the time that he was associating with known republican figures. He joined the army in 1963 as a Cadet Officer and was promoted to Lieutenant three years later.... Asked about the rumours, an angry Mr De Róiste told the *Star*: 'It's erroneous. It's lies. I have not been convicted of anything. You guys in the media have shafted my sister.'

The following day, 24 September 1997, John Donlon followed up Barry O'Kelly's article, quoting from an interview with Eoghan Harris. Donlon's article stated:

> Presidential hopeful Adi Roche has been damaged by revelations in the *Star* that her brother left the army amid allegations that he was an IRA sympathiser.
>
> That's the view of Eoghan Harris, the man who masterminded Mary Robinson's Áras success.
>
> Top political guru Harris also said that allegations about Roche regarding her 'Stalinist' running of the Chernobyl Project would strengthen her campaign.
>
> But her failure to make a clear statement on the *Star* story would do her long-term structural damage – unless she distanced herself from her brother's politics.
>
> Eoghan said: 'The *Star* story was a brilliant one. It performed a very serious, important public service.
>
> 'Adi must do more than tell us she has a warm relationship with her brother.
>
> 'She must repudiate his statement that he is a republican living in a republican country. Otherwise people will think it's her belief as well.
>
> 'I believe her foot-dragging on this is going to do more damage than the Chernobyl accusations.

'I don't think her explanation is adequate for anyone who is going to be Commander in Chief of the army. It's not a republican country, that's a matter of opinion.'

Mr Harris said he found the *Star* story very perturbing.

'The fact that her brother would want to change defence forces regulations is worrying and Adi Roche must distance herself further from it.'

The Examiner *Report*

The *Examiner* also broke the story in a front-page article on the same day, written by political correspondent Mark Hennessy with the ⅜ inch headline: 'Brother's past rises to haunt Adi'. Hennessy wrote:

Embattled presidential candidate, Adi Roche, last night refused to enter a new row after it emerged her brother was discharged from the army because of allegations that he had links with subversives.

Ms Roche declined to comment. Her spokesman was just as reticent: 'The candidate has no comment to make about something which took place when she was 14 years old.'

The former army officer, who described himself as a republican, said that if his sister became President he would want her to review the military regulations used to force him out of the army.

Dónal de Róiste left the army in 1969. 'I was in the army and was sort of pressurised to leave. They said I was linked with certain people but I was not. They said I was linked with subversives.'

'I am living in a Republic and I am a Republican. I am not a member of Saoirse or any other group. I have no difficulty with the possibility of Adi being commander of the armed forces.'

Last night, the defence forces pointed out that, under the Defence Act, Mr de Róiste was retired by the President, who at the time was Eamon de Valera.

...An army spokesman last night declined to specify

the grounds under which he was retired.

Under the regulations, he did not qualify for an honourable discharge. However, leaving the service under the section does not qualify as a dishonourable discharge.

The former army man said his former fellow officers did not put any case to him when he came under pressure to leave. 'I wanted a Court Martial. I got in contact with a solicitor. But I then left of my own accord.'

He believes his sister is very capable of holding the post of President.

'I am one hundred per cent behind her. If people have things against her bar hurt feelings, I would urge them to say so now.'

He suggested that, maybe, Fianna Fáil was behind the attacks on her. 'It's purely politically motivated.'

'Adi isn't perfect. But she is genuinely interested in the Chernobyl children. This campaign against her is nothing but insulting. She is a normal person trying to do good. She is sharp at times but she's not Stalinist,' added Mr de Róiste.

As a Cork-based broadsheet, whose sister newspaper, the *Evening Echo*, was backing Adi Roche's candidacy, the *Examiner* received a negative response to the Dónal de Róiste story. In a Mark Hennessy article the following day, headed, '"My heart goes out to Roche for the hurt she endured" says McAleese', he wrote:

> Despite the condemnation of the *Examiner* story, it must be stated it was not based upon anonymous sources – it included an official response from the defence forces Press Office and an 'on-the-record' interview with Roche's brother, Dónal de Róiste.

Veteran *Examiner* journalist Dónal Musgrave wrote:

> A Fianna Fáil TD has been positively linked with leaking information about Adi's brother Dónal, a Republican who was 'retired' out of the army under a cloud 28 years

ago. Mr de Róiste has denied membership of Saoirse, the IRA, or any such organisation.

The same Fianna Fáil politician is also known to be directly involved in efforts to acquire a tape recording of Ms Roche allegedly berating a former worker in the Chernobyl operation. Anonymous documents aimed at discrediting her have been circulated to the media and TDs in a random, cross-party mail shot to Leinster House.

In a letter to me, dated 10 April 2002, De Róiste wrote: 'The first approach in 1997 came from Neans McSweeney of the *Examiner*.' He has no positive recollection of speaking with any journalist from the *Star* newspaper. Barry O'Kelly, when contacted on 22 September 2005, could not recall positively if he or a *Star* journalist had spoken with De Róiste either.

McSweeney has confirmed that she spoke briefly with De Róiste on 22 September 1997, the day before the story broke in both the *Examiner* and the *Star* newspapers. She informed me that she conducted the interview in Irish at De Róiste's request. She recalled that there was a bit of 'hooha' the following morning when the credit of breaking the story was attributed to Hennessy, whose front-page story had 'plucked the pertinent pieces' from a story written by both herself and journalist Ralph Riegal. Subject to correction, it appears their article never appeared in the *Examiner*. McSweeney recalls that an *Examiner* editor asked her on the morning the story broke in the two newspapers: 'Did you speak to any other journalist?'

McSweeney confirmed that she had been called by a journalist the previous evening. She told the journalist, in English, about her conversation with Dónal de Róiste, earlier that same day. It was McSweeney's understanding that the journalist she spoke to was not writing a story for his newspaper and thus she felt comfortable speaking to him.

How the *Examiner* and the *Star* got hold of the 'leak' is unknown. It is interesting, however, to compare the reports of both papers, particularly the two crucial quotes: 'I'm a republican living in a republican country' (the *Star*) and 'I am living in a Republic and I am a Republican' (the *Examiner*). Both carry very different connotations, as highlighted by the comments attributed to Eoghan Harris in the *Star*.

McSweeney informed me that she quoted back to De Róiste the following crucial sentence:

> I am living in a Republic and I am a republican. I am not a member of Saoirse or any other group. I have no difficulty with the possibility of Adi being commander of the armed forces.

In an email to me, dated 25 September 2005, Neans McSweeney wrote:

> I know that I was happy with the quote as it appeared in the *Examiner*. I would have checked and double checked it. It was such a serious matter.

De Róiste had said nothing wrong, nothing offensive, nothing untoward. What was and is objectionable, however, is the twist and spin ascribed to his comments.

In addition, Dónal de Róiste had been door-stepped by photographer Jim Walpole. The published photographs show shock and fear in his eyes. He says that when he closed the door, he was engulfed by a panic attack, realising that his past, which he had, off and on, tried quietly to resolve with the army, had come back to haunt him publicly. He also felt an enormous sense of responsibility for his sister, knowing that she had already been wounded by former colleagues, and now his personal and private difficulties with the army were being used to damage her further.

De Róiste says that the principal of the school in Cork for which he was a bus driver, realising that he was traumatised by the unexpected revelations, advised him to take a few days off. It would be several months, and several encounters with a counsellor, before De Róiste would feel strong enough to fight back in defence of his good name. He is adamant that the *Examiner* quote is the accurate one and describes the *Star* quote as a Chinese whisper. He has no doubt also that the *Examiner*'s statement that a Fianna Fáil TD 'was positively linked with leaking information' about him, is true. The only question he cannot answer is who 'leaked' the information to the politician in the first place.

While the aim was clearly to damage Adi Roche's presidential campaign, the leak has also achieved another very definite outcome – the opening of a Pandora's Box, the consequences of which may haunt the defence forces and the Irish state far more than any consequential damage to the youngest and eldest children of Seán and Christina Roche.

FALLEN ANGEL

There was no way back for Adi Roche, 'the Angel of Chernobyl'. All she had was her personal integrity, which had been assaulted with mud scraped from a very shallow barrel. It was, however, mud that was sticking – the kind of mud that would require time to clear, but it was time that the media could not give during the frenzy of an election campaign.

Almost a decade after her trauma, it is heartening to see that Roche has recovered, and the loyalty of colleagues and friends has ensured the onward movement of her inspiring humanitarian efforts. She admitted to Rachel Borrill, during her interview in *Ireland on Sunday* the following year, that the viciousness of the assault almost destroyed her:

> I was literally torn apart by the dogs. It was like there was a public hanging, yet I still wasn't dead, I was still hanging on in there despite everything.
>
> There were times when I would wake up in the morning and, for a split second, everything would be all right and then, all of a sudden, this darkness would come and weigh you down, and the reality of another awful headline, an awful accusation or lie would come bouncing back in. I went through agony.
>
> I was absolutely paralysed by the speed in which it all happened and I said to myself: 'Do I need this in my life?'
>
> So I did a balance sheet of the pros and cons, and the overwhelming decision was to go on. I wanted to give it my best shot, I still had the hope and the expectation. But obviously I was hit very hard. I got a fierce battering – talk about a baptism of fire.

And she went on and so too did the accusations which, in the end, had even hardened media pundits wondering what it was all about and wondering if they too had been pawns in a bigger and more cynical game. Her rapid slide down the opinion polls began.

Within three days of the barrage of vitriol beginning, Adi Roche slipped into second place in the race for the Áras, never to recover. An *Examiner* piece on 23 September reported that the Fianna Fáil nominee, Professor McAleese, had marginally edged ahead of the young Clonmel woman. Roche was now attracting odds of 5/4. Mary Banotti 9/2, while Dana was 'becoming an increasing outsider, with betting drifting from 16/1 to 25/1'.

With the negative publicity succeeding in its political intent, a press officer for Fianna Fáil was quoted as saying, 'We have heard nothing at all about any smear campaign [against Roche] and we would not condone anything of that nature.'

An article in the *Examiner* commented:

> This comes despite the fact that prominent party members have been in regular contract [*sic*] with various newspapers alerting them to a variety of supposedly independent campaigns against Ms Roche.

Fianna Fáil's press officer stated:

> We know nothing about people – party members or not – alerting newspapers about any particular story about any particular candidate, and if anyone is doing anything of that nature then we do not condone it. Fianna Fáil would have nothing to do with anything like that. If it is true then we would not be at all happy.

Mary McAleese, whose candidacy was endorsed by the Progressive Democrats on 23 September, reacted to Roche's difficulties. Brian Dowling, writing in the *Independent* the following morning, reported that McAleese appealed to the media to exercise moral judgment and insisted that there would have to be a 'line in the sand'. Reacting to stories of former Lt Roche's 'retirement', she said:

> Adi Roche is standing for election, not her brother. My heart goes out to her for what she has endured. It is

absolutely unconscionable.

McAleese said that she had no idea whether the campaign against Roche was politically motivated, 'But whatever the motivation, it is ugly.'

Dowling also quoted Democratic Left leader Proinsias de Rossa, who condemned 'a campaign of vilification against Adi Roche'. He said that it was difficult to accept that these were a series of independent, spontaneous happenings and equally difficult to accept that there was not some degree of co-ordination.

It was also announced that Adi Roche would take leave of absence from the Chernobyl Children's Project, with an acting director appointed, pending the outcome of the presidential election.

On Friday, 27 September 1997, Adi Roche, accompanied by Labour leader Dick Spring, Democratic Left leader Proinsias de Rossa and the Green Party's Trevor Sargent, handed in her nomination papers at the Customs House in Dublin. She was, despite everything, courageously staking her right, and her claim, to a place in the race to succeed President Mary Robinson as the eighth Uachtarán na hÉireann.

With five declared candidates, the bookies were offering odds of evens for McAleese, 6/4 Roche, 7/2 Banotti, 50/1 Dana and 100/1 Derek Nally. In reality, though, Adi's race was over before it began. But still the 'leaks' continued.

On her first day of campaigning as a registered candidate, Adi Roche woke up to an article by Dónal Hickey and Edward Power in the *Examiner* which declared: 'Leaked letters reveal Belarus authorities reprimanded Roche.' The impression given at the outset of the article is that the director of the Irish Chernobyl Children's Project had been the recipient of a series of official Belarusian admonishments. However, it later emerges in the body of the article that Hickey and Power, subject to correction, based their report on only one letter, involving a rival Chernobyl project and a lifelong member of the Fianna Fáil party.

The claim was potentially even more damaging than the suggestion of a Stalinist management style, suggesting the possible mistreatment of children in the care of her charity.

In a follow-up article in the *Examiner* of 29 September, Edward Power wrote:

Letters from Russian and Belarus authorities have contradicted reports from a Fianna Fáil member that Presidential candidate Adi Roche and the Chernobyl Children's Project had behaved wrongly in dealing with ill children on holiday in this country.

Letters released this weekend by the charitable project reveal a close, amicable working relationship between officials in the former Soviet republics devastated by Chernobyl nuclear disaster which contrast with recent descriptions of Ms Roche's leadership style.

Power had been given access to letters, not 'leaked' but openly provided by the Chernobyl Children's Charity.

Edward Power's report also quoted from a statement released the day before by the Chernobyl Children's Project, which said that when Ms Roche had accepted the invitation to run for the presidency, the Project was fully aware that it would be subjected to media and public scrutiny. He quoted:

> The Project has responded readily and openly to this scrutiny. Practically all press outlets have requested and received copies of the Project's audited accounts and all of our aid programmes have been examined. The intense scrutiny which has taken place over the last week has failed to uncover any irregularities.

Roche's lack of political acumen was revealed during a one-to-one interview with RTÉ radio presenter, Pat Kenny, on Thursday, 26 September. 'I have a couple of ideas about how I would like to see Áras an Uachtaráin being the people's home,' Roche told Kenny. 'Rather than seeing it as a distinctive and separate place I am going to have this as a place of music and of sound and particularly the sound of children … I would like to see it as some kind of children's Presidency.'

When Kenny joked about a possible U2 gig in the grounds of the Áras, she blurted:

> Well you never know because I was talking to Bono yesterday after his gig in Sarajevo. We were just tossing

around some ideas and that is where I would be pulling in for example the Irish army.

I have a couple of ideas about what we can do about the tremendous amount of land that is around Áras an Uachtaráin and what it could be like during the summertime in terms of theatre and drama and music...

Suddenly her candidacy was the brunt of jokes rather than poisoned arrows from a few former associates and anonymous politicians. Fine Gael candidate Mary Banotti made an incisive statement that was akin to an old pro-boxer catching a novice with a bloody right hook:

The Áras is not a children's playground. The Áras is an institution with serious powers and serious responsibilities. We're not looking for a kind of new form of interior decorating in the Park. We are looking for a serious President who will represent the country and bring to the role judgment, experience, and hopefully, maturity.

On Saturday, 27 September, the *Star's* 'Inside File' wrote:

... some of the more cruel political animals in [Dáil Éireann] are dubbing the lovely Angel of Chernobyl, Adi Amin, after reports that she ruled the Chernobyl Project with an iron fist.

And the other joke in the Dáil is that when Adi spoke of making the Áras a safe haven did she mean a haven for her brother Dónal, who left the army in strange circumstances?

By 4 October, according to *The Irish Times*, 'Labour's dream candidate' was 'slipping into third place'. Interviewed by Maol Muire Tynan, Fergus Finlay, a close adviser to Labour leader Dick Spring and a senior Labour figure, was adamant that a 'campaign' had been orchestrated to damage Roche. The fact that the story had got into four Sunday newspapers, he argued, demonstrated that this was not the work of 'shambolic amateurs'.

On 6 October, the *Examiner* reported a disastrous plunge in the opinion polls for Roche, with a slump of 18 per cent since the first poll. From early October onwards, her political savvy, her knowledge of the role of the President and the running of her campaign were criticised widely.

Having assumed the leadership in the race for President, Mary McAleese saw her own campaign plunged into crisis by the leakage of a classified Department of Foreign Affairs document reporting confidential discussions that Departmental officials had conducted with Northern political figures. It was clear that the document had been trawled to publicise potentially damaging references to McAleese made by a senior member of the SDLP. McAleese was accused of 'pushing a Sinn Féin agenda'. While a Garda investigation was publicly announced into the leak, its findings were never reported and the Gardai have refused to inform me of the outcome of their investigation. To her credit, Roche refused to allow her campaign to become another brush to spread the McAleese smear.

ANOTHER CAMPAIGN

As Adi Roche's campaign was waning, the seeds of another campaign were beginning to take root. The article that had appeared in the *Examiner* had incensed the long-standing friend of Lt Dónal Roche, former Commandant Patrick Walshe. Throughout October, he pondered what positive action he might take on behalf of the 'retired' officer. In mid-October, he delivered a letter to all the candidates as well as the leaders of all political parties in the Republic. I am in possession of a copy of the letter he addressed to Mary McAleese, Presidential Candidate, dated 16 October 1997:

> Dear Ms McAleese,
> On 23 September 1997, the *Examiner* published a front page article under the heading 'Brother's Past Rises to haunt Adi'. The persons who were responsible for resurrecting information contained in this article did so with the intention of damaging the election prospects of Ms Roche. You are no doubt aware that Ms Roche was a young schoolgirl when the affair referred to occurred in 1969.

Of far more serious concern is the renewed effect that this information has had on her brother Dónal who was referred to in the article.

As a fellow officer serving in the army, Dónal was a friend of mine. We had a shared interest in Irish traditional music and met most weekends in Dublin and other towns to take part in music sessions. We met regularly with musicians and singers and with people who followed the traditional music scene. In 1969 Dónal was accused by the Intelligence Section of the army of 'meeting' certain people who were alleged to have been present at the music sessions. I was questioned over several days about the people we had been meeting during which attempts were made to entice me to give certain answers to questions. It was apparent to me that answers required of me were to be used to entrap Lt Roche.

Dónal's gregarious nature and his love of traditional Irish music had become his downfall. A small group of faceless people working in secret contrived a case to have an innocent man's good name taken from him and his chosen career destroyed in such a way that no trial or court martial ensued and that he could not have redress in law.

Dónal eventually left Ireland for many years. I believe that he has continued to suffer to this day from the great wrong done to him in 1969. The article in the *Examiner* will ensure that damage will continue to be caused to him.

I continued to serve as an officer in the army and retired with the rank of commandant in 1983 after twenty-two years' service. I have remained angry since 1969 because of what was done to my fellow officer and friend. There is a similarity with what happened to Captain Dreyfus in the French army in 1894. But Captain Dreyfus had the benefit of a rigged court martial. Lt Roche was convicted in secret by faceless men. The infamous Dreyfus Case caused such a public outcry in France that in 1906 all convictions against Captain Dreyfus were reversed. He was awarded a Légion d'Honneur, promoted to Major, and served in the First World War as a Lieutenant Colonel. In Ireland nearly one hundred years later no one cared that an innocent man was wrongfully condemned in secret, with no option for redress. In 1997 Dónal Roche continues to be made to suffer, publicly, for a wrong done to him nearly thirty years ago.

The dismissal of Lt Roche from the Defence Forces was finalised by the signature of the President of Ireland in 1969. It seems to me that the next President of Ireland is the only office holder in the Sate who can decide to have the case reconsidered.

Since the recent further damage to Dónal Roche occurred in the context of and as a result of the current Presidential Election Campaign I call upon you should you be elected President of Ireland to have this great injustice looked at in the hope that after many years a wrong will be set right.

Pat Kenny read out the contents of this letter on his morning radio programme as the presidential campaign entered its final ten days. For Dónal Roche, it was the first public salvo fired in his defence.

THE END OF THE RACE
With five days to polling day, Adi was sharing last place with the only male candidate, Derek Nally, at 50/1. McAleese was 4/11 favourite, Banotti was chasing her at 2/1, while Dana was attracting odds of 33/1.

By 29 October, the day before polling, an MRBI poll showed that McAleese was the 'unassailable' candidate. Roche's percentage had collapsed to 8 per cent. When the votes were counted, Roche's vote had gone down to 7 per cent.

Three days after the election, Dick Spring resigned as leader of the Labour Party. He had faced strong opposition and resentment at having overlooked Michael D. Higgins as a potential candidate and having gone outside the party to persuade Adi Roche to run for the presidency.

Speaking to me in 2002 about the presidential campaign, Adi

Roche said:

Fianna Fáil invited me to run for the Senate. Minister for Defence Michael Smith came to speak to me about it. However, I declined since, despite our family's strong Fianna Fáil background, I didn't want to get caught up in party political politics given the nature of my anti-nuclear and disarmament work.

I agreed to run for the Presidency as a rainbow coalition candidate because the invitation was from a broader base and also because the office was above party politics.

When Fergus Finlay came to speak to me about the possibility of running, I was asked if there was anything in my background that might be used. I told him about what had happened to Dónal but since it was almost thirty years ago, they didn't see it as having any bearing on my decision to run. I was completely flummoxed, therefore, when suddenly it was thrown into the ring.

It was dishonestly used. It was disgracefully used and it was cynically used. And they knew that a personal attack on me involving my family would deeply wound me. It was the final nail in the coffin.

There was no compassion or care. The aim was simply to destroy me and they didn't care what hurt they inflicted on my family. It had a horrendous impact on my parents. Here was the ghost of the past coming back to haunt them. The great social stigma and shame was, once again, back in the public eye and worse, was now a national issue. Less than a month after the election, my father was diagnosed with accelerated Alzheimer's. The doctors told us that the stress had likely hastened his condition and, by the start of the New Year, he was hospitalised.

My mother also had to deal with the near destruction of her youngest child, her eldest son and the destruction of her husband, all in the space of a few weeks. She lost two stone in weight between November and Christmas 1997.

7

PICKING UP THE PIECES

Logic is doubtless unshakable,
but it cannot withstand a man who wants to go on living.

Franz Kafka, *The Trial*

Dónal de Róiste had suddenly awoken to experience the living torture of a Kafkaesque nightmare. He drove the school bus on the morning that the 'exposé' appeared on the front of the *Examiner* and the *Star* newspapers. Before the afternoon pick-up, the principal of Coláiste Colm, Pat Kinsella, told him that journalists had been 'dogging the school'. What upset De Róiste most was that some of the children had been approached by a journalist and asked what their parents thought of an IRA man driving them to school. The *Star* and *Examiner* articles had been reported on radio and television and picked up by other newspapers. Jim Walpole's pictures were doing the rounds and other photographers were trying to find him. The rejection of Dónal de Róiste by his father had lasted all of twenty-eight years. That alone was a burden too heavy to carry. Yet, there were some in the media who saw him not as a wounded human being, but as a clown of sorts, there to be ridiculed and joked about.

Pat Kinsella could see that De Róiste was a man under great duress and suggested that he take the rest of the week off 'until the storm receded'. De Róiste's first impulse was to run away. He felt that he had neither the strength nor the personal resources within to face the demands of the media who, like his father, appeared to be hostile and to have already made up their minds about him. In the context of Adi's campaign, the juicy interpretation was to paint him as a man with a dark and sordid past. He was shocked at how apparently easy it was for the media to present inaccurate details as fact. Indeed, both he and Adi were gutted by the *Star*'s suggestion that, if she were elected, the Áras might become a safe haven for him. He seriously thought of suing the paper but could not face the risks involved in a libel action and did not have the resources to engage a team of lawyers. Furthermore, he did not then have the necessary inner strength.

His priority was to clear his head. It was more essential that he find the internal resources and resolve to face the demons of the past that had just returned to brand him with the searing mark of 'Subversive Sympathiser'. It would, however, be some eight months before he was able to take positive action in this regard.

De Róiste was aware that this was a public trauma also for his elderly parents. He was sure that his father would blame him for Adi's crisis, as he had blamed him for his loss of the officer's commission. He recalls his sister Adi and brother-in-law, Seán Dunne, telephoning him. Adi was upset and in tears; like most people, she assumed that her brother was quoted accurately in the *Star*. De Róiste, realising that his sister was under immense pressure already and that this was an additional hammer blow to her, agreed to take himself out of the limelight until the dust settled. He decided to go to a place few people might suspect, the home of Mick Burke, a friend in Urlingford, Co. Kilkenny, eighty miles from Cork.

The few days that Dónal de Róiste stayed with Mick Burke and his wife, Peggy, enabled him to see that he needed help – professional help. His mind was a spaghetti junction of angry thoughts, bitterness, confusion, disappointment, abandonment, betrayal and the near crippling feelings of hopelessness and despair.

FINDING SUPPORT

Meanwhile, Patrick Walshe had read the *Examiner* article and was infuriated by it. He was unaware of the *Star* article until De Róiste showed him a copy almost a year later. The *Examiner* piece, however, was enough to spur him into action. Motivated by the anger he felt at the unfairness of how De Róiste's 'retirement' had been used, he pondered his options and tried to recall accurately all that he could about the events of the spring and summer of 1969. His primary contribution was the composition and distribution of a letter to the presidential candidates, as outlined in the previous chapter. All the while, he was working under the assumption that De Róiste was still living in the US as he had not heard from, nor seen, him since 1985 when De Róiste had unexpectedly paid a visit to his home.

Walshe travelled to Dublin on the morning of 6 October 1997 to deliver the first of those letters. He had arranged to meet with Fergus Finlay of the Labour Party, a primary adviser on Adi Roche's presidential campaign, but when Walshe arrived at the campaign headquarters, Finlay was not to be found. He left an envelope, addressed to Finlay, with Mags Murphy of Democratic Left but says that he never received a response.

Walshe felt deeply disappointed for Adi, as well as Dónal, at how his offer to help was met by silence. He believes that a decision had been made not to get involved in the De Róiste controversy as it was considered too much of a quagmire.

I spoke with Fergus Finlay about this on 28 October 2005. He had no recollection of the events as described in the previous paragraphs but indicated that the primary focus at the time was helping Adi Roche and that the De Róiste publicity was yet another fire to be contained. 'Our sense was that we needed to protect Adi, and, if in the future we could help Dónal, we would. But that was not the issue of the moment.'

Walshe learned that De Róiste was in Ireland and eventually tracked him down. Typical of the man, he has a note in his diary stating that he called De Róiste at 2200 hours on 13 October 1997. It was a crucial phone call. He told De Róiste of his plan to contact all the presidential candidates and party political leaders, and read to him the contents of his letter. De Róiste says that the sound of the familiar and friendly voice gave him courage and strength.

De Róiste was angry when he learned about the apparent lack of interest shown by Finlay. He was also annoyed by comments made by Dick Spring and by his sister Adi in the wake of the *Star* and *Examiner* articles. The more he thought about it all, the more furious and embittered he became. His instincts told him that he needed immediate help to sort out his head before he could even consider confronting the injustices of 1969 and, now, 1997.

The first positive move he made was in spring 1998, when he called a counselling help line advertised in a local newspaper. De Róiste was referred to Anne Kelliher, a counsellor practising in Cork and Tralee. Kelliher met De Róiste for their first counselling session in May 1998. In an affidavit prepared in April 1999 for De Róiste's High Court case, she stated:

... The immediate problem presented by Dónal was that he had no sense of self or pride since he had been discharged from the army dishonourably in 1969. His vulnerability extends from the abusive interrogation that took place in 1969...

... I am of the opinion that [Dónal de Róiste] broke down at the hands of his interrogators and following his dishonourable discharge from the army he retreated into himself. His dismissal became a public matter and his position was further compounded by being rejected by his family. He became fixated and suffered the classic symptoms of a post traumatic stress disorder.... He did not get counselling and he was not believed...

When the matter of his dishonourable discharge was resurrected by the media in November [*sic*] 1997, Dónal de Róiste had to undergo the trauma and public humiliation again.... The effect of the resurrection of the matter by the media in 1997 and the public trial by the media in circumstances where Dónal de Róiste was never afforded an opportunity by the army to know the case against him and to defend himself resurrected suicidal feelings in Dónal. He was again unable to deal with the matter, but he received support from friends and former army colleagues who were retired from the army and thus were in a position to support him...

I am of the opinion that the support of his friends ... and retired former army colleagues and the counselling that I have been able to afford to him has to some level restored his dignity and self esteem and to the extent that he now has a sense of self-worth to bring this matter to the courts, to address the wrong done to him and to bring finality to the matter...

In a fashion typical of many victims ... Dónal stored his abuse deep within him where it wounded his self concept, his sense of clear boundaries, his psychological well-being and his sense of trust and belief in himself. This lack of trust and belief in himself effectively disabled him from his interrogation and enforced retirement to the point at which he has, with assistance, been able to bring this legal action.

I say that the delay in seeking assistance is as a result of the nature of the wrong done to him in that he was publicly discharged from the army with a slur in his character that caused him to be rejected by his family and society. Indeed, the slur and mark was so great that it followed him across the Atlantic to America and was resurrected some thirty years later.... The punishment is continuous and the initial abuse damages the individual self-worth and the inability to address the wrong is a symptom.

Dr Fionnuala O'Loughlin, a consultant psychiatrist, supports Kelliher's observations. Along with a sworn affidavit submitted to the High Court on 21 April 1999, Dr O'Loughlin provided a medical report on Dónal de Róiste in which she stated:

His psychological condition over the last two years would suggest a relapse of his acute symptoms of post-traumatic stress, which is not uncommon in those exposed to vivid reminders of a disturbing incident.

In her affidavit, Anne Kelliher made one other very important observation. She stated:

His rejection by the army and the enforced isolation, in that under security legislation his former colleagues could not communicate with him, left him bereft of family, friends and his former fellow officers.

Walshe tells an interesting story that gives an insight into the pressure he and Swan were feeling and how the culture of isolation around the now ex-lieutenant Dónal Roche worked.

As Christmas 1969 approached, Walshe was responsible for buying supplies for the officers' Christmas dinner at Magee Barracks, Kildare, to be held on Saturday, 20 December, that year. However, his father died on 19 December. Walshe had ordered cheese from a small cheese shop off Grafton Street and was unable to collect it due to his bereavement. He therefore asked Brendan Doherty (the 'Dog') if he could collect it and deliver it to the barracks. Doherty agreed.

Unknown to Walshe, Doherty brought former Lt Roche with him for the run to Kildare. Both men entered Magee Barracks with the cheese delivery. Early in the New Year, Doherty casually mentioned to Walshe that Roche had accompanied him to Magee Barracks with the cheese, and that Roche had spoken to some of the military personnel there. The day after learning this, Walshe went to his commanding officer Lt Col. Nolan to discuss the matter. Nolan told him that Roche's presence had been reported (he even told Walshe who had reported it), and that a file had been opened on him as a result but that he would now have it closed.

Walshe says that after Lt Roche's 'retirement', the music ended and their little group, comprising himself, Lt Gerry Swan, Lt Roche and 'the Dog', simply disintegrated. In April 1970, Walshe was sent to Cyprus on a six-month UN tour of duty. The following year, he got married, as did Gerry Swan, and the patterns of their lives changed. By then, the 'Dog' had emigrated and Roche had disappeared. No one knew where he was. It was to be fifteen years before the two friends would meet again.

8

A LONE MAN

VERSUS THE POWER OF THE STATE

I keep feeling there is some little glitch in this frame-up that I am missing which could release the logjam.

Dónal de Róiste, 7 May 2002

As previously mentioned, prior to his presidential 'retirement', in 1969, Lt Dónal Roche had consulted with solicitors Michael B. O'Maoileoin & Co., who wrote a crucial letter on his behalf (see Appendix A, Document 14). Although the defence forces prepared a draft reply to O'Maoileoin's letter, it was never sent. Since the files on Lt Dónal Roche remain open, a reply to this letter is still awaited. While De Róiste is now with a new solicitor, the body of O'Maoileoin's letter is still relevant.

The 1954 Defence Act, Subsection 47(2), and the specific Regulation under which Lt Roche was retired 'in the interests of the service', Regulation A.15, subparagraph 18(1)(f), was specifically targeted by those plotting his fast-track removal from the army because it provided a legal loophole with two corresponding benefits to them:

- It denied Lt Roche all rights, including his constitutional rights and the right to natural justice.
- It made those seeking Lt Roche's retirement 'in the interests of the service' both morally and legally unaccountable.

A summary of the 1954 Defence Act, Subsection 47(2) Regulation A. 15, Subparagraphs 18(1)(a–f), prior to a crucial 1985 amendment, is as follows:

18. (1) An officer may be retired pursuant to subsection 47(2) of the [1954 Defence Force] Act for any of the following reasons:-
(a) poor medical classification under the Defence Force Regulations Act 12;
(b) if he is undergoing treatment in a sanatorium abroad;
(c) if ... he is continually sick under the Defence Force Regulations Act 12;
(d) on being certified to be of unsound mind...;
(e) for misconduct or inefficiency;
(f) in the interests of the service.

This regulation and the powers of 'retirement' it gave to the President in 1969 are immediately tempered by sub-section 18(2) which states:

An officer shall not be recommended for retirement for misconduct or inefficiency unless or until the particulars of the alleged misconduct or inefficiency have been communicated to him and he has been given a reasonable opportunity of making such representation as he may think proper in relation to the proposed retirement.

Contrary to natural justice and Lt Roche's constitutional rights, there is a serious flaw in sub-section 18(2), as it stood in 1969, in that it covers only categories (a) to (e) in sub-section 18(1). Subparagraph 18(1)(f), 'in the interests of the service', is not covered and, therefore, an officer recommended for retirement under this specific subparagraph was effectively denied all rights of redress, as enshrined in sub-section 18(2). It was Regulation A.15, subparagraph 18(1)(f), that was invoked to achieve the fast-track expulsion of Lt Dónal Roche from the Officer Corps in June 1969.

In 1985, however, the 1954 Defence Act, Subsection 47(2) Regulation A. 15, Sub-section 18(2) was amended to include subparagraph 18(1)(f), 'in the interests of the service'. The 1985 amendment reads:

> An officer shall not be recommended for retirement for misconduct or inefficiency or *in the interests of the service* unless or until the reasons for the proposed retirement have been communicated to him and he has been given a reasonable opportunity of making such representation as he may think proper in relation to the proposed retirement.

There is a strong suspicion that the legal loophole that existed within subparagraph 18(1)(f) was exploited to remove Roche from the army. The suspicion is heightened by the fact that the Chief of Staff, in a letter (in fact, in two almost identical letters) dated 3 May 1969 (Appendix A, Documents 10a and 10b) was recommending this specific course of action, even before the full investigation into the alleged activities of Lt Dónal Roche had been completed. Lt Roche was first interrogated on 25 April 1969, just eight days prior to the Chief of Staff's letter. His alleged 'third' interview/interrogation was on 30 April, just three days before Lt General Seán Mac Eoin recommended his retirement 'in the interests of the service'.

Minds were already made up about his urgent removal even before the investigation was completed or De Róiste had been provided an opportunity to respond. It becomes clear, thereafter, that everything done by the Intelligence Section and the senior staff officers was geared to building a secret case in support of a decision already made – a decision made in secret and which they knew could not be contested. By recommending this specific regulation, the Senior Headquarters closed down from the outset all possible avenues of redress of wrongs open to the young lieutenant.

LEGAL SUPPORT

In 1997, following the trauma of the presidential campaign, Dónal de Róiste knew that he needed sound legal help if he were to make any progress in his efforts to clear his name. As previously mentioned, after his return to Ireland following the break-up of his marriage, De Róiste was involved for ten years with the Between organisation, based in Cork, which sought to relieve distress in deprived areas of Northern

Ireland by sponsoring holidays in Cork for children from both nationalist and unionist communities. The founder of the organisation, Críostóir de Baróid, a man of enormous integrity, was personally very supportive towards De Róiste and introduced him to the Irish human rights barrister, Philip Magee, SC, who in turn introduced him to solicitor James MacGuill, who had a practice in Dundalk, Co. Louth. Both agreed to take on his case *pro bono*. However, De Róiste decided to seek a practice closer to home. He was introduced to Eamonn Carroll, a partner at the practice of Noonan Linehan Carroll Coffey Solicitors, North Main Street, Cork. It was to prove a turning point for De Róiste. Carroll has been a formidable ally, providing his client with the most important legal ingredients – consistency and persistence. De Róiste states:

> Eamonn Carroll has worked diligently and *pro bono* on this case. Furthermore, something that is hugely important – he believed me!

In 1999, the year after De Róiste and Carroll teamed up, the official papers concerning De Róiste's 'retirement' were due for release under the thirty-year rule, which requires the release of various state papers, including yearly cabinet papers of the government, to be made available for public scrutiny. This usually happens on 1 January of each year. The former lieutenant, as a citizen of the Republic, applied for his papers but was refused them on the basis of 'national security'.

Papers that are withheld from release are usually those deemed likely to cause damage to the country's image, national security or foreign relations. Readers may review in Appendix A some of the documents withheld from De Róiste, and make up their own minds about the official reasons offered for their being withheld; these were released in 2002 following mounting media pressure. The cabinet minutes specific to the decision to 'retire' De Róiste have not, however, been released to the National Archives and we are unable, therefore, to assess the level and quality of consideration given to Lt Roche's case in 1969.

De Róiste's hopes of finding answers and an end to his dilemma had also been raised by the enactment of the Irish Freedom of Information Act which came into effect in April 1998. The Act has few restrictions on the information that can be made public and has, therefore, led to a sea change in the relationship between citizens, journalists, historians and government departments and public bodies.

Both the Department of Defence and the defence forces came under the scope of the Freedom of Information Act on 21 April 1998. The Act gave De Róiste, as a citizen of the Republic, the following statutory rights:

- The legal right to access information held by the Department of Defence and the defence forces
- The legal right to have official information held by the Department of Defence and the defence forces
- The legal right to obtain reasons for decisions affecting him.

Under the guidance of Carroll, De Róiste began his legal efforts to gain access to his files and to clear his name. Recalling his efforts to help his client, Carroll says:

Our first step on this journey was to seek, under the Freedom of Information Act, copies of the files held by the Department of Defence on his career and retirement. His application led to the production of the bulk of his personal file but also the refusal by the defence forces to release key documents or memoranda. The latter was crucial in helping us understand the procedures, if any, that led to his 'retirement' and the reasons why he was retired. De Róiste was advised that these documents could not be released in the interests of national security.

The refusal to release key documents left De Róiste no option but to challenge the Department of Defence and the defence forces in the High Court.

JUDICIAL REVIEW APPLICATION TO THE HIGH COURT (1998) AND SUPREME COURT APPEAL (2001)
Mr Justice Geoghegan, on 23 November 1998, gave leave to De Róiste to take his case to the High Court (Judicial Review JR438/98). Somewhat appropriately, before noon on mid-winter's day 1998,

Eamonn Carroll presented a Notice of Motion to the High Court, outlining an Order of Discovery 'of all documents in the possession, or formerly in the possession, custody, power or procurement' of the Minister for Defence and the Attorney General of Ireland, their servants or agents, in relation to all matters and issues associated with the 'retirement' of his client, former Lt Dónal Roche. In many respects, even though he still had many dark and difficult days and years ahead, it was the turning point in De Róiste's struggle for justice.

With the support of barristers Ercus Stewart, SC, and Gerard Humphreys, BL, Carroll presented seventeen grounds in support of various Orders and Declarations on behalf of De Róiste. The grounds upon which relief was sought stated that the Minister for Defence and the Attorney General had:

1. Failed to comply with the principles of natural and constitutional justice and basic fairness of procedure with regard to Lt Roche's 'retirement' from the Permanent Defence Forces.

2. Failed to comply with the Defence Act, 1954, and the Regulations made thereunder and with the principles of natural and constitutional justice and basic fairness of procedure. Lt Roche was not charged with any offence against Military Law and was not afforded the opportunity for a court martial or making appropriate representations with regard to his 'retirement'. Further, as he was not given the reasons nor notice for his proposed retirement, he was never in a position to controvert or contradict the allegations (if any) of persons unknown made against him.

3. Acted contrary to Lt Roche's constitutional rights in that they failed to abide by the provisions of the Defence Act, 1954, and the Regulations made thereunder, in particular Paragraph 18 (2) of the Defence Force Regulations A.15.

4. Failed to disclose the grounds of Lt Roche's presidential 'retirement' or how the Minister for Defence arrived at his decision to recommend his

'retirement', made known to him by a letter dated 26 June 1969 … in violation of his constitutional rights.

5. Refused Lt Roche adequate relief when he sought legal representation and/or assistance and was refused a Court Martial through which he was prepared to face his accusers and defend his reputation.

[And]

6. That their manner of implementation of the provision of the Defence Force Regulations A.15., Paragraph 18(1)(f) was in breach of the principles of natural and constitutional justice and contrary to the Constitution of Ireland.

7. That their actions had resulted in the loss of Lt Roche's good name and reputation and was so defamatory and so devastating, with such far reaching consequences, as to be in breach of legislation envisaged in the Constitution of Ireland.

8. That the military records, which disclose no military offence, recites on his record that he was retired by the President in the interests of the service, is in violation of Lt Roche's constitutional right to a good name and constitutes a secondary punishment … as to be outside the scope of the legislation enacted by the Oireachtas or regulations of the Minister and is contrary to the Constitution.

9. That the Defence Force Regulations A.15., in particular Paragraph 18, pursuant of the Defence Act, 1954, was applied in an unconstitutional manner, was unfairly discriminatory … in that Lt Roche was not afforded the opportunity to make representations in relation to the retirement and the refusal to furnish any or any adequate certificate of service and testimonial.

[And that the Minister for Defence and the Attorney General had]

10. Consistently repeated the provision of the Defence Act, 1954, Section 47(2) but have failed to provide Lt Roche with the reason for termination of his service

in the interests of the service.

11. Failed, refused and neglected to afford Lt Roche a reasonable opportunity of making such representations as he may think proper in relation to the purported retirement.

12. Not afforded Lt Roche an opportunity at any stage in any form to meet the persons unknown who were making the allegations against him.

13. Failed to meet the demand of Lt Roche to furnish any reason for his termination.

[And]

14. The implementation of the Defence Force Regulations and the Defence Act ... was in breach of Lt Roche's legitimate expectation to pursue his professional career in the Defence Forces.

15. The termination of Lt Roche's career was not done in accordance with the principles of natural and constitutional justice.

16. The Defence Force Regulations A.15., Paragraph 18(1)(f) + (2) ... are not properly delegated legislation within the meaning of the Constitution ... is impermissibly vague and wide and constitutes the imposition of a punishment that is contrary to the rules of natural and constitutional justice and contrary to the Constitution. Further, and in the alternative, it constitutes the exercise of a judicial function that is contrary to the Constitution and is also *ultra vires*, that is, beyond their legal power or authority.

17. As a consequence, Lt Roche has been unable to obtain satisfactory employment in Ireland and has had a permanent mark and scar on his character and has been subject to vilification and abuse in the eyes of the general public and his livelihood, career and reputation have been severely damaged.

De Róiste submitted a detailed nine-page sworn affidavit to the court which opened with the words, 'I am a commissioned Army Officer ...' and outlined his career details, including the fact that his annual confidential officer's report had been marked 'satisfactory'. Of significance throughout the affidavit is the fact that he openly and consistently names two people who, for reasons unknown, the Department of Defence, including most of its respondents, in this and later court proceedings, was clearly reluctant to name.

The first was Commandant Gerry O'Sullivan, Lt Roche's chief interrogator who later became Chief of Staff of the Defence Forces (April 1984–February 1986). In paragraph 8, De Róiste states:

> At Army Headquarters, I was put in a locked room. I was interrogated by Commandant Gerry O'Sullivan … Interrogation at any time went on for a number of hours. I was shouted at, threatened and physically intimidated. During a number of prolonged breaks in the interrogation, I was not advised of the duration of the break and believed that the interrogation would recommence at any time. I lost all track of date and time and now believe that the interrogation went on over a period of approximately ten days. Throughout the interrogation the questioning centred on my attendance at music venues and public bars in Dublin over the preceding period and questions centred on those also present at such music venues. I say that prior to my arrest I had travelled to Dublin and around Ireland regularly at weekends to attend traditional music events at a range of venues. On most of these occasions I was in the company of fellow army officers. I asked the interrogators what the interrogation was all about and was told 'that is for you to tell us.' I was afraid for my physical safety. I was advised that the cause of my interrogation was so serious that my family would be destroyed and that I would never work in Ireland again. I was repeatedly induced to resign my commission by being advised that it was better for me that I should do so. I was advised that if I resigned I would be paid my gratuity and that this would be 'the easier way' and I was told I could be Court Martialled and imprisoned.

At the end of paragraph 9, De Róiste says that he remembered stating that he was being wronged. 'I sought a redress but this was refused to me. I particularly recall Comdt. Gerry O'Sullivan saying "No" to my request.'

The second person named by De Róiste in his affidavit was Padraig Dwyer (sometimes referred to as O'Dwyer). In paragraph 10 of his grounding, affidavit De Róiste states:

> In the light of subsequent events I have attached significance to being asked by the interrogators whether I knew an individual by the name Padraig O'Dwyer. This person referred to had been in attendance at music pubs and venues that I had attended and had also attended the public auction at Clancy Barracks, Islandbridge. As stated above, this auction was open to members of the public to attend. In the firm knowledge of my innocence I persevered in the firm belief that all matters would clarify themselves in the course of time.

Amongst the exhibits attached to De Róiste's affidavit were:

1. The letter from the Adjutant General's office informing him of his 'retirement' by the President on the recommendation of the government, effective as of 27 June 1969.
2. Extract from *Iris Oifigiúil* dated 27 June 1969.
3. Copy of letter dated 24 June 1969 from the Secretary to the Government to the Secretary at the Department of Defence, informing him that Lt Roche had been retired by the President.
4. A Defence Forces memo, dated 30 October 1969, received in 1998 under the FOI Act, stating that a service testimonial would not be issued to Lt Roche, only a 'statement of service'. A circled notation on the document, initialled 'M.D.', states: '... the question ... is "sub judice" ...'
5. A Record of Service in the Defence Forces for the purposes of the Immigration and Nationality Act, 1952, United States of America. This document provides a summary of Lt Roche's service. It is date stamped 13 March 1978. One noteworthy

reference deals with Roche's 'Military Conduct'. Sub-headings underneath refer to 'Date of Offence – Particulars – Punishment Awarded.' Typed below these headings, in capital letters, is the answer 'NIL'.

6. Copy of *Examiner* article dated 23 September 1997, headed 'Brother's past rises to haunt Adi'.

7. Unedited copy of Dáil debates of 3 June 1998, dealt with below.

8. Copy of press statement issued by the defence forces press office, dated 22 May 1998, following an interview between Pat Kenny and De Róiste, outlining the legislation under which De Róiste was 'retired' and stating: 'There are no circumstances in which an officer of the Defence Forces has been retired in this manner except for very compelling reasons.'

9(a–e) Copies of letters sent by De Róiste to the office of President Mary McAleese, the responses of her office and the Department of Defence.

(9a) In a letter dated 21 April 1998, De Róiste pleads with the President '... to use your Presidential prerogative to right this wrong which still allows leading national newspapers to cast IRA slurs on an innocent man.'

(9b) Fergal Ó Briain, Assistant Secretary to the President, responded on 27 April 1998, stating that 'while the supreme command of the Defence Forces is vested in the President, she does not, in fact, have an executive role and is not involved in the administration or management of the defence forces ... the President regrets that she cannot intervene in this matter, or make representations on your behalf.' Ó Briain finishes by informing De Róiste that his letter will be referred to the Minister for Defence.

(9c) De Róiste replied on 12 May 1998 saying: '... I am seeking a Presidential pardon and an honourable discharge from the army because of wrongful dismissal. I feel sure you, with your legal training and Civil Rights record, will understand my case. A President fired me (unjustly) and I am appealing to a President to clear my name 29 years later.'

(9d) On 26 May 1998, Ó Briain replied stating: '...

the President ... carries out her functions in regard to the Forces under the advice of the Government. The only course of action open to this office, therefore, is to pass your letter on to the Minister for Defence for his consideration.'

(9e) On 25 May 1998, Barbara Burke, Private Secretary to the Minister for Defence, wrote to De Róiste in response to his letter to the President on 21 April 1998. Burke stated that his '... retirement was effected pursuant to subsection 47(2) of the Defence Act, 1954 and sub-paragraph (18)(1)(f) of the Defence Force Regulations A15 which provided that an officer may be retired "in the interests of the service".' She concluded, 'In the circumstances there is no action which can now be taken in the matter.'

STATEMENT OF OPPOSITION OF RESPONDENTS

The Chief State Solicitor, Michael A. Buckley, on behalf of the Minister for Defence and the Attorney General, responded with 'Statement of Opposition', dated 4 February 1999, by immediately honing in on a technicality – that of time. The first opposing point was that Lt Roche had 'failed to bring his application for leave to apply for judicial review promptly or within the time prescribed'.

Buckley further argued that since 'the decision [to 'retire' Lt Roche] was made on the 27th June 1969' (technically this is incorrect: the decision was made by the government on 20 June 1969 and became effective on 27 June 1969), Lt Roche 'has no valid and/or legitimate explanation or reason for delaying some 29 years before seeking to challenge this decision.'

The Chief State Solicitor further argued that, 'Even if the media references in the Autumn of 1997 resurrected the memory of the decision, [Lt Roche] still failed, at that time in the Autumn of 1997, to bring his application for leave to apply for judicial review promptly or within the time prescribed'.

Buckley also argued, 'The excessive and inordinate delay in bringing this matter to Court has prejudiced the Respondents in their defence ... in that three of the Army Officials who played a crucial part in making the decision which is sought to be challenged are dead.'

Finally, the Chief State Solicitor argued that the 'excessive and inordinate delay' of De Róiste had prejudiced the respondents 'in that the recollection of the other relevant Army Officials involved in the decision ... has been affected and dimmed with the passage of 29 years.'

The remainder of the state's grounding affidavit was a point-by-point rebuttal of the seventeen points of law presented by De Róiste's legal team as outlined above.

One very important admission is made by the state in its grounding affidavit lodged with the High Court. Paragraph 4(f) of the affidavit states:

> In the alternative, there was no obligation upon the Respondents in 1969, when acting in accordance with Section 42 of the Defence Act, 1954 and paragraph 18(1)(f) of the Defence Force Regulations (a)15, to disclose to or inform the Applicant of the grounds upon which the power vested in the President by the aforementioned Act and Regulations was being exercised.

AMENDMENT

In a letter to me, dated 11 August 2004, Ms Patricia Troy, Private Secretary to the then Minister for Defence, Michael Smith, TD, informed me that Amendment 93 to the Defence Force Regulations A.15., came into effect on 14 February 1985. She stated:

> Prior to the amendment, paragraph 18(2) provided that an Officer of the Permanent Defence Force should not be recommended for retirement for misconduct or inefficiency unless or until the officer had been given a reasonable opportunity to make such representations as she/he may think fit in regard to the proposed retirement. Amendment No. 93 extended these particular provisions to comprehend retirement in the interests of the service.

The Department of Defence is here acknowledging that in 1969 'these particular provisions' did not extend to the precise sub-paragraph of the Defence Act, 1954, under which Lt Roche was 'retired'. That is, of course, Regulation A.15, subsection 18(1)(f). One irony about the timing of Amendment 93 on 14 February 1985 is that it occurred when Lt General Gerry O'Sullivan was Chief of Staff.

In a six-page affidavit, also dated 4 February 1999, Commandant Denis Murphy, of McKee Barracks, echoed much of what appeared in the Statement of Opposition, filed by Michael A. Buckley, the Chief State Solicitor. Murphy, now a colonel, was a staff officer at the Directorate of Intelligence at the defence forces headquarters, where he is currently posted.

Murphy cited as an example of the prejudice facing the Department of Defence and the defence forces in contesting De Róiste's affidavit, the fact that 'All Army Officers involved in the decision [to retire Lt Roche] are either retired or dead.' He said that 'having examined and considered the relevant file pertaining to [Lt Roche], I can say that three of the Officers who were directly involved in the investigation of [Roche] are now dead.' He named these as: Col. Arthur Cullen, the DJAG; Col. Michael Hefferon, Director of Intelligence; and Lt General Seán Mac Eoin, Chief of Staff.

Commandant Murphy argued: 'the deaths of these three individuals makes it impossible … to adequately respond to [De Róiste's] claims … [and] further, that it would be grossly unfair … to face such a claim … without these crucial witnesses being able to provide evidence.'

However, the real principals in this case – Dónal de Róiste and Gerry O'Sullivan – were alive and, indeed, the files still existed. The absence of some key witnesses is certainly no bar to criminal trials for crimes up to, and including, murder, in most democratic countries, including Ireland. Moreover, Major General Joseph Emphy, who as Adjutant General had signed De Róiste's 'retirement' letter, was alive until late 2005.

Murphy also stated:

> … other members of Óglaig na hÉireann who are alive and who were involved in the decision [to 'retire' Lt Roche] have also been prejudiced…. With the passage of nearly 30 years, the recollection of individuals has inevitably been lessened … and it would be both unfair and unreliable to seek to rely on the recollection of witnesses

about an event which took place nearly 30 years ago.

Murphy rejected De Róiste's contention that he had been harassed and intimidated during his interrogations. He stated:

> [Lt Roche] makes very detailed and serious allegations about how he was allegedly interrogated by members of Oglaig na hÉireann in Easter, 1969. The [Minister for Defence and the Attorney General] deny that the alleged interrogation was conducted in the oppressive and/or torturous manner either as described by [Lt Roche] in his affidavit, or at all.

This categorical statement contradicts the argument that the passage of time prevents a proper investigation. In other words, Murphy is arguing that the passage of time prevents a proper investigation of the events, while at the same time drawing a precise conclusion in relation to those events.

Commandant Murphy's affidavit also argued that the decision to 'retire' Lt Roche was not amenable to Judicial Review on the basis that 'the decision … was made within the powers conferred upon the [Minister for Defence] and was not *ultra vires*.' That is to say, the 'decision' is beyond the legal power or authority of the court.

Murphy then dealt with the substance of De Róiste's claim. He stated that De Róiste:

> — was fully aware of the grounds and reasons for his retirement at the time…
> — had full knowledge of the investigation which was conducted in 1969
> — was aware of the reasons why he was under suspicion.

The second assertion, in particular, is not sustained by a detailed review of released documents from the 'secret' files to which Commandant Murphy had access.

'INVESTIGATION'
It appears that the last time Lt Roche was interviewed/interrogated was

by Col. Cullen, the DJAG, on 28 and 29 May 1969. A secret memo, authored by Commandant Gerry O'Sullivan (Appendix A, Document 17), states that Lt Roche informed the DJAG, on 29 May, that his solicitor had advised him 'to do nothing.' O'Sullivan also states that the DJAG had advised Roche 'of the legal position'.

There is no evidence to support the assertion that Lt Roche had, by the end of his meetings with Col. Cullen, any intimation that 'the investigation' had been concluded. Nor is there any evidence to demonstrate that Lt Roche had been informed that 'the legal position' of the Senior Headquarters Staff was the recommendation to the Minister for Defence that the government should recommend his Presidential retirement 'in the interests of the service'. It is clear that the letter informing him of his 'retirement' was completely unexpected.

Moreover, Roche was unaware that, on the day he was transferred to Boyle, 3 May 1969, a letter from the Chief of Staff addressed to the Minister (presumably the Minister for Defence) states that 'as a security precaution it has been considered prudent to transfer Lt Roche to an appointment in BOYLE.' Also unknown to Lt Roche and his solicitor was the fact that the decision to 'retire him' had already been made, just three days after his alleged third interview.

STATEMENT

In paragraph 5 of his sworn affidavit, Commandant Murphy stated that Lt Roche had 'made a statement during the course of the investigations'. This misrepresentation of the facts was also made by a serving officer of the Intelligence Branch, the principal section involved in the 'investigation' of Lt Roche in 1969. It is clear from the details revealed in his affidavit that Murphy in 1998 had access to privileged documents that De Róiste and his legal team would not get sight of until late 2002. A reading of those documents now, particularly the alleged interview between Lt Roche and the DJAG, on 28 May 1969 (Appendix A, Document 13), highlights a primary criticism being developed by the Headquarters Staff, including the Director of Intelligence – the fact that Roche refused to make a statement which, allegedly, he had previously said he would do:

> I [Col. Cullen] informed him [Lt Roche] that as he had
> volunteered on 30 Aibrean [April] to submit a statement

about the matter and as he had not done so after a month I was reluctant to do anything until he had been given the opportunity of submitting any statement he wished to make…. At 09.40 [the next day] Lt Roche again visited … my office … he informed me that the matter would not take long as <u>he would NOT make any further statement</u>. He then left.

The underlining is Col. Cullen's. The DJAG's underlined sentence is ambiguous, but what is clear is that Lt Roche did NOT make a statement, specifically on the advice of his solicitor. There is a consistent attempt throughout the documentation released in 2002 (Appendix A) to portray Lt Roche's failure to make a statement as an indication of guilt – particularly by juxtaposing Lt Roche's alleged voluntary offer to make one and his subsequent 'reneging' on the alleged offer.

Even to a layperson, the term 'statement' in the context of an investigation with legal implications has a very particular meaning. It refers to a testimony of either a material witness to, or the subject of, a matter under enquiry. In this context, a 'statement' is understood to be a declaration of facts, which the author acknowledges to be accurate and truthful, by placing his or her signature on a document that also bears the calendar date, establishing when the statement was made. There is absolutely nothing in the secret documentation released in 2002 that bears Lt Roche's signature or, indeed, the signatures of other material witnesses, either for or against Lt Roche. The most shocking aspect of the documentation released is its sheer disregard for proper and fair procedures and, as one must and should expect in these matters, unambiguous documents that are clearly signed and dated.

Murphy also suggests that Col. Cullen was directly involved in the investigation of Lt Roche, stating that the DJAG had:

… further interviewed [Roche] and read the Oath to him during the course of interviews… which took place on the 25th, 28th and 30th April, 1969. Col. Cullen was directly involved in the questioning of the Applicant. I say that an examination of the relevant file reveals that Col. Cullen also interviewed the Applicant on the 28th May, 1969….

This statement is not supported by the opening remarks of the DJAG in his report to the Chief of Staff (Appendix A, Document 13). Cullen states:

> I informed Lt Roche that the Int. rep. [Intelligence Report] on his association with ███████ had been submitted to the General Staff who had called upon me as DJAG to advise.

The Director of Intelligence, Col. Hefferon, submitted a 'Security Report' (presumed to be the Intelligence Report to which Murphy refers) with a cover letter dated 1 May 1969, the day after Lt Roche's alleged third 'interview'. There is no evidence that Cullen was involved in the interrogation of Roche prior to 28 May 1969. In his responding affidavit, De Róiste states unequivocally, 'I have not any recollection of any Colonel in uniform questioning me.' Puzzlingly, he told the court – and still maintains – that he has no memory of meeting Col. Cullen, the DJAG.

Murphy further states in his sworn affidavit that Lt Roche 'at the time of his retirement… sought and had available to him legal advice.' What Murphy did not state (perhaps because he was not aware of it) was the fact that Lt Roche's solicitor had written to the Chief of Staff and had been ignored.

Murphy continues:

> I say that on the 21st April, 1969 a report was made to the Director of Intelligence identifying [Lt Roche] as being engaged in activity which potentially constituted a threat to the security of the Defence Forces and the safety of its members.

At the time it was not known on what basis Murphy was making this statement to the court. We now know that he was quoting from a Security Report (Appendix A, Document 8b) drawn up by the Director of Intelligence, Col. Hefferon, and one, and possibly two, almost identical letters addressed to the Minister (presumably of Defence), signed by the Chief of Staff (Appendix A, Documents 10a and 10b). The Security Report states: 'A report from a confidential source was received on 21 April 1969.' The letters state: 'On the 21st April 1969 a report was made to the Director of Intelligence by a most reliable informant that a person, later identified as this Officer [Lt Roche], had been consorting with three members of a splinter group of the IRA...'

The only documentation to support these assertions is a handwritten memo, initialled 'GOS' [Gerry O'Sullivan], dated 22 April 1969 (Appendix A, Document 1). This memo, purported to be based on information supplied by a 'most reliable informant', details what Commandant Murphy's affidavit describes as an alleged meeting between Lt Roche, Padraig Dwyer and others some five or six days earlier 'which potentially constituted a threat to the security of the Defence Forces and the safety of its members'. It is also very important to state that, despite the fact that the information was, allegedly, passed to the Director of Intelligence, Col. Michael Hefferon, it was not he who wrote the memo, but rather Commandant Gerry O'Sullivan, a subordinate intelligence officer.

Commandant Murphy's affidavit further states that, 'Arising from this information [Lt Roche] was interviewed by officers of the Intelligence Section of the Army about subversive matters on the 25th ... 28th and 30th April, 1969.' He said that De Róiste had 'also admitted knowing and associating with subversive elements that he was aware had been involved, and continued to be involved, in criminally subversive activity.'

Murphy then deals with Padraig Dwyer, to whom De Róiste had referred in paragraph 10 of his sworn affidavit. He states:

> ... in 1969 Padraig O'Dwyer was a known member of a subversive group known as 'Saor Éire'. I say that in October 1968 Padraig O'Dwyer was before the Dublin District Court on charges of conspiracy and the possession of arms. I say further that an examination of the Applicant's file reveals that [Lt Roche] was also aware that Padraig O'Dwyer participated in an armed attack on members of the Garda Síochána at Ballyfermot on the 3rd October, 1968.

Nowhere in any of the files subsequently released to Dónal de Róiste in 2002 is the group 'Saor Éire' mentioned. There is no evidence in any of the notes, purporting to be records of De Róiste's three 'interviews' (Appendix A, Documents 3, 4 and 7), to support the assertion that an organisation named 'Saor Éire' was mentioned to Lt Roche during his interrogations. Indeed, the first time that Roche and Commandant Patrick Walshe heard the name 'Saor Éire' mentioned in relation to Lt Roche's retirement, was in Commandant Murphy's affidavit.

Murphy further states:

> I say that [Lt Roche] in full knowledge of this criminal activity accompanied Padraig O'Dwyer into an Army Barracks whilst he was an officer. I say and have been advised that such activity constituted a serious threat to the security of the Defence Forces.

This is a gross and unfair misrepresentation of the facts then unavailable to De Róiste and his legal team. The 'secret' files clearly establish that Lt Roche was on duty at a publicly advertised auction of surplus army vehicles, held at Clancy Barracks, Dublin, on 23 April 1969. The allegation that Lt Roche 'accompanied' Dwyer to the auction ascribes to the young officer very different motives from those of carrying out his duty.

It may also be of significance that throughout his sworn statement to the court, Commandant Murphy fails to mention an alleged very serious link between Padraig Dwyer's gang and a Sgt Shinkwin from Cork. This issue is dealt with in greater detail in Chapter 13

In his sworn affidavit, Commandant Murphy returns to the subject of an alleged 'statement' made by Lt Roche. He says:

> During the period of his interviews, the Applicant was permitted to submit a statement. On the basis of the content of his interviews, including the matters admitted in his second interview, and on the basis of his own statement, a decision was made to recommend to the Minister for Defence to retire the Applicant in the interests of the service.

In a follow-up affidavit, dated 18 February 1999, he says:

... notes made by the officer who interviewed [Lt Roche] in 1969 ... record statements made by [him] during the course of the interview.... The statement I was referring to is the statement contained within the notes which I have referred to above. I wish to clarify that there is no signed statement from [Lt Roche] on ... file. His statement is contained within the record of the interview that was conducted at that time. These notes contain sensitive material. Outside of these notes, there are no statements or letters from [Roche] or his previous solicitor on this file.

We will deal later with the assertion that 'there are no statements or letters from [Roche] or his previous solicitor on this file'. The notes Murphy refers to can be viewed in Appendix A, Documents 3, 4 and 7. The primary name that is redacted in these 'notes' is that of Padraig Dwyer. Dónal de Róiste states that he never knowingly associated with subversives or criminals. He strongly contends that the crisis that erupted around his career as an officer of the defence forces occurred because a person, or persons unknown, allegedly made false and incriminating allegations against him to the Intelligence Section of the defence forces – anonymous accusers he was never allowed to confront and allegations he was never allowed to challenge. Furthermore, it should be noted that the 'notes' referred to by Murphy were written subsequent to Lt Roche's interrogations. Their author, Commandant Gerry O'Sullivan, had sole editorial control over what he wrote. Both Lt Roche and Commandant Patrick Walshe state unreservedly that O'Sullivan took no notes during their respective interrogations.

WITHOUT RIGHTS, RANK OR RECOURSE
With regard to the legality of the decision to 'retire' Lt Roche, and the procedures adopted, Murphy states:

> ... at all material times, the Respondents acted in accordance with [Lt Roche's] constitutional rights and within the law. It should also be noted that in 1969, under Section 47(ii) of the Defence Act 1954, there was no requirement upon the Respondents to inform [Lt

Roche] of the grounds upon which the power vested in
the President was being exercised.

Here again is confirmation that Lt Roche was considered to have no
legal rights and entitlements because of the specific invocation of subparagraph 18(1)(f).

Commandant Murphy also states:

> I say that [Lt Roche] was not entitled to a trial in due
> course of law in order for him to be retired in the manner
> which took place.

He argues:

> …it is incorrect of [De Róiste] to state that the
> Respondents caused him to lose his good name and
> reputation. The decision to retire [Lt Roche] was made
> 'in the interests of the service'.

The logic of this sentence appears to be either that Lt Roche had
only himself to blame, or that the use of the specific Regulation invoked
somehow neutralised any damage done to his name and reputation.

Crucially, near the conclusion of his affidavit, Commandant
Murphy stated:

> I say and have been advised that the discretion of the
> Minister for Defence to recommend the retirement
> of members of the Defence Forces 'in the interests of
> the service' is vital for the preservation of the security
> and safety of the defence forces. If this discretion were
> to be abrogated or interfered with, the Defence Forces
> would face continuing and insurmountable problems in
> ensuring their effective administration.

There are several disturbing aspects to this statement. In the first
instance, neither De Róiste nor his legal team was disputing the
discretion of the Minister to recommend the retirement of members
of the defence forces 'in the interests of the service'. What is in dispute

is the failure to comply with the principles of natural and constitutional justice, and the application of fair procedures, with regard to Lt Roche's 'retirement'. Furthermore, the Minister, and thereby the government, does not have the right to recommend the presidential 'retirement' of any officer without ensuring that the officer has been provided with the inherent safeguards and protections provided by the Defence Act, 1954. The reality is that the Minister for Defence may, today, recommend the retirement of an officer 'in the interests of the service' pursuant of subparagraph 18(1)(f), but that officer is now protected by the 1985 Amendment to subsection 18(2), which permits various avenues of redress.

The right of redress, denied Lt Roche because of a flawed regulation in 1969, is recognised throughout the 1954 Defence Act. For example, Section 50.–(1) of the Act states that the President may dismiss an officer. However, section 50.–(2), states:

> ... an officer shall not be dismissed under this section unless or until the reasons for the proposed dismissal have been communicated to him and such officer has been given a reasonable opportunity of making such representation as he may think proper in relation to the proposed dismissal.

It may, in law, be argued that Lt Roche was not dismissed by the President but was 'retired'. The effect, however, was the same. It is clear from an analysis of the existing paperwork (see Appendix A) that an effort was made to create the impression that he was afforded every reasonable opportunity to make such representations as he thought proper in relation to his proposed 'retirement'. However, the fact that his solicitor's letter was ignored exposes the comments of the DJAG in particular (Appendix A, Document 13), and other senior officers, as a sham. There is absolutely no supporting evidence to show that the young lieutenant was being kept fully informed of serious developments pertaining to his career as a commissioned officer.

Murphy, somewhat shockingly, argues:

> ... I say and believe that certain matters within the realm of the Defence Forces must remain secret. The decision

to retire [Lt Roche] herein is, I believe, a clear example of such a matter.

The government and its agents, including the defence forces, must be held accountable to the people who elect them and who, through their taxes, pay them to act, at all times, 'in the interests' not just 'of the service', but of the common good. The health of democracy is dependent upon public accountability at all times of all agents of the state, including the defence forces and particularly its Intelligence Section.

While it is recognised that there are times when 'certain matters' must remain confidential, state agents must not be allowed to hide behind the idioms of 'secret', 'national security' and/or 'in the interests of the service', particularly when there is sufficient and justifiable public disquiet about decisions taken. The decision to retire Lt Dónal Roche is, I believe, 'a clear example of such a matter'.

The issue of privilege was pressed by Annemarie Keane, a solicitor in the Office of the Chief State Solicitor, acting on behalf of the Minister for Defence and the Attorney General. In an affidavit, dated 8 February 1999, Keane argued that before De Róiste's High Court hearing could proceed, particularly the Order of Discovery, a preliminary issue needed to be determined – that of the inordinate delay of twenty-nine-and-a-half years. She further stated that:

> ... I have examined the files which [De Róiste] seeks discovery of and these contain confidential details concerning the sources of information imparted to members of the Defence Forces during the course of their investigation of [Lt Roche] ... these files contain the statements of other officers and the names of individuals who imparted sensitive information to the investigators. I say that it is the intention of the [Minister for Defence and the Attorney General] to claim privilege over many of these documents ... it would not be appropriate for an Order of Discovery to be made at this stage of the proceedings.

Mr Justice Kinlen, who was hearing the Judicial Review, made a crucial intervention during the proceedings and ordered the respondents to 'check their files and, if possible, to supply [Dónal de Róiste] with copies of any statements made by [him]', as stated in both affidavits of Commdt Murphy and Mr Michael A. Buckley of the Chief State Solicitor's Office. Mr Justice Kinlen also asked that any letters written by [Lt Roche] or his solicitor, during the 1969 investigation, be made available.

The following day, 9 February 1999, solicitor Eamonn Carroll faxed a letter to Annemarie Keane at the Chief State Solicitor's Office with the request that her clients forward 'documents (and letters by [Dónal de Róiste] or his solicitor or on his behalf) as suggested by Kinlen J. on 8th February last, to assist us in dealing with this matter.'

The following afternoon, Ms Keane telephoned Carroll at 4.15 p.m. She advised him that notwithstanding the content of the Affidavit of Commandant Denis Murphy and the information furnished to the court on 8 February 1999, the statement of Lt Roche did not exist. She further advised Carroll that there existed only records of interviews with Roche (Appendix A, Documents 3, 4 and 7) which did not constitute a statement but that publication of these documents was being refused by the Minister for Defence and the Attorney General on the grounds that to publish same would prejudice the security of the state.

This raised the suspicion that the court had been misled, inadvertently or otherwise, in sworn affidavits by agents of the state, on the issue of an alleged statement made in 1969 by Lt Roche. There was hope in the De Róiste camp that the state's case might, consequently, collapse.

Carroll responded to the telephone call by submitting a sworn affidavit on 10 February 1999, in which he informed the court of the contents of his telephone conversation with Keane. He also pressed the issue of the alleged 'statement' made by Lt Roche:

> ... when this matter came before this Honourable Court on the 8th of February, 1999, it was confirmed to this Court by Counsel for the Respondents that the Applicant had made a statement in the course of the investigation and this Court requested the Respondents

to furnish a copy of the said statement together with copies of letters by [Lt Roche] or his solicitor or on his behalf to the Applicant before this matter was next before [the] Court on Thursday the 11th of February, 1999.

In Keane's own affidavit to the court on the same date, she stated:

> I say further that [a] Department [of Defence] official has also informed me that another file concerning the Applicant has been lost and accordingly, cannot be located within the Department of Defence. It is possible that this lost file contains statements made by the Applicant, or letters written by the Applicant or his solicitor, during the investigation.

On 18 February, Conor Kerlin, Assistant Principal Officer in the Department of Defence personnel section, stated that he had examined the Department's records and swore:

> ... I can say that there appears to have only ever been two files in the Department pertaining to [Lt Roche]. The first of these is file S 636. The S files are distinct files within the Department. A separate register of these files is kept within the Department. For the purpose of swearing these proceedings I examined the S register, which confirmed the existence of a file pertaining to [Lt Roche] ... I have sought to find this file but cannot locate it.
> ... My examination of the register revealed that file S 636 was withdrawn on the 18th June 1969 by an Assistant Secretary in the Department. This is the only record relating to this file in the S. Register.... It is the file which was referred to by Annmarie Keane, in her affidavit of the 11th February, 1999, as having gone missing. Obviously I do not know for how long this file has been missing, but it is incorrect to suggest that it has gone missing since the initiation of this discovery application. Further, if anyone did withdraw the file, this withdrawal would have been

registered on the S register. This leads me to believe that the file was not returned after it was withdrawn on the 18th June, 1969, and that this was the cause of its loss.

It is difficult to believe that documents relating to the Dónal de Róiste case were lost. We know that Intelligence documents are kept in triplicate. According to the restricted *Manual of Military Security Part I – Documents* (1954) 'not to be communicated directly, or indirectly, to the Press…':

> On discovery of the loss of TOP SECRET, SECRET or CONFIDENTIAL document, or part thereof…an immediate search will be made and such enquiries and disciplinary action will be instituted as the case may demand.
> Section XIV, Paragraphs 37 (a) and (b)

It is also difficult to accept that the file had been missing in the Department of Defence for almost thirty years. Suspicions are raised by a confidential fax, dated 23 March 1998, from a Ms Anne O'Neill of the Organisation and Personnel Branch at the Department of Defence. In a note to Captain D. O'Brien of the Official Records Section, Ms O'Neill writes:

> The second file in the Department came into existence at the time of the initiation of the proceedings herein. Re: De Róiste. As discussed, could you please forward copies of the representations which were sent from this Branch to ORS [Officers Records Section] for material for reply a number of years ago together with the replies furnished by your office. We are unable to trace our copies of these at present and the Secretary General has sought these papers a.s.a.p. please.

O'Neill's reference to 'material for reply' is with respect to a number of Dáil questions over the years, concerning the Lt Roche controversy. It would appear that documentation, upon which such replies were based, had been mislaid in 1998. There is no indication, however, that a

Department of Defence file had been missing since 1969. Commandant S. O'Giolain, Officers' Records Section, Adjutant General's Branch, in a letter dated 25 March 1998, states:

> Previous correspondence between R6 and the AG's Branch regarding [Lt Roche], date back to 1996, 1995, 1994, 1987 and 1978...

It is clear that even before Lt Roche's 'retirement' from the army became public knowledge, his file was active and being carefully managed by the Adjutant General's Office in particular. This fact is borne out by a handwritten notation added to a letter, dated 15 February 1996, received by the Adjutant General's (AG's) Office from Denis Glavin, a civil servant at the Defence Force Legislation and Personnel Branch. Glavin was forwarding correspondence received from the Office of the then Minister for Defence, Seán Barrett, TD, in connection with '... Ex-Lieutenant Dónal Roche... regarding the circumstances of his dismissal from the Force... a reply is requested before <u>26 February, 1996.</u>' The date emphasis is Glavin's.

The notation, dated 20 February, states:

> Rang D. Glavin. Explained how sensitive this case is – I indicated I would have to show it to AG and would NOT have a reply by 26 Feb.

The signature of the notation is indecipherable but the intentions are clear. Glavin's letter was received by the AG's office on the day it was dated. Why would it take more than ten days to respond to a query originating from the Office of the Minister for Defence? Why, it must be asked, even after a quarter of a century, was the 'retirement' of Lt Roche so 'sensitive'?

Glavin's letter was replied to on 27 February. It was a short two-sentence letter, sent by Captain J. Rea of the AG's Office. Rea enclosed 'a copy of a reply (dated 10 May 1995) to a previous query', and informed Glavin that the AG 'will speak to the Secretary DOD on the matter if requested to do so.'

The letter of 10 May 1995 gave a brief service record of Lt Roche and the date and regulation under which he was 'retired'. However, the final sentence is, in the context of Conor Kerlin's affidavit above, worthy of attention. It stated: 'It should be noted that previous queries were received relating to this Officer from R6 on 06/03/1978 (Cr file 3/17610) and 07/08/87.'

This correspondence, which references the Department of Defence, predates the court proceedings referred to in Kerlin's affidavit above.

Kerlin gave a third sworn affidavit on 18 March 2003, in respect of De Róiste's High Court Judicial Review proceedings following the release of the JAG's October 2002 report. He stated:

> ... [De Róiste]... makes averments in relation to the documentation available to him. In particular, he seems to make the case that, by virtue of the fact that the [JAG] made reference to a particular letter, the existence of which the Applicant was unaware of, this means that the ... Respondents are in some way in breach of a court order or, more gravely, are in contempt of court. The letter to which [De Róiste] refers is a letter dated May 30th 1969.... In that letter, [his then] solicitors, the firm of Michael B. O'Maoileoin & Co. requests information as to what charge if any was being preferred against his client. While this correspondence emanates from [De Róiste's] own solicitor, [De Róiste] states that he never got his file from his solicitor. To the extent that he suggests ... that the ... Respondents were in some way the subject of a court order requiring them to disclose the existence of documentation such as the May 30th letter, I deny this is so...
>
> ... no court order was made... as [De Róiste] suggests. Rather... a suggestion was made by Mr Justice Kinlen during [De Róiste's] Motion for Discovery that was listed for hearing on February 8th (but which was never in fact dealt with) that the Respondent should check their files and if possible, supply [De Róiste] with copies of any statements made by [him] or letters written by [his then] solicitors during the investigation conducted upon [him] in 1969 which led to his being retired by the President in the interests of the service.

Kerlin continued:

> Ms Anne Marie Keane avers that as a result of this
> suggestion, she contacted the relevant officials, in
> particular in the Department of Defence, who examined
> the file and informed Ms Keane that there was no such
> documentation. There were, however, statements on file
> made by [Lt Roche] but these would not be released
> on security grounds. She added, however that: 'the
> Department official has also informed me that another
> file concerning [Lt Roche] has been lost and accordingly,
> cannot be located within the Department of Defence. It
> is possible that this lost file contains statements made by
> the Applicant, or letters written by the Applicant or his
> solicitor, during the investigation.

Kerlin further stated:

> ... the original Departmental 'S' file which dealt with the
> Applicant's retirement in 1969 could not be located at the
> time of the judicial review proceedings. Consequently,
> the Department of Defence had to reconstitute the file
> from papers held on [Lt Roche's] military file and from
> the Taoiseach's Office. It was on 15th May 2001 that the
> 'S' file was located by chance in a safe in the Department
> of Defence. When examined, the file contained little
> material that had not previously been available during
> the judicial review proceedings other than the May 30th
> 1969 letter.

We must not lose sight of the fact that the letter in question (Appendix
A, Document 14) was sent, in the first instance, to the defence forces
and not to the Department of Defence. Lt Roche's 'secret' files also
suggest that the Chief of Staff passed the letter from his solicitor to the
Adjutant General's Office and that the Adjutant General asked that a
draft response to the said letter be prepared on Friday, 6 June 1969, and
discussed with the Secretary of the Department of Defence on Monday,
9 June 1969. It seems inconceivable that the letter in question was

not copied. The idea that the only copy in existence – presumably the original – was with the Department of Defence, is, once again, difficult to believe.

De Róiste filed a responding affidavit on 10 February 1999, in which he took issue with several of the assertions made by the state and by Commandant Denis Murphy, particularly their claim of privilege over documents he needed in order to pursue his quest for justice and the restoration of his good name. He stated:

> ... under the Constitution the administration of justice is committed solely to the Judiciary by the exercise of their powers in the Courts set up under the Constitution. Power to compel the production of evidence which includes the power to compel the production of documents, is an inherent part of the judicial power and is part of the ultimate safeguard of justice in the state.
>
> ... [It] is a confirmation... that the decisions [were] made on the basis of sources of information that I never knew and I was never given an opportunity to confront my accusers.

With the assistance of his legal counsel, De Róiste compellingly argued that a conflict of interest was developing between the judiciary and the executive powers of the state. It was arising 'with regard to the exercise of the Judicial power over the public interest involved in the production of evidence and the ... public interest involved in the confidentiality or exemption from production of documents pertaining to the exercise of the executive powers of the state'. He continued:

> It is the Judicial power which will decide which public interest shall prevail ... the duty of the Judicial power to make the decision does not mean that there is any priority or preference for the production of evidence over other public interests, such as the security of the state or the efficient discharge of executive functions of the government. I respectfully submit that it is for the Judicial power, and in this case this Honourable Court, to choose the evidence upon which it might act

in any individual case in order to reach a decision ... the Respondents have proceeded to deal with the matter of the production of documents without first dealing with the issue of Discovery ... the onus is on the [state] ... to specify in detail the nature of the privilege claimed in respect of each document and the basis of such privilege.

On 16 April 1999, Dónal de Róiste's legal team lodged 'Notice of Particulars' with the High Court. There were nineteen in total, with additional subsections. All were carefully honed requests, drawn up by his legal counsel, targeting important information concerning the mystery of his 1969 'retirement', some of which had been gleaned from statements made by the Respondents during the course of this High Court action. Amongst the requests, many of which remain unanswered to this day, are:

— Please specify if any other Army or Department of Defence officials were involved in the decision [to retire the Applicant, Lt Dónal Roche] and please identify same and their role in same.

— Please state the allegations made against the Applicant which were allegedly furnished to him for his proposed and/or purported retirement.

— Please specify the sections and sub-sections of the Defence Act, 1954 that were breached by the Applicant.

— Please specify the date on which all the documentation was furnished to the Applicant that put him in a position to controvert and/or contradict the allegations made against him.

— Please specify whether these persons who made the allegations were military or civilian personnel.

— Please specify the grounds and/or reasons for the recommendation made to the Minister for Defence to retire the Applicant pursuant of DFR A 15, Paragraph 18(2) in the interests of the service.

— Please identify the individuals who made the said recommendation.

— Please specify the representation and/or officer of

the Defence Forces who was assigned to advise the Applicant.

— Please furnish the dates and occasions when the Applicant was in possession of all necessary documentation to know the full case he had to meet and to make representation.

— Please furnish the date on which the Applicant was afforded an opportunity on which to meet the persons making the allegation against him.

— Please identify the persons involved.

— Please specify the reasons given as to why the Applicant was required to retire in the interest of the service.

De Róiste awaited the judgment of the High Court with no shortage of anxiety and trepidation. If he failed, it would demonstrate the enormous odds he was facing, and a negative judgment would be like a knockout punch. The issue at stake was whether the judiciary would accept the arguments of the Chief State Solicitor's office that his failure to bring his case to the courts represented an inexcusable delay on his part, or, recognising the trauma that had blighted his life, would compel the state and its agents to be accountable, even after a quarter of a century.

JUDGMENT

Mr Justice McCracken delivered an eleven-page judgment of the High Court on 28 June 1999, in which he stated:

> In summary ... it is my view that [De Róiste], while undoubtedly having suffered a traumatic experience, has not shown that he was so affected by that experience that he was unable to issue these proceedings over such a lengthy period. He was able to work, he was able to marry and bring up a family.... In the light of all these matters I do not think he has discharged the onus which is upon him to show the Court that there is good reason for extending the period within which this application should be made....
>
> In my view he [De Róiste] is totally blameworthy....

This is not to imply that he did anything wrong, but rather that he is the person responsible for proceedings not having been issued. I should also add that the Respondents cannot in any way be blamed for the delay....

It is also a fact that, after twenty-nine years, memories of events which took place are bound to be severely dimmed, even if the events were as unusual as they appear to have been in this case. I do not consider that the balance of justice requires that this case be allowed to proceed....

I would dismiss these proceedings not solely because of the delay in itself, but because, in addition to such delay, there is the element of blameworthiness on the part of the Applicant and the fact of possible prejudice to the Respondent.

Despite the harshness of the judgment, the court awarded De Róiste costs.

On 15 September 1999, solicitor Eamonn Carroll lodged, on behalf of Dónal de Róiste, 'Notice of Appeal' to the Supreme Court. However, on 19 January 2001, the Supreme Court closed down De Róiste's legal battle. A triple judgment upheld the High Court decision on the technicality of delay. Once again, despite the judgment, De Róiste's costs were paid by the state.

APPLICATION TO THE EUROPEAN COURT OF HUMAN RIGHTS
Following his unsuccessful High Court and Supreme Court battles, solicitor Eamonn Carroll, on behalf of his client, lodged an application with the European Court of Human Rights at Strasbourg, under the Convention for the Protection of Human Rights and Fundamental Freedom. 'Of concern again,' he admitted, 'are the time limits applicable to such an application and raised, as a preliminary point, by the Court Registrars.'

With the High Court and Supreme Court closing the door on De Róiste and the possibility of the European Court of Human Rights also shutting him down on the basis of time limits, the chances of a positive outcome in his battle to clear his name was looking very bleak.

He therefore sought the support of various journalists, including myself. My investigation of the Dónal de Róiste case is detailed in the following chapters.

9

FIRST CONTACT

As a citizen of a legitimate sovereign state, Lieutenant de Róiste was deprived of his basic civil rights. Even a soldier in the battlefield, before being shot for cowardice or rape, is accorded a court martial.

Former Garda Superintendent William Geary, aged 103

Dónal de Róiste first contacted me about his plight following the publication of my second book, *The Dublin and Monaghan Bombings*, in 2000. I had known his sister, Adi Roche and his brother-in-law, Seán Dunne, for almost twenty years and I had met Dónal on a number of occasions over the years, at their home in Cork. I had always found him to be a pleasant and courteous individual. However, until his 'retirement' was thrown into the 1997 presidential campaign, I had had no idea about this piece of their family history.

Dónal's first approach to me occurred at a time when I was heavily involved in the Dublin and Monaghan justice campaign and the production and promotion of the film *Bloody Sunday*, and I had just been asked by film director Paul Greengrass to work with him on the movie, *Omagh*. All I could do at that time was to respond with courtesy and words of encouragement. I did, however, open a file and carefully kept all his initial correspondence safe.

READING FILES

I have a note in my diary for Saturday, 27 April 2002, that states: 'The day I read Dónal de Róiste's file for the first time.' It was, in fact, a quiet Saturday afternoon and, having opened my filing cabinet, I was for some reason drawn to his name on the tab of a suspension file. Having read the first page of his first, undated, letter, I was hooked. I brought his relatively thin file downstairs and spent a quiet hour reading through it.

With the knowledge of his case that I have since accumulated, I find his written introduction to his epic struggle fascinating. It was my first insight into the efforts he was waging, almost single-handedly, against powerful, hidden and unaccountable forces within the Irish state, in particular the military establishment.

Dónal began by describing his discouragement and depression at not being able to find anyone in the media who would take up his case on a consistent basis. Under the heading 'Justice', he made a startling statement concerning his recent Supreme Court defeat:

> The only difference for me in going before Chief Justice Keane and his two pals in the Supreme Court recently, and my original interrogation, was that I now had someone to defend me. A judge is only a politician with a wig on! I was frightened but, this time, I was not alone. In neither case was I being listened to, or believed.

From reading some of the media coverage of his 'exposé' during the presidential campaign, an impression had been given that Dónal de Róiste was unstable and not entirely rational. The door-stepping photograph that appeared on the front page of the *Examiner* and *Star* newspapers on 23 September 1997 gave the impression that he was a man with a dark and hidden history. This impression, of course, played into the hands of those determined to deny him justice. There was no doubt that he was an angry, frustrated and, at times, bitter person. Unharnessed and undisciplined, he had the potential to be his own worst enemy; his acquired cynicism could be caustic and repelling to family, friends and associates. However, the more I read his correspondence, the more convinced I became of the overall consistency of his story and the more I began to understand his deep-rooted frustration and paranoia.

In his first letter to me, De Róiste described the unfolding nightmare that has haunted both him and his family for over three decades. He expressed his frustration that the High Court and Supreme Court had upheld the argument of state lawyers that there had been an inordinate delay in seeking a review of his case and, therefore, closed down any legal avenues available to him. He wrote:

The army, having maligned me during my sister's election campaign and again during question time in the Dáil, ran for cover in the High Court on the 'statute of limitations' issue! When the Chief Justice began by leaning over his bench and said to my Barrister, 'Mr Stewart, this case has been found to be both inordinate and inexcusable from the point of view of delay before Mr Justice McCracken in the High Court,' I knew I was in for a rough ride. I felt like the bus driver who thought he was an Army Officer and I squirmed. I had to remind myself that he was talking about me!

De Róiste then proceeded, with sound reason and rationality, to outline the basics of his dilemma:

I am presented with a never-ending conundrum. A real Irish snow job! I try to clear my name and get told I am out of time. I ask what I was guilty of and they say I was told at the time. I was not, nor did they have to! I ask for my files under FOI (Freedom of Information) and they say they are lost or else secret. They state that there were 'very compelling reasons' for 'retiring' me but won't tell me what these reasons were. Even criminals get told what they are being accused of. It is Kafkaesque, as Alan Shatter TD stated in the Dáil.

In letters after 11 September 2001, De Róiste expressed his fear that America's 'War on Terror' might see him being arrested while visiting his children, or denied entry into the United States. He was acutely conscious and worried about the spin created by army sources that he had been 'retired' because of his associations with Republican subversives.

He also described the trauma of his experience following his 'retirement':

For years after these tragic events I could not sleep properly or sit alone for long in a brightly lit room. It was hell for my wife to live with. I had been publicly humiliated and was thoroughly ashamed ... I felt powerless, paranoid, frightened, subject to recurring nightmares and very, very angry. The fact that my father disowned me did not help but both he and my family were not the cause of my troubles. They are victims also! I had nowhere to live and no home to go to. I stayed 'on the run' drifting from flat to flat and from job to job for a few years. Then I emigrated.

He outlined his difficulties in getting a job:

With the best will in the world any employer was going to be wary of hiring an ex-officer with 'Retired by the President in the interests of the Service' on his CV in the Ireland of the '70s. This was at a time when the war in the six counties was hotting up. I got weary of the repeated rejections.

When he went to sign on the dole, he discovered that they had no section for ex-army officers. Only three officers had been retired by the President, under 'this vicious' Section 47(2) of the 1954 Defence Act, since the foundation of the state.

De Róiste eventually found a job cleaning cars at Ryan's Car Sales, off Townsend Street, Dublin. His letter to me movingly described his fall from grace, descent into depression and sense of abandonment:

From having the cosseted life of a young officer I was suddenly made homeless and penniless and hadn't a clue for what reason or why it happened. I was very apolitical at that time. Although just 24 years old I don't believe I had even begun to exercise my vote. I lived in single officer's quarters in the barracks and had a free room and board in any town I happened to stay in that had a military facility. When they gave me 12 hours to leave I had to sleep in my car. It was disturbing for me to meet former 'comrades' as they scurried to the other side of the street to avoid me. Serving soldiers all. Guys I would have shared a drink with only weeks before! I was a military leper. If I could be done down like that so could they, if they were seen with me. I took succour in drink and I ended up committing a sort of emotional and psychological suicide.

De Róiste then referred to an officer whose name would loom large as my research developed – Commandant Gerry O'Sullivan. Whether or not Commandant O'Sullivan knew that De Róiste was an innocent man has still to be properly tested. Human beings have the facility to believe what they want, and that applies to both the innocent and the guilty. Hence, in a disputed and controversial case like the 'retirement' of Dónal de Róiste, it is imperative that the Irish state deals with all related matters in a fair, transparent and just manner. To date it has singularly failed to do this.

State lawyers displayed a somewhat bizarre shyness in acknow- ledging former Commandant Gerry O'Sullivan as De Róiste's primary and, subject to correction, sole interrogator from Army Intelligence. They failed to name O'Sullivan in both the High Court and Supreme Court hearings. The mystery of the state's reluctance to name O'Sullivan deepened when the JAG in 2002 omitted to identify him as the author of several documents she referred to in her report. Why she felt the need to do this is confusing since O'Sullivan's handwriting is easily identifiable and he had initialled a number of the documents reviewed by the JAG. Furthermore, former Lieutenant de Róiste and retired Commandant Patrick Walshe had named O'Sullivan in court affidavits. He has also been identified in a number of published press articles.

A possible major obstacle facing the former lieutenant might be the fact that O'Sullivan's career continued on the up and up while De Róiste's crashed around him. In April 1984, Gerry O'Sullivan ascended to the most powerful military position available when he was appointed Chief of Staff of the Irish defence forces.

Clearly, as he celebrated his twenty-fourth birthday in February 1969, Dónal de Róiste was a happy and carefree young man with the world at his feet and an army career that had prospects. 'I was,' he wrote, 'looking forward to going on a course to be promoted to Captain.'

He also had a healthy social life. He had a respectable young girlfriend, Mary, who was the daughter of a Garda superintendent and much liked by his family. He had many friends in and outside the army. His first letter continued:

> The ballad boom was in full swing in Ireland and my friends and I used to frequently visit Dowling's Pub in Prosperous, Co. Kildare, where the generous Pat Dowling held court and nourished some of the mighty talents we still have with us. I remember the Grehan Sisters, the Rynnes, Dónal Lunny, Christy Moore and others as they sang into the wee hours. It was a time of great artistic discovery in Ireland. The Irish musical tradition, which had been dormant for so long, was coming alive with great excitement.
>
> Once, a friend of mine … got hauled on the carpet for inviting The Dubliners to drink at Ceannt Officers' Mess in the Curragh. They had beards! I myself was paraded for having a sean-nós singer named Róisín Moylan in the mess in Athlone… Life was carefree and good…The showband craze was booming nationwide and Ireland had developed its own thriving beat group scene…
>
> I had been appointed to represent my commanding officer in a public function at the Prince of Wales Hotel, Westmeath, and was going up to Dublin to organise the annual auction of surplus army equipment. I was a busy young officer.

De Róiste then described how it had all gone terribly wrong. Amongst the documentation that De Róiste sent to me were copies of efforts made by him, following his return to Ireland, to attain meaningful employment. In response to a host of applications for a wide variety of jobs, the answer was consistent: 'We regret to inform you….' The jobs he applied for were varied and, in some instances, terribly sad when one considers what might have been if his army career had been permitted to progress unimpeded.

The second piece of correspondence in the file was dated 30 January 2001. It began:

As you can appreciate it is a bit crazy for me right now after my Supreme Court crushing, so a month or two cooling off will be good for me also. Thanks for returning my call so promptly. I would wish no one better than you to handle this! I talked with my Solicitor Eamonn Carroll and he is up for it. I want to clear my name and to do this I need to access my files. I have been denied them under 'security' or some such. Forget F.O.I. We must get going … before O'Sullivan dies or I head for Strasbourg. They will hide under the 'sub judice' rule if they can.

De Róiste then went on to discuss his love of the Irish army:

I grew up in a working class family, educated by C.B.S. and filled with love for my country. My Dad was ashamed of 'working with his hands' [sic]. My godfather Comdt Gerry Madden, was in the army and as a boy I always wished to serve my country. I was a 'scholarship boy' and thus we were able to afford a secondary education. I wanted to make my family proud of me!

There was correspondence dated 12 March 2001, which included a recounting of his interrogation ordeal, and various press cuttings, including the extraordinary story of a former member of the Garda Síochána, William Geary, who in 1928 had been falsely accused of taking a £100 bribe from Republican activists and who, at the age of 100, was finally exonerated by the Irish government.

By the time I had finished reading the file, I was outraged. I immediately called him at his Ballincollig home and discussed his case. I made a promise to Dónal de Róiste that I would help him. However, I established very clear ground rules. The first was that I reserved the right to ask him any question I felt appropriate relative to his case. The second was that if, at any time, I felt he was being less than honest with me, I would take my leave. He had no hesitation in agreeing. Since then, there have been times when De Róiste has felt uncomfortable with my probing, even on one occasion wondering if I had joined 'the other side' when I was asking hard and uncompromising questions related to Col. Hefferon's 'Security Report' (Appendix A, Document 8a). Four years later, I am still with him, because I believe that he has been telling the truth and I believe that he has been horrendously wronged by the army he loved and by the state both he and his entire family have served with loyalty and immense dignity.

Events began to move rapidly following that initial telephone call on 27 April 2002. On 1 July 2002, the Minister for Defence announced that he was asking the JAG to review De Róiste's files and, by October 2002, De Róiste and his legal team had in their possession a motley collection of documents that purported to be his classified military files.

De Róiste gave me the telephone numbers of his children in Pennsylvania, Dara and Sinead, and I spoke to them about starting an American campaign. They agreed. I mentioned that I would be in the US within a fortnight doing advance promotional work on the film *Bloody Sunday* and we agreed to meet.

The Monday following our telephone discussion, I interviewed Adi Roche in the atrium of the Civic Offices, Woodquay, Dublin. My article based on the interview appeared on page 6 of the *Star* and was headed by Adi Roche's challenge to the Taoiseach: 'Bertie, look me in the eye and then tell me my brother is a guilty man.' A subheading stated: 'Allegations in last Presidential race had terrible impact on both my parents.' The substance of the interview with Adi Roche has been recounted in the early chapters of the book. In addition, she spoke about the campaign to be launched in the United States:

> I am overjoyed that [Dónal's] children are launching this campaign in the USA. I feel very proud of them and give them my full support.
>
> They too have been robbed because their father struggled with the hurt and stain inflicted upon him which, at times, left him floundering and confused. I am delighted they have a burning desire to see justice done to their father.
>
> Dónal will recall how, as children, we were told stories of the terrible injustices heaped upon the Irish throughout our history. Fighting for justice was part of the Roche psyche. As a family we are backing our brother and his children and demanding that, once and for all, the Irish state remove the stain of suspicion cast upon Dónal

in 1969.

> This is not going away and with the involvement of Dónal's American children it has taken on an international dimension.

The *Star* also carried an editorial comment in support of De Róiste's campaign. It was, in fairness, a good comeback by the *Star* and a good start to our campaign.

On Tuesday, 7 May 2002, *The Irish Times* agreed to accept an analytical piece about the De Róiste controversy and the renewed backing of his mother and siblings. That same day, I had my first meeting with retired Commandant Patrick Walshe. From the outset, I liked him, and nothing in the intervening years has diminished my impression of a man of immense integrity and honesty with a fearless passion to see the wrong done to one of his army colleagues righted.

A week later, I left on a ten-day visit to the United States, during which I travelled by train to Washington DC to meet De Róiste's children, who travelled by car from Harrisburg, Pennsylvania. During a one-hour meeting, we discussed campaign tactics and it was agreed that they would write directly to President Mary McAleese and the Taoiseach, Bertie Ahern, and launch an American postcard campaign, aimed at the President, care of the Irish Embassy in Washington. This would run parallel to an Irish postcard campaign to the Taoiseach, care of Government Buildings, Dublin.

WILLIAM GEARY – FIGHTING A PHANTOM

During this visit, I was determined to find 102-year-old William Geary. It was clear from my initial correspondence with De Róiste that Geary's epic and 74-year struggle for justice had given him immense encouragement. Geary had become his hero and a torch of hope. De Róiste had sent me a copy of an online article from New York's *Irish Echo*, together with a powerfully constructed *Irish Times* article by the New York-born, award-winning journalist, Margaret Ward.

The latter article outlined the extraordinary story of Geary's marathon and epic campaign. Geary, then one month short of 100, talked about his struggle for justice which summed up De Róiste's dilemma also. He commented: 'I've been fighting a phantom and I don't even know what it is.'

The article reported the efforts made by Geary's godson, John P. Collins, a Bronx Supreme Court judge, who had taken up the cause of his ageing godfather. Collins had, under the Irish Freedom of Information Act, just won an important victory in that the Department of Justice in Dublin, on 'humanitarian' grounds, had agreed to release William Geary's files. The judge commented:

> It's been a tremendous disappointment that it took 70 years to release these documents. I've been sending letters for the last 30 years. Hopefully the situation can be rectified now.

Geary was born on 28 February 1899 into a farming family in Co. Limerick. Having obtained a wireless operators' certificate, he joined the crew of a merchant navy ship, and travelled to Europe, Africa, Asia, the Middle East and America, before returning to Ireland, where the fight for independence had begun. Geary helped to drill volunteers in his native Ballyagran. In the spring of 1922, a neighbour suggested he should join the newly established police force, the Garda Síochána. His application was successful and he was enlisted during the first week of May that year.

'I was happy and successful in the Garda, attaining the rank of Superintendent, 2nd Class,' he recalled later. 'But, I was dismissed on 26 June 1928, charged with bribery. It was a frame-up.' Ironically, it was on the same day, forty-one years later, that twenty-four-year-old Lt Roche was handed his presidential dismissal. Geary had been falsely accused of accepting a £100 bride from the IRA. He wrote:

> … July to the end of November, 1928, was the most unhappy period of my life. I was innocent of the charge of bribery, and although I had the feeling (bad judgment) that the Garda Síochána would soon discover a mistake was made, the suspense was unbearable. About all I did was to go to Mass on Sunday. It was so hard to meet people whose opinion of me must have been mixed, following a notice in the *Irish Independent* that I was 'dismissed for the good of the service'.

In November 1992, Geary wrote that the scars inflicted on him by his unjust dismissal from the Garda Síochána 'cannot be erased unless my innocence is acknowledged by the Republic of Ireland.'

Geary recalled the moment when his life changed. On 16 June 1928, he had been told that Deputy Commissioner Eamonn Coogan was making an inspection of Co. Clare and he was excited as he thought he 'might be complimented for the improvement of conditions in west Clare.' As he walked from the station with Chief Superintendent Duffy to meet the Deputy Commissioner at a local hotel, the first inkling of trouble he received was when his superior stated, 'Your life is ruined. You'd better tell the truth.'

He found none other than the Garda Commissioner, Eoin O'Duffy, awaiting his arrival, together with Deputy Commissioner Coogan and Chief Superintendent David Nelligan, a native of Limerick. There then began an interrogation. The Commissioner opened proceedings with the accusation, 'Mr Geary, we have evidence that you took one hundred pounds for information you gave to the Republicans.' Geary wrote:

> To this day, beyond that statement, I know nothing for I had no dealing of that nature with the Republicans. Deputy Commissioner Coogan asked me several questions (denials by me of any impropriety) and then Commissioner O'Duffy offered leniency if I admitted culpability. I had nothing to admit.

William Geary recalled weeping in the presence of Superintendent Nelligan when the two men were paired, clearly in the hope that he might confess to a fellow Limerickman. His office and lodgings were searched and that evening he was suspended from duty. On 18 June 1928, he was ordered to report to the Garda Depot, Dublin, where he stayed in the officers' quarters. All the while, he was expecting a Court of Inquiry. There was none. He wrote:

> I was dismissed from the Garda Síochána, 25 June 1928, by the Executive Council, Irish Free State [signed by William T. Cosgrave]. Before leaving the Depot, Dublin, I called on Chief Superintendent David Nelligan in his office and told him I was dismissed. He said he knew

that. He told me that if I cooperated, I would receive a job with the government. Not being able to do it, since I was not involved in a bribery, I said before leaving that he would find I was not guilty. That was the last time I saw him.

At this point I have to mention that I was an ass to believe that the Garda Síochána would make an effort to clear the name of one of its own men.

Thanks to the efforts, primarily of his godson, Judge Collins, and the journalism of Margaret Ward, the Irish government was embarrassed into righting a terrible wrong. At the age of 100, William Geary travelled from his New York apartment to meet the then Minister for Justice, John O'Donoghue. The Minister commented: 'Mr Geary's story is the story of one man's unquenchable thirst for justice.' He conferred on William Geary the status of 'a person who has retired from the Force as a Superintendent with full service'.

With the help of a friend in New York, Brian Meagher, an Assistant District Attorney in the Borough of Brooklyn, I managed to track down William Geary's godson, Judge John P. Collins, who invited me to his office in the Bronx. He listened attentively to the story of Lt Dónal Roche and kindly arranged for me to meet William Geary in his apartment in Bayside, New York, on the afternoon of 19 May 2002.

It took me all of two hours to navigate various subways and trains to Bayside. But the effort led me to an extraordinary meeting with one of the finest human beings I have ever had the privilege to encounter anywhere in the world.

William Geary was then 103 years old. He had clearly dressed up to meet me and was sporting a smart jacket, neatly pressed trousers and a colourful bow-tie. He smiled warmly and invited me into a spotlessly clean apartment. His hallway and sitting room bore testimony to a man who, despite having lived in the United States for over eighty years, retained an undying love for his native Limerick. I smiled when I saw a current edition of the *Limerick Leader* neatly folded on a table.

He told me his story which I have recounted above. He then invited me to tell him about the ordeal of Lt Roche. Not a word was missed and on a number of occasions he asked me to repeat certain details that I could clearly see he was filing away for later comment.

During a break, he made me tea and served it up with scones and jam. He questioned me intently on the Lt Roche affair. In truth, as I was still relatively new to the story, I was unable to answer many of his queries. However, after some three hours, he told me that he felt Lt Roche's experience was very similar to his own and, therefore, he would like to help him. He penned me the following message to bring back to Ireland:

19 May 2002

Delighted to meet Don Mullan who told me the sad story of Mr Dónal Roche, who has my sympathy, and he can be assured that I shall do all I can to help him.

Mr Geary died on 18 October 2004. In the interim, he and Dónal de Róiste became friends and exchanged several letters. In late September 2002, while in New York to launch his US-based campaign for truth and justice, De Róiste, together with his sisters, Len and Adi, visited Superintendent Geary and took a series of photographs of the meeting.

On 9 August 2002, a letter from Mr Geary was published in *The Irish Times*. It stated:

Sir, – 'Till then, sit still my soul; foul deeds will rise, Though all the earth o'erwhelm them, to men's eyes'. (*Hamlet*)

I am referring to the sordid, obscene dismissal of Lieutenant Dónal de Róiste, Irish Army, without trial, by President Eamon de Valera, on the recommendation of the Irish army hierarchy in 1969.

As a citizen of a legitimate sovereign state, Lieutenant de Róiste was deprived of his basic civil rights. Even a soldier in the battlefield before being shot for cowardice or rape is accorded a court martial....

From experience, I am well aware of the anguish endured by Lieutenant de Róiste on his callous dismissal from the Irish Army, the injustice, the disgrace inflicted on him, on his family. He has my sympathy.

It is incumbent on the Irish government to demonstrate that injustice shall not be tolerated, but basic civil rights held sacred, in Ireland.

William Geary also wrote to the Taoiseach on De Róiste's behalf, and sent several letters to De Róiste personally, advising him on his campaign, suggesting avenues to be explored and encouraging him to persevere. He was a man of enormous integrity and courage – a giant of honesty who dwarfed the mendaciousness of those who damaged him and the official cowards who acquiesced for decades in the concealment of truth.

Aged 103, having finally cleared his name, William Geary spent the last years of his life championing the cause of Dónal de Róiste. The clarity of his mind and a wisdom acquired from his own pain are evident in every word he wrote. Having learned of the flawed and negative report released by the JAG, Oonah McCrann, on 2 October 2002, he wrote twelve days later:

> McCrann's report, my experience too, indicates that the bureaucrats will always tenaciously hold firm, hold firm never to admit a blunder, no concession…. Always keep in mind that there was a motive for your dismissal, no accusations made until after the accident.

William Geary was convinced that the probable cause of Lt Roche's undoing was the car accident, and his refusal to lie (dealt with in the next chapter).

He was highly suspicious about Padraig Dwyer, one of the alleged 'Splinter IRA' group De Róiste was accused of associating with. He wrote on 2 November 2002:

> Think back on the day of the auction. How was it that Padraig Dwyer was there? Did he do any bidding? Would you say he was unduly friendly, close enough to record conversations? Could there be a picture of you and him taken? In all, do you suspect he could be an agent provocateur? Curious to note that it was after the auction, and your return to Athlone your trouble began.

One important development in our campaign to win justice was a series of letters published in *The Irish Times* with the designated heading: 'Dónal de Róiste Case'. It was a sign that the public was beginning to take notice.

The first letter in the series was that of his mother Christina, published on 20 May 2002. She powerfully pleaded with the Taoiseach and the Irish state to 'allow me to join my husband, knowing that "in the interests – and in the service" of truth and justice, our eldest son was, at least, given a fair chance to face his accusers and confront their accusations.' She concluded, 'Seán and I brought our family up to be decent and caring citizens, and proud to be Irish. I think we did a reasonably good job.... Is it too much to ask of our political leaders that they do the decent and honourable thing by allowing our son to clear his name?'

The next letter, published on 25 May 2002, was by veteran RTÉ journalist David Davin-Power. He endorsed the sentiments of Mrs de Róiste and stated:

> I first met Dónal de Róiste soon after his involuntary discharge from the army. I have heard nothing in the passage of 30 years to shake my view that he was shabbily treated. Moreover I have no doubt that his transition to civilian life was wilfully made more difficult by the authorities.

Davin-Power called for the re-evaluation of De Róiste's case, adding that De Róiste's life, 'has been blighted by the attitude of the state he aspired to serve.'

On the same day, *The Irish Times* published an article in which I wrote of De Róiste's efforts to clear his name. Pressure and awareness were building.

On 29 May, *The Irish Times* published a letter from the godson of William Geary, Judge John P. Collins. He was responding to my article and wrote:

> Whether Lt de Róiste is guilty or innocent – and of what – I do not know. Clearly however, on the basis of the facts

described, the lieutenant did not receive natural justice. He was denied a hearing or trial and has not seen his file.

The Irish courts, while not reaching the substance of the issues, denied any relief by reason of Mr de Róiste's delay in seeking due process. I can appreciate that he waited some years before publicly airing his complaint. My godfather did much the same. The fear, anguish and suffering are not hard to understand.

The type of issues in the Geary and de Róiste cases are not easy for any government to tackle and resolve. The last government and Justice Minister O'Donoghue took courageous action in rendering justice to William Geary. I hope the new government will take the de Róiste matter under review.

On 9 June 2002, two Sunday newspapers, *Ireland on Sunday* and the *News of the World*, carried stories about De Róiste. The *Ireland on Sunday* article, written by Patrice Harrington, drew parallels with the famous nineteenth-century case of the French Jewish officer, Alfred Dreyfus.

The *News of the World* broke the news that Hollywood film star Gabriel Byrne was backing Dónal's case. During my recent visit to New York, I had met the actor and filled him in on De Róiste's battle for justice. Byrne agreed to join the cause and to lend his name to the campaign. Indeed, he agreed, at a future date, to launch De Róiste's American campaign.

As my research continued, I kept wondering at the underlying motivation for De Róiste's difficulties. Why was he, specifically, being targeted and why the rush to get him out of the army? I could see no good reason. I carefully went through a number of ministerial answers to various Dáil questions in an effort to understand what was being said officially.

DÁIL QUESTIONS

De Róiste had tried over the years to have his case raised during Dáil Question Time. TDs who tried to help him included Bernard Allen, Tony Gregory, Joe Higgins, Alan Shatter and Trevor Sargent.

On 21 November 1984, Deputy Tony Gregory (Independent) asked the then Minister for Defence, Patrick Cooney, 'the reasons [why Lt Roche] was dismissed from the Defence Forces in June, 1969; and if there is any procedure for appeal open to him as he wishes to clear his name.'

Minister Cooney replied:

> The person referred to, who was an officer of the Permanent Defence Forces was retired in the interests of the service by the President, acting on the advice of the Government, pursuant to sub-section 47(2) of the Defence Act, 1954, and subparagraph 18(1)(f) of Defence Force Regulations A.15.
>
> The question of an appeal procedure in such a case does not arise.

Significantly, four months after Deputy Gregory's question, the specific subparagraph quoted was changed.

3 June 1998
On 3 June 1998, Alan Shatter, TD (Fine Gael) raised the following questions:

> … I am assured by [Dónal de Róiste] that he had no political affiliations [in 1969] and that is still the position. I am also assured by him that he was at no stage a supporter of militant republicanism nor did he involve himself with any subversive organisation….His treatment in the Ireland of 1969 could provide a storyline for a Franz Kafka novel….
>
> I have in my possession a letter from him dated 22 May 1998 in which he states: 'I am granting you full permission to access and make public all the files on Ex-Lieutenant Dónal de Róiste No. 08159 (1963-1969) and help clear my name.' I am asking the Minister for Defence to grant to me and to Dónal Roche access to all information and files detailing each and every allegation made against him and the reasons the Government in 1969 recommended to the then President, Eamon

de Valera, that he be dismissed from the Army. I am asking that a person independent of Government and the Defence Forces be appointed to conduct an inquiry into this matter and that Dónal Roche be given a full opportunity to refute all allegations made against him and vindicate his good name.

Ultimately an independent report should be published detailing the full background to what occurred, the manner in which Dónal Roche was treated when interrogated by the Army and clarifying whether existing records prove misbehaviour by him which justified his dismissal and whether those records stand up to critical examination and to any response that can be furnished by Dónal Roche or any other person prepared to give information about what occurred....

I am calling on the Minister for Defence to provide for Dónal Roche a just mechanism which allows this issue – once and for all – to be properly addressed in a fair manner consistent with constitutional justice.

Deputy Shatter was supported by Bernard Allen, TD (Fine Gael), who stated:

In a sense of generosity and openness the Minister should open the files to Deputy Shatter or to an independent investigator to establish the innocence of Dónal de Róiste. His life has been ruined and he has been left with a question mark over his character by faceless people operating in what is lower than a kangaroo court.

The Minister for Defence (Mr Michael Smith, TD) responded by rejecting the assertion by Deputy Allen of 'faceless people and kangaroo courts'. He placed on record 'the appreciation of all the citizens for the very fine manner in which members of the Defence Forces have carried out their duties down through the years, often in very trying and difficult times.'

An apparent implication by the Minister was that those who wished to raise the matter of possible procedural irregularities in Lt Roche's 'retirement' were, somehow, hostile to the defence forces. This, of course, is nonsense. Dónal de Róiste states clearly: 'I have never spoken against the army. I just want fair play!' Those of us involved in his campaign are all rightly very proud of the service given, and sacrifices made, by its members and their families, particularly as peacekeepers under the auspices of the United Nations, in several troubled regions of the globe. However, like all agents and servants of the state, the defence forces must be accountable, particularly when there is suspicion or public disquiet concerning decisions made. The 'retirement' of Lt Dónal Roche in 1969 is one such example.

The Minister continued:

> The allegation [of Deputy Allen] is far removed from reality. All too often we fall into the trap of judging an event which took place many years ago by the situation and circumstances pertaining in the country today. To do so is both unrealistic and unfair to the people who made the decision at the time given the circumstances which then existed.

We have to keep reminding ourselves that Lt Roche was first interrogated in April 1969 about alleged involvement with members of a 'Splinter IRA Group'. The modern IRA would not be born for another ten weeks, following the burning of Bombay Street and serious rioting in Belfast during the autumn of 1969. In the circumstances, therefore, the use of the 'Troubles' to justify the wrong done to Dónal de Róiste is disingenuous.

Minister Smith continued his answer to the questions posed by Deputies Shatter and Allen. He recited the section of the 1954 Defence Act and Defence Regulations under which Lt Roche had been retired by the President 'in the interests of the service'. He concluded:

> I have reviewed the papers in this case and I am satisfied that the matter was handled in an appropriate manner and that the decision was taken only after very detailed consideration. A decision of this type is only ever taken for the most compelling reasons. Given that this is a matter involving military security on which a decision

was made by the President, I am not in a position to
discuss it further.

What papers did the Minister review to satisfy him that 'the matter was
handled in an appropriate manner and that the decision was taken only
after very detailed consideration'? Let us recall the sworn affidavit of a
senior official of the Department of Defence, Conor Kerlin, before the
High Court on 18 February 1998, just ten weeks before the Minister
made this statement:

> ... I can say that there appears to have only ever been
> two files in the Department pertaining to [Lt Roche].
> The first of these is file S 636.... For the purpose of
> swearing these proceedings I examined the S register,
> which confirmed the existence of a file pertaining to [Lt
> Roche] ... I have sought to find this file but cannot locate
> it... My examination of the register revealed that file S
> 636 was withdrawn on the 18th June 1969.... Obviously
> I do not know for how long this file has been missing,
> but it is incorrect to suggest that it has gone missing since
> the initiation of this discovery application... [I am led
> to believe]... that the file was not returned after it was
> withdrawn on the 18th June 1969, and that this was the
> cause of its loss.

What precise files, therefore, did the Minister have available to him that
allowed him to be so certain?

3 July 2001
On 3 July 2001, Bernard Allen, TD, sought a written reply from the
Minister for Defence. The questions included:

> — if the Minister will inform De Róiste of the reasons
> for his proposed retirement in the interests of the service;
> — if the Minister will list the substance of those
> interests;
> — the Minister's further views on whether the Act,
> as written in 1969 was unjust and, therefore, had to be

amended; and

— the reason the Minister will not give De Róiste his files in order that he can clear his name.

The Minister replied:

> ... A decision to retire an officer 'in the interests of the service' is only taken for the most compelling reasons. Given that the Government decision and advice to the President concerned military security, I am not in a position to comment in further detail. However, I can say that I am satisfied that the matter was handled in an entirely appropriate and proper manner and that the decision taken was taken only after very detailed and due consideration.

In fact, as we have seen, the decision was taken at the shortest and most crowded cabinet meeting of 1969, in the midst of an election count and while an administration was in transition, and less than two weeks before the then Minister for Defence, Michael Hilliard, returned to the back benches. In his reply, Minister Smith also stated:

> Moreover, the person concerned would have been fully aware at the time of the circumstances giving rise to his retirement in June, 1969. He had been previously interviewed by officers of the Intelligence Section of the army on three separate occasions in April, 1969, in relation to a number of serious matters which had come to their attention.

In fact, Lt Roche was questioned on a single matter – his alleged association with Mr X, Padraig Dwyer. Furthermore, on the admission of the Chief of Staff, officers of the Intelligence Section of the Army had interrogated Roche – not 'interviewed' him. Furthermore, two army officers, who retired with the rank of Commandant (Walshe) and Lieutenant Colonel (Swan) have stated that all three officers attended the same venues and mingled with the same people. So, why was Roche targeted for expulsion? Again, the Minister and his Department

Dónal (back left) on a visit to his brother Conchubhar and family with his children Dara and Sinéad (first and second from left), June 1986

Adi Roche, Christina de Róiste, Dónal and Conchubhar de Róiste, 1996

Dónal, Christina de Róiste, Adi Roche, Helen Barrett (Dónal's sister) and
Conchubhar de Roiste attending the conferring of Adi with an honorary
doctorate, NUI Galway, 28 June 2002 (Photo: Carl Mullan)

Adi Roche, Sr Helen Prejean (centre) and author Don Mullan at the press conference
Buswell's Hotal, Dublin, 1 July 2002 (Photo: Carl Mullan)

Launch of the USA Dónal de Róiste Truth and Justice Campaign, Irish Arts Centre, New York, 2002. Back row (left to right): author Don Mullan, Commandant Patrick Walsh, Gabriel Byrne; Front row (left to right): Dara de Róiste, Helen Barrett, Adi Roche and Dónal (Photo: Maryann de Leo)

Superintendent William Geary (aged 103) offering advice to Dónal de Róiste on his campaign strategy, New York, 2002 (Photo: Helen Barrett)

Twenty-four sacks 'Nitrates et Engrais D7' deposited on a pallet
at the Irish Industrial Explosives Factory, Clonagh, Co. Meath, June 1974 (Photo: Patrick Walshe)

Sacks of Prills and Grade Kisi thrown together as a consequence of a storage collapse at the Irish Industrial Explosives Factory, July 1974 (Photo: Patrick Walshe)

Door secured by brush handle, Irish Industrial Explosives Factory,
July 1974. Sacks of ammonium nitrate are piled on the floor.
(Photo: Patrick Walshe)

A defence forces colleague demonstrates the ease of access to the grounds of the Irish Industrial Explosives Factory that was possible, January 1975. Note also the sagging condition of the fence top. (Photo: Patrick Walshe)

Irish Industrial Explosives Factory fence as of January 1975. Boxes containing traces of gelignite can be seen stacked at rear of photo (Photo: Patrick Walshe)

are hiding behind the excuse of 'Military Security'. The Minister continued:

> At the third of these interviews, the person in question volunteered to submit a statement in relation to the matters raised, but did not subsequently do so. Given the serious nature of the situation presented to the military authorities, they were of the opinion that to retain him in the service would be contrary to the interests of the Defence Forces and of the State.

As previously discussed, Roche went to a solicitor on 1 May 1969, the day after the 'third interview' and the advice given was to 'do nothing' until the solicitor wrote and ascertained what was happening. Tragically for Roche, and through no fault of his own, it now appears that the solicitor's firm failed to take immediate action.

According to Minister Smith:

> The Deputy Judge Advocate General was requested to advise on the matter and he himself conducted a personal interview with the officer concerned in May, 1969. The Deputy Judge Advocate General informed the officer that he had been asked to advise the General Staff in relation to the case and that he wished to give the officer concerned an opportunity to submit any statement he wished to make in relation to the issues which had been raised in the April interviews. The officer advised the Deputy Judge Advocate General that, following the April interviews, he had consulted a solicitor who undertook to correspond with the military authorities on his behalf. The DJAG informed him that no such correspondence had been received.

Following the meeting with the DJAG, Roche again consulted his solicitor who, again, told him to do nothing until after he had written; on this occasion, the solicitor did, indeed, write. The Minister's reply continues:

The Deputy Judge Advocate General took the officer through the issues raised in the April interviews, explained the gravity of the situation, advised him to consider the situation, and arranged a further meeting for the following day, at which the officer was to submit a statement. The officer raised the question as to whether he could consult his solicitor and the DJAG made it clear to the officer that there was no objection to such a course of action. When the officer returned the following day, he then advised the DJAG that he would not in fact be making any statement.

The statement is very selective in the information being offered here to Dáil Éireann. Amongst the secret memos contained in Lt Roche's files is a handwritten note by his chief interrogator, Commandant O'Sullivan, which details information given to him by the DJAG (Appendix A, Document 17). O'Sullivan states: 'Lt ROCHE informed DJAG that his solicitor had advised him "to do nothing".'

The solicitor had advised Lt Roche 'to do nothing' until after he had written to the Chief of Staff seeking clarification. The solicitor's letter was written on 30 May 1969. It remained hidden and was, allegedly, 'lost' until 15 May 2001; its existence was not revealed to De Róiste until November 2002. By the time the Minister offered the above response to Deputy Allen, the existence of Lt Roche's solicitor's letter had, on the admission of his own civil servants, been known for at least six weeks. Why did he not inform Deputy Allen of the existence of this letter? Was it because this letter might change the nature of Dónal de Róiste's case, precisely because it had been ignored by the Chief of Staff and, it seems, by the Secretary of the Department of Defence, Minister Hilliard and the Cabinet of 1969?

20 February 2002
On 20 February 2002, Deputy Joe Higgins, Independent TD for Dublin West, asked the Taoiseach the number of files withheld by his Department from the National Archives in respect of the year 1969 under section 8(4)(a), 8(4)(b) and 8(4)(c) of the National Archives Act, 1986.

The Taoiseach responded by saying that he had no role in

decisions made by certifying officers under the provisions of the National Archives Act, 1986. 'The responsibility for certifying files for retention,' he said, 'is vested by section 8(4) of the Act in officers of the Department authorised for that purpose in accordance with the provisions of the Act.' He continued:

A total of 528 files, or part files, were transferred by my Department to the National Archives at the end of 2001 to be released for public inspection on 1 January 2002 and 13 were withheld. Of the 13 withheld under Section 8(4) of the National Archives Act, 1986, ten were withheld under sections 8(4)(b) and 8(4)(c) and three were withheld under section 8(4)(a)(b) and (c). These files therefore contain certain records, release of which, in the opinion of the certifying officer:

(a) would be contrary to the public interest, or
(b) would or might constitute a breach of statutory duty, or a breach of good faith on the grounds that they contain information supplied in confidence, and
(c) would or might cause distress or danger to living persons on the ground that they contain information about individuals, or would or might be likely to lead to an action for damages for defamation...

Files of my Department in respect of the year 1969 were transferred to the National Archives in 1999 and made available for public inspection on 1 January 2000. No complete files were withheld under section 8(4)(a), (b) or (c) of the National Archives Act, 1986 by my Department in respect of the year 1969. However, some minor abstractions were made from parts of one file series under section 8(4)(b) and (c).

At the time of going to press, the Department of the Taoiseach retains an unknown quantity of documents that are relevant to De Róiste's case. These include file S 17418, which may detail the reasons, if any, given to the government by the Minister for Defence, Michael Hilliard, as justification for the decision to retire him 'in the interests of the service'.

De Róiste's solicitor, Eamonn Carroll, commented with regard to answers given to Dáil questions by both the Minister for Defence and the Taoiseach:

> Since 1998 questions have been asked repeatedly to both the Minister for Defence and An Taoiseach to explain and clarify to Dáil Members and to De Róiste the circumstances of his forced retirement and its reasons. The standard response to each Dáil Question had been that De Róiste was aware of the circumstances and reasons for his retirement, that such retirement would not have been undertaken except for the most compelling reasons and that state security and the right to protect the identity of informants must be respected. This response is something similar to the process of interrogation endured by De Róiste in 1969 – no answers need to be given as you know the answers already.

LETTERS TO THE TAOISEACH AND PRESIDENT MCALEESE

On 27 May 2002, Dónal de Róiste's children, Dara and Sinead, wrote from the United States to the Taoiseach, Bertie Ahern, TD, and President Mary McAleese. They announced the launching of their American campaign to help their father to regain his good name. They also informed both that during their next visit to the United States they would seek a face-to-face meeting if the matter were not resolved.

Meanwhile, I was becoming ever more curious as to what had driven and motivated Lt Roche's expulsion from the Irish defence forces. I was aware that the attempted linkage of Lt Roche with subversives was not compatible with the seeming lack of concern, and appalling lack of urgency that senior officers – so quick to condemn Lt Roche – displayed over the Irish Industrial Explosives factory from 1967 onwards. Urgent reports were being made by another young officer who suspected – correctly – that there was a correlation between the IRA's bombing campaign in Northern Ireland and the shameful lack of security around the Co. Meath factory. Ironically, Lt Roche's best friend in the army, Captain Patrick Walshe, was filing the reports. The reports are dealt with in Chapter 14.

I began to wonder was there another reason for De Róiste's expulsion – one that hadn't previously been thought of. The more

I thought, the more puzzled I became. Then I recalled an initial conversation I had with Commandant Patrick Walshe in which he discussed the bullying of junior officers by senior officers. He had told me, in passing, of a distressed telephone call he had received from his friend, Lt Dónal Roche, concerning a car accident about which he was being pressurised to lie. And I wondered, perchance, if this might hold the key to unravelling the entire mystery of what had happened.

CAR CRASH –

A PLAUSIBLE HYPOTHESIS

To sin by silence, when we should protest,
Makes cowards out of men.

Ella Wheeler Wilcox

In my first meeting with Commandant Patrick Walshe, on 7 May 2002, we engaged in a wide-ranging interview about the controversial 'retirement' of Lt Roche in 1969 and other matters. I was impressed by his intelligence and attention to detail, particularly his meticulous record keeping. During the interview, he spoke to me about the bullying of junior officers by senior officers. However, he did not mention a 1967 car crash in which Lt Roche had been injured.

The following week, he came to my home to give me a series of reports and photographs concerning the subject matter discussed in Chapter 14 of this book and again returned to the subject of bullying within the defence forces. It was on this occasion that he first mentioned, in passing, the aftermath of a car crash, as an example of bullying. He recalled Lt Roche telephoning him in a distressed state saying that he was coming under enormous pressure from senior officers to lie about the car crash in which he had been a passenger in a car driven by a commandant in the Transport Corps, who Roche alleged, was drunk. Walshe encouraged Roche to stay with the truth, regardless of the pressure.

At the time, I heard the story as nothing more than a passing example of internal army bullying. However, after several weeks of mulling over the case and finding no satisfactory answer, I felt that I should, perhaps, explore the car crash and satisfy myself that it was nothing more than an unfortunate but unrelated incident.

I met Commandant Walshe again in early June 2002, specifically to go over the details of the car crash as he could recall them.

Commandant Walshe informed me that he was stationed at FCA Headquarters, Birr, Co. Offaly, when Lt Roche telephoned him. Roche was then stationed at Custume Barracks, Athlone. He thought that the call had come sometime around the end of 1967 or early 1968. He is certain the call came from Custume Barracks because he drove there immediately after the phone call. (We now know, from classified documents, released in October 2002, that Lt Roche was transferred to Athlone on 3 June 1968, so it is possible that the call occurred around then.)

During my interview about the car crash, Walshe related the following:

> Dónal told me that he was being severely harassed by senior officers in the barracks. He told me it was to do with a lift he had accepted from Commandant Seán T. O'Kelly, a senior Transport Corps officer, who was returning to Cork one weekend during November 1967. He told me that Seán T. had been drinking heavily.
>
> Dónal, as I recall, said that Commandant O'Kelly was so drunk he offered to drive but O'Kelly became abusive and ordered him into the car. On the road between Templemore and Thurles a collision occurred between Seán T.'s car and a car driven by a young woman who, I understand, was badly injured.
>
> Dónal told me that Commandant O'Kelly and other officers were harassing him to make a false statement concerning the car crash. He was refusing but was coming under severe pressure.
>
> He told me he was under so much pressure that his face had broken out in blotches. In the end he stood by the truth. His stand on this incident would not have gone down well with his seniors in Athlone.

It is not possible to state categorically that the car accident was the motivating circumstance that led to the ending of young Lt Roche's promising career. However, it is clear that persons within the army not only wanted him removed, but wanted him removed fast – and with a cloud of suspicion hanging over his head. The question is why? Why was he such a threat?

Prior to the car accident, as his first four annual reports attest, Roche had been a promising young officer with a reasonably good record and every chance of advancing in the army.

On 5 June 2002, I went in search of the young woman involved in the car accident. When I eventually spoke to her, we agreed to meet the following day in the Club House of Dundrum Hotel and Golf Centre in Co. Tipperary. Her brother Maurice and a retired professional woman accompanied her. Dónal de Róiste accompanied me to the meeting because the woman was fearful that my journalistic motivation might be to cause further injury to his sister, Adi.

It was a very moving meeting. The woman asked that her privacy be respected by withholding her name from any possible articles I might write. It was clear that she still suffered, over thirty years later, from the injuries she had sustained in the crash. She was unable to sit on any of the soft sofas in the club house, requiring a chair with a straight back. Lt Roche recalled how lucky he had been. He was propelled from the back seat through the front windscreen of the overturning car he was in but had somehow escaped with only minor injuries.

The woman's brother, Maurice, said that they had believed at the time that there was drink involved and suspected a cover-up. There was talk in Templemore of officers drinking in a hotel and of a row between them.

Just before we ended the meeting, the woman reached for a bag from which she retrieved a large envelope. She told me that all her legal documents pertaining to the accident were enclosed and said that I could photocopy them. The hotel staff very kindly obliged. The documents were an unexpected bonus allowing me to read developments in the legal proceeding surrounding the car crash alongside those relating to the roller-coaster ride of Lt Roche's final year in the army.

What I discovered not only disturbed me, but led me to advance what I still believe is a plausible hypothesis regarding what may have been motivating the fast-track removal of young Lt Roche from the army.

Lt Dónal Roche had been temporarily assigned mess duties in Custume Barracks, Athlone, Co. Westmeath, and believes that this was the probable reason why he was in there on 17 November 1967. His family home was in Clonmel. Commandant Seán T. O'Kelly, who was travelling to Cork for the weekend, offered Roche a lift as far as Cahir, where his father had agreed to collect him. Sometime during that afternoon, he set off from Athlone in O'Kelly's 1967 Vauxhall Viva. O'Kelly was carrying three passengers: Lt Dónal Roche and Lt Michael Cleary, also of Custume Barracks, Athlone, and a Mrs Josephine Barry from Athlone. I have been informed by a former member of the defence forces, that Mrs Barry's husband, Patrick, was a civilian chemist, employed by the Department of Defence, stationed at the Athlone barracks.

Along the way, they stopped at Mullally's Hotel in Templemore, Co. Tipperary. De Róiste can recall neither the reason for their stop nor how long they were in the hotel, but he says that he became seriously concerned about the amount of alcohol consumed by the senior officer. He says that before leaving Templemore, he politely approached O'Kelly saying, 'Sir, I think you should hand over the keys.' He says that O'Kelly became furious and publicly dressed him down in the hotel and on the footpath as they walked to the vehicle. With his three passengers, O'Kelly left Templemore at approximately 5.30 p.m., heading in the direction of Thurles, Co. Tipperary.

Lt Gerry Swan, who had digs in Templemore at the time, was not in Mullally's Hotel in the afternoon, but remembers that when he called in later that evening, a member of staff informed him of the row involving army officers and also gave him a strange message. 'The young woman didn't know who had left the message,' Swan told me, 'but she said a young officer asked her to tell me that I would know who was enquiring when I read the obituaries the following day.'

At around 5.45 p.m. O'Kelly was in a serious crash involving a 27-year-old woman. She was travelling to Templemore in her 1965 Austin Mini to have tea with a colleague. The force of the collision was such that O'Kelly's car overturned. Garda D.F. O'Keeffe of Thurles Garda Station reported that he and colleagues arrived at the scene at 6.15 p.m. He stated:

... I found a Vauxhall Viva car [O'Kelly's] ... lying on its left side and facing in the direction of Templemore.... The driver of this car ... Commandant Seán T. O'Kelly ... was trapped in this car and was removed by Doctors J. McGovern and P. Moloney, Thurles. He was later conveyed to Nenagh Hospital by Fire Brigade ... I found [an] Austin Mini ... parked on the grass verge with its right front embedded in the wire fence on the left side of the roadway as one travels towards Templemore from Thurles.... The driver of this car ... was lying injured on the side of roadway awaiting removal to hospital. I spoke with this lady who informed me that she was driving her car from Thurles to Templemore when the accident occurred.... The vehicles apparently collided 48 feet on the Thurles side of the apex on a right hand curve as one travels from Thurles towards Templemore....

In a statement taken at the County Hospital, Nenagh, on 25 November 1967, by Garda John F. Maloney, of Nenagh Garda Station, the young woman recalled:

I left Thurles at 5.35 p.m. to go to Templemore.... It was dusk at the time and I had my headlights on. As I was about three miles out from Thurles and travelling at 35 to 40 M.P.H. I noticed a car coming from the opposite direction. I dipped my headlights and so did the driver of the other car. The next thing I noticed was that the other car was coming straight towards me. I don't remember anymore after that only that I got out of the car myself.

A copy of this statement was sent to her Templemore-based solicitor, Mr John J. Nash, a respected Fianna Fáil member of Seanad Éireann, by the Garda Superintendent's Office, Thurles.

It is interesting to contrast the young woman's statement with that given by Commandant O'Kelly. Garda Michael E. Lynam interviewed him at the Orthopaedic Hospital, Gurranabraher, Cork, on 6 December 1967, some ten days after the young woman had made her statement to the Garda Síochána. He stated:

... On 17th November, 1967 at approx. 17.30 hours I was driving a new Vauxhall Viva ... on the Templemore/ Thurles road. I was travelling on my correct side of the road and at a moderate speed. I am not a fast driver. My lights were dipped. About half way between Templemore and Thurles I saw a car ahead with dimmed lights and travelling on the wrong side of the road. I flashed my headlights as a warning, slowed down and pulled in closer to my own side. At this stage I had no reason to assume that the oncoming car would not correct its position and allow through passage, therefore I did not stop. The other car which I now believe to be GFI.922 came straight on and I felt that the driver was going to pass on my left. To stop would not have avoided an accident but would more than likely, at this stage, cause a fatal accident. To continue forward on my own side, would have led to a head-on collision, again with possible fatal results. My only alternative was to pull over to my right which I did. As I did so the other driver switched on the headlights and swung in towards me. To avoid a head-on collision, I swung hard left hoping to get through on my own side, but was struck by the oncoming car, which swung me around and caused my car to overturn. At no stage was I negligent or unaware of other road users. I was not travelling at an excessive speed, I did slow down and until the impact was in full control of my car. I am convinced that any action other than which I took would not have avoided this accident, but would have had far more serious results. As it was, only the two drivers concerned received serious injury. I had three passengers in the car, Lieuts Roche and Cleary, Custume Bks, Athlone and a Mrs Barry, c/o Mr Barry, 'The Pharmacy', Military Hospital, Custume Bks, Athlone. I have heard this statement read over to me and it is correct.

NEGLIGENCE

The woman's solicitor wrote to her c/o the Orthopaedic Hospital, Croom, Co. Limerick, on 23 April 1968. 'The issue,' he stated, 'is whether the accident was caused by your negligence or by the negligence of Commandant O'Kelly.' He continued:

> If the accident occurred as described by Commandant O'Kelly you were driving so completely on your wrong side of the road that I find it hard to credit that any sensible girl with a very moderate experience of driving would be so reckless.
>
> I am not particularly impressed by Commandant O'Kelly's statement…. From the time the danger was first noted by either party until the collision occurred was probably only a split second. In such a situation a motorist acts automatically and does not have time to think. He flashes his head lights and slows down; pulls to his own side; believes the other driver was going to pass on the left; then decided to swerve to the right; then sees the other head lights switch on from dip to high and then thinks of swinging back again to the left. All these things could happen on a straight road if one sees another car coming on the wrong side 50 to 100 yards away; but I cannot visualise them happening in the emergency which arose at this particular bend.
>
> By contrast your simple statement seems to make more sense to me…. There was no time for all the mental calculations and dipping and switching on of head lights in which Commandant O'Kelly alleges he indulged….

In the same letter her solicitor makes a critical observation which he concludes with a curious question to his client:

> There were three passengers in the other car, Lieutenant Cleary, Lieutenant Roche and Mrs Barry, all from Athlone. No statements were made to the Guards by any of them. It would be very desirable to ascertain what account (if any) these three people give of the accident. Would you be friendly with anyone in Athlone through whom you could make enquiries?

It would, indeed, have been desirable to ascertain what account O'Kelly's passengers had of the accident. The Garda 'Abstract Report' on the accident, dated 22 April 1968, notes, 'The following persons whose statements are not available may be in a position to give evidence…' and lists the names and addresses of Cleary, Roche and Mrs Barry. Why the gardaí did not take such statements isn't clear and it appears that apart from suggesting to his client that she make enquiries from friends in Athlone, the solicitor did not pursue the matter with the rigour it required. He was, after all, legally in a position to write to the Garda Síochána and request that they carry out their duty. If they had, they may have been surprised to discover a young officer who was resisting internal pressure to lie about the circumstance surrounding the accident.

The truth is that Roche was not prepared to lie. His sister, Len, recalls him arriving at their home in Clonmel later that evening:

> In 1967 we didn't have a telephone at home and I remember well the night our neighbour called to say that Dónal was on the line. I'm not sure which one of my parents took the call, only that the news was that there had been an accident and that Daddy was going to pick Dónal up, in Thurles, I believe. I recall feeling anxious and remember when he and Dad finally arrived home that Dónal was very shocked and wound up. He was horrified because the young woman who had been driving the other car was seriously injured and he said to me 'her life is ruined'. However, what stands out most clearly in my mind is what Dónal said about the person driving the car in which he was a passenger. Apparently, Dónal, realising that this man wasn't driving safely (due to alcohol consumption) suggested that he should take over and was told forcefully 'Are you, an officer, telling me, a commandant, that I'm not fit to drive?'

De Róiste's ex-wife, Leah Martin, also spoke to me about the accident. She said that during their marriage he occasionally spoke about the car accident and that he felt enormous guilt about the injuries sustained by the young woman and wondered how her life had turned out. She also informed me that her ex-husband was very clear that the senior officer driving the car was drunk at the time.

THE YOUNG WOMAN
The young woman suffered serious injuries which, to this day, affect her mobility and, at times, cause great discomfort. Her right hip socket was smashed and she sustained a broken pelvis. She spent a total of eleven months in hospital and did not return to her employment until September 1969.

She told me:

> I made my statement without the help of a solicitor. I was still suffering intensely and in a state of shock. I am absolutely sure the car was coming straight at me, on my side of the road. I remember screaming just before the impact. I don't think I lost consciousness. I kept my eyes open because I was afraid I might die. I remember seeing the passenger door was open and I somehow managed to pull myself out. I was terrified the car would go on fire.

She recalls one of the young men from the other car standing over her and asking, 'Are you okay?' She says they waited a long time for an ambulance and eventually were transferred to hospital in a Fire Brigade vehicle. Commandant O'Kelly was also in the vehicle. She recalls that Mrs Barry was also admitted to hospital.

Despite the fact that Mrs Barry was also hospitalised, it appears that no statement was taken from her. The fact that no statements appear to have been made available to the woman's solicitor from any of O'Kelly's passengers raises questions about the quality of the Garda investigation. It seems reasonable to wonder if the case was being carefully managed, off-stage.

CONDUCT UNBECOMING AN OFFICER
Former Lt Roche recalls that some time after O'Kelly had been discharged from hospital, he and a Col. Harry Byrne spoke to him at Custume Barracks. Roche says that he had made no secret of the fact that he thought O'Kelly was at fault and incapable of taking the wheel prior to the accident. He had discussed the incident with several people,

including fellow officers. He says that O'Kelly and Byrne, and other senior officers, put him under enormous pressure to change his version of events and to support Commandant O'Kelly over the 'civvy'. He stated:

> There were threats of insubordination. They questioned my loyalty and accused me of conduct unbecoming of an officer. I was accused of not standing up for a fellow officer and was warned that my persistence could affect my career. I was told that if I didn't drop saying that I had approached Commandant O'Kelly prior to the accident and asked him for his keys because he was unfit to drive, I would be considered untrustworthy and that my promotion would be held up. I was being pressurised to falsify what I knew to be the truth. The condition of the 'civvy' didn't seem to bother them. It was argued that Commandant O'Kelly's version of events was obviously the correct version since he was a transport officer. And anyway, since I was sitting in the back seat, how could I be sure of what I was saying. It was then I decided to telephone my friend, Paddy Walshe, in Birr. I had no one else to turn to for support. He encouraged me to stand firm, which I did. They knew that if I was asked to make a statement about the accident, I was going to tell the truth because I knew an innocent party had been very seriously injured because of O'Kelly's negligence.

As the months passed, the accident became a receding memory for both Roche and Walshe. Roche's army medical records record on 21 November 1967 that he was 'Involved in car accident on the Templemore/Thurles road at 1820hrs approx on the 17/11/1967'. The records also state: 'Bruising. Abdomen and Lower Chest. Not severe. Not likely to interfere with his efficiency as a soldier.'

The formal defence force document, entitled 'Report on Accidental or Self-Inflicted Injuries', Ref: A.F. 482 (Prov.), contains a section headed 'Commanding Officer's Opinion'. It was completed on 6 December 1967 by the Officer Commanding the Signal Company.

The following questions and answers are given:

(a) Was the individual on duty or warned for duty? *No*
    If so, what duty?   /
(b) Was it due to his negligence? *No*
    How far was he blameworthy?   /
(c) Was it due to his misconduct? *No*
    If so, in what way?   /
(d) Was anyone else to blame? *Involved in Motor Accident.*
(e) Court of Enquiry–
    (i)   Has any been held? *No*
    (ii)   Will any be held? /
    (iii) Date and place?   /

There are very clear instructions on the Defence Force Form A.F. 482 regarding:

> … all cases of accidental or self-inflicted injuries, involving the absence from duty of an officer or soldier, whether due to the individual's own act, or that of a comrade, or to other extraneous circumstances.

Instructions on the form clearly state:

> Full statements are to be taken by an officer from the witnesses of the accident, or, where there was no witness, from any person to whom the injured officer or soldier may have mentioned his injury immediately after the occurrence. These statements, when obtainable, will be signed by the persons making them, and by the officer who takes them, and will be forwarded with the form. Where it is intended to take disciplinary action, duplicates of these statements should be retained by the unit for use in lieu of a summary of evidence.

There is a document entitled: 'statement of Accident Details (as per GRO 43/55 Para 99H)'. While it seeks answers to some very interesting questions, it is important to understand that this is not the statement required by Form A.F. 482, above. The questions and answers are as follows:

(a) Circumstances

I was travelling in Comdt. O'Kelly's car when it was involved in an accident on the Templemore/Thurles road.

(b) (1) Name & Address of Third Party: *Not known*

(2) Name of Solicitor of Third Party: *Not known*

(3) Insurance Co of Third Party: *Not known*

(c) Reg No of Car(s) Involved: *Not known*

(d) Damage to Service Property: *Nil*

(e) Names and Addresses of Witnesses (with copies of statements): Blank

(f) (1) Name of Garda Station: Blank

(2) Name of Garda Síochána: *Not Known*

(g) Is claim being made: *Not known*

If so: *No*

Name of Solicitor to Whom Case is Referred: *Nil*

(h) Are Criminal Proceedings Being Instituted?

Not known

This document appears to have Lt Roche's signature. While Roche was, no doubt, answering truthfully, the details required by the questions were easily ascertainable by the military authorities, particularly given that three officers, and the wife of the Athlone Barracks pharmacist, were involved. A simple phone call to Templemore Garda Station, on behalf of the army, would have secured the information required.

In the classified files relating to Lt Roche, there is no statement about the car accident, as requested by Form A.F. 482. Why? Was it this form and Lt Roche's unwillingness to lie about the circumstances of the car accident that caused him his initial difficulties? Are there statements in existence from Commandant Seán T. O'Kelly and Lt (now Col.) Michael Cleary? If not, why not? Is the failure to take statements in breach of defence force regulations? Does the absence of such statements raise further questions about the quality of the enquiry and the fact that all is not right about how this matter was investigated by both the civil and military authorities, much to the detriment and disadvantage of an innocent civilian road-user?

Proceedings relating to the crash were gradually making progress through the legal system, though Lt Roche had no idea of any such developments as the failure to take a statement from him and the other passengers meant that they had been sidelined.

On 26 March 1969, the woman's solicitor received advice from a
barrister, Patrick Connolly, concerning the crash. The letter discussed
various permutations and legal tactics. Of particular interest is the
apparent assumption that O'Kelly's passengers would support the
Commandant's version of the accident. 'It is regrettable,' the barrister
wrote, 'that all of the passengers were in O'Kelly's car.' He asked
whether any of O'Kelly's passengers had been injured and expressed the
opinion that their additional claims 'may complicate matters'.

Of particular significance is the barrister's strategic advice:

> From the tactical point of view the most desirable result
> would be to get [our client's] action on first since a party
> is always in a stronger position before a Jury appearing as
> Plaintiff … a party who is more seriously injured….

On 9 April 1969, the woman's solicitor wrote to inform her:

> I have issued a Plenary Summons on your behalf in the
> High Court.

It is at this juncture that my 'plausible hypothesis' begins. The issuing of
the plenary summons by the young woman's lawyer is, I believe, crucial
to making sense of what subsequently happened to Lt Roche, starting
on 25 April 1969. Notification of the Plenary Summons and Notice
of Appearance would have been conveyed to Commandant O'Kelly.
The fact that the young woman's legal team had made the pre-emptive
strike, issuing full and unqualified proceedings, would have caused
O'Kelly deep disquiet. He was now facing a High Court action before
a jury. The likelihood of his passengers being called to testify was more
than a strong possibility, even assuming that he had managed to pull
strings to limit the scope of any investigation within the army or by the
Garda Síochána.

Commandant O'Kelly knew that Lt Roche was already refusing
to buckle under pressure. Roche's stance was in keeping with the same
rigid stubbornness of his father, Seán. As mentioned in Chapter 2, Lt

Roche's mother, stated, regarding her husband:

> Seán wouldn't tell a lie to save his life. To the point of
> being undiplomatic ... they were taught the same ... we
> were in a very truthful home, I can tell you, because you
> couldn't tell a lie to Seán.

O'Kelly and senior officers already knew that Roche was not going to
lie under oath to help his cause. He knew that if Lt Roche were called
to take the stand, he would speak the truth. He knew that Roche would
tell the court about the row they had had in Templemore regarding
his consumption of alcohol, prior to the accident. There was also the
possibility of the young woman's legal team finding witnesses to that
row since it had occurred in public.

It is possible that O'Kelly realised that if the junior officer was
permitted to testify, and assuming that his evidence were accepted, the
consequences for his own army career would be horrendous. To begin
with, his case would collapse. He would be seen to have committed
perjury and his statement to the Garda Síochána, soon to be read into
the court records, would be shown as a concoction of lies. He would be
found guilty of a very serious offence, which had resulted in grievous
bodily harm to an innocent party. Such a scenario could have left him
facing dismissal from the defence forces if convicted and imprisoned.

On 25 April 1969, Lt Roche was placed under guard and driven
to Dublin where, he claims, he was interrogated over long periods for
several days. During the period when Lt Roche was being interrogated
in Dublin, Captain Patrick Walshe, his closest ally in the army and the
officer who supported him in refusing to falsify his testimony over the
car accident, was ordered to attend an 'interview' at army HQ in Dublin.
Walshe is adamant that neither he nor Dónal de Róiste ever knowingly
associated with criminal or subversive elements.

On 26 June 1969, Roche was ordered to appear before senior
officers of Western Command, including Col. Harry Byrne, the senior
officer who, de Róiste claims, was with Commandant O'Kelly when he
was pressurised to falsify his account of the accident. He was handed a
letter, informing him that he had been retired by the President, on the
recommendation of the government, with effect from midnight. 'He
[Byrne] told me that I had been retired by the President and gave me

twelve hours to leave my barracks.'

On 7 May 1969, the young woman's solicitor wrote to her concerning a
possible out-of-court settlement on the basis of 50 per cent negligence
on each side. He continued:

> … lest the case be not settled, and in an effort to have your
> proceedings come on for hearing before the proceedings
> issued against you by Commandant O'Kelly, I issued a
> Plenary Summons in the High Court on your behalf. I
> received a Notice of Appearance, and I am now issuing a
> statement of Claim. I told the Insurance Company that
> at any time they let me hear from them agreeing to the
> figure which I mentioned, we could consider the case
> settled.

Solicitor John Nash, with the assistance of his counsel and the insurance
company, calculated that if the young woman allowed the case to go
to a full hearing, and if she won, her injuries claim would be valued at
£10,000. He also explained to her the risks involved, and consequently
advised her, on the basis of 50 per cent negligence, to settle for £5,000.
He wrote to her:

> I would recommend to you to permit me to agree that
> the case can be disposed of on the basis of 50 per cent
> negligence on each side.

Nash further stated:

> I enclose for your reference copy of Counsel's opinion
> from which you will see that he is disposed to agree with
> my view that a settlement on the basis of each party being
> 50% negligent would be in your interests.

The young woman's solicitor reasoned:

I would estimate that if there were no negligence whatever on your part you could hope to recover about £10,000; but it is very difficult to estimate what attitude a Jury would take. Sometimes I have found Juries to allow figures considerably lower than my estimate of the damages, and sometimes they allow figures considerably higher. The strange feature is that if there be one or two relatively poor people on the Jury they are inclined to allow lower damages than well-to-do people. The reason is that a person of moderate means thinks that £3,000 or £4,000 is a very substantial sum upon which he could live for a long time; but a more wealthy person would consider £3,000 or £4,000 a moderate sum.

Mr Nash advised the young woman to settle out of court. She says:

My solicitor advised me that since I was a relatively inexperienced driver, having only recently passed my test and that Commandant O'Kelly belonged to the army's Transport Section, he would be in a strong position to sway the jury in his favour. In this scenario I might lose the case altogether. He also informed me that the court might decide I was 70% negligent, in which event I would get only 30% of the damages. I was young and inexperienced regarding the law. I just knew I was not at fault so I found the whole experience troubling and traumatic. I was recovering from serious injuries and I was now facing the possibility of going to court and being found guilty of a car crash I did not cause.

My solicitor also told me that by going to court I was running the risk of having my case heard before a member of the jury who might have had a bad experience with someone in my profession and might sway the rest against me.

Her solicitor did emphasise in his letter of 9 April 1969 that the matter was one entirely for his client to decide. He wrote, 'I am giving you the benefit of my advice; but I shall not take umbrage if you refuse to accept it.' However, although she was an innocent party, her confidence in her case was being eroded and the opinion of her barrister did not help. In his letter of 26 March 1969, he wrote:

> I agree with the 'Phoenix' [Assurance Company] that the facts are somewhat tilted against our client ... Mr O'Kelly's statement to the Police is much more coherent than that of our young girl although he is inclined to be a little too involved about the accident.

In the end, the young woman settled out of court shortly before she returned to work in September 1969. She received £5,000, less expenses, on the basis of 50 per cent negligence. Her brother, a teacher by profession, was unhappy with the way the case was concluded:

> I was annoyed the case did not go to court.... I cannot recall at this distance if I spoke specifically to my sister's solicitor about the issue of alcohol. But there was a suspicion around drink and I cannot understand why he did not pursue this matter further. Indeed, I cannot understand why he appears not to have wondered why the gardaí did not take statements from the passengers in Commandant O'Kelly's car. We were, of course, young and inexperienced....
>
> On another point, Mr Nash appears to have dramatically changed his view from a position where he was not impressed by Commandant O'Kelly's statement to gardaí following the car crash to a point where he advised my sister on 7 May 1969 that Commandant O'Kelly would be in a strong position to sway the jury in his favour.

OUT OF COURT SETTLEMENT:
COMMANDANT O'KELLY V. THE YOUNG WOMAN
The young woman had been advised that the 50 per cent negligence settlement was an agreement between both parties. That was the understanding she had been given in correspondence received from both her solicitor and the opinion of counsel. However, the woman's

settlement was not the end of the affair. On 23 October 1970, she received a letter from the Phoenix Assurance Company informing her that Commandant O'Kelly was pursuing a claim against her. On 11 June 1971, solicitor Nathaniel Lacy, acting on behalf of Phoenix Assurance Company, wrote to her concerning O'Kelly's action. Lacy informed her:

> The High Court proceedings may come to Hearing anytime between now and the end of July and your attendance at the Four Courts for the Hearing of the action will, of course, be essential.

By now, former Lt Roche, reeling under the stigma of having been fired by the President of Ireland, was having a hard time trying to find suitable employment.

While awaiting further instructions from her insurance company's solicitor, the young woman had two interesting encounters. She has a memory of a member of the Garda Síochána, involved in the investigation, making what she describes as an off-the-cuff remark one day, in which he said, 'A senior officer of the Irish army had never been convicted of dangerous driving in an Irish Court and it wasn't going to happen in this case.' In the interests of accuracy, it should be pointed out that the garda's statement is not strictly true.

Sometime later, she arrived at her Thurles flat to discover Commandant O'Kelly waiting for her. Her sister, with whom she shared the flat, also spoke to O'Kelly. She says that she found O'Kelly's visit 'most peculiar'. He told her that he was taking her insurance company to court and that it was nothing personal. This was untrue. The letter she received from her insurance company, of 11 June 1971, clearly states:

> re: The High Court – Seán T. O'Kelly v. Yourself

O'Kelly said that he was sorry about what had happened but that it would be very helpful if she could come to the court simply to say that she was the driver of the other car. The woman remembers that the commandant had 'a lot of drink on him'.

She telephoned her solicitor concerning the request by her insurance company, and O'Kelly, to attend at the High Court. Remarkably, Mr Nash told her that it would be all right to go. This seems extraordinary given that his client was now being sued for negligence by O'Kelly, when it was his client's understanding that the case had already been settled on the basis of 50 per cent negligence.

A solicitor appointed by her insurance company represented her. She travelled, at her own expense, to the High Court in Dublin towards the end of October 1971. She recalls being taken upstairs for a briefing. She said that even though Commandant O'Kelly was present, and had personally requested her attendance, on this occasion he barely acknowledged her. She says that she was terrified and intimidated by the experience.

The young woman found it strange that none of O'Kelly's passengers were, like her, summoned to testify before the court. She was told that none, including Mrs Barry, would agree to attend or make a statement. It is also interesting to note that even though Mrs Barry was both injured and hospitalised, unlike Commandant O'Kelly, she did not initiate proceedings against the young woman.

At the Four Courts, she was told that one of the young passengers had lost his commission 'because he was a member of Saor Éire'. She says that upon enquiring what Saor Éire was, she was told, 'It is the political wing of the IRA.'

As she waited for the case to be heard, she was informed that it had been adjourned until 2 p.m. At 2 o'clock, a garda told her that the case had been settled out of court.

When contacted on 6 June 2002, one of O'Kelly's passengers, former Lt Michael Cleary (now Col. Cleary, Director of Engineers, McKee Barracks, Dublin), said that he had no recollection of any court case related to the accident. He said that he was 'very surprised' when Lt Roche was 'retired'. He said, 'I've never drawn a connection between the two incidents…' Col. Cleary, when asked for an interview, said that he wasn't sure if he should give one at this point, stating, 'I am still a serving officer. It is not in my personal interest that I should.' He advised that I should go through the army press office if I wanted to interview him. On 18 June 2002, the army press office sent a one-sentence response: 'Colonel Michael Cleary does not wish to be interviewed.'

As if distracted by a magician's sleight of hand, Lt Roche had, for over thirty years, directed his attention one way while an illusion was, quite possibly, being created out of his sight. In response to the question, 'Could a middle-ranking officer like O'Kelly have the influence to create such a scenario with extraordinary implications for the Irish government and the presidency over thirty years later?' retired Commandant Patrick Walshe is adamant:

> ... all that was required was a well-placed phone call to 'Security' and immediately we would have been under suspicion. The fact that Dónal and I loved Irish music and travelled frequently to various music and ballad sessions left us wide upon. Even though our love of Irish music was as genuine and as innocent as people like Christy Moore and the members of Comhaltas Ceoltóirí Éireann, for thirty years we have second-guessed our accusers wondering who it was we supposedly associated with. It's extraordinary that, in the end, it may all boil down to Dónal's refusal to tell a lie against an innocent civilian whom a drunken senior officer seriously injured.

If De Róiste's undoing is connected to the November 1967 car crash, the investigation of which appears to have disquieting irregularities associated with it, this hypothesis may hold the key to explaining the mysterious nature of his 'retirement'. If it is correct, his only apparent crime is that he was an honourable young officer who was prepared to tell the truth even though it would have had serious implications for a senior officer.

To this day, De Róiste is unrepentant for the stance he took:

> I joined the army to serve good people like the decent and law-abiding civilian injured in this crash. If, after thirty years, it transpires that my 'retirement' was for no other reason than I would, if called to testify, tell the truth about the crash in which she could have been killed, my trauma and suffering will have had a purpose.

In 2001, the Taoiseach, Bertie Ahern, said that parts of De Róiste's file were being withheld because they contained 'information provided in confidence'. The question remains as to whether Commandant Seán T. O'Kelly, or an associate, was one of the 'informants'.

THE IRISH TIMES, 29 JUNE 2002
Much of the above information was published in a two-page article in *The Irish Times* on 29 June 2002. When I initially presented the piece, together with supporting documentation, to Peter Murtagh, the then Opinion Page Editor, he was concerned about the credibility of the newspaper should my hypothesis be shot down. Following a detailed reply from me, a decision was made to proceed with publication. My detailed reply included the following summary of the key points:

— Neither De Róiste nor Commandant Patrick Walshe ever saw the connection between the O'Kelly crash and Dónal's internal army difficulties. Nor, apparently, did Col. Michael Cleary, the other military passenger. The possible connection has arisen through independent investigation and analysis of legal documents from the period.

— De Róiste and his fellow passengers were never interviewed about the accident by the Garda Síochána.

— De Róiste (and Col. Michael Cleary) were never informed of any legal developments related to the accident. Up until two weeks ago both passengers were unaware of court proceedings.

— The proximity between the issuing of the Plenary Summons against Commandant O'Kelly (circa 9 April '69) and Dónal de Róiste's arrest (25 April '69) is a cause for concern, particularly since we know from Commandant (Retd) Walshe that de Róiste had been pressurised to falsify his knowledge that O'Kelly was intoxicated when the accident happened. Walshe, an army officer who served the nation with distinction, is prepared to swear an affidavit concerning the phone call he received from Lt de Róiste and his subsequent intervention.

— It is intriguing that the only two officers who were 'interviewed' by Irish Army Intelligence at the time were de Róiste and Walshe, during which unspecified and unsubstantiated allegations were suggested.

— It doesn't take too much imagination to think through the consequences for O'Kelly if De Róiste was called, under oath, to testify before a jury and was to say, 'Sir, You were drunk!'

— When eventually O'Kelly's proceedings against the young woman reached the High Court, none of his passengers were asked to attend. This suggests irregularities in the handling of the case by the Garda and, while leaving it open to readers to draw their own conclusions, suggests to me that this case may have been managed off stage.

— It is also interesting that whoever engineered De Róiste's 'retirement' did it on the basis of Section 47(2) of the Defence Act, 1954, subparagraph (18)(1)(f) of Regulation A.15 which prescribed that an officer of the Permanent Defence Force may be retired 'in the interests of the service'.

— Subparagraph (18)(1)(f) was the only regulation in Section 47(2) which ensured that de Róiste had no comeback. This regulation was changed in 1985 to protect [officers] in Dónal de Róiste's dilemma.

When the article appeared, it was accompanied by an interview with De Róiste and another article, by Deaglan de Breadun headed, 'The sudden rise and rapid fall of Saor Éire'. De Róiste was concerned by the Saor Éire article and saw it as *The Irish Times* hedging its bets.

The morning following publication, I received an unexpected call from an *Irish Times* reader who had just read my article. The caller claimed to have heard the car crash being discussed by O'Kelly and others back in 1969. The main topic of the discussion was how to get O'Kelly out of the trouble he now found himself in.

Whether or not there is a definitive connection between the O'Kelly car crash and the ending of Dónal de Róiste's army career, there is no doubt that the article sent shock waves deep into the Department of

Defence and, quite likely, a crisis management meeting was arranged for the following Monday morning, 1 July 2002.

That same day, I chaired a packed press conference, organised by the Dónal de Róiste Truth Campaign in Buswell's Hotel, Dublin. The entire Roche family, Commandant Patrick Walshe, Joe Higgins, TD, and Sr Helen Prejean (author of the book and subject of the movie, *Dead Man Walking*) attended it.

Sr Prejean, who for many years has fought for the rights of inmates on death row, told the press conference that the case of Dónal de Róiste 'reeked of injustice'. She commented:

> For Dónal de Róiste to be retired by the president of his country, he must have done something terribly wrong. What was it? At the very least a person should be told what the charges are and given the right of fair and lawful redress. Clearly this was not done. Why? Basic justice and human rights demand a response in this case.

Speaking directly to De Róiste, one of America's most famous Catholic nuns stated:

> I think you have been given a kind of death sentence because your name has become associated with impropriety, wrongdoing, a scoundrel, and you can kill a person by killing his name. That's another kind of death.

The press conference began at 12 noon and had concluded by one o'clock. We emerged to learn that the Minister for Defence, Michael Smith, had ordered an internal investigation into the De Róiste case and that he had asked the Judge Advocate General, Oonah McCrann SC, to review former Lt Dónal Roche's files. It was announced that the Minister had asked the Chief of Staff, Lt General Colm Mangan, to hand over all files relating to De Róiste to Ms McCrann, who was to report back within a few weeks. A Department of Defence spokesperson was quoted in the *Irish Examiner* as saying, 'After that, we will have to see where we go from there.'

Hindsight is wiser than the wise and it is now clear what should have happened. De Róiste's campaign and legal team should have announced that they would engage cautiously with the process offered by the Minister but that the public should be aware that this was essentially an internal military investigation. Such a statement would have created the moral platform onto which to climb in the event of the JAG failing to deliver the expected positive outcome – a platform from which a simple statement could have been issued saying something to the effect that we had already warned the public of this possibility, but that now we required a process that was wholly independent, transparent and interested only in establishing the full and unbiased facts about this case.

De Róiste's legal team engaged with the process in all good faith. However, at an early stage it became clear, as we will see in the next chapter, that the Department of Defence was not prepared to engage on a level playing field. While the result the Department achieved from the JAG's report and attendant publicity gave it, temporarily, the high moral ground, in the long term the entire process has damaged the office of the JAG.

OTHER THEORIES

Another theory worthy of exploration surfaced in the wake of my *Irish Times* article, concerning the possible motivation for Lt Dónal Roche's 'retirement' from the army in 1969. At the beginning of September and October 2002, two articles in *Foinse*, the Irish-language newspaper, developed the theory.

The first, by Seán Tadhg Ó Gairbhí, stated that the Minister for Justice at the time of De Róiste's expulsion, Micheál Ó Moráin, was the uncle of Padraig Dwyer, the JAG's infamous and mysterious Mr X. Ó Gairbhí stated that the Minister for Justice was party to the dismissal of Dónal de Róiste in 1969. This is not entirely correct. Ó Moráin, TD for West Mayo, was absent from the cabinet meeting where the decision was taken on 20 June 1969. This was likely due to distance and the fact that he had not been re-elected to his constituency until the fourth count in the general election, the previous night.

Ó Gairbhí then discusses an interesting perspective concerning the mysterious group, Saor Éire, to which Padraig Dwyer was allegedly linked. He raised the possibility that Saor Éire, the group responsible for the murder of Garda Fallon in 1970, may, in fact, have been a pseudo group, with its origins linked to an unnamed 'senior Civil Servant of the Department of Justice'. The *Foinse* article suggested that the aim of Saor Éire was 'to discredit the IRA and collect information about those who set it up.'

The article further states:

> It is also believed that use was made of Padraig Dwyer in quite a number of other activities and events apart from the De Róiste case.

How Dwyer might have been used in the De Róiste case is not explained. However, the article correctly states that the state was not prepared to 'make available all the documentation pertaining to the [De Róiste] case.' The article concludes:

> The most common opinion now is that an injustice was done to him because he was not prepared to tell lies on behalf of a senior officer who was drunk when he injured a female driver.

Dónall Ó Maolfabhail followed up on this article a month later with one that coincided with the release of the JAG's report but it is clear from the later article that Ó Maolfabhail was of the opinion that the Minister for Defence was 'expected to exonerate De Róiste soon'. However, the journalist was not hopeful that the whole truth would be told.

The journalist states that while recognising that there was a basis for my theory about the O'Kelly car crash, he believed the case to be far more complex. Echoing the *Foinse* article of the previous month, he stated:

> It is probable that the De Róiste case is tied up with a mysterious organisation called Saor Éire and the relationship that certain Ministers in the Fianna Fáil government had with that organisation at the time.

In the October article, Ó Maolfabhail refers to discussions he had with two officers who were in the army at the time of the O'Kelly car crash but who dismissed the theory that this may have been the catalyst for

De Róiste's expulsion:

> As one of [the officers] said to me, 'Commandant Seán T
> O'Kelly was no favourite son. He wasn't in a position to
> be promoted and it was not likely that the big wigs would
> go out of their way to protect him if they thought he was
> guilty.' I agree with this opinion.

Ó Maolfabhail then outlines why he agrees with the opinion. He writes
that between February 1967 and January 1970, Saor Éire robbed over
a dozen post offices and banks but that hardly anyone was caught. The
article continues:

> On the 3rd of October 1968 however the Guards arrested
> two men, Seán Doyle and Tom O'Neill. When the two
> came before the courts on 21st January 1970, the state
> entered a *nolle prosequi*. It was understood that the two
> men would be freed and the state would be able to re-
> arrest and re-charge them. But for some reason they were
> not re-arrested.
>   On April 3rd 1970 Saor Éire robbed the Royal Bank
> at Arran Quay in Dublin. Garda Fallon was killed in this
> operation. The Gardai were angry, and rightly so. One of
> the other robbers, Joe Dillon, would have been in prison
> if it weren't for a mistake in a Ministerial Order on his
> transfer from Mountjoy Prison to Portlaoise.

Ó Maolfabhail states that around the time of the Garda Fallon murder,
Hibernia magazine published an article stating that there was a need
for an independent inquiry into the activities of Saor Éire and the
absence of government action against them. He states that within a few
weeks of *Hibernia*'s call for an inquiry, the Minister for Justice, Micheál
Ó Moráin, had resigned, allegedly for health reasons. Ó Maolfabhail
continues:

> There is no doubt that the Fianna Fáil government
> did little to stop Saor Éire between 1967 and 1970.
> Why was this? No one knows. There is a theory that

Neil Blaney was then using the organisation to run guns from America for the northern people. There is another opinion that Saor Éire was being used by certain ministers to give Sinn Féin a bad name or to spy on that party.

According to Ó Maolfabhail,

We now know that [Padraig] Dwyer [who was mentioned in De Róiste and Walshe's interrogation] was a nephew of the Minister for Justice, Ó Moráin. After the Arms Trial Dwyer was released suddenly from prison and a special guard placed on his home. If Dwyer was working for the government at the time perhaps there is a chance that Roche was fired because certain authorities feared that, because he was a Lieutenant, he might discover this fact and more.

He concludes his article:

Although I believe there is a good chance Dónal de Róiste will clear his name, I have little hope that we will ever find out why he was retired from the army. Especially if what happened to him had anything to do with that mysterious organisation known as Saor Éire.

An RTÉ journalist who was interested in a possible documentary on Dónal de Róiste put a version of this theory to me in mid-September 2005. He prefaced his remarks by stating outright that he was not interested in the car-crash theory.

My response to the RTÉ journalist is precisely my response to the theories advanced by both *Foinse* articles summarised above. First of all, Padraig Dwyer was not the nephew of the former Minister for Justice, Micheál Ó Moráin. Dwyer's widow, Margaret, has verified this fact.

To suggest that Lt Dónal Roche was expelled from the army because there was a danger he might discover the fact that Padraig Dwyer was a double agent, working for the state, suggests that Roche must have had far more than a superficial involvement with Dwyer. It is also based on the assumption that Padraig Dwyer was a government agent who had infiltrated Saor Éire, a fact of which there is no proof.

It is clear from assessing the 'secret' files released in 2002 that G2, the Irish army's Intelligence Section, is struggling to create even the most tenuous link between Roche and Dwyer, let alone Dwyer's other associates. In the end, only three pieces of evidence are recorded: (a) Roche acknowledged that he knew Dwyer as a casual acquaintance in O'Donoghue's Pub, (b) Roche had, with a friend, Brendan Doherty, taken a lift from Dwyer and a girlfriend to Galway, and (c) Roche had encountered Dwyer at a publicly advertised auction of surplus army vehicles and motor cycles in Clancy Barracks, in April 1969, where he was on duty.

Dwyer's widow, Margaret, told me that – contrary to paragraph 7 of the alleged first interview with Lt Roche (Appendix A, Document 3) – she has no recollection of ever having met Dónal de Róiste. Nor has De Róiste's girlfriend from the time – contrary to paragraph 6 of the alleged second interview with Lt Roche (Appendix A, Document 4) – any recollection of ever having met Padraig Dwyer.

Both retired Commandant Patrick Walshe and retired Lt Col. Gerry Swan state that if Lt Roche had had anything other than a superficial connection with Dwyer, or Saor Éire, they would have known – and would have reported him. Similarly, a Special Branch officer who had been tasked with monitoring the movements of Dwyer in later years and who was intimately familiar with the details of Dwyer's Special Branch file has also informed me that there is no mention of De Róiste in Dwyer's file.

The truth of the matter is that Lt Roche was targeted and was placed on a fast-track removal from the army. The definitive reason has yet to be established and may never be established. However, I am increasingly of the opinion that his alleged involvement with Padraig Dwyer, and Dwyer's alleged involvement in Saor Éire, is a distraction.

Until such time as the O'Kelly car crash is independently and exhaustively investigated, my plausible hypothesis, as outlined above, cannot and should not be discounted.

STATE-SPONSORED SPIN

The broad mass of a nation ... will more easily fall victim to a big lie than to a small one

Adolf Hitler, *Mein Kampf*

At 3 p.m. on Wednesday, 25 September 2002, Irish actor, Gabriel Byrne, at the Irish Arts Center, Manhattan, officially launched the Dónal de Róiste Truth Campaign in the United States of America. De Róiste, his old army friend, Commandant Patrick Walshe, his sisters, Len and Adi, his son, Dara, and I attended the launch.

Gabriel Byrne described the Irish government's treatment of De Róiste as 'sordid and obscene'. He likened De Róiste's experience to the fictional works of Franz Kafka and Harold Pinter and accused successive Irish governments of condemning 'an innocent man to a life of torture.' He said:

> The truth will out. Enough people know to spread the word and that is how campaigns grow. This could have happened to any person in our country and it is only by standing up against it we can prevent it from happening again.

The campaign launch was well attended by the media and was covered by all Irish-American newspapers, as well as a number of national papers in Ireland.

I had met the Irish Consul General, Eugene Hutchinson, over lunch on 16 September, to discuss various matters related to the screening of the film, *Bloody Sunday*, which had been given the honour of opening the New York film festival on 2 October. During that meeting, I discussed with him the forthcoming launch of the Dónal de

Róiste Campaign and invited him to come along himself or to send a representative to monitor it. My discussions with Mr Hutchinson were deliberate, as I wanted to ensure that the Irish government was fully informed of ongoing developments in the De Róiste campaign.

On 2 October, less than five hours before the opening of *Bloody Sunday* at New York's Lincoln Center, my mobile phone rang. The time was 12.10 p.m. and it was a call from Adi Roche. I could hear that she was in shock. She informed me that she had just received a call from Conor Tiernan, a producer with *TV3 News*. Adi said that he had briefly outlined the content of a news report TV3 was running as the lead story in its 5.30 p.m. broadcast, about the release of the JAG's report. It was clear, she said, that the report was going to be damaging to Dónal's case. Adi had not seen the report and had not been contacted by either Dónal or his solicitor, so it was all coming out of the blue. I advised her to watch the report and call me back immediately, so that I might have an idea of what it contained.

At 12.45 p.m., I spoke with Adi again. I knew instinctively from the detail she told me was contained in the report, particularly the recreation of a bar scene and a scene involving a car, that TV3 was working on a tip-off. I had worked with TV3's current affairs flagship, *20/20*, a year or two before and I knew the company's limitations. There was simply no way a detailed news report of this nature could have been put together in a couple of hours, based on a press release.

Having spoken with Adi, I tried unsuccessfully to reach Dónal de Róiste and his solicitor, Eamonn Carroll. I was told that Carroll had not yet received a copy of the report as it had arrived by post only that day. I did speak with solicitor Joe Noonan, however, who had quickly familiarised himself with the contents of the report and commented, 'It reads like a Widgery.'

It wasn't until the following day that I managed to speak with Carroll. It was clear that we had been wrong-footed. Unquestionably, serious damage had been inflicted and the Department had managed to steal the high moral ground by insisting that, despite his protestations to the contrary, De Róiste knew full well the reasons for his removal from the Officer Corps. Furthermore, the matter of the O'Kelly car crash had been dismissed on the basis of no evidence in the files to substantiate any connection with Lt Roche's army troubles.

We wondered about the timing. Was the release date of 2 October

2002 chosen because the Department knew that De Róiste's own 'media manager', with the capability of mounting a strong and robust response to the media blitz, would be swamped that day with the opening of *Bloody Sunday* on the other side of the Atlantic and, therefore, out of touch and unable to respond?

In the circumstances, De Róiste's solicitor and I felt that the best approach was to maintain our silence until we all had time to review the report thoroughly and until he had taken possession of De Róiste's army files which, the Department of Defence had announced, would now be released to him. Analysis of those documents was certainly going to be revealing.

On 4 October, at a gala dinner organised by the Irish Arts Center to honour the contribution of Gabriel Byrne to theatre, cinema and the cultural life of Irish America, one of the first people I met was the Consul General, Eugene Hutchinson, who raised the issue of the JAG's report. He mentioned her comment about my 'unsolicited correspondence'. Not having had access to the report, I had no idea what he was talking about. I realised, however, that a copy of the report had been faxed to the office of the Consul General in New York, and quite possibly to the Embassy in Washington, and it indicated that Irish officials, particularly in the Department of Defence, were carefully monitoring back in Dublin what we were doing in the US.

There was no doubt the De Róiste campaign was wounded and everyone associated with it was feeling downbeat. However, the first major boost towards recovery came that evening from Gabriel Byrne's ex-wife, Ellen Barkin. Speaking about the various campaigns for human rights that Gabriel Byrne has supported over the years – including the fact that he was the catalyst for the movie, *In the Name of the Father*, about the plight of the Guildford Four – she mentioned his support for the ongoing campaign of the Irish officer, Dónal de Róiste.

I couldn't help casting a look towards the Consul General. The knockout punch thrown by the state against De Róiste might have temporarily knocked him down, but it certainly hadn't knocked him out. The JAG's report would not be the last word and De Róiste's campaigners and supporters were not about to desert him. I was hoping that that message would be relayed back to Dublin, first thing on Monday morning.

I returned to Dublin on 6 October, anxious to discover the extent of the fall-out. I was particularly interested in discovering how the JAG had dealt with the matter of my *Irish Times* article of 29 June, which was the catalyst for her involvement. I had been informed that the family of Commandant O'Kelly was publicly calling upon me to withdraw the car-crash hypothesis. One report in the *Irish Independent* of 3 October 2002 stated:

> Author Don Mullan was urged last night to withdraw his claims that Dónal de Róiste had been forced out of the defence forces because of a car crash....
>
> Last July Mr de Róiste said he had not linked the crash with what he called his nefarious framing until questions were asked by Mr Mullan.
>
> It was suggested that Comdt O'Kelly had been drinking and that the incident was directly linked to the decision to force Mr de Róiste to retire. However, Judge Advocate General Oonah McCrann found that there was no evidence backing up the suggestion of a link between the two incidents.

This was not entirely accurate. My *Irish Times* article put forward what I described as a 'plausible hypothesis', given the close proximity between a Plenary Summons issued on Commandant O'Kelly (9 April 1969) and De Róiste's sudden and unexpected difficulties in the army (25 April 1969).

A copy of the JAG's report had been faxed to me by the Department of Defence on the afternoon of 2 October and I read it carefully upon my return from the US.

Under the heading 'Fact', the JAG made a very important point in favour of De Róiste:

> There is nothing in the documentation ... to suggest that Ex-Lieutenant Dónal Roche had come to the attention of his superiors for anything that might adversely affect his military career prior to April 1969....

Under the same heading she wrote regarding the car accident:

> ... the medical records do disclose that he was involved in
> a road traffic accident on 17ᵗʰ November 1967.... This is
> significant only because of speculation which has arisen
> in the media recently to suggest that the circumstances
> surrounding this road traffic accident were in some way
> related to the decision to retire Ex-Lieutenant Dónal
> Roche. No reference is made to the road traffic accident
> in any document other than the medical records and
> there is nothing in any of the documentation received
> which suggests any connection between the two events.

To paraphrase Mandy Rice Davies, friend of Christine Keeler in the
Profumo affair, 1965, 'There wouldn't be, would there?'

I then heard RTÉ presenter Vincent Browne, on the basis of
McCrann's statement, state at the conclusion to his programme, on 7
October:

> ... the suggestion that the reason for his dismissal
> from the army was that he was a witness to an accident
> involving Commandant O'Kelly ... is now, I would have
> thought, thoroughly debunked.

Browne had invited both Dónal de Róiste and me onto his daytime
programme, *Today with Vincent Browne*, in the summer, shortly after the
publication of my article in *The Irish Times* on 29 June. He questioned
the logic of my hypothesis and suggested that it would have made more
sense to keep De Róiste in the army than to have got rid of him. One of
his guests, however, during that programme, saw the alternative logic.
Roche had refused to lie internally and now, with a civil case pending,
if Roche were called as a material witness to the High Court, O'Kelly
would have lost control. One way to contain any possible damage he
might do was to destroy his commission and force him out under a
cloud of suspicion. What weight would the evidence of a young officer,
retired by the President on the recommendation of the government,
carry in such circumstances? Furthermore, he had been forced out of
the army under a cloud of suspicion with several unspecified innuendos
and rumours turning him into an untouchable.

Browne had been irreverently criticised following the interview by *Sunday Times* radio critic Gerry McCarthy in his column, 'Radio Waves'. On 14 July 2002, McCarthy wrote:

> For Browne, a practising barrister, this was a conspiracy theory too far. Surely, he argued, a man improperly fired from his job would have even more reason to give evidence?
>
> This overlooks the psychology of interrogation, and a man reduced to the status of non-person by presidential decree. Browne's argument comes from an abstract world of inhuman perseverance. At times, Browne himself seems to come from such a world: a place where people live to better standards, and with impossible energy levels.

Far from debunking my hypothesis, the JAG had simply ignored it. Did she truly expect to find a paper trail that might connect the two? Surely the proximity between the two deserved probing. Did, for example, the military authorities in 1967 follow proper procedures in taking statements from the three officers involved in the accident, as required by defence force regulations? If not, was this an oversight or did it suggest something more sinister? Was there a possibility that an innocent civilian woman may not have received justice because O'Kelly may have conspired with other officers to frustrate her rights? What of the Garda investigation into the accident? Was it not strange that, despite O'Kelly's having had three passengers, not one of those primary witnesses was asked by the civil authorities for a statement?

On 30 July 2002, I had sent the JAG a copy of my *Irish Times* article, together with all of the supporting evidence I had received from the young woman. On 13 September 2002, I received an acknowledgement, dated 4 September, in which she stated:

> I confirm that all relevant documentation will be included in my review of the circumstances of the retirement of Ex-Lieutenant Dónal de Róiste in accordance with the Terms of Reference governing the review.

Apparently, the JAG had decided at a very early stage that the documentation I had sent to her was irrelevant. She openly admitted that the documentation did not form part of her review. In her report, she states:

> Unsolicited written representations were received from Don Mullan ... including documentation relating to a road traffic accident in which Ex-Lieutenant Dónal Roche was involved on 17th November 1967. The said documentation does not form part of this review although the road traffic accident is referred to in the body of this report.

TV3 NEWS

The JAG's report was the lead story on *TV3 News* on the day of its publication. The news report opened with the words:

> Donal de Róiste has spent the past 35 years trying to clear his name. His sister, Adi Roche, and others have supported his claim that he was an innocent victim of a terrible injustice. But a report by the Judge Advocate General, Oonah McCrann, seen by TV3 today, tells a very different story.

In addition to photographs and archival footage, the news report also contained reconstructions of a car driving towards a bend and of a pub scene.

Having viewed the detailed news report, I found my suspicions of a possible advance tip-off from the Department growing.

In the report, there were several statements damaging to De Róiste's campaign and also statements that were potentially damaging to my reputation as a journalist. Furthermore, De Róiste had not seen the report, based on a review of classified files that were deliberately withheld from him. If reporter Conor Tiernan had received an advance briefing, as I suspected, he had not been informed that the Minister for Defence had deliberately denied De Róiste access to his files, until after the JAG had completed her report and the media had reported her 'findings'.

It is worth highlighting some of the statements the *TV3 News* coverage carried.

> ... *a report by the Judge Advocate General reveals that [Lt Roche] did know that he was being accused of being a serious security risk.*

It is clear that TV3 had not been informed during the advance briefing that a month before Lt Roche's retirement, his solicitor had written to the Chief of Staff asking 'what charges, if any' were being preferred against his client. Lt Roche was refused the right to face his anonymous accusers and their unspecified and uncontested allegations.

> *[De Róiste's] sister Adi Roche and others have supported his claim that he was an innocent victim of a terrible injustice. But a report by the Judge Advocate General, Oonah McCrann, seen by TV3 today, tells a very different story.*

This statement is quite appalling. The logic is simple: that De Róiste was, in fact, not an innocent victim – and knew it all along.

> *The report states categorically that there was no connection between the two events [the O'Kelly car crash and Lt Roche's retirement from the army].*

The report does not state categorically that there was no connection between the two events. All that the JAG said is the following:

> No reference is made to the road traffic accident in any document other than the medical records and there is nothing in any of the documentation received which suggests any connection between the two events.

Amongst the documentation I had sent to Ms McCrann was an *Irish Times* editorial of 2 July 2002, which stated: 'It can only be in the interests of justice – and of the state's reputation – that any such imputation be cleared up...' McCrann did nothing to clear up any such imputation.

The RTÉ *Six-One News* coverage was much more subdued. In fact, coverage of the De Róiste story did not make the headlines and the story was not covered until the second segment of the broadcast. Comparing how rival broadcasters had prioritised the De Róiste story convinced me that TV3 must have been offered an exclusive in exchange for the quid pro quo of the top headline. The story had national importance, but it was not, on the day, the top story. A predicted downturn in the Irish economy and the passing of a war resolution in the US were actually of far greater significance, as evidenced by the RTÉ coverage.

The Vincent Browne Show
On 7 October 2002, Vincent Browne discussed the JAG's report on his evening radio programme. The son of the late Commandant Sean T. O'Kelly and the *Irish Independent*'s security correspondent, Tom Brady, joined him. Browne opened the discussion as follows:

> We are discussing the circumstances that seemed to surround [Dónal de Róiste's] dismissal from the army in 1969 and the suggestion ... that the reason he was dismissed from the army was because he had been witness to a car accident that occurred involving a Commandant O'Kelly ... that he was dismissed because it was feared that he would give truthful evidence about the circumstances of that car accident to the detriment of Commandant O'Kelly.... Since then a ... report which was conducted by the Judge Advocate General, Oonah McCrann, has recently been published and it comes to a radically different conclusion. That it has absolutely nothing to do with that car accident.... Nonetheless, the family of Commandant O'Kelly, who is ... deceased, were very upset by the insinuations that were made in the course of our programme [in July 2002] and in the course of other programmes about their father. We have on the line David O'Kelly who is son of Commandant O'Kelly.
>
> David, I suppose you feel vindicated by the Judge Advocate General's report?

David O'Kelly responded:

> Certainly, Vincent…. This whole episode has caused a
> great deal of distress to my mother and to our family. It
> came as an absolute complete shock and the first we knew
> of this was when Don Mullan wrote a two-page article,
> which appeared in *The Irish Times* in July … Mr Mullan
> did not contact us to look for comment … and this two-
> page article… said some horrendous things about my
> father and implied that he framed Mr de Róiste … I
> think it is absolutely outrageous and far-fetched….
>
> They all suffered injuries in the car accident but the
> car accident is totally irrelevant, Vincent, to this and it
> now seems clear from the Judge Advocate's Report that
> Mr de Róiste knew all the time why he was sacked from
> the army and yet they … continued to defame and to
> vilify my father and Mr Mullan obviously realised that
> you can't legally defame the dead.

Vincent Browne, never afraid to ask the hard questions, responded to
David Kelly's comments by saying:

> I don't think that's fair now David because certainly we
> saw from the Judge Advocate General's report that [De
> Róiste] was asked about certain contacts he had made
> with a member of, I think, Saor Éire, a splinter IRA
> group. He met this guy in O'Donoghue's public house
> a few times and he attended a car auction at a military
> barracks along with this fellow, but I am not sure if he
> was fully aware that the reason he was dismissed from
> the army was because of those contacts, although he was
> questioned about it.

The reader will recall that Lt Dónal Roche was actually on duty at the
auction, and that Dwyer attended it along with hundreds of members
of the public.

O'Kelly insisted that 'the documentation would indicate otherwise.
The Deputy Judge Advocate General took him through and explained

to him each aspect of the investigation; I am actually reading from the Report here.'

Browne interjected:

> Except that he has no recollection of that … which is fair enough. I don't think that's at all clear from the Report … that he knew all along … the reasons for his dismissal.

The presenter then introduced Tom Brady, the *Irish Independent*'s security correspondent. Browne raised the crucial questions of fair procedures:

> … That he wasn't formally told what the charges against him [were] and he wasn't formally asked to reply. That he wasn't formally told that he could have legal representation… [and] in the absence of that [formality], you could argue that there was a denial of fair procedures.

Brady responded:

> Well, the procedures then were a little different … but she does conclude that he was aware at all times what was going on…. The Deputy Judge Advocate General of the time brought him through everything because looking at Dónal de Róiste's initial reaction to what was being put up to him, the Deputy Judge Advocate General was a bit concerned that he mightn't be aware of the seriousness of the charges being levelled at him so he brought him through them from start to finish.

Brady was certainly correct about the procedures in 1969 being different from what they would be today. Because of the 1985 amendment to the 1954 Defence Act, the reality is that the military authorities could not do to a serving officer today, what they did to Lt Roche then.

Browne continued:

He [the Deputy Judge Advocate General] apparently didn't say to him, 'Look you may be fired from the army as a consequence of this.'

Brady replied by stating that Lt Roche had been brought up from Athlone, that he got a grilling and, 'according to the notes that Oonah McCrann looked at… he admitted… that he knew this man who was referred to throughout this Report as Mr X.' Brady then stated: 'He was a well-known member of Saor Éire which is a splinter group of the IRA…'

There then followed an interesting exchange:

> *Browne*: Do you know who that person was?
> *Brady*: I do, yes.
> *Browne*: Who was it?
> *Brady*: I don't know whether…
> *Browne*: Has he been convicted of offences since then?
> *Brady*: Yes at the time Dónal de Róiste admitted (a) that he knew he was a criminal (b) that he knew he had served a jail sentence in England, and (c) that he knew he had been involved in a shooting incident with gardaí some months earlier and, as far as I know, he was convicted of offences connected with firing shots at gardaí.
> *Browne*: What's his name?
> *Brady*: I don't know whether we should name him or not, Vincent.
> *Browne*: Obviously if he was convicted of offences, it's all right.
> *Brady*: I think he is dead now.
> *Browne*: All right. But nonetheless there seems to have been a denial of correct procedures, and in addition, Dónal de Róiste's solicitor wrote to the army authorities and asked what specifically were the charges against Dónal de Róiste and never got a reply.
> *Brady*: There was an exchange of correspondence.

Vincent Browne correctly pointed out that there had been no reply to De Róiste's solicitor's letter asking what were the charges or case against his client. In response, Tom Brady shifted gear but raised a crucial matter regarding decisions and procedures adopted in the McCrann Inquiry. He stated:

> It had been decided, prior to the decision to have this Inquiry, to furnish all the documentation to Mr de Róiste. But then, when it was decided to bring in Oonah McCrann … the Minister for Defence decided that everything should be put on hold until she issued her report.

This point is crucial and one of the primary reasons why the High Court quashed Ms McCrann's review in 2005, following a Judicial Review.

Browne was not going to let go of the matter of the solicitor's letter back in 1969. He replied:

> All right, but the fact of the matter was that at the time when Dónal de Róiste's solicitor wrote to the army authorities asking what were the charges against him, they didn't bother replying to the solicitor.

Again, Brady failed to respond to the issue of fair procedures, instead stating, to the consternation of the De Róiste family:

> Well it is clear that, at least, if he didn't know what the charges were against him, his mother did. Because there is a report of a letter written by his mother in which she said he had been found 'not guilty' of the charges i.e. collaborating with the IRA.

It is worth considering the basis upon which Mrs de Róiste made this statement in her letter (Appendix A, Document 19). She was writing with a mother's heart. She was an intelligent woman but was not trained in legal exactitudes. Had she realised that her words would be used over thirty years later to support the injustice done to her eldest child, she would, no doubt, have chosen them differently. She was, in fact, incorrect in what she stated in her letter. Her son had not been charged with anything. But McCrann made no reference to this.

The failure to prefer charges was Lt Roche's biggest problem. The reference to 'collaborating with the IRA' was simply one of the rumours circulating at the time, and one that Mrs de Róiste had heard from her brother, Pat Murphy, in the Department of Defence. Ms McCrann also made no reference to the fact that there are two letters on file from Mrs de Róiste, both dated 21 November 1969. One letter is addressed to the Minister for Defence, from which she quoted, and the other is addressed to the Commanding Officer, Western Command. She was appealing for a character reference, given that her son 'had no previous indications from those in command that he was being found unsuitable.' She asked that her son 'be furnished with a proper reference, or else with the reasons why not.' Both letters appear to have been ignored.

Browne, a trained barrister, was not yet ready to relinquish what his legal instincts sensed was unfair. He quoted from the JAG's report:

> 'It is clear that a letter was sent by ex Lieutenant Dónal de Róiste's solicitor dated 30th May 1969 to the Chief of Staff Army Headquarters.' There they 'sought clarification of what charge, if any, was being preferred against Ex-Lieutenant Dónal Róiste. It is not clear when this letter was received and while a draft reply was prepared to the letter it would appear from the files that the draft was never finalised and the letter was not replied to.'

Browne concluded, 'That is a pretty serious breach of fair proceedings I would have thought.'

A series of rapid interjections then followed between all three participants in the discussion:

> *Brady*: I don't have the report in front of me – is there not something in the report further down where there was some correspondence and where the solicitors were asked to…
> *O'Kelly*: There was a draft reply, Tom.
> Brady: Is that what it was?
> *O'Kelly*: And she said it's unsure whether that was sent or

not, and that is the one…

Browne: No! No! She didn't say she was unsure it was sent. You see, she said it wasn't sent. She said the letter was not replied to. The draft reply was never finalised and the letter, the solicitor's letter, was not replied to. So, I would have thought that's a pretty serious denial of fair procedures and—

Brady: It's very clear from the documentation that comes out in the Report that he knew exactly why he had been called in, that he had been seen in the company of members of the IRA.

Browne: All right but I would have thought—

Brady: He acknowledged that … he had been with this man, a couple of meetings in a Dublin pub and had then gone away for a weekend break with him and his girlfriend and had then brought them to an auction of army vehicles at Clancy Barracks which at the time housed hundreds of thousands of rounds of ammunition and—

Browne: Yes, but it is also the case that he was quite open with fellow army officers that he had this contact with this guy so it wasn't something that he was attempting to conceal.

Brady: Yes, it is also clear that he was advised by several of his colleagues to discontinue the relationship.

Browne: All right but if there was something sinister about it, you would imagine he wouldn't have been telling other army officers about it.

Brady: It is not clear what his motive was. You would have to assume that he was a very naïve individual, but it hardly was suitable company for an army officer to keep – surely he was aware of that.

Browne: I don't know.

Brady: Different times, Vincent. That was 1969.

Browne: It was different times but it would have seemed to me that he was denied fair procedures. But also that the suggestion that the reason for his dismissal from the army was [because] he was a witness to an accident involving Commandant O'Kelly ... that is now, I would have thought, thoroughly debunked.

Brady: Totally ridiculous suggestion in the first place. To suggest that a Commandant could persuade the general staff – five generals – to sack somebody is ridiculous.... What also is conveniently ignored is that there was another young officer in the car at the time and it would have needed him to give a particular account, as well as Dónal de Róiste. That man, it is said, also refused to co-operate in any plan to give a false account. In fact, the man has been promoted several times since.

Brady referred to 'different times'. This is certainly true of the command structure in the army in 1969. In fact, there was only one general back then – the Chief of Staff. Furthermore, the scandals that have emerged regarding Garda corruption in Donegal and the abuse of children in church-and state-run institutions, together with the cover-up engaged in by people in authority, were also considered 'ridiculous' when first aired. Whoever 'conveniently ignored' the fact that another young officer was involved in the car crash most certainly was not this journalist. In my *Irish Times* article, published on 29 June 2002, I quote the young officer, now Col. Michael Cleary, and report that he declined to meet me for an interview.

David O'Kelly was, understandably, defending the honour of his deceased father. I accept that my 'plausible hypothesis', connecting the issuing of a plenary summons against his father with De Róiste's sudden difficulties in the army, caused distress and upset. However, the JAG did not investigate the matter as part of her Inquiry, and I deal with this matter in the following chapter.

The most important aspect of the entire radio discussion was Browne's zoning in on the issue of the denial of fair procedures. That is the crux of the Dónal de Róiste case from start to finish. If De Róiste was guilty of unacceptable associations with Mr X, Padraig Dwyer, an alleged member of Saor Éire, why was he not dismissed rather than being retired 'in the interests of the service'? The answer is simple. Before the army could have dismissed Lt Dónal Roche, irrespective of what reasons they may have had, Roche would have had available to him a whole series of protections under the 1954 Defence Act.

My suspicions that TV3 had been given an advance briefing of the JAG's report and conclusions were confirmed on 14 May 2003. TV3 journalist Laura Ryan, at my home to interview me about the Dublin and Monaghan Bombings, confirmed that Conor Tiernan had been briefed a day or two in advance of the publication of the report. This, of course, was highly significant information. Not only did it confirm my suspicions, but it again raised the whole issue of the one thing Dónal de Róiste has been denied from his first interrogation on 25 April 1969 until today – fair procedures.

When I contacted Tiernan, he told me that a source had called him the day before, outlining the gist of the story and saying that the JAG's report would be made available the following day. He said that the report was faxed to him at around 2.30 p.m. on 2 October 2002.

While I have no idea who Tiernan's 'source' was, I can guess that the contact came from the Department for Defence and that the story was offered to TV3 as an advance exclusive in return for the assurance that the story would be given top priority. Effectively, the opening remarks of the TV3 report suggested that De Róiste, based on a reading of the JAG's report, was by no means innocent. Mr Tiernan said that his story reflected only what was in the JAG's report. He pointed out that TV3 had also covered the story from De Róiste's side in the past.

It would have been helpful if the coverage had established that the JAG's evaluation was not an independent report. It was, in effect, a review of military files carried out by a person approved by the Minister for Defence and acting on Terms of Reference prepared by the same minister and reporting to the same minister. The office of the Judge Advocate General is, in fact, legally embedded in the military's legal machinery in that the JAG is the final appeal authority in the case of military courts martial. Her investigation in fact was that of 'a judge in her own cause'. Her full title is 'Judge Advocate General of the Defence Forces'. Her report has since been robustly criticised by the respected London-based human rights organisation, British Irish Rights Watch, and quashed by Mr Justice Quirke in a High Court Judgment in July 2005.

THE JAG'S REPORT
It took me several days after my return from the United States to begin to absorb the report. What particularly angered me was a submission

made by the Deputy Chief of Staff, Major General S. Brennan, on 30 July 2002, to the JAG, in which he stated:

> The suggestion that [Lt Roche's] retirement may have been connected to a civilian car accident is entirely without foundation.

He went on to refer to 'false allegations made in the media' in this regard. I did not make 'false allegations'. I reported disturbing and documented facts vis-à-vis the car accident. Contrary to assertions made by the Deputy Chief of Staff, my 'plausible hypothesis' still remains plausible. All that the JAG stated was:

> No reference is made to the road traffic accident in any document other than the medical records and there is nothing in any of the documentation received which suggests any connection between the two events.

It is hardly likely that if, as I still suspect (perhaps more strongly now than in 2002), O'Kelly's drunken collision with a young woman driving in Tipperary in November 1967 was a possible cause of Lt Roche's difficulties, a paper trail would be left behind.

It is significant, I believe, that the JAG chose not to question either Lt Roche or Lt (now Col.) Cleary about the allegation made by Roche, and supported by his family and retired Commandant Patrick Walshe, that he had vocally accused O'Kelly of causing the 'accident' because he was under the influence of alcohol. Furthermore, the young woman, who spent almost a year in hospital recovering from injuries sustained in the collision, and her family, believed that alcohol was involved and had also heard stories about officers drinking and arguing in a Templemore hotel, prior to the accident. These suspicions were reported in the *Irish Times* article and, therefore, merited attention. The fact that the JAG chose to ignore a very detailed and compelling article is, I believe, significant.

On 5 September 2002, almost a month before the JAG's report was publicised and its findings made known to Dónal de Róiste and his solicitors, Col. P.N. Ryan, Director Personnel Section, wrote to

O'Donovan Solicitors, acting on behalf of the O'Kelly family. He stated:

> I wish to inform you that your correspondence has been forwarded to the Judge Advocate General and that no records exist that would substantiate the allegations contained in the article in the *Irish Times* of the 29 June 2002 in relation to the late Comdt. S.T. O'Kelly.

I was disappointed when De Róiste's legal team omitted to establish that McCrann had not dealt with the matters raised in my *Irish Times* article. Perhaps unfairly, I felt that the apparent silence from the legal team contributed to a Department of Defence strategy aimed at making my hypothesis appear implausible, when, in reality, it was simply ignored. I was, therefore, deeply grateful to receive a copy of a letter sent to the Taoiseach by Jane Winter, Director of the London-based human rights group, British Irish Rights Watch, in which she wrote:

> She [the JAG] completely ignores important and compelling representations made by the respected researcher and author Don Mullan, which potentially shed considerable light on events…

On the Tuesday following my article, 2 July 2002, the day the Minister for Defence, Michael Smith TD, announced the JAG initiative, *The Irish Times* editorial stated:

> … In this newspaper on Saturday, the respected journalist, Don Mullan, reported details of an incident in 1967 which Mr de Róiste believes can account for his discharge….
>
> That Mr de Róiste acted with exemplary probity in regard to the drunken-driving incident is clear. If this and this alone led to his dismissal, Mr de Róiste has clearly been the victim of a monstrous injustice. If his claim is correct, army officers at successive levels, civil servants and members of the government either colluded or were

remiss in the process that led to his discharge from the army.

It can only be in the interests of justice – and of the state's reputation – that any such imputation be cleared up. Mr de Róiste asks that the files on his case be made available in order that he may answer whatever charges were laid against him. That is reasonable and it is consonant with principles of natural justice....

It is interesting to note that *The Irish Times* recognised the need for De Róiste to have his files in order that he might answer the charges. In hindsight, De Róiste's campaign should probably have engaged in a very vocal campaign to alert the public to the unfairness of the process into which Dónal and his legal team had been drawn – a process in which he would get access to the files only after the JAG had submitted her report to the Minister for Defence and her conclusions had been broadcast and spun to the nation.

Among those items released following the publication of the JAG's report was Defence Force Form (Reference: A.F. 482 [Prov.]), entitled: 'Report on Accidental or Self-Inflicted Injuries', which was partially completed in relation to Lt Roche's injuries in the car crash. This form clearly instructs:

Full statements are to be taken by an officer from the witnesses of the accident, or, where there was no witness, from any person to whom the injured officer or soldier may have mentioned his injury immediately after the occurrence.

No such statement for Dónal de Róiste appears on his files. However, there is a statement on the file in accordance with the instructions given on Form A.F. 482. It is headed: 'Accident and Injuries – statement of Witness or Injured Person – To Accompany A.F. 482'. It is dated 20 May 1966 and is signed by both Lt Dónal Roche and a senior officer. It details the circumstances surrounding a fall in which Lt Roche broke his left index finger at about 2230 hrs on 9 May 1966.

One would have thought that the O'Kelly car crash, in which there were multiple casualties, would have required similar and, indeed, more detailed statements.

Where are they? Do they, in fact, exist? Did their possible absence from De Róiste's files not exercise the curiosity of the JAG? Even if the Terms of Reference were restricted enough to allow her to consider my submission as irrelevant, surely the absence of documents indicated a potential gap and ambiguity which permitted her the latitude to explore. Indeed, how could she comment on a car accident involving Lt Dónal Roche, and suspected of being linked to his 'retirement', without referring to this anomaly?

If my 'plausible hypothesis' were proven wrong, I would unreservedly apologise, as requested, for any unintended hurt caused to the O'Kelly family. However, the woman in the car struck by O'Kelly equally deserves justice. The issues raised – for the O'Kelly family as much as for De Róiste and the injured woman – deserve to be fully examined. All parties have the right to expect that the issues raised in my *Irish Times* article be properly and fairly examined and not glossed over.

12

THE JUDGE ADVOCATE GENERAL'S
REPORT

'NOT CONSIDERED SUITABLE FOR GENERAL INTEREST'

... like a tongue
into a toothless gap, exploring the presence
of absence.

Valerie Lawson, poet

TERMS OF REFERENCE

> To enquire into the circumstances surrounding the
> retirement of ex-Lieutenant Dónal Roche, by means of
> a complete review of all relevant documents held by the
> Department of Defence and by the Defence Forces, and
> to have full access to any civil or military personnel for
> the purposes of their providing explanation in relation to
> any apparent gaps or ambiguities in the documentation
> and to report to the Minister with her conclusions and
> recommendations.
>
> The Inquirer is to be entitled, within the Terms of
> Reference, and the manner of the Inquiry contemplated,
> to take such representations in writing from any party
> whom she considers to be appropriate.

The Minister for Defence presented the first paragraph of the above
terms of reference to the JAG, Ms Oonah McCrann, SC, on 2 July

2002. Following representations by her, the Minister 'enlarged' the terms of reference on 15 July 2002 to include the second paragraph. McCrann subsequently invited submissions from Dónal de Róiste's solicitor, as well as the Department of Defence and the defence forces. A far more important addition to the terms of reference would have been the entitlement to take written and oral representations not just from those whom she considered to be appropriate, but from anyone who felt they had something to offer. Commandant Patrick Walshe, for example. And De Róiste also wished to give oral testimony. However, to accept oral evidence from Walshe and De Róiste would immediately have established the need to invite a submisssion from the former Chief of Staff, Gerry O'Sullivan. That may have been a bridge too far. The JAG states in the opening of her report:

> The Terms of Reference do not entitle me to hear oral evidence or resolve conflicts of fact.

One wonders what the purpose of her Inquiry was if she was not entitled to resolve conflicts of fact. Was the real purpose of the exercise simply to create the impression that the controversial retirement of Lt Dónal Roche had been thoroughly investigated – and resolved – and that the defence forces and the state had no case to answer?

There are key aspects of the terms of reference which – because of the private and internal nature of the JAG's Inquiry – are difficult to assess. The terms of reference are, in themselves, ambiguous. On 2 July 2002, the terms may have sounded reasonable to De Róiste and his legal team. However, in light of what has transpired and the subsequent release of some of Lt Roche's classified files, those same terms would not be accepted today. For example, the suggestion that the JAG would 'enquire into the circumstances surrounding the retirement' of Lt Roche 'by means of a complete review of all relevant documentation held by the Department of Defence and by the Defence Forces' sounds reasonable. One might have assumed that De Róiste would have all his files assessed. However, we now know that there are documents still being held by the Department of the Taoiseach and by Áras an Uachtaráin, to which the JAG, apparently, did not have access – nor did she seek such access. She does not make reference to these files in her report. She also failed to enquire from the Garda Síochána as to whether they held any files on Lt Roche or if he was named in any Special Branch files dealing with Mr X, Padraig Dwyer, or the other members of the alleged 'IRA splinter' group with which he had allegedly associated.

That the JAG should 'have full access to any civil or military personnel for the purposes of their providing explanation in relation to any apparent gaps or ambiguities in the documentation' is itself ambiguous. Did this, for example, include retired civil or military personnel or only those still in service? Even to the untrained eye, the documentation, when eventually released to De Róiste and his legal team in November 2002, was littered with gaps and ambiguities to which Ms McCrann had failed to seek answers.

THE JUDGE ADVOCATE GENERAL

The Defence Act, 1954, Section 15, states:

(1) There shall be a Judge Advocate-General.
(2) The Judge Advocate-General shall be a practising barrister-in-law of at least ten years' standing, but shall not be a member of the Defence Forces, and shall be appointed by, and hold office during the pleasure of, the President.
(3) The Judge Advocate-General shall be charged with the performance of such duties as the Government may from time to time assign to him [sic].
(4) There shall be paid to the Judge Advocate-General such remuneration as the Minister, with the consent of the Minister for Finance, may fix.

On 5 October 2001, Ms Oonah McCrann was appointed Judge Advocate General of the Defence Forces. According to the Department of Defence, the stipend of the current Judge Advocate General is €12,517 per annum. She received no additional payment for her inquiry into the circumstances surrounding the 1969 retirement of Lt Roche.

On 12 April 2004, I enquired about the criteria for appointing a Judge Advocate General and whether it was an advertised position to which prospective candidates are assessed by a government board and called to interview prior to appointment. Only after a follow-up enquiry was I given this response on 11 August 2004:

> ... the President on the advice of the government appoints the Judge Advocate General. The position is not advertised. The normal practice is for the Minister to submit a nomination to Government for approval and recommendation for appointment by the President in accordance with the relevant provisions of the Defence Act 1954.

The position is a government appointment on the recommendation of the Minister for Defence. In De Róiste's eyes this led to a situation in which there was a failure to meet the requirement that justice should not only be done but should be seen to be done.

EAMONN CARROLL, SOLICITOR,
AND THE JUDGE ADVOCATE GENERAL

The JAG, Oonah McCrann, wrote to De Róiste's solicitor, Eamonn Carroll, on 12 July 2002, enclosing a copy of the Terms of Reference. She stated:

> As you will note from the Terms of Reference, this review is confined to an examination of documentation and will not involve the taking of evidence from witnesses.
>
> In these circumstances, I do not anticipate that it will be necessary, or indeed appropriate, for any person other than myself, to participate in the review of the documentation.

The JAG wrote again on 16 July 2002, with amended terms of reference. She stated:

> ... I am anxious to deal with this matter as expeditiously as possible and if you are instructed to make written representations on behalf of your client you might notify me accordingly and I would envisage that any written representations should reach me on or before Friday, 26th July.

Carroll's practice responded to both letters, on 24 July 2002, outlining a number of concerns, including the fact that Carroll himself was on summer leave until 29 July and asked, therefore, for a time extension on the proposed date. The letter requested clarification on a number of issues:

> ... presumably other agencies and government departments [apart from the Department of Defence and the defence forces] would have been involved in processing [Lt Dónal Roche's retirement] and it would have gone before the government of the day, before being presented to the President. We therefore request that you confirm that all the documentation will be examined.
>
> We ... suggest that it would be appropriate that Ex-Lieutenant Dónal de Róiste himself be interviewed as he comes within the wording and would be a serving Officer today, but for the event that took place.

On 29 July 2002, the JAG responded:

> I am not entitled, pursuant to the Terms of Reference, to take oral evidence from any party and so I will not be interviewing Ex-Lieutenant Dónal de Róiste or any other individual in relation to the matter.

In hindsight, this was probably the moment when a red flag should have been brought to the attention of the public and concerns about the independence of the process publicly expressed. However, given the major setbacks experienced at the High Court and Supreme Court, this initiative, while flawed, was considered an important breakthrough. Until the moment when the JAG's report was published on 2 October 2002, there was optimism in De Róiste's camp that the outcome would be positive.

Nevertheless, in the opening remarks of the Submissions sent to Ms McCrann on behalf of his client, Dónal de Róiste, on 30 August 2002, Carroll expressed the following reservations:

At the outset we wish to express our serious reservations on the decision made by the Judge Advocate General not to interview parties to the events giving rise to the present impasse, who are alive and living in Ireland. Given the complexity to the matter it is submitted that the Judge Advocate General should not so limit herself to this restrictive review. Retired Lieutenant Dónal de Róiste wishes to be interviewed by the Judge Advocate General and we submit that the Terms of Reference make provision for such interview ... and all other parties to these matters and such interviews clearly come within the ambit of the Terms of Reference.

Carroll further informed McCrann that retired Commandant Patrick Walshe 'also wishes to be interviewed and to tender evidence of his experience of a similar style of interrogation as De Róiste.' Carroll stated that Walshe, 'because of his greater experience and military seniority, refused to be subjected to the interrogation methods employed'.

Carroll further stated:

It should be pointed out at the outset that ... this submission is made blind, without sight of the defence forces files, or the Department of Defence files, and without any means of reviewing all the relevant documentation held by the Department of Defence and by the Defence Forces, or other relevant files. Further, he has not had full access to any civil personnel or to any military personnel for the purpose of their providing explanations. Ex Lieutenant Dónal de Róiste does not know if there are any gaps, apparent or otherwise, or ambiguities in the documentation.

Lieutenant Dónal de Róiste does not know whether it was the Department of Defence, or any other Department Agency, that initiated the moves against him resulting in his dismissal and this is a matter which falls within the Terms of Reference 'the circumstances surrounding the retirement of Ex-Lieutenant Dónal de Róiste'.

On 4 September 2002, the JAG wrote to Carroll, reaffirming that she did not propose to hear any oral evidence from any party. De Róiste's solicitor did not receive this letter until 13 September, some nine days after it was written. I too received a letter from the JAG, dated 4 September 2002, on 13 September, acknowledging receipt of my 'unsolicited correspondence' on 30 July 2002.

Matters then took a peculiar twist when letters between the JAG and Carroll's office crossed one another in the post. On 18 September 2002, Carroll sent a holding letter to the JAG, indicating that he wished to reply more substantively to issues raised in her letter of 4 September (received on 13 September). Carroll forwarded a more substantive letter to the JAG on 20 September. However, much to his shock, he received a letter from the JAG, dated 19 September, in response to his of 18 September, stating that she had already completed her report and that it had been furnished to the Minister for Defence on 17 September.

Understandably, Carroll was taken aback. In a letter sent by fax and by post on 23 September 2002 he stated:

> We are disturbed to find that you have furnished your report to the Minister on 17th September. We do not understand the haste in despatching your report when there were matters outstanding.

He then summarised the recent flow of correspondence between his office and the JAG and continued:

> We wish to point out that the subject matter of this review has had disastrous consequences for the life of our client and his family...

Carroll outlined three principal issues of concern:

1. A presupposition that the gaps or ambiguities are only apparent and that it is already decided that the matter does not require any access to civil or military personnel for any other purpose.
2. That Lt Dónal de Róiste and ex-Commandant Patrick Walshe wish to be interviewed concerning

gaps and ambiguities in their respective interrogations.

3. That our client was retired by the President on the advice of the government pursuant to Section 47 of the Defence Act 1954 which raises the question as to whether the review of files includes the files of the Government (Cabinet) with the recommendation to the President that the officer be retired by the President. The prescribed Courts-martial Procedures of the Defence Act 1954, and regulations made thereunder, were not observed and additional questions arise as to the involvement of agencies/government department(s) other than the Department of Defence.

Carroll concluded his letter by putting Ms McCrann on notice that the possibility of Judicial Review proceedings were not being ruled out:

We are reluctant to suggest taking further steps at this juncture, but must act in the interests of our client up to and including an application to the High Court.

PUBLICATION OF REPORT

Ms McCrann did not, at any stage, seek clarification of any matters raised with her in the various submissions she received, or arising out of the documentation she was asked to review. The only person she admits to meeting, as part of her inquiry, was Major General Seán Brennan, on 30 July 2002, and that was only 'for the purpose of obtaining clarification as to some of the military terms and abbreviations used in the files'. During that meeting, Brennan confirmed to the JAG that the copy of the intelligence file she had examined was 'identical to the original intelligence file of which three copies exist'.

The additional clause entitling the JAG to take 'such representation in writing from any party whom she considers to be appropriate' is interesting. From the outset, a decision was taken to consider my written representations concerning the proximity between the plenary summons served on Commandant O'Kelly around 9 April 1969 and the start of Lt Roche's troubles on 25 April 1969, as neither 'relevant' nor 'appropriate'. Consequently, a very strict and narrow interpretation of the terms of reference by Ms McCrann allowed her to make a truthful yet meaningless pronouncement which, on the surface, appeared to 'thoroughly debunk' my hypothesis concerning the possible impact of the car crash. However, the real truth is that she had ignored my 'unsolicited' submission, including my *Irish Times* article, published on 29 June 2002, despite the fact that the article was a major part of the pressure that had led to the Inquiry.

On 28 September 2005, the Minister for Defence, Willie O'Dea, admitted as much in a written answer to Deputy Tony Gregory:

> In early July 2002, arising from a newspaper feature article on the case, published on 29th June 2002, the then Minister requested the Judge Advocate General to examine and to review the case....

Oonah McCrann, a barrister who had accepted a government appointment to the defence forces, cannot be considered an independent investigator. In the end, she carefully worked within the confines of her limited Inquiry and, consequently, my theory, far from being debunked by anything she had to say, remains compelling.

DOCUMENTS EVALUATED BY THE JUDGE ADVOCATE GGENERAL
Given that the JAG's report was quashed on appeal by the High Court in July 2005, because of her failure to adhere to fair procedures, I have decided not to include here a lengthy critique of her report. The report is available in full on the publishers' webiste, www.currach.ie. It is reproduced directly from an electronic version kindly supplied to me by the Minister for Defence following a written request.

I had enquired why the report had not been published in its entirety on the Department of Defence website, given that the website contains the press release announcing its 'findings' about Lt Roche's controversial retirement. On 22 April 2004, I was informed by the Minister for Defence's Private Secretary, Patricia Troy, that the reason for not publishing it on the website was that it was 'not considered suitable for general interest'.

This seems peculiar given the efforts the Department went to on the day of the report's publication. While the Department continues to deny that it briefed *TV3 News*, I have had it confirmed by journalist colleagues that a producer was informed, at least a day in advance, of the 'findings' and 'conclusions' of McCrann's report, as already dealt with in the previous chapter.

Correspondence from the Chief of Staff to the Minister for Defence
An interesting aspect of many of the documents reviewed by the JAG, including three allegedly addressed to the Minister for Defence, is that those in the file are written on plain sheets of paper. For example, a letter dated 3 May 1969 (of which there are two versions) from the Chief of Staff, is addressed simply to 'Aire' [Minister], which the JAG guesses is addressed to 'presumably the Minister for Defence'. The correspondence is not typed on the official headed notepaper of the Office of the Chief of Staff [Appendix A, Document 12]. In addition, the documents are marked 'secret'.

My uncertainties regarding this procedure are aroused by two facts. One is a copy of a letter in my possession – obtained from the National Archives – dated 23 May 1974, addressed to the 'Minister' and signed by Major-General T.L. O'Carroll, Chief of Staff. It is a cover letter, typed on the official headed notepaper of the Office of the Chief of Staff, accompanying a weekly analysis 'of the various types of Aid and Support supplied [by the defence forces] to the Civil Authorities covering the period 0001 hrs 13 May 74 (Monday) to 2359 hrs 19 May 74 (Sunday).' This was the week of the Dublin and Monaghan Bombings, which occurred on Friday, 17 May 1974. The letter carries the reference 'SOS 32' and is marked 'Declassified'.

Moreover, only one letter in Lt Roche's declassified files, from the period of his first interrogation on 25 April 1969 until his retirement, is typed on official defence force headed notepaper. It is, in fact, the letter informing him that, in pursuance of the powers vested in him, President de Valera was retiring him from the army with effect from 27 June 1969. The letter is typed on official headed notepaper from the Office of the Adjutant-General.

There may be a simple and rational explanation for what is either a failure by the Chief of Staff in 1969 to write to the Minister for Defence on official headed notepaper from his office, or a failure to keep on file the original versions of letters. The JAG appears not to have found questionable this procedure or the fact that there appears to be no acknowledgement to any of these letters/reports from the office of the Minister. On 4 October 2005, I wrote to the current Minister for Defence, Willie O'Dea, TD, seeking confirmation that his predecessor, Michael Hilliard, received the detailed letter(s) from Lt General Seán MacEoin, dated 3 May 1969, and enquired whether or not it had been acknowledged. On 20 October 2005, I received a telephone message from Jack McConnell, press officer to the Department of Defence, informing me that he was sending me a letter, under his name because he was the point of contact (although, he mentioned, he had not written it), in answer to several unanswered queries I had sent over the previous period.

Under the heading 'Correspondence from Chief of Staff to Minister for Defence', I was given the following answer:

> It would not be usual practice for the Minister to issue formal acknowledgements of receipt of minutes from the Chief of Staff. The Deputy Judge Advocate General's report, dated 29 May, 1969 [Appendix A, Document 13] was transmitted to the Minister with a covering minute from the Chief of Staff. It is apparent from this covering minute that the Chief of Staff had discussed Lieutenant de Róiste's case with the Minister and that the Minister was fully aware of the background to the case as recorded in the Chief of Staff's formal written report to the Minister dated 3 May, 1969. These reports were also circulated at the government meeting of 20 June, 1969 at which the Memorandum for Government was taken.

What is the usual practice therefore? Is anything sent to the Minister for Defence from the Chief of Staff ever acknowledged? Was anything sent by the Chief of Staff to the Minister for Defence relative to the retirement of Lt Roche acknowledged? Despite the serious consequences for the career of Lt Roche, there appears to have been no correspondence exchanged between the Minister for Defence – or his office – and the military authorities with regard to this matter.; not even an acknowledgement of receipt to any correspondence – whether in the form of minutes, letters or reports.

The statement in the letter that the Chief of Staff's and DJAG's reports were circulated at the government meeting on 20 June 1969, at which the memorandum for government 'was taken', is not mentioned by the JAG. On what basis, therefore, is this statement made? Has the relevant file at the Taoiseach's Department been made available to the Minister for Defence?

I have failed to get a satisfactory answer to the following question, submitted to the Department of Defence, regarding a recommendation made by the Chief of Staff and dated 3 May 1969:

> Is there any correspondence from the Minister, or his Office, seeking clarification of any matters raised in correspondence from the Chief of Staff and stating the need to ensure that Lt Roche should be afforded his constitutional rights before he [the Minister] would ask the government to recommend the retirement of Lt Roche 'in the interests of the service'? For example, the Chief of Staff, based on a Security Report from the Director of Intelligence … was recommending to the Minister that Lt Roche should be retired under Subparagraph 18(1)(f) of Section 47(2) of the Defence Act 1954, even before the investigation into Lt Roche was completed. Captain Patrick Walshe is very clear that he was interrogated later than 3 May 1969.

It seems bizarre that such a recommendation would be made to the government – even specifying the precise regulation under which it should be made – while an investigation was in progress. What is even more bizarre is the fact that the JAG didn't appear to consider this matter worthy of comment or a source of concern.

Interrogation Notes

The quality of the interrogation notes, allegedly based on three 'interviews' conducted with Lt Dónal Roche, is appallingly inadequate. The primary author of the notes is Commandant Gerry O'Sullivan, who was later appointed Chief of Staff. O'Sullivan had full editorial control over what was reported in these notes. The JAG's report does not acknowledge the authorship of the notes, despite the indisputable evidence that O'Sullivan is the author. Why?

There is absolutely no evidence that, in accordance with acceptable standards, a statement was taken from Lt Roche, which he read and signed as a true and honest account of what had transpired during any of the 'interviews' or interrogations. There is evidence that Lt Roche was being pressurised to write a statement which, allegedly, he had 'volunteered' to do at the conclusion of his third interrogation on 30 April 1969. As already stated, Roche's reluctance to make a statement cannot be interpreted as an implicit admission of guilt or of having something to hide. He was simply following legal advice.

The JAG was, herself, critical regarding the quality of O'Sullivan's notes. This was something I wished to discuss with O'Sullivan directly but he declined an invitation to be interviewed. I therefore wrote to him on 24 February 2004 about several matters, including Ms McCrann's criticism of his notes. The retired lieutenant general did not reply.

If the three 'interview' notes (Appendix A: Documents 3, 4 and 7) are a record of what transpired during the interrogations of Roche, readers should be alert to the additional detail that finds its way into O'Sullivan's 'Memo' (Document 5), 'Summary Comment' (Document 6) and, thereafter, the Director of Intelligence's letter to the Chief of Staff (Document 8a), his 'Security Report' (Document 8b), the Chief of Staff's letter(s) to the Minister for Defence (Documents 10a and 10b) and the report of the DJAG (Document 13). From where does the additional detail come, if not from O'Sullivan's interrogation notes? It is legitimate to ask whether it is, in fact, fabricated, since there is no supporting documentation.

It is also important to note that while there are comments ascribed to Captain Patrick Walshe in the Director of Intelligence's 'Security Report', there is no supporting documentation. There are no interview notes similar to Lt Roche's, despite the fact that he too underwent interrogation sessions.

In reviewing and highlighting clear gaps and ambiguities in the documentation reviewed by the JAG in her quashed report, readers should bear in mind that the various authors of military documents were producing them in the full belief that their work was 'secret' and would never see the light of day. There is a strong possibility that this may have created a false sense of security that their intentions and their methods would be hidden forever under the cloak of 'State Secrecy'.

I propose here to review in detail some of the documents considered by the JAG in her report, which, it appears, contained various gaps and ambiguities worthy of further exploration or, at least, comment. My views are those of a layperson, not a barrister. The documents I propose to review are:

1. Intelligence memo (Appendix A, Document 1)
2. Security report (Appendix A, Document 8b)
3. Third interview notes (Appendix A, Document 7)
4. Deputy Judge Advocate General's Report (Appendix A, Document 12)

Regrettably, the JAG twice declined to be interviewed by me. In a letter, dated 12 September 2005, she cited her role in preparing 'a report for the Minister for Defence', and said that she felt that 'it would not be appropriate' for her to 'discuss the contents of that report or indeed to discuss the contents of the files' that she reviewed. The reader is encouraged to refer to the documents in their entirety, published without commentary in Appendix A

(Appendix A: Document 1) Intelligence Memo
Concerning this document, the JAG states in her report:

> It appears from an initialled hand-written memorandum dated 22nd April 1969 on the intelligence file that … a 'confidential source' had reported that Ex-Lieutenant Dónal Roche was in the company of members of the Dublin IRA splinter group on the 16th and 17th April 1969…. This information appears to have set in train an investigation which culminated in Ex-Lieutenant Roche's retirement on 27th June 1969.

This is a crucial document in that everything seems to hinge on this record; apparently it was this handwritten memo that set in motion the 'investigation' into Lt Dónal Roche, which ultimately brought him to the attention of the general staff, the government and the President.

There are noteworthy aspects to this handwritten document,

initialled 'GOS' (Gerry O'Sullivan) and dated 22 April 1969, the day before the vehicle auction at Clancy Barracks.

In paragraph 1, O'Sullivan writes that 'a confidential source' has reported that an officer has been seen in the company of members of a splinter IRA group. In paragraph 4, he states that 'a reliable source' describes Lt Roche as 'rather immature and Bohemian in tastes'.

The first gap and ambiguity to be resolved is whether O'Sullivan is reporting information supplied on Lt Roche by one source or two. Are the 'confidential source' and the 'reliable source' one and the same person or two different persons? Only O'Sullivan can clarify this matter and yet, despite the fact that he was alive and well, and living in Dublin, the JAG failed to seek his help with this and other documents.

In a cover letter to the Chief of Staff, dated 1 May 1969 (Appendix A: Document 8a), accompanying his Security Report (Document 8b), the Director of Intelligence, Col. Hefferon stated the following concerning the 'confidential source':

> It has not been possible to confirm ROCHE's association with the other members of the group as reported by our confidential source. We were somewhat handicapped by our inability to question directly the original source of information although the questioning and requestioning through a third party was reasonably satisfactory.
>
> While an unsupported report must be viewed with reserve, it is significant that the report was accurate in its other aspects and my view is that it must be considered as likely to be accurate on this count as well.

The logic of this statement is, at best, confusing. Effectively, what Hefferon is saying is that the 'original source' was inaccessible and could be questioned, and requestioned, only through a 'third party'. So, was the information, as it appears from the document dated 22 April 1969, fourth hand? Can the intelligence section of the Irish defence forces unequivocally satisfy the government and the people of Ireland that, even if protected by the cloak of secrecy, they absolutely know who the source is? Or that they know who the third party was who questioned the 'source' on behalf of the intelligence services?

It is also strange that there appears to be no documented evidence of the alleged 'questioning and requestioning' of the 'original source'. What additional information did they require? What questions did they wish to be asked by the third party of the 'original source'? What answers did they get in response? Given that Hefferon's letter and Security Report are dated 1 May 1969 and Lt Roche was interrogated on 25, 28 and 30 April, are we to believe that the intelligence section had a 'third party' runner going back and forth to the original source during the interrogations? By the end of this process, within one week of his first interrogation, Roche was considered such a threat to military and state security that the military authorities were recommending his retirement 'in the interests of the service'.

In his letter to the Minister for Defence, dated 3 May 1969, the Chief of Staff described the original source as 'a most reliable informant'. On what basis did he make this assertion, given that the informant had to be contacted through a third party?

There is another reference to a 'reliable source' by O'Sullivan in a memo on which the JAG failed to comment. The memo appears to be dated 23 April 1969 (Appendix A: Document 2). The language is unclear as it describes Lt Roche as having 'attended' the auction at Clancy Barracks when in fact he was on duty there. The final sentence of the memo states:

> A reliable source reports that ROCHE may have bought
> a Land Rover.

O'Sullivan went to the trouble of listing the names of purchasers of eleven of fourteen saloons and three Land Rovers sold at the auction. Surely, even in 1969, a simple telephone call to the officer in charge of the auction would have saved him the trouble of establishing the inaccuracy of the information supplied by his informant. This instance, alone, must call into question the reliability of the original 'reliable source'. To misquote the statement of Col. Hefferon above:

> While an unsupported report must be viewed with re-
> serve, it is significant that the report was <u>inaccurate</u> in its
> other aspects and my view is that it must be considered as
> likely to be <u>inaccurate</u> on this count as well.

There are two other noteworthy aspects concerning the reliability of the 'reliable source' mentioned in this primary document. As already mentioned, in paragraph 4 of the document dated 22 April 1969, it states:

> ROCHE is described by a reliable source as rather immature and Bohemian in tastes.

In paragraph 4 of another unsigned document, referred to by the JAG (Appendix A: Document 8c), dated 26 April 1969, an alleged interview with a Commandant P. Maguire contains the following remarks:

> MAGUIRE regards ROCHE as an immature type with odd bohemian tastes, fond of beat groups, ballad singing types etc.

The language used in both sentences is remarkably similar. So much so that I decided to seek the opinion of two forensic linguists at the University of Birmingham, Professor Malcolm Coulthard and his assistant, Sue Blackwell. Both said that while a definitive opinion could not be offered, the following could be stated respectively:

> Regarding the two descriptions ... there are three not-so-common 'content' words in common, i.e. 'immature', Bohemian' and 'tastes' ... it looks highly suspicious. But I can't say as a linguist that this is enough evidence to justify a stronger statement.

Given the similarities in both sentences, it seems reasonable to wonder if Commandant Maguire might be the 'reliable source' mentioned in the first document. However, of far more significance is how a comment, allegedly made on 26 April 1969, may have found its way into an intelligence memo, allegedly written four days earlier on 22 April. It lends weight to a suspicion that the initial intelligence document may have been created retrospectively.

(Appendix A: Document 8b) Security Report
The document, marked 'secret', states:

1. A report from a confidential source was received on 21 April 1969 to the effect that:
   a. a person called 'Doc' ROCHE, believed to be in 'Supply' 1 the army had been in O'DONOGHUE's publichouse Merrion Row on 16th April. He was initially in the company of *████████ ████████ and *████████ and was later joined by *████████. He asked ████████ about *████████ and shortly afterwards left with ████████ to find ████████.

   *All members of the DUBLIN IRA Splinter Group.

The security memo (Appendix A: Document 1) is dated 22 April 1969. If this information was so sensitive, why was it not recorded immediately? The security memo has no mention of 'a person called "Doc" ROCHE, believed to be in "Supply" 1 the army'. It states clearly 'A confidential source reported that Lt ROCHE was in the company of members of the Dublin IRA Splinter Group'.

The security memo does not mention O'Donoghue's public house, Merrion Row. Nor does it mention 16 April. It states that Lt Roche was in their company 'on two days'. The dates 16 and 17 have subsequently been added to the memo. There is a further handwritten, undated secret memo (Appendix A: Document 5) in which O'Sullivan states: 'Subject met ████████ and other members of the Dublin IRA Splinter Group in Dublin on the 18th and 19th April 1969.' There is a clear conflict on the question of dates. According to Captain Patrick Walshe, during his interrogation O'Sullivan pressed him relentlessly on the subject of specific days and dates.

There are no names given in the confidential memo based on information from the 'confidential source'. Dónal de Róiste states that O'Donoghue's pub was thronged with people and that he had casual conversations with many of them but has no recollection of meeting with a specific group of people, as alleged above.

b. ROCHE returned alone about an hour later.

In the 'confidential source' memo, there is no mention of Lt Roche leaving O'Donoghue's alone. Dónal de Róiste has no recollection of this and wonders from where this information originates.

c. ROCHE met ███████████ on the following night 17th April also in O'DONOGHUEs.

The redacted name is assumed to be Mr X, Padraig Dwyer. Lt Roche acknowledged at an early stage in his interrogations that he knew Padraig Dwyer as an acquaintance in O'Donoghue's but that he had absolutely no awareness of any alleged subversive or criminal background. He states that he has no firm recollection now as to whether he met him on either 16 or 17 April, or even on both dates.

d. During some of the conversation on either 16th or 17th ROCHE mentioned the auction of army cars at Clancy Barracks on 23 April 1969 and suggested that anyone interested should come along.

It says much for the accuracy of 'the confidential source' that they were unable to state specifically when the alleged discussion took place. Given that O'Donoghue's was a very popular traditional music haunt, the 'confidential source' must have been party to the conversation in order to inform Military Intelligence of the detail. Dónal de Róiste states very clearly that he was in Dublin, on army duty, to help organise a public auction that had been publicly advertised in the national press and that he would have openly told many people of the reason for his assignment in Dublin. He is clear that he received no specific instructions from his military superiors that the auction should not be talked about and/or that it would be unwise to suggest that members of the public attend. The success of the auction would, after all, be judged on sales and the more potential buyers, the better.

2. The report was investigated and the person concerned identified as 8159 Lt Dónal ROCHE, 4 Grn S&T Coy, ATHLONE, who was attached to Clancy

Barracks from 15th April 69 for duties in connection
with the auction. ROCHE's nickname is 'DUCK'.

The confidential memo makes no mention of 'Doc' or 'Duck' Roche. It
is very definite, prior to investigation, that the person being reported on
is 'Lt Roche'.

3. The auction was kept under surveillance and Lt
   ROCHE was observed meeting and speaking
   freely to ████████ and ████████ (████████
   ████████).

Where is the evidence that the auction was kept under surveillance?
There is no supporting documentation in any of the secret files released
to Dónal de Róiste. Where are the reports of those who were tasked
to keep Lt Roche under surveillance? Equally, where are the reports of
those who received their reports? Furthermore, if the auction was kept
under surveillance specifically to see if Dwyer would make 'contact' with
Lt Roche, why was the meeting not photographed? It should be noted
that in the letter to the Chief of Staff, accompanying this report, Col.
Hefferon stated: 'in view of the extreme sensitivity of Clancy Barracks
it was felt that delay in bringing the association into the open would
NOT have been an acceptable risk'. Why, therefore, did defence forces
intelligence not plan to solidify its case against Lt Roche by catching
him on camera being 'friendly' with Dwyer?

4. ████████ and his friend left the auction about 11.30
   hrs, apparently without buying anything.

Where is the supporting evidence for this? If, in fact, Mr X, Padraig
Dwyer, was a member of 'the Splinter IRA group' as alleged in the
documentation, why was he not arrested? Why was he not, at the very
least, stopped, his presence noted and the identity of his companion
established? Would it not have been in the interests of military and state
security to establish if his companion was also a subversive?

5. In view of ████████ presence in Clancy Barracks
   and the extreme sensitivity of this post it was decided

to make a direct approach to Lt ROCHE on the basis of the meeting with DWYER at the auction. Accordingly he was interviewed at Rannog Faisneise [Intelligence Section] on 25.4.1969.

It is not established why Clancy Barracks was considered to be a military post of 'extreme sensitivity'. If the barracks was so extremely sensitive, why was a public auction held within it and the public invited to attend? Why was a press photographer given access and not only allowed to photograph the auction, but also permitted internal access to a building from which an aerial view of a section of the auction could be taken? It should also be noted that the name DWYER was not redacted in this paragraph when the document was released to De Róiste's lawyer in November 2002. Again, since Dwyer was, allegedly, a known subversive, why was he not arrested?

6. Lt ROCHE admitted the meeting with ▓▓▓▓▓▓ who was a previous acquaintance. He first met him at O'DONOGHUEs public house in about May 1968. They were introduced by a ▓▓▓▓▓▓, a guitarist with a dance band at the ▓▓▓▓▓ ▓▓▓▓▓▓.

It is clear that Lt Roche was much more open with his interrogator than Captain Patrick Walshe. Roche told O'Sullivan that he knew Padraig Dwyer as an acquaintance. Walshe told O'Sullivan that he might know him but that he required O'Sullivan to produce a photograph so that he could identify the person about whom he was enquiring. The guitarist referred to is Brian Mooney, an Australian musician.

7. He subsequently met ▓▓▓▓▓▓ on a few (2/3) occasions, always at O'DONOGHUEs and always by chance. In July he spent a weekend in Galway with ▓▓▓▓▓ ▓▓▓▓▓▓ German au-pair girlfriend and a ▓▓▓▓▓ (believed no security significance).

This paragraph, based on paragraph 5 of the first interview (Appendix A, Document 3), is the one that potentially creates the most problems for the young Lt Roche. It states that he spent a weekend in Galway with Padraig Dwyer and his girlfriend. What is not clear, because of the redactions, is the fact that a fourth person is named, Brendan (the 'Dog') Doherty. According to De Róiste, Doherty and he had planned to join Captain Patrick Walshe and Lt Gerry Swan in Galway for a weekend, and Doherty organised a lift with Dwyer. De Róiste states categorically that he did not spend a weekend with Dwyer and was never alone with him at any time. Furthermore, De Róiste points out that the only reason O'Sullivan was aware of this information was that he told him about it during his interrogation. He states that he was being truthful and, he thought, helpful. If he had felt there was anything to hide, there was no need for him to mention it, and the information would never have been known and could not have been used against him.

8. Between this and October 68 he saw ███████████ casually in O'DONOGHUES bar on about 2/3 occasions. He did NOT see him again until he met him in O'DONOGHUE's on Thursday, 17ᵗʰ April.

De Róiste states that he does not recall giving this information concerning casual encounters with Dwyer. His acquaintanceship with Dwyer was such that it is highly unlikely that he would have noted the occasions when they met. He may have met him two or three times between July and October 1968. Whether he met him between October 1968 and April 1969 he has no idea. Dwyer was only one of scores of casual acquaintances he had at O'Donoghue's pub. His friends, Commandant Patrick Walshe and Lt Col. Gerry Swan, who attended O'Donoghue's with Lt Roche, support this fact.

Readers should be aware that the reason why O'Sullivan is anxious to emphasise a gap in Roche's meetings with Padraig Dwyer, between October 1968 and April 1969, is to suggest that he had knowledge of a shooting incident, which is dealt with at paragraph 21 and paragraph 4 of the Conclusion below.

9. On that occasion ROCHE with his girl friend ███████████ a friend ███████████ with his girl friend and his sister (five in all) were in O'DONOGHUEs at the outer bar. ███████████ came in from the lounge bar, saw ROCHE asked him what he was

doing. ROCHE said he was in Dublin for the auction of army cars at Clancy Barracks on April, 23rd. ▮▮▮▮▮ said he might come along as he was interested in buying a car. ROCHE went into the back lounge with ▮▮▮▮▮, met ▮▮▮▮▮ wife and sister, chatted for a few minutes and then returned to his party at the front bar.

Even if this is true, Roche is adamant that he knew nothing of Dwyer's alleged subversive connections or alleged criminal activities. Indeed, the source memo (Document 1) clearly states in paragraph 3 that it was 'NOT possible at this stage to say whether connection is subversive or not.' Lt Roche was, and still is, a gregarious and friendly person. His girlfriend from this period has informed me that she had little recollection of visiting or frequenting O'Donoghue's pub. She has no recollection of ever meeting Padraig Dwyer.

10. He next met [Dwyer] at the auction on 23 April and spoke to him about the vehicles for sale. ▮▮▮▮▮ was with a friend ▮▮▮▮▮ whom he did not know. ▮▮▮▮▮ and his friend did not stay long and left without buying so far as he knew. He (ROCHE) did not buy anything either.

De Róiste has consistently stated that he recalls Dwyer approaching him at the public auction. Again, he knew him as an acquaintance and had no reason to be anything other than friendly and courteous, as he was with the hundreds of other members of the public who attended. He may have spoken to him about the vehicles for sale. That was the purpose of his posting – to organise and supervise an auction of surplus vehicles to be sold to the public. How long Dwyer stayed at the auction De Róiste has no idea and it was not something that particularly exercised his mind.

11. Questioned in detail about his activities over the period 15–23 April ROCHE initially protested that he could not remember. He was very vague but finally came up with the following:—

15th April (Tues) – with his girl friend – no details

16th April (Wed) – Visited a friend ███████ an Aer Lingus pilot, with an address at ████████ which he could not remember.

17th April (Thur): At O'DONOGHUE's as outlined in pars 8 and 9.

18th April (Fri): Visited friend ██████████ ████████ with his girl friend. Went to Cedar's pub.

19/20 April: Spent week-end with girl friend at his parents home in Clonmel. On night of 20th April stopped off at Kildare Barracks for drinks on the way home. Had drinks with Capt. P. WALSHE, Lt SWAN and Lt O'CONNOR.

Before the reader continues, let's do an experiment. Imagine that there is someone interrogating you. You are alone and do not have access to a diary or any form of assistance. Now, tell me immediately, where were you and what were you doing on the evening of ten days ago? How about nine and eight days ago? What about five days ago? The suggestion that young Lt Roche was vague and that he initially could not remember is likely more truthful than the exercise being thrust upon him by an all-powerful member of the Intelligence Section of the Irish army.

12. From an early stage in their association he was aware that ████████ was anti-army and anti-Establishment. ████████ frequently referred to him as 'his Free State army friend'.

De Róiste describes this as nonsense. His 'association' with Dwyer was casual. It is possible Dwyer referred to him as his 'Free State army friend' but it wasn't unusual to have his association with the Irish army commented on in various ways as it was not something he was ashamed to reveal. On the contrary, he was proud to be an officer of the Irish defence forces.

13. On one occasion ████████ told him he had been away in Connemara 'zeroing rifles' and on another he

made some passing reference to 9 mm ammunition. ROCHE did not take him seriously but did think he might have some subversive connection.

De Róiste utterly rejects this assertion, made in a secret document that he was never meant to see. It is taken from paragraph 9 of the first interrogation notes (Appendix A, Document 3) but is here given a different spin. The interrogation notes state: '… Dwyer asked him [Lt Roche] about zeroing of rifles and on another referred to 9mm ammunition but never made a direct approach to him.' It is also stated here that Dwyer told him he had been away in Connemara. This information is not recorded in the first interrogation notes. The reader should also be aware that this information is very deliberate and is inserted for a purpose. This paragraph is aimed at establishing that Lt Roche knowingly associated with subversives. The next paragraph is aimed at establishing that he knowingly associated with criminals. Note the reference to 9mm ammunition as this has a very deliberate purpose too.

14. In October he learned of ███████████ involvement in a shooting fracas with the Gardai and knew then that he was a criminal. About this stage he mentioned him ███████████ to his friend Capt. P. WALSHE and some time [later] to Comdt. P. MAGUIRE in the mess at Athlone.

De Róiste states that he learned of Dwyer's involvement in a shooting fracas with the Garda Síochána from none other than Commandant O'Sullivan, his interrogator. It was O'Sullivan, De Róiste claims, who first described Dwyer as a criminal. Walshe categorically denies any such conversation between Lt Roche and himself.

15. He did not recollect any other army person being present at his meetings with ███████████ but thought maybe his friend Capt. P. WALSHE met him once. (WALSHE denies this.)

Captain Walshe asserts that it is quite possible he was under the same roof as Dwyer in O'Donoghue's and may have met him on a number of occasions. However, he says that he did not know Dwyer's name and wished to see a photograph of him so that he could positively identify him. O'Sullivan failed to produce one. Consequently, O'Sullivan was not in a position to state categorically 'WALSHE denies this'.

16. He did not meet any other people with ▓▓▓▓▓ whom he thought was a 'loner'. ▓▓▓▓▓ told him he had been in jail in England before he came back to Ireland. He did not know '▓▓▓▓▓ or ▓▓▓▓▓.'

De Róiste has no recollection of this being discussed during his first or, indeed, during any of his interrogations. De Róiste says that O'Sullivan was the first and only person to tell him that Dwyer had been in jail in England. Furthermore, he states that he does not know to this day whether or not it is true.

17. He realised now it was foolish to have associated with ▓▓▓▓▓ but it was only a casual acquaintance and he regarded ▓▓▓▓▓ as 'unusual'. He liked to meet people like that, Bohemian types, ballad groups, etc. He knew O'DONOGHUE's pub was somewhat unsavoury but thought the crowd was 'interesting'.

It appears here that words are being ascribed to the young lieutenant that are really the thinking of a superior who scorned the idea of visiting an establishment such as O'Donoghue's pub. There is also an uncomfortable echo within this paragraph with the fourth paragraphs of the original security memo (Appendix A, Document 1) and the alleged interview with Commandant Maguire (Appendix A, Document 8c).

Moreover there appears to be an attempt from the outset to suggest that Lt Roche was not inclined to keep 'acceptable' company. The alleged interview with Commandant Maguire (Appendix A, Document 8c), describes Lt Roche as having 'odd bohemian tastes, fond of beat groups, ballad singing types etc.' Maguire also, allegedly, described Lt Roche's friend, Brendan 'The Dog' Doherty, as 'a rather unusual friend'.

Maguire is also alleged to have stated that Roche never had any trouble getting accommodation when he went to Dublin for the weekend 'as the crowd he knocked around with were the bohemian university type and there was always "a bed in a flat".' Maguire allegedly commented that he believed Lt Roche 'went away around last Xmas as a chauffeur to an American group touring round London and the Continent.' The 'American touring group' was, in fact, none other than a retired US naval captain who was delighted to hire the services of the young Irish officer who had responded to his ad and who was entitled to three weeks' leave during which they drove to London and Paris.

At this point it is worth reviewing the known core friendship group of Dónal Roche in April 1969, since it is clear that there is a very definite attempt to paint a picture of the young lieutenant as something of an eccentric and, therefore, not of a suitable calibre for the Officer Corps of the defence forces. Roche's girlfriend was the daughter of a Garda superintendent. His three best buddies, with whom he shared a passion for Irish music, were: Brendan Doherty, the son of the first CEO of the Irish Cancer Society; Commandant Patrick Walshe, who retired from the Irish army after a distinguished career; Lt Col. Gerry Swan, who also retired from the Irish army after a distinguished career; and John Roche, an Aer Lingus pilot. After his expulsion from the army, Dónal Roche lived for six months with his brother, Conchubhar, and three teachers in a Dublin apartment. Where, therefore, is the evidence of his 'unusual', 'bohemian' associations? It is all conjecture, aimed at creating an untruthful and distorted image of the young man.

18. Throughout this interview he was vague and indefinite. The impression was formed that he was deliberately so and would not be pinned down to facts. He claimed he did not know his girl friend's address nor the exact address of the friends he visited.

De Róiste has no recollection of this being discussed or even why O'Sullivan would want the address of his girlfriend and his friends. Was the intention to interview them so that O'Sullivan and the Intelligence Section might corroborate the veracity of what he was saying regarding his movements and associations? De Róiste certainly wishes they had but there is no evidence that this was ever done. His girlfriend has confirmed that she was never approached. As for the assertion that he did not know the 'exact address' of his friends, is this so strange? I suspect that, like me, the reader may have several friends to whose home they could walk or drive for a visit but when it comes to sending a Christmas card, would have to look up the 'exact address'.

> 19. Comdt. MAGUIRE was interviewed and re-
> membered a reference made by Lt ROCHE. It was
> a casual meeting in the mess. ROCHE mentioned
> that he never had any difficulty getting accommoda-
> tion when he went to Dublin for the week-end as the
> crowd he knocked around with were the university
> bohemian type and that there was always 'a bed in a
> flat'.

It is claimed that a Commandant Maguire was interviewed. However, there is no signed statement in the files from Maguire. There is only a typed document with alleged comments. There is also a suspicion concerning words ascribed to Maguire on 26 April 1969, the date of the alleged interview, and words that appear in the original 'intelligence memo' of 22 April 1969 which, allegedly, sparked the investigation. This paragraph is probably more revealing of the author than of the subject.

> 20. He went on to say that a friend he met in a pub was in
> the IRA. MAGUIRE told him he was foolish to have
> anything to do with that type of person.

This alleged admission by Lt Roche is meant to be the *coup de grâce*. It appears from this paragraph that the young lieutenant knowingly associated with a subversive and admitted such to a superior. However, there is no mention in O'Sullivan's interrogation notes of Roche having admitted to having a 'friend … in the IRA'. What the notes state is: '… he mentioned casually to Comdt. P. MAGUIRE that he knew Padraig Dwyer and Comdt. MAGUIRE advised him to avoid such people.'

The use of the word 'casual' – in paragraph 19 above; in paragraph 2 of the alleged interview with Maguire (Document 8c); and the word 'casually' recorded in paragraph 10 of O'Sullivan's 'interview notes' (Document 3) – is deliberate but also ambiguous. It is an attempt to mitigate the failure of a senior officer to report immediately an alleged association by a young member of the Officer Corps with a subversive – if, indeed, such association had been admitted. It is stated that the 'casual' conversation between Lt Roche and Commandant Maguire occurred around November 1968. If this were true, it could equally be argued that Maguire had failed in his duty as a senior officer and thereby 'endangered military security and the safety of the state'. The use of the adjective, however, is intended to absolve this member of the senior ranks of any such responsibility.

> 21. Capt. WALSHE was interviewed on 28th April, 1969. He acknowledged to be very friendly with Lt ROCHE but could not recollect ever having met ███████. He remembered ROCHE and a friend ███████ discussing ███████ involvement with the Gardai at Ballyfermot in October, 1968.

Captain Walshe utterly refutes these assertions in the Security Report and has asked on what basis they are made. For the Judicial Review of the JAG's report he swore, on 28 April 2003, an affidavit to the High Court in which he stated in forthright and unambiguous language: 'The J.A.G. chose to accept as fact for the purpose of the review two statements in the files that were attributed to me…. The Ballyfermot incident was not referred to in my interrogation at all and the first I knew of it was when I read about it in the J.A.G. report. I was shocked and angry that two fabricated statements attributed to me should have been accepted as fact by the J.A.G. without any signed statement from me in the files.'

> 22. He [Captain Walshe] was out with Lt ROCHE on the night of 23 April (day of auction). During the evening ROCHE mentioned that ███████ was at the auction in Clancy and he was sure they were seen together by 'S' branch man.

Captain Walshe utterly rejects this assertion also. Roche had no reason to suspect that the Special Branch had seen him speaking with Mr X, Padraig Dwyer. Again, there is an attempt to create the impression that

Lt Roche was knowingly associating with subversives, and that the 'contact' with Dwyer in Clancy Barracks was something other than a brief encounter. Furthermore, the above allegation, ascribed to Captain Walshe, appears as paragraph 11 in the *second* interview, not the first, as stated here. Walshe stated in his sworn affidavit on 28 April 2003: 'I was not aware during my interrogations that Lt Roche had met a Mr O'Dwyer in Clancy Barracks'.

O'Sullivan, apparently, did not keep notes of the interrogations of Captain Walshe similar to those he kept in the case of Lt Roche. The JAG did not explore this anomaly or consider it worthy of comment.

23. <u>Second interview with Lt ROCHE</u>.

Lt ROCHE was again interviewed at Rng. Fais [Intelligence Branch] on 28/4/69.

Captain Walshe was also interviewed on this day.

24. He was taken back over the details of his association with ██████████ from May 68. There was no significant change in his account up to October 1968 which he claimed was the last occasion that he had seen ██████████ until the meeting in April, 1969.

It is important for those building the case against Roche to mention October here and to begin to highlight the gap between then and their next 'meeting' in April. October was the month when Dwyer was involved in an incident at Ballyfermot, Dublin, involving the Garda Síochána, and which was covered in the *Evening Press* on 3 October 1968, with a small article in *The Irish Times* on the following day. It will later be suggested that the gap was because Roche wanted to keep a low profile and did not want to be seen with Dwyer because of the Ballyfermot incident.

25. Asked to account again for his movements in the period 15th–23rd April he made one important change. He admitted to being in O'DONOGHUEs and to meeting ██████████ twice, on 16th and 17th April 69. This accorded with the information received from our source.

The 'source' memo, dated 22 April 1969, reproduced in the photograph section, clearly shows that the numbers 16 and 17 were subsequently added. It has been pointed out that in another O'Sullivan memo, which is undated (Appendix A: Document 5), he more definitely writes the dates 18 and 19 April 1969. Apart from the 'source' memo, there is no other evidence of information received to support this highly suspect document.

Captain Walshe also recalls that O'Sullivan seemed confused about days and dates and kept badgering him to be specific about dates when he and Roche had visited O'Donoghue's. He states that, during one of his interrogations, O'Sullivan alleged that Lt Roche had stated that he (Walshe) had also 'met these people'. Walshe suspected that O'Sullivan was attempting to entrap him and immediately requested that Lt Roche be brought into his presence and asked to repeat what O'Sullivan had alleged. Walshe states that O'Sullivan was taken aback by this request. He did not bring Lt Roche into Walshe's presence.

Furthermore, stating, as paragraph 25 does, that Lt Roche 'admitted to being in O'DONOGHUEs' implies guilt when, in reality, Roche simply visited O'Donoghue's, a public house, when he was off duty.

26. Questioned as to why he omitted this second visit in his first version he claimed he had forgotten about it. He had discussed the matter with his girlfriend over the weekend and she had reminded him of the second visit.

At previously stated, Lt Roche's girlfriend informed me that she had no recollection of this conversation. It is reasonable to suspect that there is an attempt being made to suggest that Roche was not being fully honest and was deliberately holding back information as he had something to hide.

27. On the 16th (Wed) he went to O'DONOGHUEs with his girlfriend and another girl. They were in the outer bar. ████████ came from the lounge and talked to him. They spoke about ████████ case and he introduced ████████ to the girls. He told ████████ why he was in Dublin and about

the auction. ▮▮▮▮▮▮▮ said he might come along. He went back with ▮▮▮▮▮▮▮ into the lounge and met ▮▮▮▮▮▮▮ wife and sister. Shortly afterwards he returned to the outer bar where a man named ▮▮▮▮▮▮▮ had joined the two girls. Shortly afterwards they left DONOGHUEs.

Before continuing, the reader is asked to refer back to paragraphs 8 and 9 above and compare the information presented there with that in this Security Report, sent on 1 May 1969 to the Chief of Staff who, apparently, on 3 May 1969, sent it to the Minister for Defence who, allegedly, circulated it to the government at the crammed meeting of 20 June 1969 which decided the fate of Lt Roche.

If we are to accept what is presented, it appears that Ground Hog Day happened in Dublin on 16 and 17 April 1969. The Security Report states that on these dates, based on the alleged testimony of Lt Roche, the following events happened on two consecutive nights:

On Thursday 17 April (paragraph 27) and Wednesday 16 April (paragraphs 8 and 9) Lt Roche went to O'Donoghue's pub with his girlfriend. On 17 April, they were accompanied by three others. On 16 April, they were with another 'girl' and were later joined by a man. On both occasions, they were in the outer bar when Padraig Dwyer entered from the lounge bar. On both occasions, Lt Roche told Dwyer that he was in Dublin to attend the auction at Clancy Barracks. On both occasions, Dwyer said he might come along. On both occasions, Roche, allegedly, went into the back lounge with Dwyer, where he met Dwyer's wife and sister and shortly thereafter returned to the front bar and rejoined his party.

Paragraph 27 concurs with paragraph 6 of the notes of the second interview (Appendix A: Document 4) in that it states that Lt Roche introduced Dwyer to 'the girls'. The interview notes, however, state that this was the first time Roche's girlfriend met Dwyer and that 'She did not like him.' On 23 May 2004, Lt Roche's girlfriend from 1969, when asked about this statement, informed me that she had 'no recollection of ever meeting Padraig Dwyer.'

On 10 November 2005, I spoke by telephone with the widow of Padraig Dwyer. She stated that she has absolutely no recollection of ever having met Dónal de Róiste, and the scene, as described in paragraphs 8, 9 and 27 above, meant nothing to her. She said that Dónal de Róiste never visited their home, indicating that he and Padraig were not close friends. When asked if she had any awareness of Padraig Dwyer having had any association with Dónal de Róiste, she replied: 'I'd say if they had any involvement it was of a very casual nature. Very casual indeed. Meeting in the pub would be the height of it.' She said that O'Donoghue's was such a popular and crowded venue, you were likely to meet anyone and everyone there. She also informed me that her deceased husband would sometimes attend the auction of surplus Garda vehicles, as good cars were expensive and it was possible to pick up a bargain at such an auction.

Paragraph 6 of the notes of the second interview also concurs with paragraph 27 of the Security Report. The former states: 'they [Roche and Dwyer] spoke about the case'. The Security Report states: 'They spoke about Dwyer's case.' Roche refutes this. The purpose of its inclusion is to establish the growing 'evidence' that Roche was aware of Dwyer's criminal/subversive background. Presumably the 'case' relates to the Ballyfermot incident involving the Garda Síochána. This point is driven home with a sledgehammer in the next paragraph.

Paragraph 6 of the notes of the second interview contains one other piece of information which, for reasons only the Intelligence Section of the defence forces can explain, was left out of the Security Report. It concerns the man, apparently identified, who joined Roche and his two female companions on 16 April in O'Donoghue's pub. He was tall and dark and he wore dark glasses. Perhaps it was left out of the report for fear that this mysterious character might make it all sound too much like fiction.

> 28. On 17th April he was there again with his girl friend, a ▮▮▮▮▮▮ and his girl friend and ▮▮▮▮▮▮ sister. They went to DONOGHUES because ▮▮▮▮▮▮ was interested to meet a criminal type and he knew ▮▮▮▮▮▮ would be there.

This information is lifted directly from paragraph 12 of the first 'interview' (Document 3). It is essential for the author of the report to establish that Lt Roche knowingly associated with criminals and subversives. It is essential to establish that he was fully aware of the alleged criminal background of Padraig Dwyer. So here's the scenario we are asked to believe: on 17 April 1969, or thereabouts, a male acquaintance of Lt Roche and his girlfriend, had the following idea:

> *Male acquaintance*: I'd be interested in meeting a criminal. Do you know any, Dónal?
> *Roche*: Actually I do. He's called Padraig Dwyer. He's a criminal and he'll be in O'Donoghue's on 17 April. Let's all head down there and I'll introduce you to him.

It is simply not plausible and how the JAG was not concerned by the discovery of references such as these is baffling.

De Róiste is equally baffled as to why the military authorities felt the need to redact the names of his friends and associates. He would especially like to know the identity of his friend who is alleged to have expressed the wish to meet 'a criminal type', should such a person exist. De Róiste suspects that the reason why the names of his friends have been redacted, particularly in this scenario, is that they would immediately refute the allegations.

Roche's girlfriend of 1969 said that she had absolutely no recollection of this incident. Indeed, she stated: 'I couldn't imagine anyone in my company asking that.' She went on to say that she remembered Dónal Roche as being 'a straight and honest person'.

29. They did meet ▮▮▮▮▮▮ and chatted together for a while. His girlfriend would not speak to ▮▮▮▮▮▮ as she did not like him.

Presumably, as the daughter of a Garda superintendent, she would not like Dwyer because he was supposed to be a criminal. But the real truth is, she didn't have to like Dwyer because this simply did not happen.

30. Recounting the meeting at the auction on the 23rd he said ▮▮▮▮▮▮ asked him about various cars and he told him about them. At one stage ▮▮▮▮▮▮ friend said to him that he should be careful talking to them as ▮▮▮▮▮▮ was being watched by the Special Branch.

In paragraph 3 above, we read that 'the auction was kept under surveillance' because of Lt Roche's 'contact' with Mr X, Padraig Dwyer. Now we read that Special Branch, whose presence had been observed by Dwyer's companion at the auction, was watching Dwyer. Roche refutes this and while he recalls meeting Dwyer at the auction, he says that he met him and greeted him as a member of the public.

The reference to the Special Branch is important because Padraig Dwyer was the subject of Special Branch surveillance. I met with a Special Branch officer who investigated the activities of Dwyer for several years and, indeed, shadowed him. I discussed the Lt Roche case and the Clancy Barracks auction, and the Special Branch officer said that he recalled nothing about Roche, or the Irish army, in any of the files relating to Dwyer. The significance of this will become even more apparent later.

> 31. In the evening of 23 April he was out with Capt. WALSHE and mentioned to him that ███████ was at the auction and that he was sure that they had been seen together.

As stated above, Captain Walshe not only refutes these assertions, but has lodged a sworn affidavit with the High Court to that effect. Furthermore, if Roche was engaging in something illicit and knew that he was being watched, why would he openly greet Padraig Dwyer at a public auction and in an army barracks?

> 32. ROCHE continued to deny that he met ███████, ███████ or ███████ on the 16th April or that he ever knew them. He claimed not to have been worried about his relationship with ███████ and did not feel that there was any security hazard in it. Asked why he felt no worries about a known criminal and subversives being in Clancy Bks he said he was sure the Special Branch would have been watching him and he felt no responsibility to report it.

This is a distortion. The real issue, which the JAG did not invite Commandant Gerry O'Sullivan to answer, was why, if they had identified a 'security hazard' in 'known criminals and subversives being in Clancy Bks', all of the 'criminals and subversives' were not arrested? If we are to believe the scenario presented, known criminals and subversives were watched by the military and the Garda Síochána entering a sensitive military post and were watched leaving, without being stopped, questioned, arrested, or even photographed.

> 33. He repeated that no subversive suggestion about ammunition, arms or military plans had ever been made to him by ▪▪▪▪▪▪▪ or anyone else. He realised now in the light of the enquiry that he had been foolish but felt he had done nothing wrong.

The first sentence of paragraph 33 is true because Roche's alleged 'relationship' with Dwyer was no deeper than the 'relationship' that Captain Patrick Walshe had with Dwyer. The second sentence is likely the opinion of O'Sullivan.

CONCLUSION

> 1. Lt ROCHE has known ▪▪▪▪▪▪▪ for almost a year. He met him fairly regularly between May 68 and October 68 including spending a weekend with him in Galway.

Roche knew Padraig Dwyer as a casual acquaintance whom he met on odd occasions when he went with companions, including other officers, to O'Donoghue's bar. He took a lift to Galway from Dwyer who was with a female friend and Roche was with his friend, Brendan (the 'Dog') Doherty. Roche and Doherty did not spend the weekend with Dwyer. Military Intelligence knew about the lift to Galway only because Roche told them. If he had felt he needed to conceal anything about his 'relationship' with Dwyer, he had no need to reveal this and O'Sullivan would have been none the wiser. It should also be noted that the lift to Galway occurred in July 1968, over two months before the Ballyfermot incident involving the Garda Síochána.

2. He was aware that ██████████
a. was a generally undesirable character.;
b. had served a jail sentence in England;
c. was decidedly anti-Army and anti-Establishment.

According to De Róiste, a and c above are the opinions of O'Sullivan, ascribed to him. As for point b, this is not recorded in any of the three interview notes and is added to reinforce the allegation that Roche knowingly associated with a criminal.

3. He had suspicions at least that ████████ had some subversive connections (talk about 'zeroing of rifles' and '9mm ammunition' – connect with para 13). He also referred to him to Comdt. MAGUIRE as being 'in the IRA'.

Why is there no signed statement from Commandant P. Maguire confirming the contents of their alleged conversation? Where is the evidence that he discussed 'zeroing of rifles' and '9mm ammunition'? I mentioned earlier the importance of remembering the reference to 9mm ammunition. Can the reader remember precisely where I mentioned this? Roche was, apparently, expected to remember the significance of an alleged reference to 9mm ammunition and to connect it with a court martial of a certain Cork-based army sergeant dealt with in Chapter 13.

4. In October he became aware that ████████ had been involved in a shooting fracas with the Gardai at Ballyfermot and was charged with offences arising from it. Newspaper reports at the time adverted to the possibility of a political and subversive background to this incident.

There are two press cuttings placed at the front of Lt Roche's G2/C/491 file. The C/491 is the Military Intelligence Section's designation for 'Members engaged in Subversive Activities'. The first cutting is taken from the front of the Dublin *Evening Press* of 3 October 1968 and details an attempted bank robbery earlier in the day, which had been foiled by gardaí who 'came under fire'. The article states that following a high-speed chase through Ballyfermot and Drimnagh, during which shots were fired, four men were arrested at Kilworth Road. A rifle and three loaded revolvers were recovered.

The second cutting, dated 4 October 1968, is taken from *The Irish Times*. It is not a main headline and is written on a two-inch column, seven inches deep. The article has two headlines: 'Shots fired at garda patrol car' and 'Four men remanded on arms charge'. Under the second heading, *The Irish Times* reports:

> Four men appeared in the Dublin District Court yesterday on charges of conspiracy and the possession of arms.
>
> They were: Seán Doyle (30), Silogue Road, Ballymum; Simon O'Donnell (23), no fixed address; Thomas O'Neill (30), no fixed abode, and Padraig Dwyer (26), of Marshfield Road, Inchicore.
>
> They are charged with conspiring and with the possession, at Cooley Road, Drimnagh, yesterday, of one rifle, three pistols and a quantity of ammunition.
>
> They were remanded in custody for one week.

The two press cuttings, which have nothing whatsoever to do with Lt Roche, are placed on his file to lend weight to the allegations being made against him. The incident received front-page headlines in the *Evening Press* over two days, but the subdued reportage of *The Irish Times* on 4 October is the only article that names the four people involved in the shootout, including Padraig Dwyer. There can be little doubt that the other three names are the names that are redacted throughout Lt Roche's 'secret' files, including this Security Report.

The incident was a local talking point and did not receive headline national news coverage, as is clear from the *Irish Times* article. Neither Roche nor Walshe can remember hearing about the incident, and both are adamant they had no idea that anyone they knew was involved in any such incident. Furthermore, they were stationed in the midlands and there was no reason why the incident should have impacted on them. There was certainly no briefing in the army about the incident which was a matter being handled entirely by the Garda Síochána.

5. Despite this knowledge he met ▮▮▮▮▮▮▮ on successive nights (16/17th April) in O'DONOGHUES. He discussed his (▮▮▮▮▮▮) case with him, told him what he (ROCHE) was doing in Dublin and at least concurred with his intention to visit the highly sensitive army post at Clancy Barracks.

The points made here have already been dealt with under paragraphs 1a–1b, 5 and 27 above.

6. He met him at the auction and advised him about the cars. Though reminded of ▮▮▮▮▮▮ position by his friend – 'Special branch men are watching him' – he took no protective action to assist military security.

Dwyer approached Lt Roche at a well-attended public auction. The statement 'he took no protective action to assist military security' is meaningless. Indeed, it can be argued, the 'watchers' 'took no protective action to assist military security'. Why was Dwyer not apprehended? The whole purpose of the alleged 'watch' placed on the auction was to see if Roche and Dwyer would connect. Once they had, surely both men should have been immediately arrested and interrogated. Why did that not happen?

7. ROCHE's association with ▮▮▮▮▮▮ is clearly established. There is NO evidence to indicate that the association had become subversive though ROCHE should have been fully aware of the potential danger.

On what basis is Lt Roche's association 'clearly established'? What is being admitted to here is actually the fact that there is NO evidence of a subversive connection between Roche and Dwyer and his group. There is an opinion, stated as fact, that there was a danger of the association becoming subversive, but it is all conjecture. If Lt Roche's 'retirement' was to be achieved – unopposed – 'in the interests of the service', something more substantial would be required. As it stood, the case was not strong enough.

Enter Sgt John Shinkwin. Who? Precisely.

8. In the light of the experience of the SHINKWIN
   case and the known extremism of the Group of
   which ▮▮▮▮▮▮ is a member it is very likely that
   an approach would have been made if the association
   had not been uncovered.

The immediate question one finds oneself asking is 'Who is Shinkwin?'
And what does this have to do with Lt Roche, six days after his first
interrogation? Remember, this report is dated 1 May 1969, and,
allegedly, Roche's third and final interview had occurred the previous
day, 30 April. A review of all three 'interview notes' (Documents 3,
4 and 7) will reveal that there is absolutely no mention of Shinkwin.
The Shinkwin case was not mentioned either during Captain Walshe's
interrogations. So, why is it here? Indeed, is there a genuine connection?
   This matter is, I believe, of such significance that Chapter 13 is
entirely devoted to what I call the Shinkwin Affair. And again, it
is important not to forget the alleged mention of 9mm ammunition,
because this, apparently, is the link between Lt Roche and Sgt
Shinkwin.

9. The fact that ROCHE did not meet ▮▮▮▮▮▮
   during the period October/April may be accounted
   for by the SHINKWIN case and the shooting
   incident which both occurred about this time.
   ▮▮▮▮▮▮ was in custody for some weeks arising
   from the latter. Additionally ROCHE was away for
   three weeks at the end of December/beginning of
   January acting as a chauffeur/guide to an American
   touring London and France. He obtained this by
   answering an advertisement in the newspaper.

The fact that Roche did not meet Padraig Dwyer during the period
between October 1968 and April 1969 was for no other reason than
that Dwyer was not in O'Donoghue's pub when he visited there and
he had no reason to miss him since Dwyer was not on his list of friends
or acquaintances who would be missed. And as regards his trip abroad

at Christmas, he had annual leave and responded to an advertisement either in a newspaper or posted on a notice board in the barracks. The person requiring a driver was a retired US naval officer, whom De Róiste remembers as Captain Bill from Florida. Lt Roche says that he saw this as an adventure. Not only would he get a chance to travel with a former naval officer from the US, but he would have the opportunity to visit the sights of London and Paris, and get paid at the same time.

10. The only evidence to connect ROCHE with others in the group is that of the original confidential report. An unsupported report of this nature must be taken with reserve but it is pointed out that:-

a. The report was very accurate in all other matters.

b. It clearly pointed to ROCHE as the person concerned.

c. It reported him as being in O'DONOGHUES on two nights (16/17th) – a fact not admitted by ROCHE until his second interview.

d. It reported an arrangement to attend the auction which occurred.

10 (a–c) have been dealt with above. However, the assertion at 10 (d) needs to be clarified. Where is it reported that 'an arrangement to attend the auction' was made? Paragraph 2 of the original 'confidential' memo (Appendix A, Document 1) simply states, 'During the conversation ROCHE mentioned that there was an auction of army vehs at Clancy Bks on 23rd April 69 and that he would advise on a good car if anyone wanted to buy one.' This is simply word-of-mouth advertisement in addition to the ads placed in all the national papers. What is reported in the source memo is not 'an arrangement'. Subparagraph 10 (d) above is quite simply spin.

11. Coupled with the fact that these four, ▮▮▮▮▮▮▮, ▮▮▮▮▮▮▮, ▮▮▮▮▮▮ and ▮▮▮▮▮▮ [those named in the *Irish Times* article above] are all known to knock around together and to frequent O'DONOGHUES pub it remains a strong possibility that ROCHE did meet them there on the 16th April and may have

known them previously.

One senses that the author of this report is clutching at straws and attempting to convince – even himself – that Roche's associations were deeper than they actually were. As the conclusions of the Security Report are now being made, did its author realise that the case against Roche was, in fact, really very weak? The next two conclusions would suggest this.

> 12. He can deny this because he knows that direct evidence connecting him with them has not been produced.

That conclusion speaks eloquently for itself.

> 13. ▮▮▮▮▮▮▮ is a thoroughly bad character. He has a jail record in England, is awaiting trial on charges here and was one of the four who planned to attack LAHINCH Camp last August in collaboration with ex Sgt SHINKWIN.

Even if all of the above were so, what does it have to do with Lt Roche?

> 14. Any association by a member of the Defence Forces with him or his group constitutes a security hazard. When the member is an officer this hazard is increased very considerably.

What association? There is absolutely no evidence of anything other than a casual acquaintance.

There was a distinct possibility that the removal of Roche from the defence forces could be considerably delayed if the Minister for Defence, the government, or even the President, queried the basis of the proposed recommendation for his retirement. Remember, this Security Report is dated 1 May 1969 and the Chief of Staff, allegedly, sent it with a covering letter to the Minister for Defence two days later, with the recommendation that Roche be retired 'in the interests of the service'. This was also the same day that the Chief of Staff had, as a 'prudent security precaution', moved Roche from Athlone to Boyle.

There are two appendices attached to the 'Security Report', which can be read near the end of Appendix A, Document 8b. The second Appendix gives broad details of Lt Roche's army career. The first Appendix, however, is far more significant. It specifically deals with the alleged connection between Padraig Dwyer and his group, and Sgt John Shinkwin, the subject of my next chapter.

However, before concluding this chapter, which has broadly reviewed some of the documentation available to the JAG, there are two further significant documents that must be highlighted.

THIRD INTERVIEW NOTES

Nowhere in the Security Report we have just considered, including the appendices, is there any reference to the alleged 'third interview' on 30 April 1969. This document (Appendix A, Document 7) is interesting in that it appears to have been added retrospectively. It also differs from the two previous interview notes in that it does not specifically state where the interview took place. Its sequence in the documentation, as noted by the JAG, follows the Security Report, which she observes, 'makes no reference to the third interview'. The notes of the third interview are typed and, once again, unsigned, and their authorship undeclared. There is a date on this document, '1/5/69', which is handwritten.

There are six paragraphs in this document. Paragraphs 2 to 5 deal with an alleged additional memory Lt Roche had concerning a brief encounter with a Lt Leo Casey in O'Donoghue's pub on the evening of 16 April 1969. Roche allegedly thought that Casey might also have met Dwyer. The notes state that Casey confirmed meeting Roche 'by appointment' around 21.35 and leaving at about 22.00. Casey, it is alleged, said that Roche was at the bar 'with two girls and a man who had a guitar'. The notes state: 'He did not remember being introduced to anyone' though he did see 'ROCHE speak to a man in the lounge but did not know what was said.' Paragraph 5 observes that 'This information helps little beyond confirming that ROCHE was in Donoghue's [*sic*] between 21.35 hrs and 22.00 hrs on 16th April, 1969.'

Paragraphs 1 and 6 of the alleged 'third interview' notes are more important. As typed, paragraph 1 reads:

Further to the security report on Lt Dónal ROCHE
of 30 Aibreán [April] 69 the following additional
information was submitted.

However, the word 'was' is scored out and the word 'is' has been inserted
by hand. The sentence thus reads:

Further to the security report on Lt Dónal ROCHE
of 30 Aibrean [April] 69 the following additional
information is submitted.

This change is significant. The first sentence, as typed, is a retrospective
statement. The second sentence, with the handwritten insertion, is
present tense.

This sentence also suggests that the Security Report was written on
30 April 1969, and not 1 May 1969, as dated. The handwritten addition
of the date '1/5/69', in the same pen as the word 'is', may have been
added to camouflage the fact that this entire document was written
much later with a specific purpose in mind. And what might that
purpose have been? Paragraph 6 holds the key. It states:

At the conclusion of this interview Lt ROCHE said he
wished to submit his account of this matter in writing.
He was advised he was free to do this if he wished and
that if he submitted one it should be through the OIC
Ceann [Command OC]. Cft. MADIGAN, who was
present at this stage, was informed accordingly.

It should be noted that Lt Roche was *not* asked to make a statement. It
is stated that he 'wished to submit his account of this matter in writing'.
He was told that he was free to do so, but with conditions. It must
be through his Command OC – in other words, through an officer
who had no involvement in the entire process. Yet later he is accused
of refusing to submit a statement. The purpose, it seems, is to suggest
retrospectively that Lt Roche was afforded fair procedures throughout
and that his alleged 'voluntary' offer to submit his account of the matter
in writing was greeted with openness. It should be recalled that in
paragraph 12 of the first interview notes (Appendix A, Document 3),

it is stated: 'At an early stage he [Lt Roche] refused to answer questions and asked for a solicitor.' Roche may have been young and naïve but he was no fool. He absolutely refutes the assertion that he offered to submit his account of the matter in writing. He was more concerned about getting a solicitor, although he felt that the solicitor he did get failed to defend him properly in the end.

It should also be noted that while there is no evidence of anyone other than O'Sullivan being present during the first and second interrogations, remarkably a Commandant MADIGAN happens to be present at the precise moment when Roche offers to submit his account in writing. Why might this be so? It establishes the 'fact' that there was a witness to support the allegation. It was now the word of two senior officers against a young lieutenant.

It is, however, recorded in quite a clumsy manner. The final sentence of the document states:

> … Cft. MADIGAN, who was present at this stage, was informed accordingly.

Again, we have a confusion between present tense and past tense. If Commandant Madigan 'was present' – why would there be a need to 'inform him accordingly'?

It is my suspicion that this document was written retrospectively, backdated, and that its primary purpose was to create the illusion that Roche had voluntarily offered to make a statement and subsequently reneged on his offer.

DEPUTY JUDGE ADVOCATE GENERAL'S REPORT

In a document marked SECRET (Appendix A, Document 12), addressed to An tAire [the Minister], the Chief of Staff, Lt General S. Mac Eoin, wrote:

> In accordance with your request I arranged for [Lt Dónal Roche] to be interviewed by the Deputy Judge Advocate General. This interview took place on 28/29 Bealtaine [May] 1969.
>
> The report of the Deputy Judge Advocate General dated 29ú Bealtaine 1969 is attached hereto and

reinforces the conclusions already arrived at by me after consultation with the Adjutant General, the Quartermaster General, the Assistant Chief of Staff and the Director of Intelligence.

The DJAG is the defence forces' chief legal officer and, unlike the JAG who is a civilian barrister-at-law, is a member of the forces. As such, it is the duty of the DJAG to ensure that proper legal procedures are adhered to in accordance with the Defence Force Act 1954.

It is clear that even before the DJAG was asked to conduct his 'interview', minds had already been made up, and, in the minds of high-ranking officers – especially in Intelligence Section – Lt Roche was guilty, but specifically of what? Where was the hard evidence, apart from innuendoes and attempts to build a case that was little more than guilt by association?

To this day, Dónal de Róiste cannot clearly remember meeting the DJAG, Col. Arthur Cullen. He says that he encountered a number of senior officers and it is possible one of them was Cullen but there is much in Cullen's report for which he simply cannot account.

The DJAG's report requires separate and detailed analysis. However, in the context of the military authorities' failure to reply to a legal enquiry from Lt Roche's solicitor, it is disquieting that at no stage did the army's most senior legal officer advise the young lieutenant of his corresponding rights under the Defence Act 1954. The only apparent step he took was to read the Oath of Allegiance and then proceed to suggest that Roche had not honoured the Oath by his actions. Indeed, by his own admission, the DJAG states that he advised Lt Roche that there would be no objection to his consulting a solicitor, but only after Lt Roche, allegedly, asked the question. I have been advised that it would not be normal to expect the DJAG to make an executive recommendation in this instance. His job should be solely to advise on a matter of law.

It would also have been helpful if the current JAG, Ms McCrann, in her review of the secret files held on Lt Roche, had attempted to ascertain the identities of the two people who had drafted the response to Lt Roche's solicitor. Their identities are important to establish since there are wider implications if the office of the DJAG was engaged in drafting that response, within days of the DJAG having conducted his formal 'interview' with Roche.

The DJAG's 'secret' report to the Chief of Staff, dated 29 May 1969, states:

> In accordance with your directions this officer reported to my office yesterday for interview.
>
> The interview commenced at 14.05 hours.
>
> I informed Lt Roche that the Int. rep. [Intelligence Report] on his association with ██████████ had been submitted to the General Staff who had called upon me as DJAG to advise.

In the Chief of Staff's undated and 'secret' letter – addressed to the Minister for Defence – he states that this encounter happened at the Minister's request (Document 12). The DJAG had a responsibility to Lt Roche to establish this fact, if true. The Senior Headquarters Staff had requested the DJAG to meet Roche, precisely because the Minister, allegedly, requested that he should. He stated:

> I informed him that as he had volunteered on 30 Aibreán [April] to submit a statement about the matter and as he had not done so after a month I was reluctant to do anything until he had been given the opportunity of submitting any statement he wished to make.

It is alleged that Lt Roche volunteered a written statement in the presence of two officers, Commandant Gerry O'Sullivan, his prime interrogator, and Commandant Madigan. Roche robustly denies this assertion. Roche had been advised not to make a statement by his solicitor and was under the assumption that, as he had been moved to Boyle, Co. Roscommon, his solicitor had the matter in hand.

> Lt Roche then stated that on the Friday after his final interrogation by the Int Sec on 30/4/69 he had consulted his solicitor (Mr Michael O'Maoileain), who had undertaken to write to the Director of Intelligence and to Officer Commanding, Western Command. I informed him that these letters had NOT been received.

This suggests that Roche was confused and surprised, having been under the assumption that O'Maoileoin had written, as he had said he would at the beginning of May, to the Chief of Staff and his Commanding Officer.

> Lt Roche did not appear to me at this stage to be very seriously concerned about the matter so I proceeded to take him through his statements in Int Sec. He agreed with the accuracy of the report and on further questioning admitted to being aware that Sgt Shinkwin had been court-martialled and convicted of stealing and selling 9mm ammo.

How could the DJAG take Lt Roche 'through his statements' when no such statements exist in his files? Was he reading from the O'Sullivan notes? The O'Sullivan notes contain only assertions to the effect that Roche admitted this/denied that etc. De Róiste has no idea where the DJAG got the impression that he had taken him 'through his statements'. He was seriously worried and had been hoping that the matter had blown over. Indeed, his girlfriend from the time, when asked if Dónal was under stress, said: 'Of course he was under stress. I am sure it took an awful lot out of him.'

De Róiste utterly refutes the assertion by the DJAG that he 'agreed with the accuracy of the report.' Furthermore, he has absolutely no recollection of the case of Sgt Shinkwin being discussed with him by the DJAG. It must also be noted that this is the first time that Shinkwin was, allegedly, raised with Lt Roche. This immediately calls into question the entire role of the DJAG in this encounter. By, allegedly, confronting Roche with Shinkwin, Col. Cullen was, wittingly or not, continuing the interrogation of Roche. He was certainly not acting with the level of independence one might expect from the army's senior legal person whose job it is to ensure fair procedures and guard against abuse.

If, as is alleged, Lt Roche admitted to being aware of the Shinkwin court martial at which Sgt John Shinkwin was convicted of stealing and selling 9mm rounds of ammunition, the case against Roche would be strengthened. There are several leading statements throughout the documentation that are working towards making a link between two unconnected episodes. Here is an example:

> On one occasion ▮▮▮▮▮▮▮ told him he had been away
> in Connemara 'zeroing rifles' and on another he made
> some passing reference to 9mm ammunition. ROCHE
> did not take him seriously but did think he might have
> some subversive connection.
> Colonel Hefferon, Security Report to Chief of Staff, 1
> May 1969. (Appendix A, document 8b, paragraph 13)

And here is the clincher. Written by the Chief of Staff on 3 May 1969
to the Minister for Defence and, apparently, circulated at the cabinet
meeting on 20 June 1969, at which Lt Roche's fate was finally decided:

> Sgt SHINKWIN pleased [*sic*] guilty ... and was
> sentenced to six months' imprisonment. This case
> was well publicised in the army and in the public press
> and it is inconceivable that Lt Roche did not associate
> Dwyer's reference to '9mm ammunition' with the case
> of Sgt Shinkwin. (It is known that this ammunition was
> sold to ▮▮▮▮▮▮ – alias ▮▮▮▮▮▮▮ ... a member of the
> splinter group of the IRA.
> (Appendix A, Document 10a, paragraph 3.3).

It is important to keep reminding oneself that there is absolutely no
mention of Shinkwin in the three interrogation notes (Documents 3,
4 and 7). This is, allegedly, the first occasion that the case is raised with
Roche, and Roche has no memory of its ever having been discussed
with him.

Col. Cullen, the DJAG continued:

> I asked him if this Int Rep, taken as a whole, did not
> indicate that he must be considered a security risk and he
> replied that that [*sic*] this is what the Int Sec had told him
> and added 'I don't appreciate what I am guilty of.'

After four years of research, I still don't appreciate what he was guilty of either.

> I then went through the report in the minutest detail and his answers were consistent with those already given to Int Sec: on some matters his answers were glib and practically flippant on others evasive, for instance, I asked him if there was any significance in the fact that he had ceased to meet ███████████ in October 1968? He replied that there was not – he had not had the opportunity as he had not been in Dublin. I suggested to him that one reason was that Shinkwin had been tried in October and that another might be the Ballyfermot incident. He said that he wasn't sure if it had been October, it might have been in September. I then suggested that the reason why he ceased to meet ███████████ in September was that it was in that month that Shinkwin had been arrested and charged. Lt Roche then said that possibly it had been as early as August? I suggested that if it was August the cause might have been that it was in August that the 9mm ammo. had been stolen and sold. At this Lt Roche smiled and shrugged his his [*sic*] shoulders and said that he couldn't remember anyway.

Cullen was continuing the interrogation of Lt Roche here, although he had, allegedly, been asked to advise on the legal position. In another SECRET memo (Appendix A: Document 17), dated 12 June 1969 (one week before the memorandum for government was prepared, and just two weeks before Lt Roche's expulsion), Commandant O'Sullivan stated:

> Lt ROCHE was interviewed by DJAG at 1430 hrs on 28. Bea (May) 69.
> He was advised of the legal position…

There is no evidence that the DJAG offered Lt Roche any legal advice throughout their encounter. Nor did he advise him of the legal position, or indeed of the fact that his retirement 'in the interests of the service' had been proposed to the Minister for Defence on 3 May. It is deeply disconcerting that Ms McCrann appears to have seen nothing untoward in this.

It is also clear that the DJAG was seeking an admission of guilt and pressurising Lt Roche into making the much-desired written statement. He states:

> I told him that the facts disclosed a very serious state of affairs and I read to him the oath taken by him when he was commissioned and that the report seemed to suggest that he was not being true to either the words or spirit of his oath. I advised him that he should go away and seriously consider his situation and that he should call on me the following morning at 10.00 hours with his statement.
>
> The interview ended at 15.10 and as he was leaving my office Lt Roche asked if there would be any objection to him consulting his solicitor. I replied 'Certainly not.'

The next sentence is spun in a manner that is deliberately aimed at giving the impression that Roche is unwilling to make a written statement because he knows he is guilty and would, therefore, incriminate himself. Cullen's signed report states:

> At 09.40 this day Lt Roche again visited me in my office. I asked him to sit down and he informed me that the matter would not take long as he would NOT make any further statement. He then left.

This is not supported by the 'secret' O'Sullivan memo of 12 June 1969 (Appendix A, Document 17), which states:

> … ROCHE said he proposed to see his solicitor.
>
> At 0940 hours on 29 Bea (May) 69 Lt ROCHE informed DJAG that his solicitor had advised him 'to do nothing'.

Again, it is disconcerting that Ms McCrann failed to make reference to the conflict that existed between two reports of the same event. In this instance I am inclined to believe that the 'secret' memo of O'Sullivan is the accurate record of what transpired. It reflects the advice that was given by Lt Roche's solicitor who told his client 'to do nothing' because he would now write to the Chief of Staff, which, of course, he did.

The DJAG then proceeded to drive the final nail into young Lt Roche's coffin:

> From the Int. Reps and from my own interview with him and having regard to his manner of answering questions and his general demeanour in this context and his refusal to make a statement (though he had volunteered to do so) I am satisfied beyond all doubt that this officer's retention in the Forces constitutes a grave security risk.

The DJAG makes his assertion that 'beyond all doubt' Dónal's continued service constitutes a grave security risk based to a large extent on these pieces of conjecture:

a. Roche's general demeanour
b. Roche's alleged refusal to make a statement
c. Roche's manner of answering questions.

Hardly convincing 'evidence' upon which to be so categorical.

THE QUASHING OF THE JUDGE ADVOCATE GENERAL'S REPORT

There is no doubt that the choreography put in place to publicise and spin the JAG's report caught us all by surprise, and the conclusions Ms McCrann came to were deeply damaging to Dónal's developing campaign. However, the manner in which the office of the JAG was used to underpin a thirty-three-year-long injustice against a young Irish officer has damaged the independence of the office.

The McCrann report not only derailed De Róiste's growing campaign – it almost destroyed it. But it ultimately failed. Eamonn Carroll, De Róiste's solicitor, quietly and energetically worked behind the scenes with Ercus Stewart SC and Gerald Humphries to rebuild the legal case. First, they sought leave to judicially review the JAG's report. In the course of a preliminary hearing, on 17 November 2003,

Mr Justice Quirke expressed the view that the decision to withhold documents due for release under the Freedom of Information Act amounted to conspiracy. Counsel for De Róiste, Ger Humphries, in a summary note to Eamonn Carroll, wrote: 'We had not used the word "conspiracy", but he [Judge Quirke] said the effect of it would be to pervert the enquiry'.

Mr Justice Quirke also directed the state to swear an affidavit regarding the 'discovery', on about 15 May 2001, of the missing file which contained the letter from De Róiste's solicitor, dated 30 May 1969 (Appendix A, Document 14).

On 16 January 2004, Conor Kerlin, a principal officer at the Department of Defence, swore the following affidavit about the missing file:

> According to the best of my knowledge, information and belief and having made inquiries within the Department I say that … in relation to the missing file… the said file was untraceable within the Department until May 15 2001. On that date a Department Official found the file by chance while searching in the safe of the Secretary General of the Department for some unrelated papers. The official in question was not involved in any way with the matters related to the de Róiste case but was aware that the file had been missing and immediately realized the significance of the find and brought the matter to the attention of the then Private Secretary to the Secretary General who then informed the Secretary General of the position. All communications between officials of the Department in relation to the finding of this file were verbal.

Mr Justice Quirke gave leave for a full judicial review of the JAG's report. It was held on 21–23 June 2005. With regard to the procedures adopted for Ms McCrann's report – particularly the decision not to give Dónal de Róiste and his legal team access to his files until after her report had been published – Conleth Bradley, SC, a new addition to De Róiste's cause, stated in his opening remarks:

The review could only be described as a sham, given the
fact that Dónal was invited to participate in the review
notwithstanding the fact that he complained of having
no documentation in circumstances where a decision
had been made to give him the documentation, with that
decision embargoed until after the review, the self-same
review which decided to give him the documentation.
Were the circumstances surrounding Dónal's retirement
not so serious, the aforementioned would be laughable.

On 28 July 2005, Mr Justice Quirke issued his judgment. He quashed
Ms McCrann's report, including her conclusion that the decision to
retire Lt Dónal Roche in 1969 had been 'reasonable'. Judge Quirke
granted De Róiste a declaration that the report was void and had no
effect. Vivion Kilfeather, writing in the *Irish Examiner*, reported:

He [Mr Justice Quirke] said the decision to recommend
Mr de Róiste's retirement in 1969 had been deemed by
the courts to have been lawfully made. However, there
had been no determination by the courts or by any tri-
bunal as to whether or not the decision to recommend
his involuntary retirement was 'reasonable'. The JAG
(Oonah McCrann SC) inquiry was a process which was
'apparently undertaken to make such a determination' he
said.

Mr Justice Quirke also found that De Róiste had not been granted fair
procedures. In his conclusions he stated:

By failing to provide the applicant with access to the
relevant documents the JAG and the Minister deprived
the applicant of the opportunity to make meaningful
and informed representations to the JAG within the
process directed towards the vindication of his right to
his reputation and good name....
That was patently unfair to the applicant. It
comprised a failure to provide him with fair procedures
and a failure to observe the principles of natural and

constitutional justice in the conduct of the process. No explanation has been offered on behalf of the respondents by way of justification or mitigation. It remains therefore unexplained and inexplicable.

The failure to provide fair procedures were by no means trivial, insubstantial or technical in nature. It inhibited and may well have prejudiced the capacity of the applicant to make fair and adequate representations to the JAG....

It was a moment of relief and cause for celebration for it was the first legal victory that De Róiste had achieved. In essence, however, as the final sentence of Mr Justice Quirke's judgment indicates, all that had been achieved was the quashing of the JAG's report on the basis of unfair procedures:

The decision made in 1969 to recommend the applicant's retirement from the Defence Forces remains unaffected by any order made in these proceedings.

De Róiste's presidential retirement, on the recommendation of the government, is unaffected and, therefore, his long and epic struggle to clear his name continues.

This fact was made clear by the response of the current Minister for Defence, Willie O'Dea, TD, to Deputy Tony Gregory's enquiry as to whether, in view of the quashing of the JAG's report, any steps were being taken to re-open the case.

On 28 September 2005, Minister O'Dea responded:

A decision to retire an officer 'in the interests of the service' is only taken for the most compelling reasons. The government advice to the President was on grounds of security. I am satisfied that the matter was handled in an entirely appropriate and proper manner in 1969 and that the decision taken then was taken only after very detailed and due consideration....

... the recent High Court judgment in the matter of the report of the Judge Advocate General specifically and only related to the actual procedures utilised by the Judge Advocate General in the course of her review and examination of this matter in 2002. The substantive issue, namely the Government decision in 1969 to recommend the retirement of this individual from the defence forces by the President, remains entirely unaffected by the judgment of the High Court, a point specifically emphasised within the text of that recent judgment itself…

SUBVERSION

Oonah McCrann has every right to feel aggrieved and betrayed by the Minister's assertion above, which appears to blame the procedures utilised by her, as Judge Advocate General, for the collapse of the state's case. In truth, Mr O'Dea's predecessor, Michael Smith, no doubt acting on advice from the very civil servants who drafted the above parliamentary response, played a very active role in the procedures that resulted in the High Court quashing of the report. It is, therefore, quite appalling that they now appear to be shifting all blame for the quashing of Ms McCrann's report onto the office of the Judge Advocate General. At the conclusion of this disappointing and deeply flawed process, the most damaged entity appears to be none other than that office.

It is clear that the state is not ready to review openly the substantive issues of the Lt Dónal Roche case. It is still hiding behind the issue of 'national security'. Although the Minister for Defence was prepared to state that he was 'satisfied that the matter was handled in an entirely appropriate and proper manner in 1969 and that the decision taken then was taken only after very detailed and due consideration', several requests by me for an in-depth on-camera interview have been ignored.

The following chapter deals with a matter that requires transparent public scrutiny. If, as I suspect, information was misrepresented in order to 'beef up' the case against Lt Dónal Roche, the only conclusion that can be drawn is that justice and truth were subverted and the government and President were misled by senior officers of the defence forces – and civil servants – in their decision to retire Lt Roche 'in the interests of the service'.

13

THE SHINKWIN AFFAIR

Treason shall consist only in levying war against the State, or assisting any State or person or inciting or conspiring with any person to levy war against the state, or attempting by force of arms or other violent means to overthrow the organs of government established by this Constitution, or taking part or being concerned in or inciting or conspiring with any person to take or to take part or be concerned in any such attempt.

The Irish Constitution (Article 39)

The following additional information on the Lt Dónal de Róiste affair was added to the Security Report reviewed in the previous chapter and sent by the Director of Intelligence, Col. Hefferon, to the Chief of Staff who, in turn, sent it to the Minister for Defence:

> SECRET
> <u>ADDITIONAL INFORMATION</u>
>   The persons mentioned in the report received are
> ██████████, ██████████, ██████████ and ██████████.
>   They are members of the IRA splinter group and are amongst the most extreme members in it.
>   ██████████, ██████████ were all connected with the SHINKWIN case of August last year. ██████████ was the chief contact. He collected the ammunition from SHINKWIN and paid for it. ██████████ met SHINKWIN with ██████████ at a later date and arranged a raid on LAHINCH Camp on 27th August, 1968.
>   ██████████, ██████████ and ██████████ were three of the four (██████████ was the fourth) who went to LAHINCH on 27th August 68 with the intention of

raiding the camp and only changed their mind at the last
minute.

███████, ███████, ███████ and ███████
were the four involved in the shooting incident with the
Gardai at Ballyfermot in October 68. They are currently
awaiting trial for this.

The Group are believed to have been involved in bank
raids and ███████ is awaiting trial for the Newbridge
raid. Some of them are also suspected of being involved
in the Newry bank raid.

███████ returned from England about 18 months
ago. He came to Garda notice in the summer of 1968 as
associating with the Splinter group but was not positively
identified until the investigations into the SHINKWIN
case.

He was the driver of the car at LAHINCH and again
at Ballyfermot. He is currently employed as a fitter with a
central heating firm.

███████ was one of the two men sentenced for
setting fire to the Fianna Fáil HQ in Mount Street on 21
October, 1967.

Members of the group were reliably reported to
have planned an attack on a post in Cork (believed to be
FERMOY) in the summer of 1968 but did not go ahead
with it because the Cork group were against it.

THE SHINKWIN COURT MARTIAL

The Shinkwin court martial was covered in the national press on 9
October 1968. It is interesting to note that in Lt Roche's 'subversive
file', intelligence officers have added press cuttings from the *Evening
Press*, dated 3 October 1968 and *The Irish Times*, dated 4 October 1968,
giving details of the so-called 'Ballyfermot shootout' between Dwyer,
his associates and the Garda Síochána. However, there are no press reports of the Shinkwin court martial of the same week. in his file. Why?

The following composite account is based on the reports in *The Irish
Times* and *Cork Examiner* of the court martial of Sgt John C. Shinkwin,
on 9 October 1968. The *Irish Times* headline states: 'Sergeant Admits
Ammunition Theft – Money was the motive' and the *Cork Examiner*

headline states: 'Took Ammunition "For Financial Motives Purely"'.

Sgt Shinkwin, aged thirty-two, was attached to Command Training Depot, Cork. He was married with four children under the age of eight. He resided at Crosshaven, Co. Cork, and had served overseas with the defence forces on five occasions in the Congo and Cyprus. On 8 October 1968, he was ordered to appear before a general court martial at Collins Barracks, Cork, presided over by four senior officers. Lt Col. M.N. Gill, solicitor, Adjutant General's Branch, was judge advocate; Captain M.K. Bradley, BL, was prosecutor, and Captain P. Kelly was defending officer. Sgt Shinkwin pleaded guilty to three charges:

(1) Stealing 1,300 rounds of 9mm ammunition valued at £17.13s 6d at Collins Barracks on 16 August 1968;
(2) Selling the ammunition to a person unknown in Cork city on the same date; and
(3) Being absent without leave from Collins Barracks from 1800 hours on 12 September to 1700 hours on 17 September.

After the plea, the President of the Court, Col. M.A. O'Byrne, asked the judge advocate, Lt Col. Gill, to explain to the accused the implications of pleading guilty. Lt Col. Gill said that if the court accepted the pleas of guilty, the only function left to it was to pass sentence.

'Of course,' he informed Sgt Shinkwin, 'you will have the opportunity of giving evidence in mitigation of punishment. This evidence you may or may not give on oath, and you will have the opportunity of calling witnesses to your character. Your defending officer may address the court in mitigation of punishment.'

Sgt Shinkwin's defending officer told the court that he had discussed the position and the plea with the accused, and the accused was aware of the implications. The President then stated that the court was accepting Sgt Shinkwin's plea of guilty.

The judge advocate said that the finding of the court would be subject to confirmation. The procedure on the pleas of guilty was that the accused might now make a statement in reference to the charges, after which a summary of evidence, relevant to the charges, would be read. Sgt Shinkwin declined to make a statement, after which the President said: 'At this stage I consider it expedient, in view of the powers and responsibility placed on me as president of this court under Section 194 of the Defence Act (1954) and in the interest of defence and security to close the court and I do so order that this part of the trial shall be closed.'

Upon resumption of the open session of the court martial, Commandant Henry Goldsboro, and Commandant J. A. McMahon, under whom Sgt Shinkwin had served in Cyprus, spoke on his behalf, referring to his service as 'satisfactory' and his conduct 'exemplary'. Both officers agreed that while in Cyprus Sgt Shinkwin had been a credit to his country and the army.

McMahon stated that as OC of Command Training at Collins Barracks, Sgt Shinkwin had been under his command. He had been an able and efficient instructor who could always be relied upon to be present for his period of instruction and to carry out his duties efficiently. 'On September 15th,' McMahon said, 'he handed himself up to me and since then he co-operated fully with me and others in the investigation.'

Called by the prosecution, Capt. James Hayes, Adjutant of the Command Training Depot at Collins Barracks, produced a record of Sgt Shinkwin's service and character. He had no military convictions before this court martial.

The judge advocate said that Shinkwin had now been in custody for twenty-two days, and had not been paid. He had first joined the army in 1952 and again in 1960 for a period of nine years. He held both Cyprus and Congo UN medals.

NO SUBVERSIVE CONNECTION

The defending officer, Captain Patrick Kelly, then addressed the court in mitigation of punishment. He informed the court that, on Sgt Shinkwin's own sworn statement, the offence was committed purely for a financial reason. He stated:

> Sergeant Shinkwin had no connection or sympathy with subversive elements either here or in Great Britain.

Let us at this point bear in mind the linkage being made in the 'secret' documents on Lt Roche's files in which a very definite connection was alleged between Padraig Dwyer, his alleged associates in the 'Splinter

IRA group' and Shinkwin. Kelly continued:

> With regard to the financial motive for this offence, this Sergeant who had given excellent service for ten years was involved in a most unfortunate accident, an accident which you could admit could happen to very many people. He was carrying out a work of mercy in that he was driving an injured person to hospital. It was unlikely on the spur of the moment he would think he was not insured when driving the car. It was unfortunate he did have an accident and that it involved him in very serious debt.
>
> Up to the time of the accident his service was exemplary, as he said himself he had some H.P. debts. But he budgeted wisely and was able to meet them. But out of the blue he was saddled with an extra £200. I think you will admit that an extra £200 out of the blue for a sergeant with a wife and family of four children who had just established his home was an impossible imposition particularly when he was ordered to pay the £200 within six months. Very little consideration was needed to realise this was an impossible position to pay back so much out of a salary of £12 a week.

Captain Kelly concluded his defence:

> What is the point now of inflicting detention or imprisonment on the accused? He is not a danger to the state and in so far as he does not sympathise with those subversive elements, neither is he a thief in the strict sense of the word.

After members of the court had spent about half an hour considering the merits of the case, the president announced the following:

- Sgt Shinkwin was sentenced to six months' imprisonment without hard labour,
- He was reduced to the rank of private, and

> • He was discharged from the Irish defence forces.

After the Judge Advocate had told the accused that the sentence was subject to ratification and that he had the right of appeal, the proceedings were closed.

ANALYSIS

As previously stated, the above is a composite account of the Shinkwin court martial based on press reports of 9 October 1968. It is interesting that four senior officers turned up at the court martial to testify on behalf of Shinkwin's good character. These testaments contrast starkly with the absolute silence of any senior officer – particularly Lt Roche's Commanding Officers in Athlone and Boyle – who might have attempted to defend Lt Roche or even offer a statement on behalf of his good character. Roche had received a fourth consecutive 'satisfactory' rating in his officer report for the year ended 31 December 1968. Why the sudden silence and abandonment?

Several illuminating points arise from the press reports. For example, Shinkwin was found guilt of stealing 1,300 rounds of 9mm ammunition on 16 August 1968 and selling them 'to a person unknown' in Cork city on the same date. There is absolutely no mention of subversives and certainly not a hint of any of the redacted names that the intelligence reports contain. Yet all the so-called intelligence documents from Dónal de Róiste's files link Shinkwin with members of the same splinter IRA group that included Mr X, Padraig Dwyer. In the 'Additional Information' to the Hefferon 'Security Report' of 1 May 1969, quoted above, the alleged link between Shinkwin and those involved in the Ballyfermot shooting is made clear. Yet the court martial heard nothing about Shinkwin helping Dwyer and the others to plan an attack on Lahinch Camp on 27 August 1968, as alleged in the same 'Additional Information' attached to the Security Report. From where, therefore, does this information emanate? Given the treasonous implications, why was it not included with the charges Shinkwin faced?

The Irish Times of 9 October 1968 clearly states:

> Addressing the court on behalf of the accused [Shinkwin], Captain Paddy Kelly said, that on the accused's own sworn statement the offence was committed purely for a

financial reason. He had no connection or sympathy with subversive elements either here or in Great Britain.

There is nothing in the reports to suggest that the court contested this testimony.

This has huge implications also regarding the statement by the Chief of Staff to the Minister for Defence in his letter of 3 May 1969. In that letter, he writes:

> Sgt SHINKWIN pleaded guilt to all the charges and was sentenced to six months' imprisonment. This case was well published in the army and in the public press and it is inconceivable that Lt Roche did not associate [Dwyer's] reference to '9mm ammunition' with the case of Sgt Shinkwin. (It is known that ▉▉▉▉ – see above – is a member of the splinter group of the IRA. It is also known that during his period of absence without leave Sgt Shinkwin was associating with the four members of that splinter group in LAHINCH – ▉▉▉▉ [▉▉▉▉], ▉▉▉▉ and ▉▉▉▉ and it is further known that this group planned an attack on LAHINCH camp then occupied by troops).

There are two very important points arising out of this statement by the Chief of Staff. The first concerns his assertion that 'it is inconceivable that Lt Roche did not associate Dwyer's reference to "9mm ammunition" with the case of Sgt Shinkwin.' If there was no subversive connection, as pleaded by Shinkwin's military advocate at his court martial; and given that Dwyer and his companions did not feature in the *Irish Times* and *Cork Examiner* reportage of the court martial, how and why is it 'inconceivable'? Furthermore, on the published sworn testimony of Shinkwin, he 'had no connection or sympathy with subversive elements'. So, even if Roche had read the media reports, the reality was that Shinkwin could have sold the ammunition to any of a whole range of people who were not subversives. It might have been to a member of a gun club or to licensed gun enthusiasts or hunters.

The second important point is this: the Chief of Staff states in his letter to the Minister: 'It is also known that during his period of absence without leave [12–17 September 1968] Sgt Shinkwin was associating with four members of that splinter group in Lahinch ... and it is further known that this group planned an attack on LAHINCH Camp then occupied by troops).' This directly contradicts the 'Additional Information' added to Col. Hefferon's 'Security Report' (Appendix A, Document 8b) which states:

> ██████████ met SHINKWIN with ████████ at a later date and arranged a raid on LAHINCH Camp on 27th August, 1968 ... ████████, ████████ and ████████ were three of the four (████████ was the fourth) who went to LAHINCH on 27th August 68 with the intention of raiding the camp and only changed their mind at the last minute.

The dates suggested by the Chief of Staff to the government are at variance with the undisputed public evidence given at the Shinkwin court martial. These dates are exactly the same in both *The Irish Times* and *Cork Examiner* reports, and there is just one small discrepancy in the time – the *Cork Examiner* states 1600 hours and *The Irish Times* states 1800 hours on 12 September.

Both the Ballyfermot incident and the Shinkwin court martial were covered in the national press in the same week. Why are copies of the press cuttings of the Shinkwin affair not attached to Lt Roche's military files, along with the press cuttings of the Ballyfermot shooting incident? Both, let us remember, are clearly linked in the case being built against Lt Roche, and both incidents are, allegedly, interconnected by virtue of the 'subversives' involved, so why omit press cuttings on one? Or was there a danger that the coincidence of both unconnected events appearing in the press in the same week might raise suspicions?

We must never lose sight of the fact that Lt Roche's case was never intended to see the light of day. The vast majority of the documents he eventually received in 2002, after the 'findings' of the JAG's Inquiry had been published, are marked 'Rúnda' and/or 'Secret'.

There is one final very important piece of the jigsaw. I have interviewed a member of the Garda Síochána's Special Branch who, for several years, had responsibility for monitoring the movements and activities of Padraig Dwyer. The officer informed me that he had read the Special Branch files on Dwyer and he had absolutely no recollection of any mention of Dwyer's alleged connection with either Lt Roche or Sgt John Shinkwin. He told me:

> If there had been any reference to Dwyer's connection with any member of the Republic's security forces, it would have jumped out at me immediately and would have caused me to pay particular attention. I do not recall seeing any such reference in his files.

In addition, I discussed the 1968 Ballyfermot bank robbery incident and the Shinkwin affair with Padraig Dwyer's widow, Margaret, during two telephone conversations on 10 November 2005. Mrs Dwyer knew about the Ballyfermot incident but said that she knew nothing of Shinkwin. During the second conversation, she said that she had been thinking about the name Shinkwin from our first conversation, but she had no recollection of it, although it is an unusual name.

Clearly, these matters require further investigation. On this occasion, the investigation must be entirely independent and in the public domain.

SERGEANT JOHN SHINKWIN

On Friday, 14 May 2004, I spoke briefly by telephone with former Sgt John Shinkwin and his wife. Mr Shinkwin, now in his late sixties, is in failing health. I briefly outlined the Lt Roche case to him and informed him that the JAG had mentioned his name in her report and that classified documents in Roche's army files linked him (Sgt Shinkwin) with the same people with whom Roche was being linked. I informed him that the files stated that he had sold ammunition to subversives and that he was linked to four names that were redacted but which we had a reasonable idea were: Sean Doyle, Simon O'Donnell, Thomas O'Neill and, positively, Padraig Dwyer. Upon hearing the names he responded, 'They mean nothing to me at all.'

I asked him about the alleged plan to raid Lahinch army camp and he said that he had absolutely no idea what this was about. Again, I repeated the four names of people with whom Sgt Shinkwin is alleged to have conspired to attack Lahinch barracks in August 1968, and he seemed to be completely at a loss to know what it was all about.

On Friday, 22 July 2005, Commandant Patrick Walshe and I travelled to Cork city where we met with Sgt Shinkwin's defending officer, then Captain Patrick Kelly; he had retired from the army after a distinguished career, with the rank of lieutenant colonel. Having made Lt Col. Kelly aware that we wished to discuss matters related to Lt Roche's 1969 retirement 'in the interests of the service', I began by asking him, 'Are the names Sean Doyle, Simon O'Donnell, Thomas O'Neill and Padraig Dwyer known to you?'

Having pondered carefully he answered, 'No.'

I informed him of the alleged connection between Sgt Shinkwin and the aforementioned four people. I then appraised him of Lt Roche's case and the alleged connection with the Shinkwin case, as discussed above. I also informed Lt Col. Kelly about my conversation with the former Special Branch officer who had monitored the career of Padraig Dwyer, and I brought to his attention the fact that the press reported that the President of the Court Martial, Col. M.A. O'Byrne, had, 'in the interest of defence and security', closed the court, which resulted in part of the trial not being heard in public. I asked Lt Col. Kelly if any of the details concerning Shinkwin and the four alleged subversives were discussed during the closed session. He said that as far as he could recall, the details as outlined above were not discussed during the closed session of the court martial.

I also reminded Lt Col. Kelly that, following the resumption of the public session of the court martial, he had stated that Sgt Shinkwin:

> ... had no connection or sympathy with subversive elements either here or in Great Britain... He is not a danger to the state and in so far as he does not sympathise with those subversive elements, neither is he a thief in the strict sense of the word.

Lt Col. Kelly made the following comments:

- The names of the four alleged subversives meant nothing to him.
- He had no awareness that the Shinkwin case was being linked to Lt Dónal Roche's 'retirement'.

- He said that the Shinkwin case was no 'big deal' at the time. It got coverage but was not a major talking point in the army.
- He had no awareness of Shinkwin's involvement with a Splinter IRA group as alleged in Lt Roche's files.
- He said that nothing as stated in the secret documents 'rang a bell' with him.
- He said that if there had been other matters related to Sgt Shinkwin that were not brought up at the court martial, and of which he had not been made aware – such as the matters we were discussing with him – he would consider that he was being made a fool of.

Lt Col. Kelly then agreed that the following statement attributed to him could be published in relation to our meeting:

> The assumption was he [Sgt John Shinkwin] sold ammunition to an individual or some group. But who they were wasn't known to me. My memory is that his reason for selling it was due to financial hardship.
>
> It was pre 1969, so the North hadn't erupted, other than the Civil Rights Movement. I certainly don't remember any suggestion of a connection between Sergeant Shinkwin and the names of the four people you gave me, and their alleged involvement with an IRA Splinter Group.'

CONCLUSION

It appears to me that it is not without significance that, in all the sworn affidavits made in 1999 by Commandant Denis Murphy (an officer of the Directorate of Intelligence), who had full access to various secret documents related to Lt Roche, including the Security Report and the DJAG's report, he judiciously avoids making reference to Shinkwin.

It is not without significance that the Deputy Chief of Staff, Major General S. Brennan, in his submission, on behalf of the defence forces, to the JAG on 30 July 2002, while reviewing the secret documentation by way of making the army's case against Lt Roche, also judiciously avoids making reference to Shinkwin.

It is not without significance that in all of the oral and written answers delivered in Dáil Éireann by successive Ministers for Defence, while they have, on occasion, quoted extensively from the report of the DJAG, they have judiciously avoided making reference to the alleged connection with Sgt Shinkwin.

It is not without significance that in any of the press releases issued on the Lt Dónal Roche controversy, the Department of Defence judiciously avoids mentioning Shinkwin. In background notes, issued with various press releases, the report of the DJAG is summarised, but there is no mention of Shinkwin. This is curious given that the DJAG alleged in his report to the Chief of Staff, on 29 May 1969, that he had got an admission from Lt Roche that he was aware of the Shinkwin court martial.

It may also be significant that the JAG, Ms Oonah McCrann, makes only passing reference to Shinkwin in her report. Perhaps she cannot avoid mentioning the case which is used with such effect in the various reports penned by the Director of Intelligence, the Chief of Staff and the DJAG. All three of their documents were, allegedly, passed to the Minister for Defence and, apparently, distributed to the government on 20 June 1969. All three use Shinkwin in building the case for Lt Roche's expulsion. Yet, McCrann reduced the Shinkwin case to a passing footnote on page 9 of her report. Why?

If Shinkwin was actually guilty of what is alleged, *vis-à-vis* Mr X and his associates, it should have merited greater attention in the civil courts at the time, in the General Staff's submission to the JAG in 2002 and, indeed, in the JAG's report. If true, the Shinkwin case would demonstrate not just the danger posed by Padraig Dwyer, and his group, but also the threat to military and state security posed by Lt Roche who allegedly:

(i) Knowingly associated with such dangerous subversives and criminals, and

(ii) Was aware of the Shinkwin court martial and, given the alleged comment by Dwyer about 'zeroing of rifles' and '9mm ammunition', must have connected Dwyer with the Shinkwin case.

Indeed, the Chief of Staff argued that it was 'inconceivable' that he would not have made the connection.

The Directorate of Intelligence, senior staff officers, officials of the Department of Defence and the Minister for Defence make no reference to Shinkwin today because, I believe, they know that the connection is a malicious lie that cannot be erased from the documentation. A malicious lie that was fabricated to strengthen the case against Lt Roche, and which was passed to the Minister for Defence, as fact, and as part of the supporting 'evidence' to justify the recommendation that the government and President 'retire' Lt Roche 'in the interests of the service'. Consequently, it may be that Ms McCrann could only downplay its significance, but could not ignore it, because of the possibility that its significance might be discovered subsequent to the release of the documentation to Lt Dónal Roche.

It is also significant that Shinkwin's court martial was reported in the press during the same week as the Ballyfermot shoot-out (9 October and 3/4 October 1969 respectively). If Dwyer and his associates were guilty of colluding with Shinkwin in the manner described in Lt Roche's files, they were all guilty of nothing less than treason, and Shinkwin, having surrendered himself to military authority on 17 September 1968 and, reportedly, having fully cooperated with their investigations, should have been the state's chief witness in the arrest and conviction of 'a most active, extremist Group of Splinter IRA' (Security Report, 1 May 1969).

Instead, it appears that this information, if true, was ignored and Dwyer and his gang were permitted not only:

(i) To endanger the lives of members of the Garda Síochána during the very week that Shinkwin was facing his court martial because of his alleged involvement with them, but also

(ii) To endanger military and state security by their associations with a serving officer of the defence forces, Lt Dónal Roche – an alleged association that led to Roche's presidential 'retirement', but with no consequences to them.

It simply is not plausible.

14

SUPERMARKET FOR BOMBERS

The greatest scandal in the history of the Irish state.

Colonel James K. Cogan

The language used by the Director of Intelligence, the DJAG and the Chief of Staff in describing Lt Roche as a grave security risk to both the military and the state is harsh and uncompromising. There is absolutely no compassion, no room for compromise or a process that would allow the young officer to defend himself.

There is zealotry in the urgency of these powerful men in ridding the defence forces of a young officer they consider not up to the standard of loyalty required. Yet, these men were part of a system that utterly failed in its duty to ensure that the very people with whom they accused young Lt Roche of consorting were denied the raw materials for a ruthless and devastating bombing campaign on the island.

A review of the photographs contained in the illustrated section of this book will demonstrate the scandalous lack of security around the Irish Industrial Explosives Factory at Clonagh, near Enfield, Co. Meath, which led Captain Patrick Walshe to report the matter aggressively to military superiors. He also informed retired Col. James K. Cogan who communicated in detail his concerns to the Department of Justice and to the Taoiseach of the day, Liam Cosgrave. Patrick Walshe emphasises that 'all photographs were taken by me during weekends when there were no employees or management in the factory'.

In April 1974, Walshe was given responsibility as an officer of the Depot Artillery for the administration of the security guard at the factory. He recognised that all was not right there. He immediately began to report his concerns, fearful that there was a correlation between the IRA's relentless bombing campaign in Northern Ireland and the lack of security at this particular factory. Security there was the responsibility of the Department of Justice. The military guard was at the factory at the request of that department.

Walshe described the lack of security thus: 'It was a supermarket for bombers with no one on duty at the check-out.' He continued:

> What added to my anger at this inexplicable security lapse was that, not so long before, Lt Dónal Roche had been thrown out of the defence forces 'as a security risk' yet here now, in full view, was not just a security risk but a frightful breach of state security.

Walshe, however, has always maintained that the culpability of the factory management was minor compared to that of the Department of Justice. That department did not appear, he says, to have been at all concerned by the state of affairs at the factory.

What follows is disturbing reading. The Clonagh Explosives Affair is one of the great unexplored scandals of modern Irish history. The entire nation owes a debt of gratitude to Commandant Patrick Walshe, who tried to blow the whistle on the scandal in the hope of saving lives. It will become obvious that if Dónal de Róiste had, in any shape or fashion, compromised his fellow officers or betrayed his oath of allegiance to the state he swore to serve, with loyalty and dedication, he would have received no succour from Walshe.

THE PANDORA'S BOX

Who was it in 1997 that saw the potential of Dónal de Róiste's controversial 1969 'retirement' from the defence forces as a stake to destroy the heart of his sister Adi Roche's presidential campaign? Whoever leaked an account of his misfortune to the press has succeeded only in opening up a Pandora's box, the ramifications of which have yet to be fully realised.

Commandant Walshe is particularly appalled at the unfounded innuendo that Dónal de Róiste knowingly associated with subversives, and questions why de Róiste was 'retired' and he was not, given that both men frequented the same public establishments and associated with the same people. What makes Commandant Patrick Walshe such a powerful and credible advocate for the cause of Dónal de Róiste is his handling of an unrelated matter – what one senior officer described as 'the greatest scandal in the history of the Irish state'.

THE CLONAGH AFFAIR

On 1 April 1974, Captain Patrick Walshe was stationed at Magee Barracks, Kildare, when the garrison was assigned military logistics responsibility for guarding the Irish Industrial Explosives Factory at Clonagh, near Enfield, Co. Meath. Captain Walshe had been for several years an instructor in ballistics and gunnery at the Artillery School, Kildare, and was not unfamiliar with the technology of explosives.

From the moment Walshe set foot in Clonagh, he was alarmed at the lack of security around the factory, which had stocks of up to 2,000 tons of explosive-grade material. He was aware of the potential consequences of this and suspected a possible linkage with the IRA's bombing campaign in Northern Ireland.

Walshe's concerns were such that he immediately began to document the security flaws at Clonagh and report them to his defence forces superiors. During a ten-month duty assignment at the factory, he prepared and submitted thirty-two detailed reports, including over one hundred photographs, highlighting the easy access to Clonagh for anyone who might wish to avail of its deadly stockpile. He felt the need to deliver so many reports because of what he considered a carefree attitude being adopted by people in authority, including members of the government, who were made aware of the situation in great detail.

The Department of Justice had sole responsibility for the control of commercial explosives within the state. All of Walshe's reports and recommendations were approved by, and forwarded to, the Chief of Staff's branch, by his Commanding Officer, Lt Col. M. Fitzsimons. According to Walshe:

> A great many reports on security concerns around the factory were likewise submitted by NCO guard commanders. I remember one particular NCO who concluded his report by stating, 'Security duty at this place is a nightmare that you think will never happen but it is.'

Walshe states, 'It is my belief that all reports were forwarded by the Chief of Staff to the Department of Justice.'

Returning the Serve

Walshe was particularly alarmed when the Dublin and Monaghan bombs exploded on 17 May 1974, killing thirty-three civilians, and he feared that it was an act of retaliation by the British for the lack of security at Clonagh. British military intelligence has long been suspected of colluding with the UVF to carry out the synchronised attacks. Responding to a question about the attacks on Dublin and Monaghan in Peter Taylor's 1999 BBC documentary, *Loyalists*, David Ervine of the Progressive Unionist Party chillingly described them as a way of 'returning the serve'. Walshe believes that the explosives used in the Dublin bombs on 17 May 1974 originated at Clonagh and had been intercepted by security forces in Northern Ireland.

Information has recently surfaced which has lent weight to Patrick Walshe's fears. Indeed, his suspicions that Clonagh was a supply source for the IRA bombing campaign in the North was confirmed prior to Christmas 2002 by former Taoiseach Dr Garret FitzGerald in his book, *Reflections on the Irish State*, in which he makes the following statement:

> I particularly recall how furious I was in the mid-1970s at the discovery that the British army in Northern Ireland had known for 18 months that explosives being used by the IRA were being stolen from a particular explosives factory in our state but had not told us about this, apparently because they preferred to use this leakage as a propaganda weapon against us than to save lives in Northern Ireland by stopping it.

FitzGerald, in an interview with me on 25 January 2003, confirmed that the factory he was referring to was the Irish Industrial Explosives Factory, near Enfield.

Walshe was appalled when he read these comments and said:

> I am by no means defending the British army, whose intelligence services were, I believe, responsible for orchestrating the Dublin and Monaghan bombings. But it is not accurate to say that the entire cabinet did not know. I am shocked that Garret FitzGerald, who was Minister for Foreign Affairs, was not aware of the

situation at Clonagh since information about the lack of security there had been communicated in detail to other ministers of his government.

LAX SECURITY DURING THE TERM OF
'THE LAW AND ORDER GOVERNMENT'
Walshe has made available to me his reports, contemporaneous notes and photographs, all of which he passed to defence forces superiors, beginning on 5 April 1974. They detail what one former senior army officer, Col. James K. Cogan, described in a 1984 affidavit as 'a scandalous and criminal lack of security' at the factory. Cogan (to whom Walshe was related by marriage) shared Walshe's concerns and says that he personally informed a cabinet minister of the Clonagh affair in mid-April 1974 at Leinster House. A member of the Fine Gael party, he had access to government ministers.

When first informed of details of the scandal, Cogan commented that there was little doubt but that British military intelligence was aware of what was going on. Cogan's affidavit details the content of a memorandum he claims he handed to the cabinet minister. It contained the following information:

(a) The very extensive factory premises were unfenced in any meaningful sense;
(b) Fully prepared explosives and raw materials were being left in the open within sight and easy reach of the public road;
(c) There was an almost incredible laxity in storage and accountancy – the manner of stacking would defy accurate tally;
(d) There was little or no supervision of the comings and goings of employees;
(e) There was a military guard on the factory. Its duties were confined to protection of the premises against external aggression – it had no powers in relation to the internal workings;
(f) The installation was such a maze of stores, offices, mixing bays and blast walls that it would be easy for an employee to dump a quantity of explosive outside

the immediate perimeter without detection.

The gravity of the situation at Clonagh is gauged by reference to mere snippets from former Commandant Walshe's reports. On 1 July 1974, for example, he presented his commanding officer at Magee Barracks, Kildare, with a detailed report and supporting photographs. It included references to:

> Quantity (probably one bag, 50 kg) of substance resembling ammonium nitrate deposited on roadway about 500 yards from main entrance to plant...
> Cellophane sack marked 'ammonium nitrate' and containing a quantity of substance found secluded in weeds...
> Quantity of substance on roadway and roadside about 100 yards from main entrance to plant...
> Ammonium nitrate prills (four sacks, 40 kg) outside F5.
> The perimeter fence of the compound was only 25 yards from this [large and secluded] quantity of ammonium nitrate which was visible over an extensive area beyond the compound fence.

It should be noted that this situation pertained some ten weeks after Col. Cogan personally appraised a government minister of the situation at the Clonagh factory and six weeks after the Dublin and Monaghan bombings.

FACILITY FOR MISAPPROPRIATION

Patrick Walshe's contemporaneous commentary to his military superiors concerning the Clonagh affair is revelatory. He expressed concern that three months had elapsed and his recommendations had not been implemented. He expressed deep disquiet that a facility existed from which explosive materials could be taken with minimal risk of detection. He also stated:

> It is apparent that a double standard of custody and control of dangerous substances exists.... Over one year

ago ... quantities of sodium chlorate as small as two kilograms were withdrawn from hardware and chemist shops throughout the country. This substance was stored in military custody under high security conditions.... The implementation of that procedure rings hollow when compared with the present situation evident at Clonagh.

Sodium chlorate was used as a weed killer, but could easily be converted into a very effective explosive.

Captain Walshe expressed concern that no consideration appeared to have been given to the serious responsibility for ensuring 'that these dangerous substances are prevented from getting into the hands of subversives.' He recommended urgent action 'without further delay'. He expressed the opinion that the immediate closure of the plant and impounding of all materials into safe custody might be necessary until such time as management at the factory met some basic security commitments.

Walshe collected samples of unsecured material that he found in the factory compound. He states: 'Samples of all materials collected by me were analysed by ordnance officers, who confirmed that they were prime explosive materials and blast-effect improvers.'

INCREASING ALARM

Walshe became increasingly alarmed at the lack of response to his reporting. Yet another report, dated 4 September 1974, concluded that, 'until such time as ALL deficiencies are corrected ... there can be no reasonable assurance that the source of bomb-making material in unauthorised hands has not come from the Irish Industrial Explosives Plant at Clonagh.'

Walshe says that the response to his persistent reporting was attempts by very senior officers to inhibit his efforts. The most serious of these was a written admonishment, of which he has recently acquired a copy, from the Chief of Staff, Major General O'Carroll. His commanding officer was directed to read the document to him. Walshe later learnt that the admonishment, as well as being unjustified, was illegal. Walsh also states:

A fellow officer had reported on the matter in November 1974, directly to Patrick Donegan TD at his constituency office. Donegan, who was Minister for Defence, complained about the officer's action to the Chief of Staff who promptly paraded him and informed him that his future military career would be leant upon severely for reporting to the Minister.

Of many reports forwarded by NCO guard commanders at the factory, all were ignored. To my knowledge not one officer from the Chief of Staff's Branch was sent to Clonagh to confirm or otherwise the validity of our concerns.

In late October 1974, a Garda investigation into the theft of explosives at Clonagh was conducted. Two army privates were convicted of stealing small quantities of substances from the factory. Ex-Commandant Walshe told me that he fully co-operated with the investigation and furnished it with a full set of his reports. He is, however, critical of the Garda operation against members of the defence forces and believes it was a contrivance to discredit the persistent reporting from Magee Barracks when, in reality, people in more senior positions, and in the political administration, should have been held accountable for the scandalous lack of security.

According to Walshe, Lt Col. M. Fitzsimons, Officer Commanding, Magee Barracks, told him that a verbal communication had been passed down to him from the Department of Justice stating: 'they could not understand what we were doing all the complaining about since it was our own soldiers who were stealing the stuff.' Walshe states that Fitzsimons added, 'We are only wasting our time reporting.' Shortly afterwards, Walshe says, the Commanding Officer made a recommendation that the military guard at the factory be withdrawn as it could not accomplish its function. Col. Cogan believed that the purpose of the military guard was to provide 'a cloak of respectability' for the operation.

Walshe continues:

In mid-November 1974 I could no longer contain my anger at the way the reports to Defence Forces

Headquarters were being ignored. I wrote a letter summarising our efforts at reporting. The letter was addressed 'To Whom it May Concern'. The letter stated: '…Exercise of my lawful responsibilities as a [commissioned] officer has been a complete failure.' I also wrote, 'The state has failed in a disgraceful way to guarantee the security of its citizens.' According to the custom of the Service, reports should be signed with the name, rank and appointment of the officer. In breach of the custom I signed the detailed document: 'Patrick Walshe Citizen'.

Stringent efforts were made by Defence Force Officers to compel me to soften the tone of the document and to sign it in conformity with the custom of the Service. I did not relent. I had the full moral support of Lt Col. Fitzsimons for my course of action. The document was transmitted, unamended, to the Chief of Staff. Colonel Cogan also delivered a copy of the document directly to An Taoiseach, Liam Cosgrave. Despite this, still no action was taken.

On 6 February 1975, unexpectedly, the military security duties at Clonagh were transferred to another unit. The Chief of Staff and security officials in the Department of Justice had failed to silence us, so the duty was returned to 'safer hands'. I had pointed out in my 'Citizen' letter that 'there can be no confidence in the State Security System until the officials responsible for the scandal at Clonagh are identified and dealt with.'

In an interview I conducted with Dr FitzGerald, he told me that he personally had no knowledge of Captain Walshe's efforts to stem the flow of explosives to subversive elements. He was unaware that a fellow minister had been apprised of the situation pertaining to the Clonagh factory in mid-April 1974, and that the Taoiseach of the day, Liam Cosgrave, was personally aware of the situation at the factory by not later than 9 September 1974. He expressed surprise at learning that Col. Cogan had felt the need to seek an urgent meeting with Cosgrave to inform him of the deteriorating situation at the factory, saying, 'You would have thought the government, having been informed, would have done something about it.'

While expressing the opinion that this was an interesting line of inquiry and should be pursued, he did not, however, accept that the Irish government knew about the situation at Clonagh before the British army. He said:

> They may or may not have reacted adequately to concerns about security but that doesn't mean that they knew or believed that explosives were actually leaking out. You wouldn't expect any government to allow that to happen if they thought that.

INEXPLICABLE

When shown photographs taken by Captain Walshe detailing the lack of security around the Clonagh factory, Garret FitzGerald had this to say:

> It is inexplicable that this information was furnished and no action was taken. I don't understand it. It's totally out of kilter with anything I would have known about my colleagues. It's a problem. The allegation always was that Cosgrave and the cabinet went over the top with security [in relation to] the IRA, not that they were ever neglectful. So that's why it is surprising.

Patrick Walshe's suspicion that the 1974 Dublin and Monaghan bombings were related to the Clonagh scandal and that their aim was to teach the Republic a lesson also needs to be examined. The Garda handling of the forensics in the aftermath of the bombings is deeply disquieting.

CHAIN OF CUSTODY

It is known that bomb debris related to the biggest unsolved mass-murder case in the history of the Republic of Ireland disappeared for eleven days in the immediate aftermath of the explosions. It was then delivered to a forensics laboratory outside Belfast, by which time all explosive traces had effectively disappeared. In the course of my research for my book, *The Dublin and Monaghan Bombings* (Wolfhound Press, 2000), the Garda Commissioner failed to explain this anomaly and also failed to state whether the Republic's police could establish a chain of custody for the debris, especially for the eleven days it took to reach a forensic laboratory.

Detective Ted Jones of the Garda Ballistic Section did manage, however, to deliver small quantities of debris from Parnell Street, the first of the four bomb targets, to Dr James Donovan, then at the State Laboratory, on 20 and 23 May 1974. In his analysis of the debris, Dr Donovan detected 'the presence of two blackened prills of ammonium nitrate'.

On 24 March 1999, I interviewed Dr Donovan, who made the following statement which, in the light of Captain Walshe's revelations, may have a profound significance. Dr Donovan said:

> I feel that the ovide prills of ammonium nitrate, blackened as they were, must have had some significance or else somebody would have come and talked to me. But when my own authorities did not do so, I find that strange.

As can be clearly seen from the photographs, large and unaccountable quantities of prills were lying about the unsecured compound, easily accessible over a single-stranded barbed-wire fence. Prills are a granular form of explosive-grade ammonium nitrate, easily converted into an industrial explosive.

When asked if the apparent disappearance, for eleven days, of the forensics related to the Dublin and Monaghan bombings might be linked to the fact that someone in authority may have known that the source of the explosives was actually from within the Irish state, FitzGerald responded:

> I see the possible relationship between the two events, which is news to me. I was always thinking in terms of the explosives being used in the North. I hadn't related it back down here.

Responding to the revelations that the explosives used by British Intelligence to bomb Dublin and Monaghan may have originated at the Clonagh factory, Angela O'Neill, who lost her father and had two young brothers seriously injured in the Parnell Street bombing, said:

This revelation is shocking and raises strong suspicions about how the Irish government responded to the attack and why we, and all other innocent victims, were abandoned for over 25 years. An Garda Síochána have a lot of explaining to do in light of the Clonagh revelations.

The Garda Commissioner should explain to the nation, and more especially the victims of the 1974 bombings, the true reasons why his force was, it appears, negligent regarding the urgency of having the bomb debris analysed for the purpose of apprehending the perpetrators. The question must be asked if persons in the Garda, or agents of the state, suspected or knew that the explosives used in the Dublin and Monaghan bombings came from Clonagh and realised the enormous political fallout if this information became public. Garret FitzGerald agreed that this was a line of inquiry that must now be investigated.

CONCERNED FOR THE STATE

Ex-Commandant Patrick Walshe has distinguished himself as an officer loyal to the state and, more especially, to the protection of lives, north and south. When Garret FitzGerald was informed of Walshe's detailed and forthright reporting on Clonagh, motivated by his suspicion that there was a definite correlation between the Provisional IRA's bombing campaign in Northern Ireland and the lack of security at the Co. Meath factory, FitzGerald responded:

If what you are telling me about him is true, I would have a very high regard for his loyalty. He seems to have been a very vigilant person, concerned for the interests of the state. He did his duty.

FitzGerald was then told that ex-Commandant Walshe's best friend in the army had been Dónal de Róiste and that their friendship endures to this day. He was asked to comment on the apparent anomaly between Walshe being an officer of such high calibre and unquestionable loyalty to the state and, on the other hand, his keeping company with an officer accused of recklessly compromising state and military security by cavorting with republican subversives. He responded: 'You are quite right to relate the two things, I can see that. You are right.'

FitzGerald's final words to me are, unquestionably, relevant to both the Dónal de Róiste case and the Clonagh affair. He said:

> Nothing should be covered up. I have always had that view. If you make a mistake, admit it. No cover-up ever lasts. It always comes out anyway.

Walshe also stated:

> Dónal Roche was accused of being in breach of his oath. I believe he was not. However, I believe the very senior officers that set him up for dismissal and attributed to me two statements that they had fabricated in their case to the government were the ones who were in breach of their oaths. Likewise, the senior defence forces officers and officials in the Department of Justice who tolerated and covered up the scandal of the explosives were in breach of their oaths and their duty to the innocent, trusting citizens of this state. That cover-up has continued to this day. The brazen injustice that was perpetrated on Dónal Roche because he loved traditional music and talked to people in public houses has likewise continued and is being sustained by senior defence force headquarters staff and civil servants in the Department of Defence.

Walshe's final comment to me was:

> Military Intelligence found acceptable the information from a 'confidential source' that was, allegedly, 'questioned and re-questioned through a third party'. They then used this information in the creation of the case to remove

Lt Roche from the defence forces as a 'security risk'.
Quite obviously, the information from their 'source'
was of greater security significance than the persistent
reporting on the explosives scandal by Lt Col. Fitsimons,
his officers and his NCOs. All these grave reports were
ignored, whereas the information used to destroy Lt
Roche was eagerly taken on board. It is just not possible
to comprehend that serious security reports from their
fellow soldiers, of many ranks, were ignored, while a
report from a shady 'confidential source' was acted upon.

CONCLUSION

The intuitive words of Dónal de Róiste's elderly mother, already quoted,
still ring true. Dr FitzGerald's final comment simply adds weight and
urgency to the case. After four years of exhaustive research, I have found
nothing to cause me to doubt the consistent pleas of Dónal de Róiste
that he was never given the opportunity to defend himself against
unspecified allegations and anonymous accusers from 1969 until the
present day.

That cover-up has continued to this day. When Dónal was arraigned
in April 1969, the factory at Clonagh had been operating for some time
in flagrant breach of even minimal security requirements. That situation
continued up to April 1974, when Patrick Walshe's garrison took over
military security duties there. In the meantime, the sustained bombing
campaign in Northern Ireland had commenced. What was the staff of
the Directorate of Intelligence doing during this time?

As recently as 28 September 2005, the current Minister for Defence,
Willie O'Dea, TD, was still holding the line regarding the 'retirement'
of De Róiste. Referring to the High Court decision to quash the report
of the JAG, he stated in Dáil Éireann:

> ... the recent High Court judgment in the matter of
> the report of the Judge Advocate General specifically
> and only related to the actual procedures utilised by the
> Judge Advocate General in the course of her review and
> examination of this matter in 2002. The substantive issue,
> namely the government decision in 1969 to recommend
> the retirement of this individual from the Defence

Forces by the President, remains entirely unaffected by the judgment of the High Court, a point specifically emphasised within the text of that recent judgment itself.

Of particular significance in the High Court decision was the directive from the Minister for Defence that Lt Roche's files be withheld from him until after the JAG had completed her report and his department had attempted the choreography of the final burying of his case with a media blitz. This included a known press leak, aimed at damaging his cause in the public mind and, especially amongst the media.

Background notes circulated to the media at the time of the publication of the JAG's report, concluded with the following paragraph:

> Based on an assessment of the facts as outlined ... the military authorities in 1969 concluded that Lt Roche potentially constituted a security risk and on that basis his retirement in the interests of the service was recommended. It is emphasised that in such circumstances there is no legal requirement for a person to be tried with an offence under military law or the ordinary criminal law. This principle was upheld by *Finlay P in The state (Donnelly) v Minister for Defence* (H.C unreported, October 9 1979) where he stated that there was a 'clear public necessity' that the military authorities should have the discretion to remove persons considered to be a security risk.

As we have seen from our neighbours across the Irish Sea, the law, on occasions, fails to deliver justice and has, on several occasions, delivered the 'appalling vista' of gross miscarriages of justice. With due respect to Mr Justice Finlay, as members of the public, we have the right to disagree with his opinions and judgments. The Donnelly referred to above is Corporal Michael Donnelly, a military policeman who, like Lt Roche, appears to have been targeted and his removal from the defence forces orchestrated for very questionable reasons. Since the paragraph above has also appeared in answers to parliamentary questions in Dáil Éireann related to the 'retirement' of Lt Dónal Roche, and at the conclusion of the submission made, on behalf of the defence forces, to the JAG by Major General Seán Brennan, Deputy Chief of Staff (Operations), I decided to research Donnelly's case. My research is made available as Appendix B of this book. It too makes for disturbing reading.

At the heart of the matter is the potential for abuse by military authorities – indeed, anyone in authority – who are provided with unrestrained latitude as to how they might interpret subjective matters such as state and military security. In this regard, I was quite shocked by assertions made by Major General Brennan at the conclusion of the submission to the JAG, dated 30 July 2002. He concluded:

> ... Faced with a similar situation today, where an officer of the Defence Forces was unable or unwilling to explain his association with subversive elements, the General Staff would have no hesitation in making the same recommendation for the retirement of that officer as it would consider such action to be essential for the preservation of the security of the Defence Forces and of the State.

Commandant Walshe angrily responded to this statement by Major General Brennan:

> This comment 'unable or unwilling to explain' by Brennan is nothing short of mischievous in so far as it refers to Lt Roche. Brennan chooses to ignore Lt Roche's solicitor's letter to the Chief of Staff requesting information on what charges, if any, were being preferred against him. He also ignores the fact that Lt Roche had been advised by his solicitor to do nothing until such times as a reply had been received by his solicitor from the Chief of Staff.

Furthermore, how could an officer explain his association with subversives if none existed? Even after her examination of the files, the JAG, Ms McCrann, seemed less than convinced that Padraig Dwyer (Mr X) was a subversive. On page 19 of her report she refers to 'Mr

X's ... possible subversive links' and on page 15 she writes that Mr X 'possibly had subversive connections'. So, under the circumstances, are we to believe that Lt Roche was 'retired' for having recognised and acknowledged non-subversive connections with a man with 'possible subversive connections'? It doesn't make sense.

If someone makes an allegation against an officer, no matter how ridiculous, and if the accused cannot explain it, is it all right to discharge him? It is a strange view of justice – the presumption of guilt, rather than innocence.

The reality is that Major General Brennan would not get away today with what was done to Lt Roche in 1969. Even if he and his fellow senior staff members were to recommend to the government the retirement 'in the interests of the service' of a serving officer, they would be restrained by an amended Defence Force Act which would require them to provide the officer with basic rights and procedures that would, it is hoped, protect the officer's constitutional rights and his or her rights to natural justice:

> An officer shall not be recommended for retirement for misconduct or inefficiency or in the interests of the service unless or until the reasons for the proposed retirement have been communicated to him and he has been given a reasonable opportunity of making such representation as he may think proper in relation to the proposed retirement.
>
> 1954 Defence Act, Section 47(2), Regulation A 15, Sub-section 18(2)

Given the assertions made in the defence force submission by Major General Brennan, there are many officers who can be very grateful that the loophole in the 1954 Defence Act was closed in 1985.

Echoing the mantra of his predecessors, the Minister for Defence, Willie O'Dea TD, also stated in his written response of 28 September 2005:

> A decision to retire an officer 'in the interests of the service' is only taken for the most compelling reasons. The government advice to the President was on grounds

of security. I am satisfied that the matter was handled in an entirely appropriate and proper manner in 1969 and that the decision taken then was taken only after very detailed and due consideration.

There are many citizens who do not agree with the Minister, and will not until justice is not only done, but seen to be done. It is hoped that the effect of this book will be to increase public disquiet and increase the pressure on the government, once and for all, to do the decent thing and give Dónal de Róiste an independent, transparent and fair process. This includes access to all files, including those retained by the Department of An Taoiseach.

Until this is done, the words of Dónal de Róiste's recently deceased mother, Christina de Róiste, stand as a damning indictment of powerful men in the first decade of the new millennium whose ears and eyes are closed:

> I believe my son Dónal is innocent. I believe he was wrongfully 'retired'. I believe the case against him was so spurious that he was denied proper procedures. I believe the government have been misled in the information presented to it by Dónal's accusers and that our one-time great hero, Eamon de Valera, may, in turn, have been wrongly advised.

CLOSING STATEMENT

DONAL DE RÓISTE

Foul deeds will rise
Though all the earth o'erwhelm them, to men's eyes
William Shakespeare, *Hamlet*

When I joined the army, willing to serve my country, little did I imagine that the army would try to destroy me. The great US Civil War General, William Tecumseh Sherman, said it best when he declared that military fame was: 'To be killed in the field of battle and have our names spelled wrong in the newspapers.' I have achieved the latter and hope at this stage of my life to avoid the former. In some ways I am still twenty-four years old, shocked and frightened, locked in a barred room under armed arrest.

This book was written to clarify my difficulty in seeking justice. For the past thirty-seven years, I have consistently declared that I am innocent and suffered for trying to defend myself. This book goes a long way towards restoring my good name. It focuses on areas of governmental secrecy and on the fairness that is crucial in a democracy. My story questions the power of the state versus the rights of the individual in Ireland and has been compared to that of the French Captain Dreyfus, who was wrongly convicted of treason in the 1890s and forced to endure prison, isolation and shame before being cleared and recommissioned. I persuaded Don Mullan, an investigative journalist renowned for his work in the field of justice and civil rights, to examine my story. I am honoured to be associated with his efforts on my behalf.

In 1997 I was living quietly in Ballincollig, Co. Cork. I unexpectedly received a phone call from a journalist from the *Cork Examiner*. I was rushing out to work at the time and was taken completely by surprise. Out of politeness, I agreed to talk to her for a few minutes. She asked, among other things, whether I was a Republican. I answered that since the official designation of the state is the Republic of Ireland, I was. She asked about my past service in the army with particular emphasis on the reasons for my forced expulsion by President de Valera in 1969. I told her truthfully that I had been falsely accused and framed and that I had refused to resign my commission. I sensed that she had a hidden agenda and realised that that long-forgotten and shameful episode in my life must have been leaked to the press, in order to damage the presidential campaign of my sister, Adi Roche.

The 1997 presidential election was a dirty campaign. A selective version of my interview appeared in the *Cork Examiner*, the *Star* and other papers. They had a field day at my expense with lurid headlines such as: 'Brother's past rises to haunt Adi' and 'De Róiste denies he was ever a member of the IRA or Saoirse.'

Although Adi had started as odds-on favourite, her campaign rapidly slumped in the polls. A picture appeared in the press of me slamming the door of my house, trying to get away from door-stepping photographers. The intense pressure provoked a nervous breakdown. No one was given the opportunity to have a good word for me and those who tried to defend me were ignored. I relived in my head the horrors of my 1969 arrest and interrogation. I could not eat or sleep. I needed medical attention to recover and I was diagnosed as suffering from post-traumatic stress disorder. Reporters analysed every area of my life. After being denied justice in the Dáil and ignored for years, I was now subjected to trial by media. Of course, I was found guilty, again.

Reporters asked the children on my school bus how their parents felt about having an IRA man driving them. Some people shouted 'Up the 'RA' to annoy me. I was called a terrorist to my face. At Christmas 1997, I was barred from participating in a charity performance in an army barracks with Cantairí Mhúscraí, my local choir. I dreaded becoming unemployed and having to emigrate again. Finally, I had to leave my home and take time off work to survive the merciless onslaught.

I contacted the legal firm of Noonan Lenihan Carroll & Coffey to see if they could help me to defend myself and to attempt to restore my good name. Eamonn Carroll agreed to take my case, and explained in considerable detail the difficulties we faced and the long odds of trying to access the courts. Six months later, in 1998, we got to the High Court in order to seek a judicial review and thereby to access my files. Although I had unsuccessfully attempted to do this on my own with the help of various politicians during the previous thirty years, I was cautiously optimistic about finally getting access to the files to see what the government's case against me was. I thought this would only be a matter of form in a modern democracy, which prides itself on its openness and accountability – especially in light of the new Freedom of Information Act. How wrong I was!

The state claimed in court that I had signed a confession but rejected the judge's suggestion that I be given my files, and then fought the case by stating that I was out of time. They also told the court that some crucial files relating to my case were 'missing' since 1969. It was not until 2002, after numerous court battles, a Judge Advocate General's review and many newspaper articles by the intrepid journalist who wrote this book, that I finally gained access to my army files.

The files contained the original false allegations made by a secret informant against me in 1969. There was also an unanswered letter from my solicitor dated 30 May 1969. It was addressed to the Army Chief of Staff, General MacEoin, asking what charges, if any, were being made against me. I now felt utterly betrayed by our justice system. I believe it is reprehensible and offensive to ignore a solicitor's letter. I was also under the impression that holding back such a letter from the courts was an illegal act. The files show how secret informants operate and are protected and how, in times of political paranoia, false accusations can be made to assume the power of facts. This book reveals the depth of the military bungling and state obfuscation in my case.

The truth will set us free, we are told, but it is obvious here that truth is in scarce supply and seems to have been the first casualty of the JAG's review. It is to their eternal shame that none of the journalists who contributed to the damaging articles had the decency to ask me for my version of events. My family and I believe that, in my case, President de Valera was misinformed and thus got it wrong.

My principal complaint has been that as a serving army officer, in good standing, I did not get the basic human rights accorded even to criminals. I was forcefully retired after repeated interrogations and accusations 'in the interests of the service'. This was done secretly, under the notorious Section 47 (2) of the Defence Act 1954. Defence Forces Regulations A.15, Paragraph 18(1)(f) (since amended) which states that 'the President may retire any officer for any prescribed reason'. I was retired without charges, trial or conviction, and I was also denied my references for service rendered. My career was ruined, job prospects blighted and my good name destroyed. While living in the US in the late 1980s, I applied for citizenship. The immigration officials asked why I had been retired from the army by the Irish President. I had no satisfactory answer to give them as I never got to face my accusers and was not told what I had been found guilty of. Any time I raised the question in the Dáil the mantra was always the same – '...the matter was handled in an entirely appropriate and proper manner in 1969 and the decision ...was taken only after very detailed and due consideration.'

My father was a proud working man who simultaneously held two jobs during the 1950s when unemployment and emigration were commonplace in our society. When I was commissioned as an army officer in 1965, he was happy for me. Dad was born in the revolutionary year of 1916 and his family contributed to the first Dáil loan. Out of loyalty to the Free State, he joined the Irish army during the Second World War (the Emergency). He was part of the new post-colonial state and very conscious of being a member of the first generation to live in a partially free Ireland. He loved the Irish language and spoke it fluently. He was also a Fianna Fáiler and a Dev man, with all the angst associated with it. Angry civil war discussions were not unusual in political conversations in my youth. My father had to live in a small Irish town after my public disgrace. I had to go abroad to find work. He was crushed by this foul deed, done in secret by the President and state he loved. He suffered the disgrace of having a son fired from the military, and this was shameful and inexplicable to him. He was a simple, truthful man. When the media dragged it all up again in 1997 and disgraced his family by attacking his youngest daughter, he was shocked. Reporters even phoned him and my mother in bed one morning. Eventually he started slipping into Alzheimer's disease and died in January 2002. Sadly we did not become reconciled.

When Don Mullan agreed to investigate my case, he stipulated that he needed two ground rules in order to protect his freedom and journalistic integrity. These were:

- He could ask any questions of me in relation to my 'retirement' from the army.
- If he believed me to be untruthful, he would walk away.

I told Don that I feared the power of the state, which had spent large amounts of public money trying to crush my struggle.

In 2001, my case was denied in the Supreme Court as it was deemed out of time. My delay was both 'inordinate and inexcusable', the judges said. The trickery used to ensure this verdict is clearly explained in the book. In cooperation with former army comrades, Commandant (retired) Patrick Walshe and Lt. Col. (retired) Gerry Swan, Don Mullan posed a hypothetical question concerning the aftermath of a car crash in which I was involved in 1967. I had refused to lie on behalf of the drunken senior officer who was driving. Mullan's article, which suggested that following this event I was not highly thought of among senior army personnel, was published in *The Irish Times* on 29 June 2002. For me the article helped explain why none of my seniors spoke up in my defence in 1969. The piece created so much public interest in the de Róiste case that the then Minister for Defence, Michael Smith TD, decided to head off any further criticism by announcing a Judge Advocate General's review in order to clarify the matter. This had the effect of gagging me under the sub judice rule, and my campaign flagged. I believed that this was a case of the army investigating itself. The process lacked the transparency which the case demanded.

The JAG failed to investigate the car-crash incident and gave no better explanation for my forced 'retirement'. She refused to interview me or Commandant (retired) Patrick Walshe. Her report was published in October 2002. McCrann concluded that the President was right to retire me. She gave no coherent reasons for drawing such a conclusion. She did allow me access to the files I had been denied, but only after she had concluded her review. I was devastated.

Undaunted, my legal team got a High Court judicial review of her findings and, three years later, in July 2005, Mr Justice Quirke quashed the JAG findings and stated that I had not got 'fair procedures'. This has always been my contention, from the day I was placed under armed arrest on Friday, 25 April 1969. The axiom 'justice delayed is justice denied' has no bearing on my case, it seems.

In the era of war on terror, this book is a salutary warning on the abuse of state power. It follows the struggles of a falsely accused individual, documenting his futile attempts to prove his innocence or even get a fair hearing. It raises questions about the level of openness and accountability in our democracy. It also raises questions about the use of informants. It questions the connection or lack of it between the executive and the legislative branches of our government. It queries individual and group responsibility and accountability, and challenges the unfettered power of the state. It asks what 'interests of the service' are served by my never-ending punishment.

It is said that the law is what separates us from barbarism and humour separates us from animals. To be mis-labelled a terrorist by the faceless forces of the state and punished *in perpetuum* is anathema to democracy. No smoke without fire, they said. You must have done something wrong for them to arrest you. That is the kind of thinking that led to Hitler's Germany and the 1890s burning of Bridget Cleary.

Like my father, I joined the army to serve my country. My family could not afford to send me to college and the army provided me with a great career opporunity. I believe that to this day it is considered an honour to be called up. I never had any quarrel with the army. I can assure Óglaigh na hÉireann, the President, and the government that they have nothing to fear from me; nor do they have anything to fear from the truth.

'An error does not have to become a mistake unless we are unwilling to correct it,' US President John F. Kennedy said. This book shows the errors at the heart of the Donal de Róiste case. I trust that the President, on the advice of the government, will correct this error before it becomes a historic mistake. This is too young a country to be reduced to sustaining what Bernard Allen TD referred to as 'a kangaroo court'.

AFTERWORD

LIEUTENANT COLONEL (RETIRED) GERRY SWAN

I knew Dónal for a comparatively short period between 1966 and 1969. Our military paths never crossed but within that short time-frame we were regular companions at Dowling's of Prosperous, a noted music venue and at virtually every Fleadh Ceoil, beer festival and major equivalent music festival in the country. I got to know Dónal extremely well during this period and formed an opinion of his character which I have never had reason to change. He was gregarious and carefree, at times lacking in seriousness and discretion, but he could not be and never was knowingly disloyal to his oath of allegiance to the constitution of Ireland.

This is the full import of what happened to Dónal. One moment he was enjoying what, in the Ireland of the time, was regarded as a very high-status career with the support and friendship of his peers and the admiration of his family. Without warning and in the space of a few weeks, he became an out-of-work pariah, not only shunned by his army contemporaries but disowned forever even by his father. This was not the end of it. Because of the grounds of his dismissal, his work prospects were very poor and it came as no surprise, that, having been so ill-treated, he suffered post-traumatic shock and that his life fell apart.

Don Mullan's investigation has been motivated by his renowned regard for justice. It is an effort to get at the truth in the hope that one of the state's most cloistered institutions might yet correct one of its mistakes, so devastating in its consequences for Dónal de Róiste, and improve both its practices and itself in the process. Dónal's persistent struggle to clear his name over more than thirty years is probably the strongest evidence of all that he was no subversive. Mullan deals severely with those immediately involved in investigating Dónal. Perhaps their actions might generously be described as overzealous. In any event, they do appear to have made up their minds prematurely and to have drawn the wrong conclusions.

Don Mullan has here given us an incisive, detailed and thorough account of the factors which led to Dónal de Róiste's sudden and unexpected dismissal from the defence forces in 1969. I cannot recall exactly who first informed me of it but I do recall that it came as a bombshell and I remember saying, 'This is a terrible mistake, but the truth will out in time.' I did not envisage then just how long it would take.

APPENDIX A

(Two key documents, the report of the Judge Advocate General (October 2002) and the High Court judgment of Mr Justice Quirke which quashed the JAG's report (July 2005) are available on the Currach Press website www.currach.ie.)

DOCUMENTS REFERRED TO IN JUDGE ADVOCATE GENERAL'S REPORT

DOCUMENT 1
[Handwritten, dated and initialled]
SECRET
1.   A confidential source reported that Lt. ROCHE was in the company of members of the Dublin IRA Splinter Group on two days, [the dates 16/17 have been subsequently added to this memo] in April, 69. It was apparent that he knew ████████ and ██████████████ well.
2.   During the conversation ROCHE mentioned that there was an auction of Army vehs at Clancy Bks on 23rd April 69 and that he would advise on a good car if anyone wanted to buy one.
3.   NOT possible at this stage to say whether connection is subversive or not.
4.   ROCHE is described by a reliable source as rather immature and Bohemian in tastes.
5.   Dif Fais Ceann 1 was briefed on the background info on 22/4/69. Fif Fais Cean O will attend the auction at Clancy Bks on 23 April.
GOS Cpt 22/4/69
SECRET

DOCUMENT 2
[Handwritten, dated and initialled]
SECRET
Memo
Lt. ROCHE attended the Auction at Clancy Bks.
████████████ was also present. They were friendly to gether [*sic*]. A third unidentified person, fair haired, slim build was also there.
████████████ and companion left at 12.30 [crossed out] hours approx.
A reliable source reports that ROCHE may have bought a Land Rover.
GOS 23/4/69
[The numeral '3' in this date appears to have been superimposed over another number].
SECRET

DOCUMENT 3
[Typed, undated and unsigned]
SECRET
INTERVIEW with (0.8159) Lt. Donal ROCHE on 25.4.1969, at Rgn, Fais,
1.   I informed Lt. ROCHE that I was inquiring about two civilians he had met at the auction at Clancy Bks on 23 April, 1969.
2.   He said one of them was a ████████████ who was a previous acquaintance.

342

The other was a friend of ███████ whom he did not know but believed his name was ███████. He was aware that ███████ was a criminal who had been involved in an incident with the Gardai at Ballyfermot last year.

3.   He first met ███████ at O'Donoghue's, a public house in Merrion Row, about May or June of last year. They were introduced by a mutual friend, ███████ ███████, presently with a dance band at the ███████, ███████, ███████.

4.   He subsequently met ███████ on a few (2/3) occasions, always at O'DONOGHUE's and always casually.

5.   In July he spent a weekend in Galway with ███████, ███████ girl-friend, a German au pair girl and a ███████.

6.   Between this and October he saw ███████ casually on a further 2/3 occasions in DONOGHUE's [sic]. He did not see him from October until Thursday, 17th April 1969, when he again met him in O'DONOGHUE's.

7.   ROCHE went there with his girl-friend, ███████, a friend ███████ and his girl-friend and ███████ sister. They were in the outer bar. ███████ came in from the lounge bar, saw ROCHE and asked him what he was doing in Dublin. ROCHE said he was up for an auction of Army cars in Clancy Barracks. ███████ said he might come along as he was interested in buying a car. He went back into the lounge with ███████, chatted to ███████ wife and two other women for a few minutes and then returned to his party at the front bar.

8.   He next met ███████ at the auction on 23 April and spoke to him about the vehicles for sale. ███████ and his friend did not stay long and left without buying so far as he knew. He (ROCHE) did not buy anything at the auction.

9.   From an early stage he knew ███████ was anti-Army. ███████ frequently referred to him as his 'Free State Army friend.' On one occasion ███████ asked him about zeroing of rifles and on another referred to 9mm ammunition but never made a direct approach to him.

10.   He learned that ███████ was involved with the Gardai when his friend, ███████ rang him and drew his attention to the press reports of the Ballyfermot incident. This was about November 1968. About this time he mentioned casually to Comdt. P. MAGUIRE that he knew ███████ and Comdt. MAGUIRE advised him to avoid such people.

11.   The only army person he could recollect being with him when he met ███████ was Capt. Patrick Walshe of Kildare and this was on only one occasion.

12.   Questioned about his activities since coming to Dublin for the auction on 15th April ROCHE was very vague and protested that he could not remember. Pressed for details he came up with the followings:

15th April (Tues) – with his girl-friend – no details

16th April (Wed) – Visited a friend ███████ an Aer Lingus pilot with an address at ███████, ███████, which he could not remember.

17th April (Thurs) – At O'DONOGHUE's pub as outlined in paras 6&7.

18th April (Fri) – Visited friend, ███████, ███████, ███████, with his girl-friend. Went to Cedars pub.

19/20 April: Spent weekend accompanied by girl-friend, at his parents home in Clonmel.

On night of 20th April stopped off at KILDARE Bks. For drinks on the way home. Had drinks with Capt. P. WALSHE, Lt. SWAN and Lt. O'CONNOR.

13.   He denied ever meeting any other people with ███████ other than his friend at the auction. He did not know ███████, ███████ or ███████.

He knew ████████████ held 'peculiar views' and was aware from October that he was a criminal. He realised he was foolish to associate with ████████████ but it was only a casual acquaintance, there was never any approach made to him and he regarded ████████████ as being 'unusual'. He (Roche) liked to meet people like that, Bohemian types, ballad groups etc. He knew O'DONOGHUEs pub was somewhat unsavoury, but thought the crowd there was 'interesting'.

14.   Throughout the interview Roche was vague and uncertain about his movements. I formed the impression that this was deliberate and he would not be pinned down to facts. He claimed he did not know his girl-friends address, nor the exact address of the friends he visited.

15.   At an early stage he refused to answer questions and asked for a solicitor. He claimed he thought initially that he was being questioned on a matter resulting from theft of items at Clancy during the auction. When informed that it was a security investigation he understook [sic] to cooperate but continued to be vague and indefinite.

16.   Towards the end of the interview he said he knew he was finished in the Army but would not retire as he wanted to see what 'they would do with him'. I feel that this was a bravado touch and a determination not 'to be chickened.'

17.   The interview terminated circa 1700 hours and on instruction of S. Fais, I informed Lt. ROCHE that he would be returned to Athlone that evening but would be likely to be required for further questioning in a few days.

SECRET

DOCUMENT 4
[Handwritten, undated and unsigned]
SECRET
Seconded Interview with Lt. Roche 28/4/69

1.   Lt Roche arrived at Rng Fais at 1615 hours.

2.   I informed him that I was continuing the previous interview and checking on some points in his statement.

3.   I took him back over his association with ████████████ from May 1968. There was no substantial change in his statement up to October 68 which he claimed was the last time he saw ████████████ until April 69.

4.   He asserted that his relationship was a purely casual one. He was aware that ████████████ was a 'wild' one and anti Army but he (ROCHE) did not take him seriously.

5.   Asked to account again for his movements in the week prior to the Auction, ROCHE made one important change. He admitted being in O'DONOGHUES and meeting ████████████ twice, on 16th and 17th April 69.

6.   On 16th (Wed) he went in with his girl friend and another girl. They were in the outer bar. ████████████ came out from the lounge and talked to him - they spoke about the case. He introduced ████████████ and the girls – this was the first time his girl friend had met ████████████. She did not like him. Roche and his friends were joined by a ████████████ tall dark with dark glasses. They left sharply afterwards.

7.   On the 17th April he went to ████████████ O'Donoghues with his girl friend, a friend ████████████ and two other girls. He [or is it she?] went because ████████████ wanted to meet a criminal and ROCHE knew ████████████ would be there. They did meet ████████████ and talked to him for a few minutes.

8.   Questioned why he mentioned only one meeting at the first interview he said he had forgotten but his girl friend reminded him of the two visits.

10.   Recounting the meeting at the auction he said ████████████ asked him

344

about various cars and he told him about them, sometimes going away to enquire about them [the word 'it' is scored out and replaced by the word 'them']. At one stage ██████████ friend ███████████ (███████████) said he should be careful talking to them as '█████████ was being watched by the Special Branch'.

11.   That night (Wed 23 April) he was out with Capt ███████████ and mentioned to him that █████████ was at the auction and he was sure that he was seen talking to him. (██████████ confirmed this in the interview with him).

12.   Pressed and questioned about meeting other people with ██████████, ROCHE denied this emphatically. He was not worried about his relationship with ██████████ until the auction when he realised he might be seen but he was satisfied that he was able to control the relationship. NO suggestion about ammunition or military plans was ever made to him by ████████.

13.   ROCHE went as a chauffeur 'guide to an American around XMAS, 1968, travelling with him to London and the Continent. [Note to myself: See Comdt. Maguire interview, 26/4/69, paragraph 5].

SECRET

DOCUMENT 5
[Handwritten, undated and unsigned]

SECRET

Memo

1.   Subject met ████████ ██████████ █████████ and other members of the Dublin IRA Splinter Group in Dublin on the 18th and 19th April 69.

2.   He met █████████ at the Auction in Clancy Bks on 23 April 69.

3.   Believed to have had arrangement to meet members of the Group in O'Donoghues pub on night of 23 April 69 but not confirmed that he did so.

4.   ██████████ Formally lived at ████████ █████████ Contact of SHINKWIN. Received ammunition from SHINKWIN.

One of the Group at Lahinch Camp on 26 Aug.

Presently on bail on charges arising from incident with Gardai at Ballyfermot.

██████████ lives at ████████ met SHINKWIN with ██████████ in Cork on 17 Aug 68 when raid on Lahinch Camp is believed to have been planned.

Also involved in Ballyfermot

██████████ Drove car at LAHINCH] on 28th Aug. Involved in Ballyfermot. Was in Cork but bail withdrew and is now in Mountjoy since 23 April 69. [This is the date of the Auction].

This is the most active sub group of the IRA splinter Group. Saw at Cork and believed to have been involved in the Newry bank raid and other raids in the Republic.

They are associated with ██████████ █████████. ██████████ ██████████ is probably the local leader.

SECRET

DOCUMENT 6
[Handwritten (O'Sullivan?), undated and unsigned]

SECRET

Summary

Comment

1.   A Confidential source reported on 21st April that;

a.   ROCHE was in DONOGHUES pub on 16th April [Memo has added dates of 16 and 17] and there met ████████ and ████████. He later met ████████ ████████ there and left with ████████ to meet ████████. The source reports that ROCHE appeared to be well acquainted with them.

b.   ROCHE met ████████, at least, on the following night (Thurs) also in O'DONOGHUES.

c.   ROCHE arranged to meet ████████ at the auction in Clancy Bks on 23 April 69.

d.   ROCHE had not previously come to notice.

Comment

a.   Is supported [the word 'correct' has been crossed out and replaced by the word 'supported'] only in that ROCHE admits meeting ████████ but no one else on 16th April.

b.   Is correct in Donny (?) ROCHE'S own statement.

c.   Is correct in that they did meet at the auction. Though ROCHE denies that he invited ████████ but He did tell him about the auction.

2.

a.   The report that ROCHE know others than ████████ in the group i.e. ████████ ████████ and ████████ is unsubstantiated.

b.   ROCHE'S relationship ('knowledge' has been scored out and replaced by 'relationship) with ████████ is supported by his own Statement, that of Comdt. MAGUIRE and Capt. WALSHE.

c.   ROCHE'S meeting with ████████ at the Auction is substantiated by witnesses i.e. Oif Fais and Oif Fais Cuita Cean O and 'S' Branch man present at Clancy. Anyway, ROCHE admits it.

Comment

It is considered therefore that in assessing the security significance of this case the source report that he knew others in the group should be viewed with reserve ('disregarded' has been scored out and replaced by 'viewed with reserve') and the case judged on his relationship with ████████ solely.

Analysis of ROCHE'S relationship with ████████

3.

a.   ROCHE knew ████████ at least from MAY 1968. He met him fairly frequently between then and October 69, including spending a week-end in GALWAY with him.

b.   He was aware during this period that ████████ was a wild, undesirable character and that he was Anti-Army and anti-Establishment.

c.   ROCHE had suspicions at least that he might have IRA connections (He told Comdt MAGUIRE that one of his friends was in the IRA - and in the context of this it is obvious he meant ████████).

d.   During this period on at least two occasions firearms were discussed – Once about zeroing of rifles and the other about 9mm ammunition.

e.   ROCHE made no effort to avoid ████████ and did not report his relationship with him.

f.   In October he became aware that ████████ had been involved in a shooting fracas with the Gardai and was a criminal. He still did not disclose his relationship with him.

g.   There is no evidence to connect ROCHE with ████████ from October 68 – April 69 though in the circumstance of the meeting on 16th April there is the possibility that they had met in the interim.

h.   ROCHE met ▓▓▓▓▓▓▓ in Donoghues [*sic*] on the 16th April. He talked to him quite openly, told him what he (ROCHE) was doing in Dublin, discussed ▓▓▓▓▓▓▓ case and left it open for ▓▓▓▓▓▓▓ to come to a sensitive Army post.

i.   ROCHE went back again on 17th April apparently deliberately to meet ▓▓▓▓▓▓▓ which he did.

j.   He met him again at the Auction in Clancy and advised him about cars. Though reminded again of ▓▓▓▓▓▓▓ position when warned by ▓▓▓▓▓▓▓ friend ▓▓▓▓▓▓▓ that 'S' branch people were watching him, ROCHE took no protective (?) action to advise Army Authorities about ▓▓▓▓▓▓▓ presence.

Note   ROCHE made not attempt to conceal his contact with ▓▓▓▓▓▓▓ at the Auction.

k.   ROCHE was obviously concerned that he had been seen with ▓▓▓▓▓▓▓ (witness his comment to Capt. P. WALSHE).

l.   ROCHE did not disclose his meeting with ▓▓▓▓▓▓▓ on 16th April until second interview.

Assessment

(1)   ROCHE maintained a relationship with ▓▓▓▓▓▓▓ for about a year.

(2)   He was aware for most of its time that ▓▓▓▓▓▓▓ was undesirable and from October to April that he was a criminal awaiting trial for a serious offence.

(3)   Despite this he met ('sought out' crossed out and replaced by 'met') ▓▓▓▓▓▓▓ on successive days in April 69 and on the Second occasion clearly sought him out.

(4)   He discussed his position freely with ▓▓▓▓▓▓▓ and told him about an auction at Clancy Bks.

(5)   He was openly friendly with him there.

(6)   In normal circumstances a case like this would have been developed further. In view of the sensitivity of Clancy Bks it was decided to make an early direct approach. This is a measure of the potential seriousness of this case.

(7)   There is no evidence to indicate a Subversive connection between ROCHE ▓▓▓▓▓▓▓ but in the light of the SHINKWIN case and the known militancy of the Group of which ▓▓▓▓▓▓▓ is a member it is most likely that such an approach would have been made had not the association been uncovered.

Final Comment

While Lt. ROCHE may have been more foolhardy than criminal, he displayed a serious degree of irresponsibility ('a grave lack of respon' is scored out and replaced by 'a serious degree of irresponsibility') in his continuing association with ▓▓▓▓▓▓▓ and potentially endangered military security.

He must be rated as a serious security risk.

SECRET

DOCUMENT 7

[Typed, unsigned, with [O'Sullivan's?] handwritten date of 1 May 1969]

SECRET

0.8159 Lt. Donal ROCHE

1.   Further to the security report on Lt. Donal ROCHE of 30 Aibrean 69, the following additional information is ('was' is crossed out and replaced by 'is') submitted.

2.   At a third interview on 30.4.69 Lt. ROCHE said he had now remembered that he had met a Lt. Leo CASEY, Air Corps in Donoghues [*sic*] on the night of the 16th April. This was by previous arrangement, He thought CASEY met ▓▓▓▓▓▓▓ with him.

3.   Lt. CASEY confirmed meeting ROCHE by appointment on 16th April. He (CASEY) arrived there at about 21.35. ROCHE was at the bar with two girls and a man who had a guitar. He did not remember being introduced to anyone.

4.   He saw ROCHE speak to a man in the lounge but did not know what was said. He (CASEY) left at about 22.00hrs.

5.   This information helps little beyond confirming that ROCHE was in Donoghue's between 21.35 hrs and 22.00 hrs on 16th April, 1969.

6.   At the conclusion of this interview Lt. ROCHE said he wished to submit his account on the matter in writing. He was advised he was free to do this if he wished and that if he submitted one it should be through the OIC Ceann [Commanding Officer]. Cft. MADIGAN, who was present at this stage, was informed accordingly.

1/5/69. [Date is handwritten and appears to be O'Sullivan's writing]
SECRET

DOCUMENT 8A

[Typed cover letter to Security Report [Document 8b], dated 1 May 1969 and signed by Colonel M. Hefferon, Director of Intelligence]
SECRET
G2/C/491
[This document is dated 1 May 1969. Why did O'Sullivan ask that a new file in the 491 category be opened on 12 June 1969 when, as these references clearly establish, it already had been opened?]
Ceann Foirne [Chief-of-Staff]
Uasail, [Sir]

1.   The security report on the alleged association of 0/8159 Lt. Donal ROCHE with members of a subversive group is submitted herewith. Appendix A giving background security data on the Group and Appendix A personal record of Lt. ROCHE – are also enclosed.

2.   It has been established that Lt. ROCHE has known ▮▮▮▮▮▮▮▮, a member of the Group, for almost twelve months. His most recent contacts were on the 16th and 17th April and the 23 April, 1969. On the latter date he met him at the auction of army vehicles at Clancy Barracks. This meeting resulted in ROCHE being approached directly to explain his conduct.

3.   As you are aware we would have preferred to develop this case more fully before moving on ROCHE but in view of the extreme sensitivity of Clancy Barracks it was felt that delay in bringing the association into the open would NOT have been an acceptable risk.

4.   It has not been possible to confirm ROCHE's association with the other members of the group as reported by our confidential source. We were somewhat handicapped by our inability to question directly the original source of information although the questioning and requestioning through a third party was reasonably satisfactory.

5.   While an unsupported report must be viewed with reserve, it is significant that the report was accurate in its other aspects and my view is that it must be considered as likely to be accurate on this count as well.

6.   As outlined in Appendix A this is a most active, extremist Group of Splinter IRA. They have had a record of violence and armed robbery over the last year. On two occasions they have threatened military security with proposed attacks on posts and on a third by inciting an NCO to steal 1,300 rounds of ammunition (SHINKWIN case). It will be recalled that ex.-Sgt. SHINKWIN, CT Depot, Cork, was sentenced by court martial for the theft of 1,300 rounds of 9 mm ammunition at Cork last September.

7.   The association of a member of the Defence Forces with any of this Group is unquestionably a threat to military security, even if actual subversion cannot be proven and such an association claimed to be 'innocent.'

8.   I am unable to see how an officer who has acted in the manner of Lt. ROCHE can merit the trust and confidence of his superiors to perform his duties as an officer. I have no hesitation in assessing him as an extremely serious security risk.

9.   Background security information on the main activities of this Group is given in Appendix A to the report. It is suggested that a preliminary reading of the Appendix will facilitate the reading of the report itself.

Signature CORNAL
(M. Ó hEibhrin)
[Cornel Hefferon]
STIURTHOIR FAISNEISE
[Director of Intelligence]
1 Bealtaine, 1969
RESTRICTED

DOCUMENT 8B
[Typed]
Security Report: 0.8159 Lt. Donal ROCHE, 4 Grn S&T Coy
RESTRICTED
Security Report: 0.8159 Lt. Donal ROCHE, 4 Grn S&T Coy [Pages 1-5]

1.   A report from a confidential source was received on 21 April 1969 to the effect that:

a.   a person called 'Doc' ROCHE, believed to be in 'Supply' I the Army had been in O'DONOGHUE's publichouse Merrion Row on 16th April. He was initially in the company of *███████████ and *███████ and was later joined by *███████████. He asked ███████ about *███████ and shortly afterwards left with ███████ to find ███████.

b.   ROCHE returned alone about an hour later.

c.   ROCHE met ███████ on the following night 17ᵗʰ April0 also in O'DONOGHUEs.

d.   During some of the conversation on either 16ᵗʰ or 17ᵗʰ ROCHE mentioned the auction of Army cars at Clancy Barracks on 23 April 1969 and suggested that anyone interested should come along.

2.   The report was investigated and the person concerned identified as 8159 Lt. Donal ROCHE, 4 Grn S&T Coy, ATHLONE, who was attached to Clancy Barracks from 15ᵗʰ April 69 for duties in connection with the auction. ROCHE's nickname is 'DUCK'.

3.   The auction was kept under surveillance and Lt. ROCHE was observed meeting and speaking freely to ███████ and ███████ (███████).

4.   ███████ and his friend left the auction about 11.30 hrs, apparently without buying anything.

5.   In view of ███████ presence in Clancy Barracks and the extreme sensitivity of this post it was decided to make a direct approach to Lt. ROCHE on the basis of the meeting with DWYER at the auction. Accordingly he was interviewed at Rannog Faisneise on 25.4.1969.

6.   Lt. ROCHE admitted the meeting with ███████ who was a previous acquaintance. He first met him at O'DONOGHUEs public house in about May

1968. They were introduced by a ████████, a guitarist with a dance band at the ████████ ████████.

7.   He subsequently met ████████ on a few 92/3) occasions, always at O'DONOGHUEs and always by chance. In July he spent a weekend in Galway with ████████ ████████ German au-pair girlfriend and a ████████ (believed no security significance).

8.   Between this and October 68 he saw ████████ casually in DONOGHUEs bar on about 2/3 occasions. He did NOT see him again until he met him in O'DONOGHUE's on Thursday, 17th April.

9.   On that occasion ROCHE with his girl friend ████████ a friend ████████ with his girl friend and his sister (five in all) were in O'DONOGHUEs at the outer bar. ████████ came in from the lounge bar, saw ROCHE asked him what he was doing. ROCHE said he was in Dublin for the auction of Army cars at Clancy Barracks on April, 23rd. ████████ said he might come along as he was interested in buying a car. ROCHE went into the back lounge with ████████, met ████████ wife and sister, chatted for a few minutes and then returned to his party at the front bar.

/ ....

* All members of the DUBLIN IRA Splinter Group.

10.   He next met [Dwyer] at the auction on 23 April and spoke to him about the vehicles for sale. ████████ was with a friend ████████ whom he did not know. ████████ and his friend did not stay long and left without buying so far as he knew. He (ROCHE) did not buy anything either.

11.   Questioned in detail about his activities over the period 15-23 April ROCHE initially protested that he could not remember. He was very vague but finally came up with the following:-

15th April (Tues) – with his girl friend – no details

16th April (Wed) – Visited a friend ████████ an Aer Lingus pilot, with an address at ████████ which he could not remember.

17th April (Thur): At O'DONOGHUE's as outlined in pars 8 and 9.

18th April (Fri): Visited friend ████████ ████████ with his girl friend. Went to Cedar's pub.

19/20 April: Spent week-end with girl friend at his parents home in Clonmel. On night of 20th April stopped off at Kildare Barracks for drinks on the way home. Had drinks with Capt. P. WALSHE, Lt. SWAN and Lt. O'CONNOR.

12.   From an early stage in their association he was aware that ████████ was anti-Army and anti-Establishment. ████████ frequently referred to him as 'his Free State Army friend.'

13.   On one occasion ████████ told him he had been away in Connemara 'zeroing rifles' and on another he made some passing reference to 9 mm ammunition. ROCHE did not take him seriously but did think he might have some subversive connection.

14.   In October he learned of ████████ involvement in a shooting fracas with the Gardai and knew then that he was a criminal. About this stage he mentioned him ████████ to his friend Capt. P. WALSHE and some time to Comdt. P. MAGUIRE in the mess at Athlone.

15.   He did not recollect any other Army person being present at his meetings with ████████ but thought maybe his friend Capt. P. WALSHE met him once. (WALSHE denies this).

16.   He did not meet any other people with ████████ whom he thought was

a 'loner'. ████████████ told him he had been in jail in England before he came back to Ireland. He did not know '██████████ or ██████████.'

17.　He realised now it was foolish to have associated with ██████████ but it was only a casual acquaintance and he regarded ██████████ as 'unusual'. He liked to meet people like that, Bohemian types, ballad groups, etc. He knew O'DONOGHUE's pub was somewhat unsavoury but thought the crowd was 'interesting'.

18.　Throughout this interview he was vague and indefinite. The impression was formed that he was deliberately so and would not be pinned down to facts. He claimed he did not know his girl friend's address nor the exact address of the friends he visited.

19.　Comdt. MAGUIRE was interviewed and remembered a reference made by Lt. ROCHE. It was a casual meeting in the mess. ROCHE mentioned that he never had any difficulty getting accommodation when he went to Dublin for the week-end as the crowd he knocked around with were the university bohemian type and that there was always 'a bed in a flat.'

20.　He went on to say that a friend he met in a pub was in the IRA. MAGUIRE told him he was foolish to have anything to do with that type of person.

21.　Capt. WALSHE was interviewed on 28th April, 1969. He acknowledged to be very friendly with Lt. ROCHE but could not recollect ever having met ██████████. He remembered ROCHE and a friend ██████████ (connect with Para 7) discussing ██████████ involvement with the Gardai at Ballyfermot in October, 1968).

22.　He was out with Lt. ROCHE on the night of 23 April (day of auction). During the evening ROCHE mentioned that ██████████ was at the auction in Clancy and he was sure they were seen together by 'S' branch man.

23.　<u>Second interview with Lt. ROCHE</u>

Lt. ROCHE was again interviewed at Rng. Fais on 28/4/69.

24.　He was taken back over the details of his association with ██████████ from May 68. There was no significant change in his account up to October 1968 which he claimed was the last occasion that he had seen ██████████ until the meeting in April, 1969.

25.　Asked to account again for his movements in the period 15th-23rd April he made on important change. He admitted to being in O'DONOGHUEs and to meeting ██████████ twice, on 16th and 17th April 69. This accorded with the information received from our source.

26.　Questioned as to why he omitted this second visit in his first version he claimed he had forgotten about it. He had discussed the matter with his girl friend over the weekend and she had reminded him of the second visit.

27.　On the 16th (Wed) he went to O'DONOGHUEs with his girlfriend and another girl. They were in the outer bar. ██████████ came from the lounge and talked to him. They spoke about ██████████ case and he introduced ██████████ to the girls. He told ██████████ why he was in Dublin and about the auction. ██████████ said he might come along. He went back with ██████████ into the lounge and met ██████████ wife and sister. Shortly afterwards he returned to the outer bar where a man named ██████████ had joined the two girls. Shortly afterwards they left DONOGHUEs.

28.　On 17th April he was there again with his girl friend, a ██████████ and his girl friend and ██████████ sister. They went to DONOGHUES because ██████████ was interested to meet a criminal type and he knew ██████████ would be there.

29.　They did meet ██████████ and chatted together for a while. His girlfriend would not speak to ████████ as she did not like him.

30.   Recounting the meeting at the auction on the 23rd he said ████████ asked him about various cars and he told him about them. At one stage ████ friend said to him that he should be careful talking to them as ████████ was being watched by the Special Branch.'

31.   On the evening of 23 April he was out with Capt. WALSHE and mentioned to him that ████████ was at the auction and that he was sure that they had been seen together.

32.   ROCHE continued to deny that he met ████████, ████████ or ████████ on the 16th April or that he ever knew them. He claimed not to have been worried about his relationship with ████████ and did not feel that there was any security hazard in it. Asked why he felt no worries about a known criminal and subversives being in Clancy Bks he said he was sure the Special Branch would have been watching him and he felt no responsibility to report it.

33.   He repeated that no subversive suggestion about ammunition, arms or military plans had ever been made to him by ████████ or anyone else. He realised now in the light of the enquiry that he had been foolish but felt he had done nothing wrong.

CONCLUSION

1.   Lt. ROCHE has known ████████ for almost a year. He met him fairly regularly between May 68 and October 68 including spending a weekend with him in Galway.

2.   He was aware that ████████
a.   was a generally undesirable character.;
b.   had served a jail sentence in England;
c.   was decidedly anti-Army and anti-Establishment.

3.   He had suspicions at least that ████████ had some subversive connections (talk about 'zeroing of rifles' and '9mm ammunition' – connect with para 13). He also referred to him to Comdt. MAGUIRE as being 'in the IRA'.

4.   In October he became aware that ████████ had been involved in a shooting fracas with the Gardai at Ballyfermot and was charged with offences arising from it. Newspaper reports at the time adverted to the possibility of a political and subversive background to this incident.

5.   Despite this knowledge he met ████████ on successive nights (16/17th April) in O'DONOGHUES. He discussed his (████████) case with him, told him what he (ROCHE) was doing in Dublin and at least concurred with his intention to visit the highly sensitive Army post at Clancy Barracks.

6.   He met him at the auction and advised him about the cars. Though reminded of ████████ position by his friend – 'Special branch men are watching him' – he took no protective action to assist military security.

7.   ROCHE's association with ████████ is clearly established. There is NO evidence to indicate that the association had become subversive though ROCHE should have been fully aware of the potential danger.

8.   In the light of the experience of the SHINKWIN case and the known extremism of the Group of which ████████ is a member it is very likely that an approach would have been made if the association had not been uncovered.

9.   The fact that ROCHE did not meet ████████ during the period October/April may be accounted for by the SHINKWIN case and the shooting incident which both occurred about this time. ████████ was in custody for some

weeks arising from the latter. Additionally ROCHE was away for three weeks at the end of December/beginning of January acting as a chauffeur/guide to an American touring London and France. He obtained this by answering an advertisement in the newspaper.

10. The only evidence to connect ROCHE with others in the group is that of the original confidential report. An unsupported report of this nature must be taken with reserve but it is pointed out that:-

a. The report was very accurate in all other matters.

b. It clearly pointed to ROCHE as the person concerned.

c. It reported him as being in O'DONOGHUES on two nights (16/17ᵗʰ) – A fact not admitted by ROCHE until his second interview.

d. it reported an arrangement to attend the auction which occurred.

11. Coupled with the fact that these four, ███████████, ███████████, ███████████ and ███████████ are all known to know around together and to frequent O'DONOGHUES pub it remains a strong possibility that ROCHE did meet them there on the 16ᵗʰ April and may have known them previously.

12. He can deny this because he knows that direct evidence connecting him with them has not been produced.

13. ███████████ is a thoroughly bad character. He has a jail record in England, is awaiting trial on charges here and was one of the four who planned to attack LAHINCH Camp last August in collaboration with ex. Sgt. SHINKWIN.

14. Any association by a member of the Defence Forces with him or his group constitutes a security hazard. When the member is an officer this hazard is increased very considerably.

Additional background information on the Group concerned is given in Appendix A attached.

Personal particulars on Lt. ROCHE are at Appendix A attached.

RESTRICTED

RESTRICTED
APPENDIX 'A' [Page 6]
ADDITIONAL INFORMATION

The persons mentioned in the report received are ███████████, ███████████, ███████████ and ███████████.

They are members of the IRA splinter group and are amongst the most extreme members in it.

███████████, ███████████ were all connected with the SHINKWIN case of August last year. ███████████ was the chief contact. He collected the ammunition from SHINKWIN and paid for it. ███████████ met SHINKWIN with ███████████ at a later date and arranged a raid on LAHINCH Camp on 27th August, 1968.

███████████, ███████████ and ███████████ were three of the four (███████████ was the fourth) who went to LAHINCH on 27th August 68 with the intention of raiding the camp and only changed their mind at the last minute.

███████████, ███████████, ███████████ and ███████████ were the four involved in the shooting incident with the Gardai at Ballyfermot in October 68. They are currently awaiting trial for this.

The Group are believed to have been involved in bank raids and ███████████ is awaiting trial for the Newbridge raid. Some of them are also suspected of being involved in the Newry bank raid.

███████████ returned from England about 18 months' ago. He came to Gardai

353

notice in the summer of 1968 as associating with the Splinter group but was not positively identified until the investigations into the SHINKWIN case.

He was the driver of the car at LAHINCH and again at Ballyfermot. He is currently employed as a fitter with a central heating firm.

███████████ was one of the two men sentenced for setting fire to the Fianna Fail HQ in Mount Street on 21 October, 1967.

Members of the group were reliably reported to have planned an attack on a post in Cork (believed to be FERMOY) in the summer of 1968 but did not go ahead with it because the Cork group were against it.

RESTRICTED

DOCUMENT 8C

[Typed, unsigned, undated, authorship undeclared despite the use of 'I' in opening paragraph]

Interview with Comdt. MAGUIRE.

1.   I spoke to Comdt. MAGUIRE on Saturday, 26th April. He remembered the incident that Lt. ROCHE spoke about.

2.   It was a very casual meeting in the Mess. ROCHE mentioned that he never had any trouble getting accommodation when he went to Dublin for the weekend as the crowd he knocked around with were the bohemian university type and there was always 'a bed in a flat'.

3.   He went on to say that one friend he met in a pub was in the IRA but that though they were on opposite sides they were friendly. MAGUIRE told him he was foolish to have anything to do with that type of person.

4.   MAGUIRE regards ROCHE as an immature type with odd bohemian tastes, fond of beat groups, ballad singing types etc.

5.   He believes he went away around last Xmas as a chauffeur to an American group touring round London and the Continent.

6.   He has frequently had a rather unusual friend to stay with him at Athlone, known as the 'DOG'. Maguire does not know his first name.

DOCUMENT 9 [DUPLICATE OF DOCUMENT 7 ABOVE]

DOCUMENT 10A

[Typewritten, Signed by Lt General S. MacEoin, dated 3 May 1969]
SECRET
0.8159 Lieutenant Donal ROCHE
An tAire. [The Minister]
This officer, born on the 12th February 1945, entered the Military College as a Cadet on the 7th October, 1963. He was commissioned on 29th September, 1965. He is at present serving with the 4th Field Company, Supply and Transport Corps. Prior to being awarded a cadetship he had approximately three years' service with An Forsa Cosanta Aitiúil.

I attach hereto a SECRET file from the Director of Intelligence which sets out in detail the investigations carried out by Officers of the Intelligence Section, into this Officer's associates. The contents of that file are summarised hereunder and from the facts disclosed, for the reasons set out below, after consultations with the Adjutant General and the Director of Intelligence summarised hereunder and from the facts disclosed, for the reasons set out below, after consultations with the Adjutant General and the Director of Intelligence and after much deep and anxious thought I am to recommend that Lt. Roche is retired by an tUachtaran pursuant to the powers vested in him by Section 47 (2) of the Defence Act, 1954, for the reason prescribed by the Defence Force Regulation A 15, paragraph 18 (1)(f), that is to say,

'in the interests of the service.'

Consequent on this and in view of the material stored in Clancy Barracks and the demands of military security, Officers of the Intelligence Section of Army Headquarters interviewed Lt. Roche on the 25th April. He was again questioned on the 28th and 30th April.

The conduct of Lt. Roche on being first interviewed by the Intelligence Officers may also be significant – he denied being in O'Donoghue's on the 16th April and said that he was only there on the 17th. At the second interview on the 28th April he admitted being in O'Donoghue's on both the 16th and 17th April and to meeting ████████ there on both occasions.

Full details of the various interrogations of Lt. Roche appear on the attached file and taken in conjunction with the known facts the following appear:

1.   Lt. Roche has known ████████ since at least May 1968 and met him fairly frequently between then and October 1968 and in fact spent a weekend with him in Galway.

2.   Up to October 1968 Lt. Roche was aware that ████████ was a generally undesirable character, that he has served a jail sentence in England, and he was decidedly anti-Army and anti-Establishment. From ████████ talk about 'zeroing rifles' and '9mm ammunition' Lt. Roche must at least have been suspicious that ████████ belonged to or has associations with a subversive organization and even at this state his oath of loyalty which he has solemnly made on his commissioning and his sense of responsibility as an Officer of the Forces should have dictated to him his immediate duty of reporting to his superiors his knowledge of ████████ and ████████ likely associations.

3.   Two matters of importance and significance emerge from the questioning of Lt. Roche. If Lt. Roche's statement is correct his association with ████████ ceased from OCTOBER '68 until APRIL '69, Lt. Roche quoted ████████ as referring to '9 mm ammunition.' On the 8th October 1968 No. 810740 Sergeant John SHINKWIN of Command Training Depot, Southern Command, was tried by General Court-martial in Cork and charged with:

1.   On or about 16th August 1968 STEALING 1300 rounds of 9mm ammunition.

2.   On or about 16th August 1968 SELLING 1300 rounds of 9 mm ammunition.

3.   Absence with Leave [sic] from 12 Sept to 17 Sept 1968.

Sgt SHINKWIN pleased [sic] guilty to all the charges and was sentenced to six months' imprisonment. This case was well publicised in the Army and in the public press and it is inconceivable that Lt. Roche did not associate ████████ reference to '9 mm ammunition' with the case of Sgt. Shinkwin. (It is known that this ammunition was sold to ████████ – alias ████████ – see above – a member of the splinter group of the IRA. It is also known that during his period of absence without leave Sgt Shinkwin was associating with four members of that splinter group in LAHINCH – ████████ and it is further known that this group planned an attack on LAHINCH Camp then occupied by troops.)

On the 3rd October 1968 an armed attack was made on members of the Garda

Siochana at Ballyfermot by at least four men – [REDACTED] (see above) [REDACTED] (see above) [REDACTED] [REDACTED]. Lt. Roche admitted that he knew of [REDACTED] participation in this attack.

All of these matters were known to Lt. Roche when, as he states, he renewed his acquaintanceship with [REDACTED] in April 1969. His remarks to his fellow officers corroborate this – see the statements of Comdt. Maguire and Capt. Walshe. See also Lt. Roche's statement that when his friend [REDACTED] expressed a desire to meet a criminal type Lt Roche took him to O'Donoghue's because he knew that [REDACTED] would be there. Lt. Roche in speaking to Capt. Walshe referred to the auction in Clancy Barracks and to the presence there of [REDACTED] and that they had been seen together by the Special Branch.

As a security precaution it has been considered prudent to transfer Lt. Roche to an appointment in BOYLE.

S. Mac Eoin   LT. GENERAL
(S. Mac Eoin)
CEANN FOIRNE [Chief-of-Staff]
3 Bealtaine, 1969 [3 May 69]
RUNDA [SECRET]

DOCUMENT IOB
[Typewritten, Signed by Lt General S. MacEoin, dated 3 May 1969. This document is almost identical to the one above but for the following changes]:

It is headed <u>AIRE.</u> [MINISTER] and addressed to Uasail [Sir]

1st paragraph: 4th Field Company is described as 4th Garrison Company.

2nd paragraph: in addition to the Adjutant General and the Director of Intelligence, the Quartermaster-General and Assistant Chief of Staff are included.

5th paragraph: "- he denied being in O'Donoghue's..." reads: "- he avoided mentioning being in O'Donoghue's..."

5th paragraph: "... he said that he was only there on the 17th", reads: "... and said only that he was there on the 17th."

Fact 3 (3): "Absence with Leave from 12-17 Sept 1968" is changed to "Absence without Leave..."

Fact 4, last sentence: The name 'DWYER' is unredacted leaving the final sentence to read: "Lt. Roche admitted that he knew of DWYER'S participation in this [the Ballyfermot] attack."

This Officer... is at present serving with the 4th Field Company, Supply and Transport Corps...

This Officer... is at present serving with the 4th Garrison Company, Supply and Transport Corps...

DOCUMENT II
SECRET
RESTRICTED
<u>Reg.</u>
Please open new file in 491 series in name of 0.8159 Lt. Donal ROCHE and pass to me.

GoS   12/6/69
File h/with.   Initials R? 12/6/69.
RESTRICTED

SECRET

[Undated letter to Minister, from the Chief of Staff, Lt. Gen S. MacEoin]
SECRET
0.8159 Lieutenant Donal ROCHE
An tAire. [The Minister]
Uasail, [Sir]
In accordance with your request I arranged for this officer to be interviewed by the Deputy Judge Advocate General. This interview took place on 28/29 Bealtaine [May] 1969.
The report of the Deputy Judge Advocate General dated 29u Bealtaine 1969 is attached hereto and reinforces the conclusions already arrived at by me after consultations with the Adjutant General, the Quartermaster General, the Assistant Chief of Staff and the Director of Intelligence.
S. Mac Eoin   Lt-General.
(S Mac Eoin)
Ceann Foirne. (Chief of Staff)
SECRET

[Report of the Deputy Judge Advocate General, Col. Arthur Cullen, dated 29 May 1969]
SECRET
OFFICE OF THE DEPUTY JUDGE
ADVOCATE GENERAL
29 Bealtaine 1969
0.8159 Lieutenant Donal ROCHE
An Ceann Foirne. (Chief-of-Staff)
Uasail, [Sir]
In accordance with your directions this officer reported to my office yesterday for interview.
The interview commenced at 14.05 hours.
I informed Lt Roche that the Int. rep. [Intelligence Report] on his association with ████████ had been submitted to the General Staff who had called upon me as DJAG to advise. I informed him that as he had volunteered on 30 Aibrean [April] to submit a statement about the matter and as he had not done so after a month I was reluctant to do anything until he had been given the opportunity of submitting any statement he wished to make. Lt Roche then stated that on the Friday after his final interrogation by the Int Sec on 30/4/69 he had consulted his solicitor (Mr. Brendan O'Maoileain, 144 Baggot St. Dublin – Tel 62879) and his solicitor had undertaken to write to the Director of Intelligence and to Officer Commanding, Western Command. I informed him that these letters had NOT been received.
Lt. Roche did not appear to me at this stage to be very seriously concerned about the matter so I proceeded to take him through his statements in Int Sec. He agreed with the accuracy of the report and on further questioning admitted to being aware that Sgt Shinkwin had been court-martialled and convicted of stealing and selling 9mm ammo. I asked him if this Int Rep, taken as a whole, did not indicate that he must be considered a security risk and he replied that that [sic] this is what the Int Sec had told him and added 'I don't appreciate what I am guilty of.' I then went through the report

in the minutest detail and his answers were consistent with those already given to Int Sec: on some matters his answers were glib and practically flippant on others evasive, for instance, I asked him if there was any significance in the fact that he had ceased to meet ███████ in October 1968? He replied that there was not – he had not had the opportunity as he had not been in Dublin. I suggested to him that one reason was that Shinkwin had been tried in October and that another might be the Ballyfermot incident. He said that he wasn't sure if it had been October, it might have been in September. I then suggested that the reason why he ceased to meet ███████ in September was that it was in that month that Shinkwin had been arrested and charged. Lt. Roche then said that possibly it had been as early as August? I suggested that if it was August the cause might have been that it was in August that the 9mm ammo. Had been stolen and sold. At this Lt Roche smiled and shrugged his his [*sic*] shoulders and said that he couldn't remember anyway.

I told him that the facts disclosed a very serious state of affairs and I read to him the oath taken by him when he was commissioned and that the report seemed to suggest that he was not being true to either the words or spirit of his oath. I advised him that he should go away and seriously consider his situation and that he should call on me the following morning at 10.00 hours with his statement.

The interview ended at 15.10 and as he was leaving my office Lt Roche asked if there would be any objection to him consulting his solicitor. I replied 'Certainly not.'

At 09.40 this day Lt Roche again visited me in my office. I asked him to sit down and he informed me that the matter would not take long as he would NOT make any further statement. He then left.

From the Int. Reps and from my own interview with him and having regard to his manner of answering questions and his general demeanour in this context and his refusal to make a statement (though he had volunteered to do so) I am satisfied beyond all doubt that this officer's retention in the Forces constitutes a grave security risk.

Ath 1 Cullen   Col. DJAG

RESTRICTED

DOCUMENT 14

[Letter to Chief-of-Staff from Lieutenant Roche's solicitor]

OUR REF. BMcD/md   YOUR REF.

Chief of Staff

Army Headquarters,

Dublin 7_____

Re: First Lieutenant Donal Roche
        formerly of 4th Garrison, Transport Division,
        Athlone, Co. Westmeath and now of
        19th. Battalion, Boyle, Co, Roscommon.

Dear Sir,

We act for 1st. Lieutenant Donal Roche who has instructed us to act on his behalf with regard to various serious accusations and charges made against him by the Army.

Our client states that he has been brought before various officials and officers of various ranks and accused of misconduct, indiscretion, being a security risk etc. On one occasion he was charged with the offence of being a security risk and on another occasion gross misconduct and so on, with the result that our client does not know where he stands. He is being pressurised and badgered which is quite unfair, due to the fact that he has not yet been formally charged and notice given to him, and an opportunity afforded him to make his own case in his own Defence. Every action that has been taken up to now against him has been completely to his prejudice.

We must point out that in the Defence Act, 1954 there are various protections given to officers which have been ignored in our client's case.

Our client would therefore like to know what charge, if any, is being preferred against him.

Yours faithfully,
Michael B O'Maoileoin & Co
MICHAEL B. O'MAOILEOIN & CO.

DOCUMENT 15
[Draft response by army to Lt Roche's solicitor]
Messrs Michael B. O Maoileoin & Co,
Solicitors,
144, Lower Baggot Street
Dublin 2
Lieut. Donal Roche
A Chara,
I am to acknowledge your letter of 30th May 1969 addressed to the Chief of Staff in reference to this Officer.

If your Client thinks himself wronged in any matter by any officer he should take action in accordance with Section 114(1) Defence Act 1954.

[It is clear from the unsent reply to O'Maoileoin's letter of 30 May 1969 that it is a first draft that was mulled over and finalised by a second (perhaps more senior) hand. While the JAG is correct in stating that O'Maoileoin' letter 'was not replied to', I disagree with her assertion that 'the draft was never finalised.' It was finalised but not typed and sent.

It is interesting to note that the second hand does not, in any significant way, alter the logic of the first draft. The following is the first draft with the input of the second hand in parentheses.]

A Chara,
I am (directed?) to acknowledge (the receipt of) your letter of 30th May 1969 addressed to the Chief of Staff in reference to this Officer.

If your Client ['this officer' has been crossed out] thinks himself wronged in any matter by any officer he should (it is open to him to) take action in accordance with Section 114(1) (of the) Defence Act 1954.

(mise, le meas)

DOCUMENT 16
[Undated, unsigned, O'Sullivan handwritten memo, naming Lt Roche's solicitor]
RESTRICTED
Lt. Roche's solicitor is Mr. B. O'MAOILEOIN, 144 Lr. Baggot St. 2. Dublin.
RESTRICTED

DOCUMENT 17
[Secret Memo, dated 12 June 1969, initialled 'GOS'(Gerry O'Sullivan) Handwritten]
SECRET
Memo
Lt. ROCHE was interviewed by DJAG at 1430 hrs on 28. Bea (May) 69.

He was advised of the legal position and informed that he had until 1000 hours on 29 Bea 69 to submit an explanation of his conduct. ROCHE said he proposed to see his solicitor.

At 0940 hours on 29 Bea (May) 69 Lt ROCHE informed DJAG that his solicitor had advised him 'to do nothing.'

DJAG informed CF & Adm accordingly.

12/6/69

GOS

SECRET

DOCUMENTS 18 AND 19

[Handwritten letters by Mrs Christina de Róiste to 'The Officer Commanding', Custume Barracks, Athlone and An t-Aire Cosanta, dated 21 November 1969]

'Awbeg', Western Park, Clonmel, Co. Tipperary.

21-10-'69

The Commanding Officer, Custume Barracks, Athlone, Co. Westmeath.

Dear Sir,

My son, Donal Roche, served in the Western Command of the Army as a Lieutenant, and was retired without a reference on, approximately, June 27th 1969.

As his parent, I wish to know why he now has to face the future without a reference, having been found not guilty of the charge which was made against him, and having been given no previous indications of unsuitability.

You are well aware that in this life a person's most treasured possession is his character, hence my request.

I have informed An t-Aire Cosanta.

Yours sincerely, (Mrs.) C. Roche.

An t-Aire Cosanta,

Geata na Páirce,

Baile Átha Cliath.

A chara uasail,

My son, Donal Roche, served in the Western Command, Custume Barracks, Athlone, as a Lieutenant in our Irish Army.

He was retired on, approximately, June 27th 1969, without a character reference.

He had been found not guilty of the charge made against him, which was collaboration with the I.R.A. He had no previous indications from those in command that he was being found unsuitable. Why, therefore, does he now have to face a future without a character reference after giving six years service in our National Army?

In this life, our most treasured possession is our character. Therefore, as his parent, I wish him to be furnished with a proper reference, or else with a reason, why not.

Mise, le mór mheas, (Bean) Creasa De Róiste.

APPENDIX B

THE MICHAEL DONNELLY AFFAIR

A 'Background' note accompanying the Department of Defence press release headed: 'Inquiry into the circumstances surrounding the retirement of ex-Lieutenant Dónal Roche in 1969', issued on 2 October 2002, states:

> Based on an assessment of the facts as outlined above, the military authorities in 1969 concluded that Lt. Roche potentially constituted a security risk and on that basis his retirement in the interest of the service was recommended. It is emphasised that in such circumstances there is no legal requirement for a person to be tried with an offence under military law or the ordinary criminal law. This principle was upheld by Finlay P. in The State (Donnelly) v. Minister for Defence (unreported, October 9 1979) where he stated that there was a 'clear public necessity' that the military authorities should have the discretion to remove persons considered to be a security risk.

Like Dónal de Róiste, ex-Corporal Michael Donnelly is fighting an epic three-decade battle to clear his name of charges made against him by nameless and faceless people. It is a problem for individuals like De Róiste and Donnelly that they cannot know, for the purpose of defending themselves, who their 'reliable' accusers are – if they exist – and what the justification is for acting on the 'information' attributed to them.

BORDER INCIDENT

In 1970, aged seventeen, Michael Donnelly joined the defence forces, following in the footsteps of several generations of his family who lived in Ballyfermot, Dublin. He did full-time border duty with the FCA before joining the regular army in March 1971. In 1972, something happened which was later to be slanted against him.

The incident occurred in February of that year when his unit was called upon to investigate trouble on the border. Having dismounted from his vehicle, Donnelly was running to a position with a General Purpose Machine Gun (GPMG) when he accidentally discharged a few shots. Almost immediately, a previously unseen British army helicopter rose above a tree line a couple of fields away and departed the area.

The following day, Donnelly was charged with 'negligence'. However, after a discussion between the patrol commander and the Officer Commanding at Castleblaney Military Camp, the charge was dropped and it was concluded that the incident had been an 'innocent mishap'. His only punishment was to pay for the spent ammunition. It is important to note that the charge, before being dropped, was negligence. There was never any question of malicious intent, particularly regarding the helicopter.

The incident was clearly considered to be of no consequence as, within a month, Michael Donnelly was accepted into the ranks of the 2nd Garrison Military Police Company (2 Grn MP Coy) a respected branch of the defence forces, requiring an exemplary record. In August 1972, his military career was looking promising when he was promoted to the rank of corporal.

NEW YEAR DRAMA

The New Year, however, began with drama, when a GPMG was stolen from a secure location within Clancy Barracks, Dublin, allegedly while Donnelly was on duty. The young corporal had just started main gate duty when, at 8.20 a.m., he received a call from the orderly sergeant to say that a magazine was missing. Donnelly says that he immediately put in place the requisite procedures, stopping all vehicles and pedestrian traffic from leaving Clancy Barracks. Ten minutes later, the orderly sergeant telephoned Donnelly again to say that it was actually a GPMG that was missing.

In 1995, some 22 years after the theft, Donnelly was perturbed when he discovered a previously unseen *Evening Herald* article, dated 2 January 1973, which stated, 'Both Gardai and army officers were surprised that a weapon of such bulk could be removed from the barracks – unobserved by the sentry on duty.'

It was an ominous sign of things to come. The fact that Donnelly had been trained in the use of the GPMG, and that he had been involved in a border incident with the same weapon, appears to have awakened suspicions that there might be a correlation between the stolen weapon and the fact that Donnelly, as 'the sentry on duty', had failed to observe its removal from Clancy Barracks.

As with the incident involving the GPMG on the border, all seemed to be forgotten when, on 5 April 1973, Corporal Donnelly was given a commendation for intervening in an incident at the Curragh Detention Camp. Provisional IRA inmates had been about to assault a fellow inmate when Donnelly intervened to save him. Commandant J. Enright wrote to the Governor and the Provost Marshall, stating his belief that Cpl Donnelly's performance during the incident was 'worthy of the highest praise.'

GUILTY UNTIL PROVEN INNOCENT

Unknown to Donnelly, however, forces were at work against him. Just two years later, on 23 April 1975, he was detained while coming off duty, and taken to an interview room. Once there, his Commanding Officer (C/O), Captain P. J. O'Brien and members of the army's Special Investigation Branch (SIB) interrogated him throughout the night. He was released, under guard, to his billet, at 8 a.m. At 4 p.m., after little sleep, he was allowed to eat. As a corporal, he was entitled to eat in the NCOs mess but his SIB guards brought him instead to the general canteen where he was forced to eat in isolation. Donnelly states: 'It was deeply embarrassing. I really began to feel under a lot of strain then. I felt they were psychologically trying to break me at that time.' Apparently, Donnelly, like De Róiste was guilty until proven innocent.

At 5 p.m., his second interrogation session of 23 April began. Donnelly says that Captain O'Brien commented, 'I don't like to see any man railroaded. The way you answer my questions will decide if you stay in the army or not.' According to Donnelly, O'Brien was later to refuse him access to the army's legal officer and to block his request for a court martial.

At around 7 p.m., two officers from the Garda Síochána's Criminal Detective Unit arrived but Donnelly says that they introduced themselves as Special Branch. He remembers one in particular who was openly aggressive. 'He accused me of being a member of the IRA and of stealing the GPMG from Clancy Barracks in 1973. He also asked me if I knew Peter and Harry Claine and other names I did not recognise.'

Corporal Donnelly truthfully informed the Garda officers that he did know Harry Claine and, to a much lesser extent, his brother, Peter. Harry and he were friends and, until recently, had been colleagues in 2 Grn MP Coy. He would, in time, be best man at his wedding. Indeed, Donnelly points out, Harry Claine had been given an honourable discharge with a good conduct record on 27 July, the previous year. What he didn't know at the time was that the Garda officer questioning him actually lived in the same neighbourhood as Harry Claine, on Decie's Road, Ballyfermot.

Donnelly is still confused about this line of questioning and wonders what he or Harry Claine had been guilty of. He recalls the fact that while Harry Claine's brother, Peter, had republican sympathies, so too had Tomás Mac Giolla, whose brother Michael was a senior legal officer in the defence forces. Furthermore, when Harry had been given his honourable discharge the previous year, his 'Protection Certificate' informed him that 'in case of emergency' he was to rejoin '2 Grn MP Coy, Collins Barracks, Dublin'.

Donnelly's CO, Captain P.J. O'Brien, further interrogated him that day. According to Donnelly, O'Brien became irate and accused him of attempting to shoot down a British army helicopter in retaliation for Bloody Sunday. 'I couldn't believe what I was hearing,' Donnelly told me. 'The incident of 1972, which had been investigated at the time and of which I had been cleared, was now being used to damage me.'

INTERVIEW WITH SUPERIOR OFFICER

In an action that he admits was born of desperation, he managed to outwit his CO by making a formal written request to see a legal officer of the permanent defence forces. It was a clever move by the young corporal because it forced the defence forces and the Garda Síochána to show their hand. He is anxious to point out that he voluntarily made his statement to a superior officer, Company Quartermaster Sergeant (CQMS) Joe Heffernan, after being cautioned.

He was formally interviewed by Heffernan, at Collins Barracks, on the afternoon of 25 April 1975. Heffernan asked him if he knew Peter and Harry Claine and if he had visited Peter Claine's house in Tallaght, having travelled to it in a Cortina car, registration number GIO 66 [a car owned by Harry Claine] on an unspecified date. He said 'yes' to all three questions, stating that on the one and only occasion he had visited Peter Claine's home, it was to help Harry to deliver a carpet. He was then asked if he knew that Peter Claine was a member of Sinn Féin. He said that he had an idea. Heffernan then suggested to him that it was foolish to be in Peter Claine's company. Donnelly replied, 'It was seldom I was in Peter's company.' Heffernan pressed him, 'Did you not think it was foolish?' Donnelly replied, 'I did not think there was any harm in it.'

The young corporal was then asked if he had given Peter Claine '… any information concerning the activities of the military police or any other unit of the force?' He replied, 'I did not.'

He was then asked about an article that had appeared in the Sunday World, concerning conditions in the Curragh Detention Centre. Journalist John Keane had penned the article in June 1974 and his source had allegedly been two unnamed members of the military police corps who complained about working conditions and general morale in the army. Donnelly replied, 'I know nothing about it nor was I involved in any way with these articles.'

He was then asked if Peter Claine or his brother or any of their friends had been 'involved in the compiling of these articles?' Corporal Donnelly replied, 'I don't know.'

In February 1989, having been made aware of the allegations made against Donnelly, journalist John Keane wrote to the Minister for Defence, Michael Noonan, stating that he was the author of the Sunday World article and that his memory of the interview was crystal-clear. 'Michael Donnelly was not one of the two men … I interviewed,' he stated.

Heffernan also asked Donnelly if he knew a prisoner in the Curragh Detention Centre, named 'Doocey'. He replied, 'I know him to see from doing duty in the prison.' He was then asked a question, the implications of which he was not to understand until two decades later. Heffernan asked him, 'Did you ever refer to him [Doocey] as Dooley?' Donnelly replied, 'Not to my knowledge.' Heffernan continued, 'Why should information be forwarded to the effect that you did call him Dooley?' Corporal Donnelly responded, 'I have no idea.'

Through the Freedom of Information Act, Donnelly recovered a military document which, apparently, solved the mystery. The document says that a Sgt John Jordan, MPC, made a report in which he alleged that on 22 February 1975, in the NCOs' mess, he overheard the young corporal refer to Doocey as Dooley. Based on this allegation, Donnelly was, without his knowledge, deemed to be the source of a second *Sunday World* article, dated 23 February 1975, which had used the name Dooley instead of Doocey!

Sgt Heffernan also asked Donnelly where he had been the night before the GPMG was taken from Clancy Barracks. He said that, since he was 'on early [duty] the next morning', he had slept in the barracks. He was then asked, 'Do you know who took the GPMG or do you know where it is?' Donnelly replied, 'I have no idea who took the GPMG or where it is or anything about it.'

The final question was whether he knew a person with the surname Rice. 'I do not,' Corporal Donnelly replied. To this day, he does not understand the implications of this question.

OTHER ALLEGATIONS

In another document released under the FOI, dated 28 July 1976, the following is stated: 'Subject [Donnelly] first came to notice in 1974 when he was suspected of passing information to the newspapers...'

The document also states, 'In July 1974 he was reported to be an associate of the following....' A large area of redaction then follows. The document further accuses Corporal Donnelly and an accomplice of approaching serving soldiers in the Parkside Hotel in May 1975 and suggesting to them 'the necessity for a "Soldiers' Union".' The document further states, 'the subject is also suspected of involvement in the theft of a GPMG from Clancy Barracks in January 1973.' Finally, to ex-Corporal Donnelly's astonishment, the document states: 'Donnelly is also alleged to have been involved in a series of robberies with others, and it is reported that his house, which is thought may be 207 Balrothery Estate, Tallaght, was being used as a 'safe house'. (The house, in actual fact, belonged to Peter Claine.)

DISCHARGE LETTER

Corporal Michael Donnelly was given a dishonourable discharge from the Irish defence forces on 25 April 1975. The discharge letter, which he first saw in 1977 in the High Court, stated:

This Cpl has associated with known members of a subversive group (OIRA) and has visited a house which is under surveillance by the Special Branch. Reliable information discloses that he was involved in the theft of the GPMG from Clancy Bks. He was stationed in Clancy Bks at that time. He was also involved in newspaper articles which appeared in the 'Sunday World'. These articles were critical of conditions in the Curragh Detention Centre and in the army in general. Donnelly did duty in the Curragh Detention Centre at that time.

O/C 2 Grn MPC [Captain P.J. O'Brien] has carried out a thorough investigation into this Cpl's background and involvement in these incidents.

He is satisfied that Donnelly was concerned in illegal activities.

It would be very difficult to take disciplinary action against this Cpl as the evidence is 'circumstantial' [sic]. In the circumstances I would recommend that he should be discharged 'service no longer required' as I am satisfied that he is a serious security risk, especially in his employment as a Cpl in the MPC.

The letter is signed: 'Intelligence Officer, Eastern Command.'

It is worth emphasising that the three words used to taint the young military policeman prior to his discharge, in most of the incidents used to destroy his military career, are vague generalities: 'suspected', 'reported' and 'alleged'. There is not one piece of concrete or compelling evidence to support his removal from the permanent defence forces. This is clearly acknowledged in the final paragraph of his discharge letter, above, with its strange logic whereby vague 'circumstantial' so-called evidence can be construed to satisfy the intelligence officer that Donnelly is 'a serious security risk' and should, therefore, be discharged, 'service no longer required'.

The letter also states that Donnelly's CO, Captain O'Brien, 'carried out a thorough investigation into this Cpls background and involvement in these incidents' and 'he is satisfied that Donnelly was concerned in illegal activities.' Given the vague generalities used in attempting to link Donnelly with 'security risk' activities, and given that his senior officers did not appear to know his correct address, there must be serious doubts about the thoroughness of Captain O'Brien's investigation, and questions about the motivation for wishing to have Donnelly removed.

The first paragraph of the intelligence officer's discharge letter outlines the case for Donnelly's removal, citing four reasons: (1) Associating with members of a subversive group; (2) Visiting a house under surveillance by the Special Branch; (3) Involvement in the theft of the GPMG, and (4) involvement in the *Sunday World* article. The most serious allegation is the third, which, the letter reveals, is attributed to a 'reliable' informant. Who?

Corporal Donnelly requested and was refused a court martial. He told me, 'They gave me the punishment but never gave me the trial.'

THE JUDGE ADVOCATE GENERAL

Like Dónal de Róiste, Donnelly is determined to force the state to provide him with a fair and transparent procedure to clear his name. However, having watched de Róiste's experience with the Judge Advocate General, Donnelly has instructed his lawyers not to accept a process whereby the military's civilian legal appointee investigates the military.

His experience of both the military and civil justice system has made him cautious. He told me, 'I came into this a bit naive, believing in Irish justice. Now I have learnt that the Law is not about Justice. The law is about the law.' On 30 January 1989, Tomás Mac Giolla, TD, wrote to Col. Patrick J. Ghent, Deputy Judge Advocate General, stating that Michael Donnelly was 'still very concerned at the manner of his discharge especially on behalf of his family and is anxious to have his name cleared.' Mac Giolla asked the DJAG if Donnelly 'has any entitlement to a Court Martial or what other procedure may be open to him to pursue the matter.'

Ghent responded two weeks later: 'An entitlement to a court-martial does not arise where no charges are preferred. I am not aware of any procedure which may be open to him to pursue this matter.' It sounds like de Róiste's experience all over again.

Donnelly has also tried to seek redress through the civil courts. His battle to date has been epic and very costly. He has worked since his discharge as a labourer with

Dublin Corporation, to support his family, and in the evenings and at weekends as a doorman and, more recently, a taxi driver, to pay for legal bills associated with his campaign to clear his name. On 9 and 10 March 1977, he took his case to the High Court, and in 1982 to the Supreme Court. On both occasions, he was forced to fight blind, with no access to his files. And on both occasions, the courts ruled against him. The Supreme Court also awarded costs against him and he was sent a legal bill in excess of £40,000. At first he was stunned at the harshness of his treatment but then politely informed his legal team that he could not and would not pay the courts' costs and that if they wished, they could send him to prison. Amazingly, he was not pursued for costs.

ANONYMOUS LETTERS

There have been several bizarre occurrences throughout Michael Donnelly's years of campaigning. On two occasions, in August 1979 and in 1984, anonymous handwritten letters with no address, but signed 'John O'Reilly', were sent to Dublin Corporation, stating that Donnelly was leaving work 'to visit a married woman in the Ballyfermot Area' with whom, the letters alleged, he was having an 'affair'. Dublin Corporation investigated the anonymous allegations 'but found no evidence'. Donnelly has no doubt that there was malicious intent and suspects that part of the aim of the letters was to get him sacked and force him to take the immigrant boat and thus remove both himself and his campaign to clear his name.

Another similarity with the de Róiste case is that Michael Donnelly's father, in the immediate aftermath of his discharge, disowned his son. Unlike de Róiste, however, Donnelly was reconciled with his father in 1980, shortly before he was married. Thereafter, until his death in 1997, Donnelly's father supported his son's quest for truth.

In 1981, however, Michael Donnelly was given a copy of a letter marked 'Confidential'. The letter, given to him by someone he describes as 'a sympathetic military source', was dated 6 March 1977 (three days before his High Court hearing). It is signed by his former CO, Commandant P.J. O'Brien, and carries the reference APM/A/154. The body of the letter is preceded by the number, rank and military attachment of his brother, Patrick Donnelly, who was then a corporal in the military police. Both Michael and his brother were taken aback by the contents of the three-sentence letter, sent by O'Brien to the office of the Assistant Provost Marshal, Eastern Command. The letter states:

> Attached please find communication received by me from the father of the above-mentioned.
> I have acknowledged receipt of Mr. Donnelly's letter and informed him that it had been passed to his Officer Commanding.
> Forwarded for your attention and necessary action.

Donnelly's 'sympathetic military source' told him that the communication referred to in Commandant O'Brien's correspondence was a handwritten letter purportedly from his father. He was told that the letter made reference to his brother Patrick and another brother, both of whom were still in the army, and included negative and uncomplimentary comments about Michael. Michael Donnelly says that he confronted his father about this and that his father denied ever having written to Commandant O'Brien or of having received any communication from him. His brother Patrick told me that he is mystified as to why his father would write to O'Brien in the first place and that at no stage did O'Brien ever discuss with him the contents of any letter from his father. Both brothers believe that no such letter exists or, if it does, that their father is not the author of it.

In a further twist to the saga, on 17 May 1999, Michael Donnelly wrote to the Information Commissioner, under the Freedom of Information Act, concerning the above, seeking access to the 1977 file APM/A/154. On 1 July 1999, the Information Officer replied:

> The defence forces has checked with the Intelligence Office, the Director of Military police and the Department of Defence and it cannot locate a file with the reference number APM/A/154/77...

POLITICAL SUPPORT

Amongst the politicians who, over the years, have written on Donnelly's behalf is the Taoiseach, Bertie Ahern. While Minister for Labour in 1989, he wrote to the Minister for Defence, Michael Noonan, regarding the matter of 'anonymous letters' and the role that they might have played in his dismissal. He also wrote to Donnelly on 17 January 1989, stating: 'I assure you I will do what I can to help you with this case and when I have further news I will be in touch with you again.'

One politician who has been a stalwart in supporting Donnelly's campaign to clear his name is Pat Rabbitte, TD. Some of Rabbitte's handwritten notes related to Donnelly have even turned up in army Intelligence files released under the Freedom of Information Act. In a brief conversation with this journalist on 12 June 2003, Rabbitte stated that over several years of contact with a person, it is possible to get a feel for their integrity. 'I would go to the wire for Michael Donnelly,' he said.

One cannot but admire Donnelly's tenacity and determination to pursue the recovery of his good name. His files are overflowing with letters to a variety of people he thought might be able to help. Included amongst responses he has received are letters from the UN Commission for Human Rights; the Foreign & Commonwealth Office, London; Chris Mullen, MP; the British Embassy; the Northern Ireland Office; Office of the First Minister (Designate) and Deputy First Minister (Designate) the Northern Ireland Assembly; Áras an Uachtaráin; the Garda Síochána and RUC Headquarters, Belfast.

A letter from the RUC, dated 31 July 1997, responds to an offer by Donnelly to make himself available to assist with an investigation into an alleged machine-gun attack on a British army helicopter in February 1972. The letter, signed by R.B. Maxwell for the RUC Chief Constable, states:

> ... The RUC has no record of a helicopter in Northern Ireland being fired upon on the dates in question. As there is no evidence of a crime having been committed there will be no investigation into the matter.

'A CIVILIAN' ALLEGEDLY ADMITS TO STEALING A MACHINE-GUN WITH HELP OF MILITARY POLICEMAN FRIEND

According to Donnelly, his CO, Captain O'Brien, stated in a sworn affidavit that he was acting on information received from the Garda Síochána. According to Donnelly, information was received from the Garda Síochána in May 1973 which stated, 'a soldier living in Ballyfermot was involved in the theft of a machine-gun.' Donnelly told Magill that further information was received in June 1974, alleging, 'a civilian had been overheard in a pub claiming he had stolen the machine-gun, with the help of a PA [Military Policeman] friend.' Donnelly says that further information was received on

23 April 1975, the day of his arrest, claiming that 'the civilian' (presumably a 'reliable source') had stated: 'the PA friend who had helped him steal the machine-gun from Clancy Barracks had also fired on a British army helicopter in 1972'.

Donnelly remains puzzled as to why the 'civilian' was never arrested and sentenced for admitting to stealing the weapon and why both he and the 'civilian' were not brought before the civil courts to face charges. Even at this remove, he challenges both the army and Garda Síochána to produce the 'civilian', as he is willing to face the charges and allegations levelled against him.

FORMER COMMANDING OFFICER DECLINES INTERVIEW

Meanwhile, Michael Donnelly, like Donal de Róiste, continues his lonely struggle to clear his name. It is clear that his long campaign is beginning to gather support. Recently he was informed that the respected London-based human rights organisation, British Irish Rights Watch, was prepared to examine his case with a view to supporting his quest for public accountability and a fair and independent review.

Donnelly has managed to get some important information through the Freedom of Information Act. However, he believes that further important information is being withheld. He told me:

> I don't believe I have access to my full files. For example, my Police notebooks have disappeared. In 1997 I was informed that my Statement of Evidence was 'no longer available', yet it turned up in documents released under FOI in August 2002. I firmly believe that there are files related to me which I am being denied. I am of the opinion that these files would be of assistance in helping to prove my innocence – not in assisting the authorities to prove my guilt. I have absolutely nothing to fear from the truth and I challenge the Military Authorities and the Department of Defence to deal with my case in an open and public way.

On Tuesday, 17 June 2003, I contacted Donnelly's former CO, Captain O'Brien, for a cover story I was writign for *Magill* magazine. O'Brien retired as head of security at RTÉ some years ago. He was asked for an interview concerning the case of former Corporal Michael Donnelly and his role in his eventual discharge. O'Brien informed me: 'it's an army matter and you should go through the army for your information.' When asked why he was reluctant to be interviewed, he said, 'I think you know my position.' He was informed that *Magill* was in possession of documentation, including statements made by him, and that the magazine wished to discuss these with him. He responded, 'No thanks.'